How to Become an Environment-Friendly Miner

About the Author

The author as a member of the Indian Administrative Service (IAS) has worked in senior positions under the State Government of Bihar and the Central Government. He had long experience of working in the mining and non-ferrous metals sectors for about thirteen years under the State Government and the Central Government. After retirement he had held a constitutional post as the State Election Commissioner. He also worked as Chairman of the Expert Appraisal Committee (Mining) for three years under the Ministry of Environment and Forests, Government of India. This (the Expert Appraisal Committee) is a Statutory Committee which is mandated to appraise all applications for prior environmental clearance from the government and to make appropriate recommendations for grant or rejection of any application for environmental clearance in respect of any mining project.

The author also had worked as short-term Consultant of the Commonwealth Secretariat, London twice on "Industrial Opportunity Survey" in Vanuatu and "Setting Up Mineral Based Industries" in Tonga, both South Pacific Island countries.

He has authored a book under the title "*Emerging Grassroots Power*", a Critique on Elections to the Panchayats and Municipality, based on his personal experience in conducting elections to the local bodies in Bihar after a gap of more than two decades published for Institute of Social Sciences, New Delhi by Concept Publishing Company Pvt. Ltd., New Delhi.

How to Become An Environment-Friendly Miner

A HANDBOOK

M.L. Majumdar
I.A.S. (Retd)

CONCEPT PUBLISHING COMPANY PVT. LTD.
NEW DELHI-110059

ISBN-13: 978-93-5125-174-3

First Published 2015

Published and Printed by

Concept Since 1974

Concept Publishing Company Pvt. Ltd.
A/15-16, Commercial Block, Mohan Garden
New Delhi-110059 (India)
T: 25351460, 25351794, *F*: 091-11-25357109
E: publishing@conceptpub.com, W: www.conceptpub.com
Editorial Office: H-13, Bali Nagar, New Delhi-110 015, India.

Cataloging in Publication Data--Courtesy: D.K. Agencies (P) Ltd. <docinfo@dkagencies.com>

Majumdar, M. L. (Makhan Lal), 1940- author.
How to become an environment-friendly miner : a handbook / M.L. Majumdar.
pages cm
Includes index.
ISBN 9789351251743

1. Mines and mineral resources--Environmental aspects--India. 2. Environmental impact analysis--India. 3. Miners--Training of--India. 4. Mining law--India. I. Title.

DDC 333.850954 23

Prof. (Dr.) Gurdeep Singh
VICE CHANCELLOR
Vinoba Bhave University
Hazaribag-825301 (Jharkhand)

Mobile: 9431711184
Ph. No.: 06546-264279, 261938 (O)
06546-264066, 262342 (R)
FAX : 06546-267878 (O), 264066 (R)
Email : s_gurdeep2001@yahoo.com

Ref. No.: VBU/VC/589/15
Date: 18/05/2015

Foreword

Our mother earth is the most precious gift of the Universe. It is the sustenance of "nature" that is key to the development of the future of mankind. It is the duty and responsibility of each one of us to protect nature. It is here that the understanding of the Environment comes into the picture.

India is endowed with significant mineral resources which include fossil fuels, ferrous and non-ferrous ores and industrial minerals. These non-renewable resources are finite. Many of these resources are located in environmentally sensitive area. Mining of these resources inevitably gives rise to significant environmental and social impacts and it requires careful impact assessment followed by environmental management plan.

Environmental Impact Assessment process has been well developed and in practice the world over particularly in India to effectively manage the degradation of our environment due to various developmental activities including mining.

Shri M L Majumdar, formerly Chairman, Expert Appraisal Committee (Mining), Ministry of Environment and Forests, Government of India, an experienced administrator, has come out with a very comprehensive and useful book in "How to Become An Environment-Friendly Miner". The material in the book is well presented in an integrated manner in lucid language with homely examples. This has made the book very rich in content and would prove to be a very valuable document both for the students as well as for the teachers and all the personnel engaged in mining. It doesn't require heavy intellectual input to understand the hidden massage sought to be conveyed in the book which even a layman associated with mining industry would never miss.

I would like to compliment Shri Majumdar for such an excellent job and contribution to the society. I am confident that this book would be of great help to all those who are interested in understanding the environmental aspect of mining in all its ramifications. The book is also a useful guide for mining fraternity and the consultants in the preparation of a practical and pragmatic Environment Impact Assessment Report and Environment Management Plan while seeking prior environmental clearance for any mining project.

Dr. Gurdeep Singh
Vice Chancellor
Professor (HAG) and Chairman
State Environment Impact Assessment Authority, Jharkhand

Preface

Having worked in the mining sector, as Secretary, Department of Mines and Geology, Government of Bihar, then comprising present State of Jharkhand, a major mineral bearing State and as Director, Joint Secretary and Additional Secretary to the Government of India in the Ministry of Mines for a fairly long period, which is not a common feature for a civil servant in the administrative system of our country, I could not find myself ever in a situation when I would be inclined to subscribe to the sweeping statement that miners as a class have no concern at all for the protection of the environment even though they supposedly make huge profits out of their mining activities. My belief is, and not without reason, that a miner is also concerned about the need for a fully conscious responsibility in protecting the environment in the areas of his operations. During my tenure of three years as Chairman of one of the two Expert Appraisal Committees on Mining, constituted by the Ministry of Environment and Forests (MoEF), Government of India, in terms of the Notification No.S.O.1533(E) dated September 14, 2006 issued by the Ministry, popularly known as 14th September Environment Notification, I came across number of cases in which the lessees (the words miner, lessee, project authority, project proponent have been used by me as synonyms) have, of their own, reported certain imaginative and innovative measures taken by them which only indicate that they have been taking reasonably well thought of mitigating steps to protect the physical environment and following a reasonably well-conceived Corporate Social Responsibility (CSR) Policy, themselves, at least a majority of them, perhaps not realizing or not bothering to advertise that they have been doing so, thereby making valuable contribution to the maintenance of the environment of the area. I will give one such example without naming the person. She was a lady lessee from the State of Karnataka, perhaps belonging to a traditional benevolent landed family. The consultant, who made a presentation on her behalf, could not fully convince the Committee about the CSR activities being carried on by the project proponent. One of the members of the Committee suggested that we should directly ask the lessee concerned to clarify the issues raised by the Committee. While giving consent to the suggestion of the member I had some initial hesitation about such an approach as I was still under the impression that a miner, that too a lady with the limitations imposed on her in visiting such work sites under the relevant mining laws, might not always be in a position to elaborate the CSR activities being executed by her organization. We (the Committee) were amazed to see that the lady gave a very interesting presentation on various activities being done by her for the socio-economic benefit of the people as also for the conservation of the ecology and protection of the environment of the area though without using the nuances that are used by a professional consultant. She was effective in convincing the members about the activities and the benefits thereof. The Committee had similar experience in many more cases. In fact, after the revised (April, 2008) Model Terms of Reference, prepared by the Committee for the preparation of Environmental Impact Assessment (EIA) Report and Environment Management Plan (EMP) on mining projects, the Committee could see a markedly qualitative difference in the preparation of the Environmental Impact Assessment (EIA) Report and Environment Management Plan (EMP) by the project proponents. The Committee itself got lot of new ideas from some of the lessees which were subsequently incorporated as additional Terms of Reference in the Model Terms of Reference notwithstanding the fact that cynics and sceptics would argue that the lessees might be doing things just to please the Committee . But one cannot miss the point that it is a welcome change, if not for anything, at least for the fact that a miner has applied his mind to the larger issues of protecting the environment and I consider this as no mean achievement for the Committee which has at least achieved some success in impressing upon the miner to apply his mind to the issue even if it is only to satisfy the Committee as the critics would like to say. One can show the magnanimity in having a small bit of confidence in the bona fide of a miner. I only wish that they(critics) could spare some of their idle time to interact with some of the lessees and find for themselves the state of affairs rather than blaming the entire mining fraternity. As in any other group of people, there is no denying the fact that there are black sheep among the miners as well.

My long association with the mining sector and specially my three years' experience as Chairman of the Expert Appraisal Committee on Mining constituted by the Ministry of Environment and Forests have convinced me that if proper guidelines are issued to the miners, and the concerned officers of the State Governments and the Central Government explain the implications of various Acts and Rules framed thereunder on environmental protection through Seminars and Workshops organized at convenient locations we could have much better results. One can imagine the lack-lustre attitude on the part the concerned authority which is proved by the fact that even after more than 3 years of operation of the Environment Notification till August 2009, when my Committee's tenure of three years ended, the authority was yet to come with a list of accredited consultants for the preparation of EIA Report and the EMP for the benefit of the miners, many of whom specially the small miners whose number is quite large, do not know how to go about it. In the process there has been mushroom growth of self-styled consultants with no or very little expertise for the job so much so that many of the so-called consultants do not even know the distinction between a pre-feasibility project report as required under para 6 of the Environment Notification and a Mining Plan to be approved by the Government under Section 5(2) (b) of the Mines and Minerals (Development and Regulation) Act 1957, (MMRD Act). It was only in December 2009 that the MoEF had come out of its "slumber of indifference" to this critical requirement by issuing a circular on the accreditation of consultants for preparation of EIA Report and the EMP. I shall comment in detail on this half-baked circular in Chapter 14 on the Role of the Stakeholders.

In this book, one can call it (book) a critique if one so likes, I have made an attempt to demonstrate how it is possible to execute mining projects and at the same time to protect the environment. This is possible if we have the courage to repose certain amount of confidence in the bona fide and sincerity of a miner, and the MoEF issues detailed and practical guidelines on how to act on the contents of the 14th September Notification and the subsequent amending Notifications as per the usual practice followed by the government in such cases. In fact, I have selected the title of the book "*How to become an Environment-Friendly Miner*" having that in mind and perhaps it is not for nothing.

This book could as well be a useful one relevant for any other industrial activities. Since, however, I have been associated for a fairly long period of about 16 years with the mining industry, I found it easy to deal with the environmental issues concerning mining industry.

Author

Acknowledgements

Without the generous help of Federation of Indian Mineral Industries (FIMI) and in particular of Shri R.K. Sharma, Secretary General (FIMI), it would not have been possible for me to complete this book. I would express my grateful thanks to FIMI for allowing me to utilize its staff and the computer network in giving practical shape to the book. I would specially thank Mr. Madan Sonar and Mr. Dinesh Girdhar who took extensive dictation and typed the same. Mr. Dinesh Girdhar took great pains in typing the final version of the book. I would also thank Mr. Gour Sundar Saha in putting all the annexure to the book in their proper order. I would also specially thank Mr. Shiv Singh Rana who could find time even in his otherwise busy schedule to make photocopy of several draft copies and also the final draft copy of the book.

I would like to thank many of my acquaintances for suggesting improvements in the final version of the book. I would like to express my grateful thanks to Prof. Gurdeep Singh of the Indian School of Mines, Dhanbad for the time and pains he has taken to go through the final draft of the book and for giving a 'Foreword' to the book.

I have been greatly influenced by the views of Dr. S.R. Wate, presently Director, National Environmental Engineering Research Institute (NEERI), Nagpur as a Member of the Expert Appraisal Committee (Mining) while conceiving the general outline of the book. I express my sincere thanks to him.

It took lot of my private time at home and without the endurance of my wife Ranjita, this book would not have been possible. I acknowledge her invisible contribution to making my dream to write this book a reality.

I would also like to thank M/s. Concept Publishing Company Pvt. Ltd., who had published my first book, for agreeing to publish this book as well.

Apologies

The narrative of the facts and conclusions drawn and the suggestions given may apparently give an impression that a "know all" self image of the author is sought to be established. It is far from that. As I have been driven by my own experience of working in the mining sector for about thirteen years under the State Government and the Central Government at Senior levels and the experience of working as Chairman of Expert Appraisal Committee on Mining under the Ministry of Environment and Forests, Government of India for three years the narrative could not be otherwise. I am also at ease to forcefully argue that mining and environment can and should go hand in hand. I think the readers will accept my apology for any deviation from the conventional way a Book on any subject is usually authored.

While giving my views and suggestions on how the miner could be a saviour of the environment I could not help making critical comments on the Constitution and the functioning of the very Committee of which I was the Chairman for three years, activities of a certain section of miners, role of Non-Governmental Organizations (NGOs) and an indifferent attitude of the Ministry of Environment and Forests. While I am grateful to the Ministry for appointing me as Chairman of one of the two Expert Appraisal Committees (Mining) that gave me a true insight in various issues concerning environment protection and roles of various players therein, I will be failing in my duty as a former Chairman of the Committee and also as a retired civil servant with long association with the mining sector if I do not share my experiences and offer my suggestions, may be unsolicited for that, for the benefit of all stakeholders for the cause of environment. My criticism, including that on the functioning of the Committee, is without any malice to anybody and inspite of this, if anybody feels aggrieved and offended, I sincerely apologise for that. All my criticism is with a view to impressing upon all concerned to remove the deficiencies that have been pointed out at various places in this book so that the intention of the Government in harmonizing various mining activities, nay, all developmental project activities, with the protection of environment, fructifies. There has been repetition of certain expressions throughout the book and this has been done deliberately for a clear and instant understanding and is not intended to have a boring effect on the reader who, I am sure, can always allocate some extra time for such repetitions which are a necessary evil.

Environmental issues are quite large and complex but, for the sake of convenience, I have arbitrarily divided the whole thing in seven critical segments.

This book is meant for the benefit of the miners as a class. The existing players in the field would perhaps find that there is nothing written in this book which they did not know and this may be true. But the future miners and specially small miners whose number is quite large may find the book relevant. A book of this nature would surely have contents which are not unknown to many but that need not limit either the narration of facts or the conclusions reached for the benefit of the larger mining and environment fraternity. This book, like any other book on any subject, is no exception and would be of interest to some while not so to many others.

With my limited command over vocabulary I have taken extensive help of the Oxford English Dictionary in selecting appropriate words and the meaning thereof as assigned by the Dictionary.

M.L. Majumdar

Contents

Chapter – 1

Introduction

There are various laws for the protection of environment and conservation of forests enacted by the Central Government and various agencies are involved in ensuring a reasonably clean environment in which one can live a tolerably pollution free life while enjoying the benefits of various developmental activities. Since this book is concerned only with mining activities, that too in ferrous and non-ferrous minerals, I do not make any comment on the pollution created as a result of other developmental activities like river valley projects, power projects, coal mining, etc. unless there is a need to make reference to such projects by way of comparison between the extent of hazards created by such projects and the environmental issues thrown up by mining projects.

There are mainly three Central Acts, the Environment (Protection) Act, 1986, the Forest (Conservation) Act, 1980, and the Wildlife (Protection) Act, 1972 and the Rules made thereunder with which a miner should be fully conversant before taking up any mining projects. There are certain other Acts/Notifications etc. under which the miner is required to obtain certain clearances before taking up any mining operation. These Acts, etc. are the Water (Prevention and Control of Pollution) Act, 1974 (the Water Act) and the Rules framed thereunder, the Air (Prevention and Control of Pollution) Act, 1981 (the Air Act) and the Rules framed thereunder, Coastal Regulation Zone (CRZ) Notification, 2011 and the Hazardous Waste Management, Handling and Transboundary Movement Rules. The relevance and criticality of the above Acts, Rules etc. would be elaborated in Chapter-5, Part-B on the preparation of EIA report and the EMP.

A new Act, namely, the Scheduled Tribes and other Traditional Forest Dwellers (Recognition of Forests Rights) Act, 2006 has been enacted by the Central Government which is equally important and it is essential that every lessee gets familiar with the implications of the relevant provisions of this Act which has far reaching bearing on his CSR policy affecting the livelihood of such forest dwellers.

I do not think that there is any need now to emphasize the fact that a mining project including the beneficiation process is responsible for creating environment problems not only in the areas of its operations but also in the surrounding areas. Such areas could be the lease-hold areas (plant area in case of a beneficiation/processing plant) and its surroundings including the route through which the mined minerals are transported to its next place of use including the points from which the minerals would be marketed either for export or for domestic consumption. Therefore, a miner simply cannot afford to take a casual approach in the discharge of his duty in protecting the environment. The miner can always claim, and he can not be faulted for that, that he is exploiting the minerals only for the economic development of the country and ultimately for the benefit of the population. If a miner pauses for a while and makes an introspection he will himself realize that if environment is not protected, the health of the very people, for whom all these economic activities are ostensibly meant, would not permit such people to enjoy the avowed benefit of the economic activities. Therefore, it is ultimately in the interest of the society of which the miner is a part that the mining activities must ensure a tolerable environment in all its ramifications.

There are legal provisions for strictly enforcing the conditions to ensure that a miner carries out his mining activities in such a way that the environment is not adversely impacted, and if impacted adversely, which is more often than not the case, corrective actions are taken to restore the environment to the extent people find it liveable. There is an ethical aspect also involved in the whole process. In our country and perhaps in most of the countries, minerals are located mostly in the forest areas and therefore exploitation of such mineral wealth would have adverse impact on the forest cover, flora and fauna, besides interfering with the normal livelihood of the scheduled tribes and other traditional forest dwellers who have been living there for generations and who depend upon the forest for their very survival. Therefore, the miner should consider it as his moral duty to ensure that his activities do not interfere with the normal way of life of the forest dwellers, whether human being or fauna and other forest elements. Examples are better than precepts and I will highlight this ethical aspect by giving two concrete examples that came to my notice as Chairman of the Expert Appraisal Committee. In one case, a major public sector unit in the iron and steel sector, while presenting its case to the Committee, made a very forceful plea to the Committee for environmental clearance by arguing that for mining in the particular region, which is also known for its rich bio-diversity, the company has taken great risk as the forest dwellers are hostile to the proposed activities. It was explained to the officer, who happened to be of a very senior level in the company, that mineral iron ore has been lying underground in the area for years and the tribals and other traditional forest dwellers have been living there for generations in perfect harmony with the forests and the wildlife. But who had asked the company to come to the area by taking so-called great risk for the exploitation of the minerals? Answer given by the officer was that their activities were for the economic upliftment of the people and they wanted to mine the area for making steel which is an essential element for developing infrastructure in the country. The reaction of the Committee was that if the company was exploiting the mineral wealth and thereby creating a negative impact on the normal vocation and source of livelihood of the forest dwellers in the area, the company should think whether it is its moral responsibility or not to spare a little thought and do something for protecting the environment. The officer agreed and assured the Committee that they would come up with a reasonably well thought of package for the protection of the environment and economic package for the benefit of the forest dwellers which, indeed, the company did, at least on paper.

In another case, a large private sector unit made a presentation before the Committee for mining bauxite in a tribal area. The deposit would last only for five years. On the rehabilitation package for the affected families, about 230 in number, the proposal of the company was that all these families were to be shifted to a different location and after five years when the mining would be over, they would be brought back, an admission that the attachment of the affected families to the places where they have lived for generations is too strong to ignore, to their old location for resettlement there. It does not require any comment that such an inhuman approach can be projected to a Government Committee before which the company presented these families as if they (affected people) were grazing cattle who could be shifted at will. It is understood that the company had managed to get the environmental clearance subsequently.

It does not require any emphasis to tell a miner that he needs the environmental clearance from the competent authority before starting any mining project for which elaborate procedure has been prescribed by the Central Government in the Ministry of Environment and Forests (MoEF) through Notification No. S.O.1533(E) dated 14th September, 2006. It is now more than six years old and most of the miners are familiar with the

Notification. However, the Notification itself needs further elaboration. I have attempted some comments by way of clarification on this Notification in the next chapter.

A miner extracts the minerals from underground. For extracting the minerals, breaking and degradation of lands are inevitable. Dust will be created in the process of mining as also during crushing. Even simple mining of sands involves digging of lands. Every mining activity will have an impact not only on the environment, including forest land, but also on the livelihood of the local people. Therefore, a miner has to prepare an Environmental Impact Assessment (EIA) Report, i.e., a report that contains the likely impacts of the proposed mining activities on the physical and social environment as assessed by the miner himself. It is not necessary that all impacts as a result of mining will only be adverse. There may be a case in which mining may result in positive impact. The Committee had come across certain cases when the lessee, who was also the owner of the land, reported that after the mining of bauxite which was mostly an outcrop, up to a depth of few meters only, the post mining lands had become fertile for agricultural purposes. Mining also creates many gainful economic activities thereby generating employment opportunities for the local people. Similarly, in certain areas exhausted mine pits would be a source of perennial water for use by the local people for irrigation and other purposes. Therefore, every miner has to prepare an EIA report. Model Terms of Reference framed by the Committee would be a helpful guide in doing the job.

After the EIA report has been prepared, the next stage would be to enumerate mitigating measures to counter the adverse impact likely to be created on account of mining activities. For example, if mining activity affects adversely the productivity of the farm land due to dust and other pollution, the mitigating measures would involve controlling the dust and to compensate the farmer to the extent productivity of the land gets affected due to mining. This is called Environment Management Plan (EMP), i.e., a management plan to mitigate the effects of adverse impacts on the physical and social environment due to mining activities.

To prepare the EIA report and the EMP, the miner must have base line data of various constituents of the environment in the area as obtaining prior to the mining operation and then prepare the EMP related to the adversely impacted constituents.

One very important element has been introduced by the 14th September Environment Notification, and that is public consultation, popularly known as public hearing. Since mining activity will have an impact on the local population, they have great stake in the operation as it would adversely impact their livelihood besides health and environment as a result of degradation of lands and felling of trees, etc. In the public hearing, affected people will raise various issues ranging from employment, health and drinking water facilities. The miner has to explain to the people during public hearing the steps proposed to be taken to mitigate the likely adverse impacts. The proceedings of the public hearing become an integral part of the procedure for the grant of environmental clearance. For the benefit of the miner, I have allocated a full chapter in this book on public consultation.

After all the procedural requirements have been completed, the miner has to submit his EIA report alongwith EMP, proceedings of the public hearing, a copy of the pre-feasibility project report and giving the required information in the prescribed form to the Central Regulatory Authority (CRA) i.e., Ministry of Environment and Forests for grant of environmental clearance. The completed papers are placed by the Ministry before the Expert Appraisal Committee (EAC). The project proponent can himself, or through a representative including the consultant who has prepared the EIA report and the EMP, can make a presentation before the Expert Appraisal Committee in which, besides giving details of the project, technology to be used etc., steps proposed to be taken to address the issues raised by the people during the public hearing are clarified. There are about 10-15 members in the Committee. The project proponent should be ready with convincing clarifications on various issues raised by the Committee. Once the Committee is convinced with the proposed mitigating measures projected by the lessee, the Committee recommends the project to the Ministry for according environmental clearance. While recommending environmental clearance, the Committee invariably prescribes certain conditions to protect the environment. The recommendations of the Committee form the basis on which the Central Government takes a view on the question of grant or otherwise of environmental clearance for any project. The importance of the Committee can be appreciated by the fact that the Central Regulatory Authority (CRA), i.e. the Ministry of Environment and Forests (MoEF) shall normally accept the recommendations of the Committee and in case the Ministry does not agree with the recommendations it shall request the Committee for its reconsideration. If, however, the Committee, on reconsideration, does not change its earlier recommendations, the Ministry can take its own decision. Usually the Ministry accepts the recommendations of the Committee as these recommendations are put in the website of the Ministry and become public document and any decision contrary to the recommendations of the Committee can be challenged in a Court of Law. I am emphasizing this fact just to impress upon the project proponent that the Committee has been given a very important role in the entire process and, therefore, it has to be convinced by the project proponent about the merit of his proposal. The procedure as explained above shall be, *mutatis mutandis,* applicable in respect of 'B' category projects to be considered by the State Level Expert Appraisal Committee.

If the Ministry accepts the recommendations of the Committee a clearance letter is issued to the project proponent incorporating the conditions prescribed by the Committee. The Ministry of Environment and Forests has also certain standard general and special conditions which are also invariably added, as applicable in a particular case, to the list of conditions prescribed by the Expert Appraisal Committee. Once such a clearance is given, the miner is empowered to start mining operations provided he has got other clearances including clearance under the Forest (Conservation) Act, 1980, if required, and after obtaining the statutory permission from all the concerned authorities, most importantly "consent to establish the unit", i.e., permission of the State Pollution Control Board under the Air Act and the Water Act to start the project activities. For 'B' category cases the clearance is granted by the State Level Environment Impact Assessment Authority.

For the benefit of project proponents, the Expert Appraisal Committee under my Chairmanship has prepared a Model Terms of Reference for the preparation of the EIA report and the EMP and the same were revised in April, 2008 which are also in the website of the Ministry of Environment and Forests. The Terms of Reference have been called model as the same will stand modified on case to case basis depending upon a specific project. But an attempt has been made by the Committee to devise the model terms of reference in a way that it would, *mutatis mutandis*, generally be applicable in all mining projects. As regards processing plant, the Ministry has certain set of terms of reference and I must admit that the Committee could not make any attempt to prepare a model terms of reference for the processing plant. This is mainly on account of the fact that I found that the Ministry did nothing to make an assessment of the working of various Committees after their formation which resulted in certain amount of frustration and I was not inclined to continue as Chairman for the full tenure of three years. In fact, I submitted my resignation some time in March 2009 but the Minister refused to accept my resignation and on his personal request I continued as Chairman till the end of the tenure of the

Committee in August, 2009. But the Committee was seriously considering further revision of the model terms of reference besides preparing terms of reference for the processing plant.

In the subsequent chapters various issues concerning protection of the environment starting with detailed analysis of the Environment Notification of 14th September, 2006 in Chapter-2 have been dealt with.

Since the Scheduled Tribes and other Traditional Forest Dwellers (Recognition of Forest Rights) Act, 2006 has introduced certain new elements with far reaching impact on mining activities I have allocated one full chapter to the relevant provisions of this Act and their implications. I have allocated a full chapter to the functioning of the Expert Appraisal Committee, NGOs and the Ministry of Environment and Forests under the title Role of the Stakeholders.

While giving any practical example I have in mind mostly iron ore (at times some other minerals) mineral as this (iron ore) mineral is abundantly available in the country.

Chapter – 2

14th September Notification

For executing any mining project including expansion of an existing project as also beneficiation plant, a lessee would require prior environmental clearance for the project which is granted by the Ministry of Environment and Forests (MoEF), Government of India under the Environment (Protection) Act, 1986. The project proponent is required to file an application in the prescribed Form-I as modified by the 1st December, 2009 Notification referred to in the succeeding paragraph along with an Environment Impact Assessment (EIA) report and the related Environment Management Plan (EMP) and a copy of the pre-feasibility project report to the Central Regulatory Authority, i.e. MoEF.

The action to be taken and the procedures to be followed in obtaining the required environmental clearance have been elaborated by the MoEF vide their Notification No. S.O. 1533 (E) dated 14th September, 2006 hereinafter to be referred to as the 14th September Notification. There have been three major amendments to the above Notification, one dated 11th October, 2007 vide Notification No. S.O. 1737 (E) and another dated 1st December, 2009 vide Notification No. S.O. 3067 (E) while the last one dated 4th April, 2011 vide Notification No. S.O. 695 (E) issued by the MoEF. For the benefit of the project proponent, these amendments have been appropriately incorporated in the original, i.e., 14th September Notification. The updated 14th September Notification with the amendments referred to above has been kept as Annexure-A to this book for a convenient and comprehensive reference.

The practical application of the 14th September Notification in the preparation of the EIA report and the EMP for obtaining environmental clearance would be explained later in this book. In the present chapter, I have made an attempt to explain the procedural part so that a lessee is familiar with the implications of the various requirements enunciated under the 14th September Notification and subsequent three amending notifications referred to in the preceding paragraph.

Para 2 of the 14th September Notification makes it clear that there are two categories of projects or activities for which prior environmental clearance shall be required. This has been included in the Schedule to this Notification. Mining projects come under Item No. 1(a) of the Schedule with which this book is concerned. Whatever, has been stated in this book is only in respect of ferrous and non-ferrous minerals. There are two categories of mining projects as Category 'A' and Category 'B'. Mining projects in a lease hold area which is equal or more than 50 hectares shall be considered as Category 'A'. However, asbestos mining shall always be treated as Category 'A' even if the lease hold area is less than 50 hectares. Though not stated in the Notification, the intention is obvious as the impact of environmental pollution that would affect human beings and other living things is quite serious and therefore such cases (mining of asbestos) should be treated separately. If the lease hold area is less than 50 hectares but not less than 5 hectares, the projects would be treated as Category 'B'. A lease hold area of less than 5 hectares was kept out of the purview of the 14th September Notification. In the light of the Supreme Court ruling, environment clearance shall be required for lease hold area of less than 5 hectares also. The authority competent to grant environmental clearance for Category 'A' project is the Central Regulatory Authority (CRA), i.e., the Central Government in the MoEF while for Category 'B' projects the competent authority is the State Environment Impact Assessment Authority (SEIAA) *which should not be confused as the State Government*, as the State Government does not have the authority under the Environment (Protection) Act, 1986 to exercise the power of granting environmental clearance. The Central Government can, under Section 5 of the Act, delegate certain other powers under the Act to the State Government(s) with the option to revoke such delegated powers as and when deemed fit. Even the SEIAA is to be constituted by the Central Government in the MoEF for which the procedure has also been prescribed under the 14th September Notification.

Mineral prospecting is exempted from the requirement of environmental clearance. This provision is the amended version after the qualificatory expression "not involving drilling" was deleted by the Notification dated 11th October, 2007.

Sub-paras (i), (ii) and (iii) of para 2 enumerate the projects or activities that require prior environmental clearance. It is clear that not only the new projects or activities but also expansion or modernization of existing projects or activities and any change in product mix beyond the specified range would require environmental clearance.

Para 3 of the 14th September Notification deals with the composition of the SEIAA which will deal with the cases falling under Category 'B'. Sub-para (7) of para 3 is significant and a lessee needs to be fully conversant with its implications. The original sub-para (7) of the Notification merely states that all decisions of the SEIAA shall be taken in a meeting, i.e., not in a file by circulation as is the practice quite often followed and that such decision shall be unanimous. The stipulation that decision shall be unanimous was definitely impractical as it can not be expected that all the three members including the Chairman shall have identity of opinion on each and every project. While the expression "consensus" has a flexible connotation, the expression "unanimous" does not leave any scope for any dissenting voice. Thus sub-para (7) has been modified by the Notification dated 1st December, 2009 referred to earlier. Amended sub-para (7) provides that the decision of the SEIAA shall ordinarily be unanimous but if that (unanimity) is not possible, the decision shall be by majority. To obviate any scope for incorrect or controversial decision by the majority, the amended sub-para (7) makes it mandatory that in case of difference the details of the views, for and against, shall be clearly recorded in the minutes and a copy of such minutes shall be sent to the MoEF. This will give an opportunity to the Central Government to scrutinize a case and take a view if any intervention by the Central Government is called for, though such an eventuality (intervention by the Central Government) is not stipulated in the amending Notification. Thus, an element of transparency in the working of the SEIAA has been introduced by the amending Notification dated 1st December, 2009 and if the project authority is aggrieved by the majority decision it can always take recourse to available legal and administrative remedial actions.

Para 4 of the Notification gives the categorization of projects and activities which has been elaborated above. To assist the Central Level Regulatory Authority and State Level Regulatory Authority, there will be two Expert Appraisal Committees, one for Category 'A' projects and the other for Category 'B' projects. At the Central Level, the Expert Appraisal Committee (EAC) shall consist of professionals and experts as provided for under Appendix-VI to the 14th September Notification. There have been some amendments in the Appendix-VI vide MoEF Notification dated 11 October, 2007 referred to earlier. Most of the modifications are by way of correcting certain omissions which are of clerical nature. However, there is one important addition to the list of experts or professionals who could also be member of the EAC. An expert on Public Administration or Management could also be considered for appointment as a member of the EAC. Para 4 of the Notification that specifies certain expertise and experience for a person to become the Chairperson of the EAC have been deleted by the Notification of 11th October, 2007. The number of members of the EAC shall not exceed fifteen with a provision that the Chairperson can exercise the discretion to co-opt any expert for a particular meeting of the Committee i.e. such a co-opted member shall not be routinely invited for each and every meeting. The EAC is, therefore, a fairly representative body to be in a position to give appropriate recommendations to the Ministry. EAC shall have a tenure of three years and there is a provision for giving only one more tenure of three years. Thus, no member or Chairperson shall be on the EAC for more than six years. To ensure that the meeting can be conducted in the absence of Chairperson, there is a provision for nominating one of the members as the Vice-Chairperson and such Vice-Chairperson shall be nominated only by the Chairperson. In order that the Chairperson or any member does not become a victim of vindictive or arbitrary decision by the Government, the appendix provides that no Chairperson or member may be removed prior to expiry of his/her tenure without a cause and proper enquiry. Though a provision has been made for removal of the Chairperson and the members, I have come across a specific case in which the MoEF has rewarded a particular person by giving him one extra tenure of three years on the newly constituted EAC even though the conduct of the particular person was found to be of unbecoming nature and integrity doubtful justifying instant removal.

All Category 'B' projects and activities will be considered by the State or Union Territory Level Expert Appraisal Committee (SEAC) whose recommendations will be essential for the SEIAA to take a view on the proposal for granting environmental clearance. Para 4 of the 14th September Notification makes an interim arrangement for dealing with Category 'B' projects in respect of States/Union Territories in the absence of a duly constituted SEIAA or SEAC. As per the original provision of the Notification such Category 'B' projects would be treated as Category 'A' projects and to be considered by the Central Government. There has been minor modification in sub-para (iii) of para 4 by the Notification dated 1st December, 2009. By this amendment, a Category 'B' project in a State or Union Territory where there is no duly constituted SEIAA or SEAC shall continue to be a Category 'B' project (and not treated as Category 'A' project) and shall be considered at the Central level. In other words, a Category 'B' project shall not automatically become a Category 'A' project simply because it will be considered at the Central level. That is to say, absence of SEIAA or SEAC does not alter the category to which the particular project belongs.

By the same Notification dated 1st December, 2009, it has been specified under "Note" after the Schedule that if a Category 'B' project is located, wholly or partly, within 10 km from the boundary of: (i) Protected areas notified under the Wildlife (Protection) Act, 1972; (ii) Critically polluted areas as identified by the Central Pollution Control Board from time to time; (iii) Eco-sensitive areas as notified under Section 3 of the Environment (Protection) Act, 1986, such as, Mahabaleshwar Panchgani, Matheran, Pachmarhi, Dahanu Doon Valley, and (iv) inter-State boundaries and international boundaries it shall be treated as Category `A' project for the purpose of grant of environmental clearance by the MoEF. In other words, a project proponent is required to submit his proposal for environmental clearance in respect of the project falling under the above specification(s) to the Central Regulatory Authority i.e., MoEF. If there is an agreement between the respective States or Union Territories sharing the common boundary to the effect that the stipulated distance of 10 km could be reduced or could be completely done away with, there will be no need for treating a Category `B' project as Category `A' project. In other words, such Category `B' project will continue to be treated as Category `B' project provided such a project does not fall under the purview of (i), (ii) and (iii) above. This means that Category `B' project coming under the purview of (i), (ii) and (iii) shall remain unaffected by any agreement between the respective States or Union Territories sharing the common boundary. Theortically there can be a possibility in which a project may fall within 10 km from the common boundary shared by three (could be more) States. In such a situation, if any one of the common boundary sharing States declines to enter into an agreement for reducing the distance of 10 km or declines to agree that the stipulation could be completely done away with, the Category `B' project in question will be treated as Category `A' project.

Para 5 of the 14th September, 2006 Notification deals with the scope of work of the Expert Appraisal Committee, one at the Central level which, as already explained, will be known as Expert Appraisal Committee (EAC) and the other at the State or Union Territory level which will be known as State Expert Appraisal Committee (SEAC). This Committee will screen, scope and appraise the mining projects or activities in Category 'A' and Category 'B' as the case may be. The Committee shall meet at least once in every month. The para also talks of the composition of the Committee etc. which will be explained in greater detail later. The members of the Committee shall be competent to undertake site visit while appraising a particular proposal. The Committee shall function on the principle of collective responsibility. The Chairperson of the Committee has a very critical role as he/she will be required to function as a friend, philosopher and guide for all the members and he/she shall try his/her best to ensure that the recommendations of the Committee are by way of consensus. However, difference of opinion among the members whose number could be anything between 10 and 15 cannot be ruled out. The Notification envisages difference of opinion and in such a situation the views of the majority shall prevail. During the entire tenure of three years, the Committee of which I was the Chairman had no occasion to take a view which were not by way of consensus.

Para 6 of the 14th September, 2006 Notification deals with the filing of application by the project proponent before the MoEF for prior environmental clearance. The application is required to be filed in the prescribed Form-I. Form-I is prescribed in respect of mining projects. The filled in application form alongwith EIA report and the EMP, a copy of the pre-feasibility project report and proceedings of the public consultation shall be submitted by the project proponent to the MoEF with a simple forwarding letter. Without going into details, it would be useful if I make small elaboration on the requirement of pre-feasibility project report reserving my right to give further details in appropriate place later. The reason for having a pre-feasibility project report is to assure the regulatory authority that the proposed mining project or activity shall be financially viable after meeting all expenses on executing the project as also expenses to be incurred on protecting the environment including conservation of flora and fauna besides giving a reasonable return to the project proponent as otherwise the project proponent could execute the project without doing anything for the protection of environment. I will come back to this subject later for a comprehensive presentation in Part-A of Chapter-5.

Vide 1st December, 2009 Notification, there have been major modifications in Form-I in respect of basic information. There are now 24 items against which the project proponent is to give the required information which relate to the basic information about the project, its location, name and address of the project proponent, etc. This was long over due as the Committee had persistently taken the view that the original form on basic information was grossly inadequate. In fact, there was another form, which was known as Annexure-II, which was more informative than even the amended version of Form-I. There is no change in the Form in respect of other paragraphs (II) to (VI). However, by the above Notification few important additions have been made at the end of Form-I. The first addition is on the undertaking to be given by the applicant about the correctness of the information given in the form. In addition to the above undertaking, the amended form would impose certain obligations on the project proponent which have been explained under NOTE at the end of the form. These are as follows:

- If the project involves clearance under CRZ Notification, 2011, the project proponent is required to submit, alongwith the application, a CRZ map giving the required information as also the status of the requisite clearance by the Coastal Zone Management Authority concerned under the provisions of the CRZ Notification, 2011, if necessary.
- If the project is located within 10 km of the National Parks, Sanctuaries, etc., as referred to earlier, the project proponent is required to submit the relevant map duly authenticated by the Chief Wildlife Warden.

The last one is on the requirement of a signed authority, in case the project proponent so decides, in favour of a person to present the case before the Committee or to sign any paper on behalf of the project proponent so as to ensure that only the authorized person makes the submission to the Committee.

Para 7 of the 14th September, 2006 Notification explains in details the various stages involved in the prior environmental clearance process for new projects. However, it does not mean that these stages would not be relevant for expansion/modification cases. There are four stages i.e., screening, scoping, public consultation and appraisal. These stages are briefly explained in the sequel.

Stage (1) – Screening

Screening is applicable only in respect of Category 'B' projects and activities. Since, the area involved in Category 'B' project is less than 50 hectares, an assessment is required to be made first if further environmental studies for the preparation of EIA report is essential. Such a decision will be taken by the State Level Expert Appraisal Committee (SEAC). This will basically help smaller lessees who may not have enough financial resource for undertaking detailed environmental studies which are essential for larger projects. Thus the SEAC will take a conscious decision on the matter so that smaller lessees do not find the project financially unviable. But it is quite possible that even for smaller area, in some cases, there could be the possibility of serious environmental issues and therefore, detailed environmental studies would be required for such projects before the same are appraised prior to the grant of environmental clearance. Thus the nature of the project and its location will determine if detailed environmental studies are required to be undertaken or not. There cannot be a rule of thump that a small project would not entail any environmental issue. If the SEAC comes to the conclusion that a particular project and its location are of such nature that it would have impact on the environment, the SEAC shall direct accordingly and such type of project will be termed as Category 'B-1' requiring EIA report. The remaining projects where environmental studies are not required will be termed as Category 'B-2' and such project would not require an EIA report. The Ministry of Environment and Forest (MoEF) will issue the necessary guidelines in this regard. There has been some amendments in this respect vide Notification dated 1st December, 2009. It provides that even in respect of Category 'B-2' project appraisal shall be made on the basis of the prescribed Form-I and EIA report if a particular project is exempted from Public Consultation. In other words, if there is a Public Consultation, an EIA report will not be required. But if the Public Consultation is not mandatory or the project has been exempted from Public hearing, an EIA report would be required. It really means that if there is a Public Hearing, the various issues on environmental pollutions would be raised by the members of the public and the response of the project proponent thereto would serve the purpose of an EIA report and the EMP.

The MoEF is yet to issue the required guidelines on the requirement or otherwise of preparation of an EIA report in respect of Category 'B-1' or Category 'B-2' projects even though the 14th September Notification is more than six years old. Thus, there is still confusion in the minds of project proponents under Category 'B' projects.

Stage (2) – Scoping

For obtaining prior environmental clearance on any project or activity, the project proponent is required to file an application before the MoEF alongwith duly filled in Form-I, EIA report, EMP, proceedings of the public hearing and a copy of the pre-feasibility project report. The project proponent may suggest his own terms of reference for the preparation of EIA report and EMP to the EAC for Category 'A' project and SEAC for Category `B' project. While considering the proposal for prior environmental clearance referred to it by the MoEF, the Committee determines the terms of reference on the basis of the information furnished by the project proponent in the prescribed Form. The EAC or the SEAC may, at its discretion, accept the terms of reference submitted by the project proponent, if any, with or without modifications. The Committee may also organize a site visit by a sub-group of the Committee. This entire process is called scoping. This is a very important exercise to be undertaken by the Committee as, if the Committee comes to the conclusion that a particular project is not fit to be granted environmental clearance it may recommend the proposal to the regulatory authority, i.e. MoEF for rejection and the MoEF may reject the application at this stage itself. However, such a case of rejection shall have to be communicated to the applicant in writing within 60 days of the receipt of the application. As the applicant is not given an opportunity to be heard, the decision of the MoEF to reject his application alongwith reasons therefor is to be conveyed to him so that he can exercise his option to take available legal or administrative action in case he feels aggrieved by the decision of the regulatory authority. Since, such a rejection is in violation of the principle of natural justice, all cases of request for prior environmental clearance are processed in terms of the 14th September Notification. In the entire process, the framing of the Terms of Reference is very critical as the terms of reference must address all relevant environmental concerns for the preparation of an EIA report based on which the EMP is also prepared. The Committee is required to determine the Terms of Reference for each project that comes before it for appraisal. Since it is not a practical idea to frame terms of reference in each and every case as that would take unusually long time which will delay the entire process of appraisal, the Committee has framed a terms of reference which is called model. The first model terms of reference was prepared some time in November 2007 and based on the experience gathered by the Committee the Model Terms of Reference was revised in April 2008 which has been followed by the Committee till its tenure ended in August, 2009. It is understood that the next committee also followed the same model terms of reference. For an instant reading, a copy of this Model Terms of Reference has been kept at Annexure-B. This is also available on the website of the MoEF. A perusal of the Annexure would indicate that the Committee has made an attempt to cover environmental concerns likely to come up in executing a mining project. The committee never thought that the Model Terms of Reference with all its ramifications shall apply equally in each and every mining project. Nevertheless, a project proponent would find it very easy to identify the issues that need to be considered in detail in respect of his project. To that extent the Model Terms of Reference has a universal application. In fact, the Committee was considering further elaborating the Model Terms of Reference based on the experience gathered subsequently. But due to certain circumstances, briefly referred to in the Chapter on Introduction, I was not inclined to make any attempt on further revising the Model Terms of Reference.

Stage (3) – Public Consultation

Public Consultation, popularly known as Public Hearing, is a very significant stage introduced by the 14th September Notification. Detailed procedure for the conduct of public hearing has been provided for in Appendix-IV to the Notification. The original Appendix-IV has been substituted by a new Appendix-IV by the 1st December, 2009 Notification. At this stage I will only briefly state the most important aspects of Public Consultation while giving details of the procedure as also its relevance in the preparation of the EIA report and the EMP in Chapter-4. In a nutshell, public consultation is a methodology by which the material concerns of the local people who will be affected due to the mining operations to be carried on by the miner are ascertained and are effectively addressed by the project proponent. Needless to say that any mining activity would impact the environment of the surrounding areas which will affect the air quality, water quality as also the total physical environment of the area and larger the operations wider is the impact on the environment. The operations will also affect the productivity of the land which will have an adverse impact on the economic conditions of the people. It will also interfere with the normal movement of the people including their cattle besides affecting the forest cover and the fauna of the area. No doubt, the mining operations would also create direct and indirect employment opportunities for the local people. However, such employment opportunities would not automatically neutralize the likely adverse physical environment affecting health and life of the people. Therefore, it is essential that the miner knows in advance the likely reaction of the local populace who will be directly impacted because of the mining operations so that the miner, while preparing the EMP, can address the bona fide concerns of the local people. This will indirectly help the miner to get the willing support of the local people. This will be an asset whose value cannot be quantified in terms of cash but the good will created thereby would be enormous compared to the financial involvement. The Public Consultation will also give an opportunity to the miner to create certain basic facilities like drinking water, health care services, etc. even before mining actually starts.

Stage (4) – Appraisal

This is the most crucial stage in the entire process as the project is subject to a very critical and detailed scrutiny by the Expert Appraisal Committee both at the Central level and at the State level. It is not enough that the miner has prepared a thorough EIA report and convincing EMP including the steps proposed to be taken by the project proponent to address the concerns expressed by the people during public consultation. Though the proceedings of the Public Consultation are to be submitted to the regulatory authority, the Expert Appraisal Committee goes into each and every concern raised during the public hearing and judges if the response of the project proponent thereto are adequate. The practice followed by the Expert Appraisal Committee at the Central level is that the project proponent himself or through an authorized representative who could be the consultant who has prepared the EIA report and the EMP makes a video presentation of the project, the EIA report and the EMP consistent with the Terms of Reference which were earlier approved by the Committee. The project proponent is required to give an authentic map of the lease-hold area and its buffer zone (10 km radius) and the Committee invariably insists on the submission of such a map based on the satellite imagery. This map provides all the details like forests, water bodies, lands, hills and everything else that are physically and technically possible to show on the map. At the end of the presentation each and every member of the Committee may raise some doubt and the project proponent is to clarify those doubts. The project proponent is required to indicate the steps proposed to be taken for mitigating adverse impacts and needless to say that such steps should be realistic and pragmatic for which the project proponent is required to give the financial outlay. In this context the pre-feasibility project report becomes an important guide as the pre-feasibility project report, even without giving the details of the cash flow statement, internal rate of return, etc., gives a fairly reasonable idea about the profitability of the project and the surplus cash to be generated which will be available for executing the various mitigating steps including the socio-economic activities as a part of the CSR policy. Since the Committee consists of about 10-15 members who are experts in various fields, the project proponent should be ready to answer any doubt raised by any member. No doubt the Chairman tries to arrive at a decision by consensus, but if some of the genuine concerns expressed by the member(s) cannot be satisfactorily explained by the project proponent, the Chairman also would find it difficult to come to a commonly acceptable conclusion.

Grant or Rejection of Prior Environmental Clearance

After appraisal of the project and if the Expert Appraisal Committee is satisfied that it is a fit case for which prior environmental clearance can be accorded, it recommends grant of environmental clearance to the regulatory authority, i.e., MoEF at the Central level and SEIAA at the State level. For the sake of convenience and for the purpose of this book I have used the expression MoEF as the regulatory authority which shall mean the SEIAA also. The regulatory authority normally accepts the recommendations of the Committee and in case the regulatory authority disagrees with the recommendations of the Committee, it shall request the Committee for reconsideration for the reasons that will be recorded by the regulatory authority. The recommendations of the Committee are very important as the regulatory authority shall normally accept the recommendations. This puts enormous responsibility on the Expert Appraisal Committee as its recommendations cannot be a casual or half-hearted one. It is quite possible that the Expert Appraisal Committee may, on reconsideration, change its opinion. However, during the tenure of the Committee headed by me for three years, it has not changed its first recommendation even on reconsideration on the request of the regulatory authority. The Committee has reconsidered the matter in an open mind and had always taken an objective view. There has been only one case in which on a reference from the Regulatory Authority for reconsideration the Committee modified the recommendations but that modifications did not run counter to the basic recommendations of the Committee. In fact, in the process, the Committee modified the recommendations because the proposed changes suggested by the project proponent were found to be more environment friendly as the changed scenario would have resulted in less land degradation and consequent less adverse physical environment. However, the Committee insisted that the project proponent was required to come before it with its modified proposal and the regulatory authority considered that the Committee's stand was procedurally correct.

While recommending a particular case the Committee also prescribes certain conditions for compliance by the project proponent and these conditions are meant for protecting the environment. While conveying the sanction letter, the Ministry also prescribes certain conditions relevant to the specific project. The recommendations of the Committee including its recommendations for rejection are always with sound reasons and these recommendations become public documents and are put on the website of the Ministry and the miner as well as the general public have access to these recommendations which are instantly in public domain.

There are few more relevant aspects in the process of grant of environmental clearance. These are explained below.

Time schedule of various activities has been indicated in the 14th September Environment Notification. The project proponent is required to submit complete information and all the relevant documents to the regulatory authority. These documents are referred by the Regulatory Authority to the Expert Appraisal Committee for its appraisal. The Expert Appraisal Committee has been given 65 days' time to complete the procedure and submit its recommendations to the regulatory authority, i.e., MoEF. The Committee itself is required to submit its recommendations within 5 working days after the meeting is over. The MoEF is required to take a decision on the recommendations of the Committee within 45 days. Thus a total of 110 (65+45) days are available to the Committee and the Ministry to come to a final decision. However, if the regulatory authority remits the case back to the Committee for reconsideration, the Committee is required to give its opinion within 45 days and thereafter the regulatory authority shall convey its final decision within another 45 days. But these are exceptions and there are not too many cases where the regulatory authority requests for reconsideration.

Validity of Environmental Clearance

The environmental clearance granted by the MoEF is valid for a period not exceeding 30 years for mining projects. This is in accordance with the provision of Section 8(1) of the Mines and Minerals (Development and Regulation) Act, 1957 (MMDR, Act) which provides for grant of mining lease for a period not exceeding 30 years. It is quite possible that the Ministry must have kept the above provision of the MMDR, Act in mind while determining the period of validity for environmental clearance. Since any mining project will have a gestation period of 2-5 years depending on the nature and extent of the ore as also the size of the lease-hold area, the validity of the environmental clearance must take this also into account. Moreover, the project proponent always indicates the life of the project and therefore all these factors are taken into account in fixing the period of validity of the environmental clearance.

Post Environmental Clearance Monitoring

Grant of environmental clearance is not the end of the process. In fact, post environmental clearance monitoring as prescribed under Para-10 of the 14th September Notification is very significant. This has been elaborated by inserting a new sub-para by the 1st December 2009 Notification. The gist of this para is that the project proponent is required to inform the public of the environmental clearance granted to the project along with the environmental conditions and safeguards through advertisement at his cost in at least two local news papers besides displaying the same on the website of the project proponent permanently. MoEF as also the SEIAA would make all these documents as in the public domain. There is also another requirement that has been introduced by the 1st December, 2009 amendment under which the project proponent is required to send copies of the environmental clearance to the Heads of local bodies, i.e., Panchayati Raj Institutions and Municipal Bodies. In addition to the concerned officers of the Government, all these authorities would have to display the copies of the environmental clearance for 30 days in a conspicuous place in their respective office. The basic purpose is to inform the local people about certain activities for which environmental clearance has been granted with various terms and conditions so that the informed section of the public can keep a constant vigil on the activities of the project proponent and on the status of compliance with the terms and conditions prescribed by the Ministry.

Transferability of Environmental Clearance

After the grant of environmental clearance, the ownership of the project may change on account of normal business transactions or on account of demise of the original owner of the project or due to any other reason. A question will come up about the transfer of the environmental clearance granted by the regulatory authority. The provision of the relevant laws shall apply in such cases also. Thus, if a lease has been transferred to another entity, environmental clearance granted would also be transferred to the legal transferee of the lease. For such transfer of the environmental clearance granted by the MoEF, separate consideration by the Expert Appraisal Committee is not required as the Committee has considered the project as such and the ownership of the project was not relevant for the Committee to arrive at a particular view. However, two "no objection", one by the transferor and the other by the regulatory authority shall be required before the environmental clearance can be transferred to the new entity. The terms and conditions and the validity period shall remain the same. Though not mentioned in para-11 of the 14th September Notification, it is common sense that the new owner has to apply to the regulatory authority i.e., MoEF with documentary evidence that the mining lease and other relevant assets have been transferred to him alongwith "no objection" from the original owner for effecting the transfer of the environmental clearance. However, if the change of ownership has been due to the demise of the original owner, the lease and the relevant assets will stand transferred to the legal heir of the original owner. Application for transfer of the environmental clearance shall, in such a contingency, i.e., demise of the original owner, be accompanied by legally acceptable (could be Court order or WILL, etc.) document to prove that the new entity is the legal heir. The terms and conditions of the original environmental clearance and the period of validity shall remain unchanged, that is, only the ownership will be changed in case of a transfer.

Chapter – 3

Forest Rights of the Scheduled Tribes and Other Traditional Forest Dwellers

In this chapter I have made an attempt to explain the implications of certain provisions, relevant in the context of mining activities, of a new Act enacted by the Parliament. The Act under the title the Scheduled Tribes and Other Traditional Forest Dwellers (Recognition of Forest Rights) Act, 2006 (No. 2 of 2007), which I will also refer to, for the sake of convenience, as the Forest Rights Act, notified on January 2, 2007 and the Scheduled Tribes and Other Traditional Forest Dwellers (Recognition of Forest Rights) Rules, 2007 framed under the Act, have introduced certain new elements a miner should necessarily be conversant with. As stated in Chapter-1 on Introduction, I have started with the assumption that whatever I have said in this book is applicable in respect of iron ore mineral in the forest areas where the scheduled tribes and other traditional forest dwellers have been living for generations. This has been done deliberately as it becomes easier to explain relevant provisions of the Act and Rules, etc. in a more instructive and convincing manner. Even though the major part of my career involving my working in the mineral sector has been spent in non-ferrous minerals and metals sector, as Chairman of the Expert Appraisal Committee, I found that cases of iron ore mines are of typical nature and therefore I must take the case of iron ore mines for the purpose of this book. However, what I have stated in this book shall, *mutatis mutandis*, apply in respect of other minerals as well.

Evidence shows that occurrences of iron ore are in the remote forest areas. Though there are iron ore occurrences in other areas but commercially exploitable iron ore are located mostly in the forest area and this is also the area where tribal population and other forest dwellers live. Before I deal with the implications of relevant sections of the Act and the Rules framed thereunder it would be of immense help to a miner if he is informed of certain basic facts which, though are well known to all of us, have not been given the importance they deserve. The Act and the Rules framed thereunder do only codify them with a view to conferring legally valid forest rights on the traditional forest dwellers, which rights they have been, even otherwise, enjoying for generations.

It is a well-known fact that every State has a list of scheduled tribes as notified by the President of India under Article 342(1) of the Constitution of India. Every State will have its own list of tribes who are listed in the schedule and are called scheduled tribes in the concerned State. Like wise, there are certain other people who do not come in the category of any tribe, whether scheduled or otherwise, but have been traditionally living in the forest for generations. It is pertinent to explain the import of the expression "generation" for proper understanding of the expression "other traditional forest dwellers". This has been clarified in the form of explanation to sub-section (o) of Section 2 of the Act. The explanation makes it clear that the word "generation" means a period comprising of twenty-five years, may be, perhaps due to the fact that the ground reality is such that a man of that age, traditionally residing in the forest, would be expected to have a family with his children who become the generation next for the community. This, in practical terms, would mean that in the family line starting with the father, his son(s) and his grand son(s) living in the forest would be taken as traditional forest dwellers. The main sub-section (o) makes it clear that "other traditional forest dwellers" means any member or community who has for at least three generations prior to the 13th day of December, 2005 primarily resided in, and who depend on, the forest or forest land for *bona fide* livelihood needs. Thus while there is no doubt about the status of the scheduled tribe people living in the forest for generations, in case of other traditional forest dwellers, it has to be proved that such dwellers must have been living in the forest for at least three generations prior to the reference date i.e. 13th day of December, 2005 and who must be dependent on the forest or forest land for bona fide livelihood needs for the intended benefits under the Forest Rights Act. Thus if such dwellers only live in the forest area, may be for many generations, but they do not depend on the forest land or the forest for their bona fide livelihood needs, they would not be entitled to the benefits envisaged under the Act. This seems to have been done deliberately as there are cases where some one including tribal or non-tribal must have built their own residential complex in the forest only for living purposes but their source of livelihood is not provided by the forest, as such people would be earning their livelihood needs outside or could be even inside the forest area in various commercial vocations like trade, business and services. Thus in order to enjoy the benefits of forest rights as traditional forest dwellers under the Act such forest dwellers must satisfy two conditions, namely, they must have been living in the forest for at least 75 (25 years × 3 generations) years prior to 13th Day of December, 2005 and not after this date and that they must be dependent on the forest or forest land for their bona fide livelihood needs. As regards a tribal, in order to be entitled to the benefits under the Act, the particular tribe to which he belongs must find a place in the Schedule as notified under Article 342(1) of the Constitution of India and not otherwise.

We commonly use to say that tribal people collect various Minor Forest Produce (MFP) that includes all Non-Timber Forest Produce of plant origin including bamboo, brush wood, stumps, cane, tussar, cocoons, honey, wax, lac, tendu or kendu leaves, medicinal plants and herbs, roots, tubers, etc. and it is a common scene in any forest area to see tribal people, mostly women, carrying head-load of these minor forest produce and walking long distance to sell the surplus quantity of these forest produce in the weekly market while part of it are consumed by them. These forest dwelling tribal people depend on the forest and forest land for their bona fide livelihood needs. As stated earlier, there are certain traditional non-tribal forest dwellers who would be similarly depending on the forest or forest land for their bona fide livelihood needs.

The expression "bona fide livelihood needs" has been defined not under the Act but under sub-rule (1) (b) of Rule 2. Bona fide livelihood needs would mean that such forest dwellers shall have the right through production or sale of produce resulting from self-cultivation of forest land for the fulfilment of sustenance needs of self and family. Self-cultivation of forest land will be as provided for under clauses (a), (c) and (d) of Section 3 of the Act extracted later in this chapter. Self-cultivation would entail right to live in the forest land for habitation or self-cultivation for livelihood, right of ownership, access to collect, use, and dispose of minor forest produce within or outside village boundaries and certain other rights like use of water bodies for fishing, cattle grazing lands etc. In layman's language this would mean that a forest dweller can exercise his forest rights only if he would engage in doing any work for his bona fide livelihood personally or through his own family members and not otherwise like through any hired persons except when physically incapacitated to do so.

The *Times of India* in its Delhi edition dated 9th September, 2012 has reported that the Government of India have made certain amendments in the Rules under which tribals and other forest dwellers can store and trade in minor forest produce besides meeting their consumption requirements. Thus, such people will enjoy the right to transport and store the minor forest produce for trade purposes beyond their bona fide livelihood needs without any hindrances. In other words, the definition of "bona fide livelihood needs" has been expanded to include activities beyond personal use.

Many of us would be claiming that we are fully aware of these practices of collecting minor forest produce by the tribal and other traditional forest dwellers for their livelihood needs. But we are totally ignorant, though our vanity does not allow us to admit that (ignorance), of the fact that these forest dwellers have been living there for generations on the land and that while collecting the minor forest produce they are also doing an immense and unnoticed act of conservation of biodiversity and maintenance of ecological balance and thereby such traditional forest dwellers are conserving the forest while ensuring their livelihood needs. We are equally ignorant that most of the forest dwellers do not have a legal documentation that recognizes their rights over the land where they have been living for generations and that there is no effective law that ensures their livelihood and food security. The above noted Act has codified these issues with the provisions for conferring on such scheduled tribes and other traditional forest dwellers a legal stamp in their forest rights which are theirs very own for generations. A similar, though not identical, case is that of non-tribal share croppers (in some States they are called *bargadaars*) who do not have any crop land of their own and in some cases they do not have even a home-stead land to construct their own dwelling house on. Such people are engaged, by the local land owners including some very small land owners who consider farming below their dignity, to cultivate their land for raising various crops and in lieu therefor they get a share of the crops raised on the land for their livelihood. In some States like West Bengal, rights of such *bargadaars* have been recorded but in many States such share croppers are at the mercy of the land owners who would take recourse to various tricks to deny continued right to work as a share cropper on the same land as under the existing regulation of these States if a share cropper works on a particular piece of land for a minimum number of three years or so, he acquires the right to continue farming on the same land. It is not uncommon to see many plots of land remaining fallow for one year so that the share cropper hired by the land owner does not have the continued right to cultivate the same land in the fourth year as there was a break, artificially, if not deceitfully, created though.

Before I proceed to explain the provisions of the Act relevant for a miner, I would also bring it to the notice of the miner that if his socio-economic activities as a part of the CSR policy takes into account the fact that if the miner takes few small steps that will allow an uninterrupted opportunity to the scheduled tribes and other traditional forest dwellers to ensure their traditional rights for sustainable use of the forest it will benefit most the miner. The Act itself does not define the expression "sustainable use" but it accepts the meaning of this expression as given under sub-section (o) of Section 2 (Definitions) of the Biological Diversity Act, 2002 (No. 18 of 2003) notified on February 5, 2003 as enacted by the Parliament: This sub-section (o) is extracted hereunder:

> "(o) "sustainable use" means the use of components of biological diversity in such a manner and at such rate that does not lead to the long-term decline of the biological diversity thereby maintaining its potential to meet the needs and aspirations of present and future generations"

The reading of the above sub-section makes it clear that the forest products and other products on the forest land should be used in such a way that in the long run biological diversity does not get impacted adversely and that even after regular use of the forest products the future growth of the biological diversity remains unhindered. In other words, the biological resources like plants, animals, etc. and the eco-system should be allowed to grow even after consumption of a part of the forest produce. The scheduled tribes and other traditional forest dwellers are an integral part of the forest and they know it very well that for their sustenance they must use the forest products and forest land in a way that allows the forest to grow thereby making such forest dwellers the natural conservators of forests. An example (repeated elsewhere in this book) is called for here. A forest dweller would collect minor forest produce, a dry branch of a standing tree, for using it as fuel by cutting the branch. But he would never cut any green branch that has life in it much less the tree itself as he knows that if he does so he would only kill his opportunity to collect such branches in future. It will not be an exaggeration if one comes to the conclusion that there is no better manpower than these scheduled tribes and other traditional forest dwellers to protect and conserve the forest and the ecological balance in the area.

Having explained certain salient facts, it is necessary to tell the miner about the purpose of giving such a boring background especially when he is already aware of such things. The purpose is that when the miner is mining in a forest area, there will be certain destruction of forest cover which will interfere with the normal vocation of the scheduled tribes and other traditional forest dwellers and therefore his socio-economic package must take note of the necessity to create a situation which would provide to the forest dwellers an uninterrupted source of their livelihood needs. I give here only one example, elaborating the details later while dealing with the subject on Environment Impact Assessment (EIA) and Environment Management Plan (EMP) in Part-B of Chapter 5 and in Chapters 10 and 11. Since, the forest dwellers would be grazing their cattle for which either they would have community grazing land or they would be grazing their cattle in the open forest area. Any mining operations in the area would interfere with the free movement of the cattle for grazing purpose. Therefore, the miner has to find an alternative convenient place for grazing purposes or must take steps to develop an alternative grazing area for the cattle.

I would deal with certain concepts introduced in the Forest Rights Act and which are exclusively relevant for a miner who will be exploiting the mineral resources in a forest area where the scheduled tribes and other traditional forest dwellers have been living for generations. The Act deals with the issue of recording forest rights in favour of such forest dwellers. Section 3, extracted after this para, deals with the forest rights. These rights include the right to hold and live in the forest land under the individual or common occupation for habitation or for self-cultivation for livelihood; right of ownership, access to collect, use and dispose of minor forest produce which has been traditionally collected within or outside village boundaries; other community rights of uses or entitlements such as fish and other products of water bodies, grazing (both settled or transhumant) and traditional seasonal resource access of nomadic or pastoralist communities. It is useful to clarify the meaning of the words 'settled' and 'transhumant' in the context of grazing of cattle for a clear understanding. Grazing land can be a definite, i.e., already settled piece of forest land over which the community as a whole has right for grazing its cattle. But some times due to various reasons grazing land has necessarily to be different in different seasons. The word "transhumant" is a combination of two words, "trans" meaning beyond and "humant" meaning, etymologically (by origin), ground or region. In other words, transhumant grazing means seasonal moving of live stock from one region to a different region depending on the exigencies of circumstances. This is important in view of the fact that mining activity may also interfere with the grazing rights of the nomadic or pastoralist communities in different regions.

Section 3 also clearly provides that the forest right shall also mean the right to protect, regenerate or conserve or manage any community forest resource that such forest dwellers have been traditionally protecting and conserving for sustainable use. These rights are basically not only rights but also a duty which the holders of such rights consider enjoined upon themselves without perhaps knowing that they have a duty to protect the forest even though they might be doing so for their bona fide livelihood needs. This particular forest right is very significant for a miner to know as here is a group of people whose skills and talents can be put to beneficial use of the miner himself by encouraging them through very little financial support for conserving the forest which is likely to be adversely affected due to mining activity.

The forests rights of the scheduled tribes and other traditional forest dwellers have been listed in Section 3 (1) of the Forest Rights Act which is extracted below:

Forest rights of Forest dwelling Scheduled Tribes and other traditional forest dwellers

"3. (1) For the purposes of this Act, the following rights, which secure individual or community tenure or both, shall be the forest rights of forest dwelling Scheduled Tribes and other traditional forest dwellers on all forest lands, namely:

(a) Right to hold and live in the forest land under the individual or common occcupation for habitation or for self-cultivation for livelihood by a member or members of a forest dwelling Scheduled Tribe or other traditional forest dwellers;
(b) Community rights such as *nistar*, by whatever name called, including those used in erstwhile Princely States, *Zamindari* or such intermediary regimes;
(c) Right to ownership, access to collect, use, and dispose of minor forest produce which has been traditionally collected within or outside village boundaries;
(d) Other community rights of uses or entitlements such as fish and other products of water bodies, grazing (both settled or transhumant) and traditional seasonal resource access of namadic or pastoralist communities;
(e) Rights including community tenures of habitat and habitation for primitive tribal groups and pre-agricultural communities;

(f) Rights in or over disputed lands under any nomenclature in any State where claims are disputed;
(g) Rights for conversion of *Pattas* or leases or grants issued by any local authority or any State Government on forest lands to titles;
(h) Rights of settlement and conversion of all forest villages, old habitation, unsurveyed villages and other villages in forests, whether recorded, notified or not into revenue villages;
(i) Right to protect, regenerate or conserve or manage any community forest resource which they have been traditionally protecting and conserving for sustainable use;
(j) Rights which are recognised under any State law or laws of any Autonomous District Council or Autonomous Regional Council or which are accepted as rights of tribals under any traditional or customary law of the concerned tribes of any State;
(k) Right to access to biodiversity and community right to intellectual property and traditional knowledge related to biodiversity and cultural diversity;
(l) Any other traditional right customarily enjoyed by the forest dwelling Scheduled Tribes or other traditinal forest dwellers, as the case may be, which are not mentioned in clauses (a) to (k) but excluding the traditional right of hunting or trapping or extracting a part of the body of any species of wild animal;
(m) Right to *in situ* rehabilitation including alternative land in cases where the Scheduled Tribes and other traditional forest dwellers have been illegally evicted or displaced from forest land of any description without receiving their legal entitlement to rehabilitation prior to the 13th day of Decemeber, 2005."

Another important and significant provision i.e. sub-section (2) of Section 3 is in respect of forest land that would be required by the Government for creating certain facilities like schools, dispensary or hospital, anganwadis, fair price shops, drinking water supply and water pipelines, rain water harvesting, etc. which is extracted below:

"(2) Notwithstanding anything contained in the Forest (Conservation) Act, 1980, the Central Government shall provide for diversion of forest land for the following facilities managed by the Government which involve felling of trees not exceeding seventy-five trees per hectare, namely:

(a) schools;
(b) dispensary or hospital;
(c) anganwadis;
(d) fair price shops;
(e) electric and telecommunication lines;
(f) tanks and other minor water bodies;
(g) drinking water supply and water pipelines;
(h) water or rain water harvesting structure;
(i) minor irrigation canals;
(j) non-conventional source of energy;
(k) skill upgradation or vocational training centers;
(l) roads; and
(m) community centres;

Provided that such diversion of forest land shall be allowed only if,—

(i) the forest land to be diverted for the purposes mentioned in this sub-section is less than one hectare in each case; and
(ii) the clearance of such developmental projects shall be subject to the condition that the same is recommended by the Gram Sabha."

This sub-section makes it very clear that for the above activities, the provisions of the Act shall prevail upon the provisions of the Forest (Conservation) Act, 1980. In other words, permission for the above activities on forest land shall be given by the Central Government by diversion of forest land for non-forest activities under the Forest (Conservation) Act, 1980 almost in a routine way as stipulated under the above sub-section (2). However, there is some restrictions like that felling of trees shall not esxceed seventy-five per hectare, the forest land to be diverted for any one of the above purposes shall be less than one hectare and that such activities need the recommendation of the Gram Sabha. If a miner is not allowed to utlise the forest land for any of the purposes noted above without prior permission of the Central Government (which may be at times difficult or even impossible to get), he can always participate in the above activities by making his own contribution to the Government

Agencies executing such activities thereby creating a good will among the local paper. If, however, the miner can procure the permission from Government to create any of the facilities like setting up a primary health centre or a school for the locals he can himself directly take up the work.

The role of the Gram Sabha assigned under the Act is significant and a complete departure from the usual practice followed by the Government in getting recommendations through the official hierarchy. The Gram Sabha has been given the authority to initiate the process of determining the nature and extent of forest right and its recommendation is essential in any resettlement proposal or economic package concerning forest dwellers. This is basically on account of the fact that the Gram Sabha is fully conversant with various rights and needs of any particular person or of the community. In order that the Gram Sabha does not get dominated by few influential persons, a specific provision has been made that the quorum of any meeting of the Gram Sabha shall be not less than two thirds of all members of such Gram Sabha. Gram Sabha has been defined under sub-section (g) of Section 2 of the Act and according to the definition all adult persons of the village shall be members of the Gram Sabha with full and unrestricted participation of women. With this definition of the Gram Sabha along with the provision of quorum of not less than two thirds members of the Gram Sabha, it goes without saying that any recommendation of the Gram Sabha shall be most appropriate and genuine for conferring forest rights on the scheduled tribes and other traditional forest dwellers and for executing any economic package. The Act specifically ensures that the consent of the Gram Sabha shall be free from any pressure and this is clear from the wording of sub-section (2) (e) of Section 4 of the Act extracted below:

> "(e) the free informed consent of the Gram Sabhas in the area concerned to the proposed resettlement and to the package has been obtained in writing"

For a complete understanding of the functions of the Gram Sabha it will be useful to go through the provision of Rule 4 which is extracted below:

> **"4. Functions of the Gram Sabha.** (1) The Gram Sabha shall—
>
> (a) initiate the process of determining the nature and extent of forest rights, receive and hear the claims relating thereto;
>
> (b) prepare a list of claimants of forests rights and maintain a

register containing such details of claimants and their claims as the Central Government may by order determine;

(c) pass a resolution on claims on forest rights after giving reasonable opportunity to interested persons and authorities concerned and forward the same to the Sub-Divisional Level Committee;

(d) consider resettlement packages under clause (e) of sub section (2) of section 4 of the Act and pass appropriate resolutions; and

(e) constitute Committees for the protection of wildlife, forest and biodiversity, from amongst its members, in order to carry out the provisions of section 5 of the Act.

(2) The quorum of the Gram Sabha meeting shall be not less than two thirds of all members of such Gram Sabha.

Provided that where there is a heterogeneous population of Scheduled Tribes and non-Scheduled Tribes in any village, the members of the Scheduled Tribe, Primitive Tribal Groups (PTGs) and pre-agricultural communities shall be adequately represented.

(3) The Gram Sabha shall be provided with the necessary assistance by the authorities in the State."

It is outside the concern of a miner to know how a particular forest dweller has been conferred upon certain rights under the Act. The procedure has been prescribed in the Act and the Rules framed thereunder. The legal documents for such rights have been prescribed under the Rules as Annexure-II (Individual Holder) and Annexure-III (Community Holder). These documents are signed by senior officers of the State Governments including District Collector/Deputy Commissioner. The miner will be perfectly within his right to prepare any scheme under his CSR policy for providing required gainful economic package to a forest dweller keeping in mind and not inconsistent with the recommendations of the Gram Sabha. It is also in the interest of the miner to do so as thereby he will have the support not only of the individual beneficiary but also of the entire village which will be an asset which cannot be quantified in terms of cash in carrying out his mining activities in the area. This is a new concept and the miner is well advised to have a good rapport with the villagers in general and not exclusively with some influential persons.

It is a fact that the miner will have some practical difficulties in a State where no election to Panchayats has taken place. Once elections to the three-tier Panchayat Institutions in a State take place it becomes easier to identify Gram Sabha under a Gram Panchayat and depending on the jurisdiction of the village(s) over the lease-hold areas and its surroundings, a miner would know definitely what are the forest rights and the location where such rights are to be exercised and accordingly he can prepare a package as a part of his CSR policy for the scheduled tribes and other traditional forest dwellers falling within the buffer zone of the mining activities. Core zone means the lease-hold areas and buffer zone means an area within 10 km radius of the lease-hold areas and, therefore, the miner will have wide option to prepare some economic packages to give effect to the forest rights as recommended by the Gram Sabha and finally approved by the district level committee. Since, the Sub-divisional Officer and the District Collector/Deputy Commissioner are Chairman of the sub-divisional level committee and district level committee respectively, a miner will have a vary trying time to pursue the matter at various levels from the village to the district level, but it is worth it keeping in mind that in the process he will not have to face a hostile local people all the times.

In the process for obtaining environmental clearance from the Ministry of Environment and Forests (MoEF) it will be quite pertinent to mention here that with proper rapport with the Gram Sabha, and its approval of the proposed economic activities to be included in the package as a part of his CSR policy, the miner will find it very easy to get the support of the local people in the public hearing that would be conducted as a part of the requirements under the Environment Notification of 14th September, 2006.

Chapter – 4

Public Consultation

Public consultation, commonly known as public hearing, is a very important and significant step in the entire process in obtaining environmental clearance for any mining project or activity. The original notification has prescribed the procedure for conduct of public hearing in Appendix-IV to the notification. This Appendix-IV has been substituted by a new Appendix-IV by the 1st December, 2009 notification. The substituted Appendix-IV is not materially different from the original Appendix-IV, except that the substituted Appendix-IV makes conduct of public hearing more transparent besides adding certain elaborations here and there.

It is important to understand the import of the expressions "Public Consultation", "Public Hearing" and "Public Meeting" so as to appreciate the significance of public consultation as distinct from that (significance) of public hearing or public meeting. There is a qualitative difference between the expression "Meeting" and the expressions "Hearing" or "Consultation". The meaning of the expression "meeting" can be best understood by a very familiar example of, say, public meeting addressed by a politician usually during the period of elections. In a public meeting the speaker delivers a speech and the audience has the obligation (so assumed by the speaker) to listen to the speaker, and the audience is also supposed to applause intermittently by repeating the slogans or by clapping hands at the call of the supporters of the speaker who will be positioned at different vintage points among the crowd to ensure that their leader (speaker) leaves the meeting place fully satisfied and convinced about the efficacy of the magical power of his or her oratory. In a public meeting the public (the crowd) are not heard. Rather the speakers are to be compulsorily heard by the crowd present in the meeting.

In contrast to public meeting the role of the public in public hearing is reversed. In other words, the public in a public hearing in the context of a mining project is to be patiently heard by the project proponent. It is not enough that the concerns raised by the public in such a public hearing are heard by the project proponent but the project proponent is under the obligation to address the concerns expressed by the public present in the meeting. This can be further elaborated by giving a reference to the procedures followed in our legal system by a trial court. An example will make it clear for a miner to appreciate the importance of public hearing. In a criminal court an accused is tried for the offence allegedly committed by him. Even if the accused knows and admits in the court that he has committed the alleged crime, say murder, and he had the *mens rea*, that is, the motive or criminal intent to commit the offence of murder, the trial court shall punish the accused only after giving him full and reasonable opportunity of being heard. That is, even if the accused pleads guilty, the trial court will punish him only after hearing him. Thus the views of the accused are to be assessed and appreciated by the trial court with cogent reasonings and depending on the nature of the evidences the trial court would decide the quantum of punishment to be imposed on the accused.

The expression "Consultation" has a meaning similar to the expression "Hearing" as explained in the preceding para. Here again an example will be useful to explain the connotation of consultation. Suppose the project authority proposes to provide drinking water facility in a village falling within the boundary of his mining lease or within the 10 km. radius, he would always like to select the site after consulting the village people or the head of the Village Panchayat. When the project proponent undertakes consultation he's under obligation to take note of the views of the villagers about the appropriate site for the purpose. The project proponent cannot select the site without giving due consideration to the views of the villagers. In other words, in the matter of consultation the opinion of the people consulted takes a pre-eminent status. It needs no emphasis to tell the project proponent that if views of the local people or at least majority of people in case of difference of opinion, are honoured, the project proponent would get instant support of the local people in the execution of his project.

It is now amply clear that public hearing in the context of mining project is not a simple process of hearing the public. A miner should always keep it in mind that the proposed mining activities to be undertaken by him would have impact on the physical and social environment not only in the leasehold area but also in its surroundings. This impact could be both adverse and positive, though mostly adverse. In the process of executing the project there would be degradation of lands, dust pollution, adverse impact on productivity of lands, health of the people, flora and fauna. Depending on the velocity and direction of the wind, dust generated on account of extraction of minerals and transportation to the destination would create dust pollution and vehicular pollution that could adversely impact not only the productivity of lands but also the cropping pattern in distant places en route. No doubt there will be some positive impact due to mining activities. Thus the project would generate employment opportunity for the local people directly in the project activities and also in ancillary activities, if any, besides indirect employment opportunities like opening tea stalls, road side eateries and transport activities. However, the immediate concerns of local people would be the adverse impact on the lands, water bodies and grazing lands for their cattle. The most vocal demand that would be invariably raised during public hearing would be employment to the local people especially to the land oustees.

The project proponent must anticipate the demands of local people to be raised during public hearing. Therefore, he should be ready with steps that he proposes to take to address the concerns expressed by the people in public hearing. I will briefly discuss three types of demands and concerns likely to be encountered by the project authority in public hearing at this stage while going into more details later in the context of the subject on the preparation of Environment Impact Assessment (EIA) Report and Environment Management Plan (EMP) in Chapters 5 and 11.

A common demand would be employment to the local people. It would be beneficial for the miner to give some positive response without making any impractical promise which cannot be kept. It is always possible to announce in the public hearing that no outsider shall be given employment in the project if the required manpower is locally available. There will be no dearth of unskilled persons locally and hence the project proponent straight way can give the assurance for employing the local people on all unskilled jobs. It is also possible to assure the public that if locally employable young boys and girls are available for employment in skilled and semi-skilled jobs with required training the project proponent would take necessary steps in that direction by appropriately training such persons at his cost. The project proponent can not take the plea that skilled manpower is not locally available and hence the local boys and girls can not be considered for employment in his project. This is a fallacious argument as the project proponent can not expect the local people to train their wards in certain vocations relevant for the project which was not in existence even in the wildest imagination of the local people. Therefore, the project proponent can arrange for imparting training to the eligible local boys and girls in certain skills that would be required for the project proponent in mining as well as office function or for self employment with some financial assistance.

Another common problem likely to be faced by the local people especially in the tribal areas is the loss of grazing lands for their cattle as the mining activities would definitely interfere with the free movement of the cattle and hence there would be demand for cattle grazing land. The project proponent can always assure the villagers during public consultation that alternative grazing area could be developed by him at convenient places selected by the local people even before the start of mining activities.

Adverse impact on the productivity of agricultural lands is inevitable on account of mining activities and therefore any apprehension of the villagers about lower yield of their crop-lands is a reality and consequently demand for higher compensation will be raised. In such a situation the project proponent can assure the public that he would assess the extent of damage to the productivity of lands in consultation with the officers of agriculture department of the government and would pay the compensation accordingly and periodically.

It would also be useful for the project proponent to indicate the financial implications for each of the above steps that have been suggested and this can be announced in the public hearing itself so as to create a positive impression and a sense of confidence in the minds of the local people. Since it is essential for the project proponent in terms of para 6 of the 14th September Notification to prepare a pre-feasibility project report, the project proponent could indicate the amount of funds that he would keep earmarked for such socio-economic activities. To make it more convincing the project proponent can also indicate that all expenses on socio-economic activities shall be a part of the project cost and therefore the required funds will always be available during the life of the project.

The above examples would show that public hearing can be put to maximum advantage of the miner as, if he succeeds in creating a positive impression among the people likely to be adversely affected by the proposed mining activities, he would create an asset of goodwill which would facilitate his execution of the project with a friendly people around. Hence, the project proponent should not have any apprehension that the public at large are necessarily hostile to the project. To his surprise it could just be otherwise.

It is always advisable to prepare the complete EIA Report and the EMP before going for public hearing. If the EIA Report and the EMP are ready, the project proponent can explain to the public, in the presence of the local District Collector or his nominee and the other State Government officials including the officials of the State Pollution Control Board, the extent of impact, both positive and adverse, and the proposed mitigating steps and the financial outlay for the purpose. If this can be accomplished in the beginning of public hearing itself, the public present in the hearing would likely to appreciate more, rather than disclosing the proposed mitigating steps after the concerns and demands are raised by the public. Since, the miner will be the first to be called upon by the District Collector or his nominee, who will preside over the public hearing, to present his case he should utilise this opportunity to explain the various steps with financial outlay for the socio-economic benefits of the local people. The miner should keep it in mind that time is essence and he should not miss the first available opportunity to forcefully disclose his plans. After the public hearing is completed the project proponent may have to modify the EIA report and the EMP taking into account the outcome of the public hearing before submitting the same to the Regulatory Authority.

I would now explain the procedural and other details for conduct of public hearing as prescribed in the Appendix-IV to the 14th September Notification. Before I go into the procedural details I would like to, at the risk of repetition, emphasize that it will be a grave mistake if the project proponent takes the public hearing as a routine exercise. More so, he should not make any attempt to ensure that only select number of people whom he considers to be friendly or at least not hostile is present in the public hearing. A perusal of the procedure for conduct of public hearing as prescribed under Appendix-IV would make it very clear that the public hearing shall be a transparent exercise with widest possible participation by the local affected persons and that the concerns of the people are given due consideration and are addressed adequately. It is not for nothing that the procedure prescribes wide publicity and the proceedings are videographed so that the Regulatory Authorities are satisfied that all the genuine concerns of the local people who would be affected by the mining operations have been taken care of. To make the proceedings authentic and effective the local District Magistrate or an officer subordinate to the District Magistrate who shall not be below the rank of Additional District Magistrate, assisted by a representative of the State Pollution Control Board (SPCB) or the Union Territory Pollution Control Board (UTPCC), as the case may be, shall supervise and preside over the entire public hearing process. It is also mandatory that the proceedings of the public hearing shall be displayed on the notice board or at any other conspicuous place at the office of the 3-tier Panchayati Raj Institutions like Village Panchayat, Block Panchayat and Zila Parishad, District Magistrate and the SPCB or the UTPCC for wider publicity. It is incumbent on the concerned SPCB or UTPCC to display the proceedings on its website for general information. It is open to any person to send comments on the proceedings directly to the appropriate Regulatory Authority and also to the project proponent. Thus, the completed proceedings of the public hearing become a public document in the eye of law and the same becomes a part of the procedures in obtaining environmental clearance for the project. Thus, if any project proponent fails to appreciate the importance and relevance of the public hearing he shall be taking a great risk. In fact, any practical and pragmatic minded project proponent can, as said earlier, make most of the public hearing and to his advantage. And as we proceed further it would be amply clear that financial involvement in adequately addressing the genuine and bona fide concerns of the local people is insignificant compared to the benefit in the form of goodwill of asset. It needs no emphasis that executing a mining project or for that matter any industrial or developmental project with a hostile population around is a bad entrepreneurship. With the present level of awareness among the people even in remote areas, if a project proponent can even think that he can execute his project without willing support of the local populace he shall do so at his own peril.

The primary responsibility is cast on the applicant, that is, the project proponent. To start with, the applicant is required to make a request to the Member Secretary of the concerned SPCB or UTPCC by a simple letter for arranging the public hearing on his proposed mining project. It is quite possible that the project site covers areas that might fall in more than one district or State or Union Territory. In such a situation the applicant shall make separate request to each of the concerned SPCB or UTPCC for holding the public hearing. Since it is a request through a simple letter no particular proforma for such a request letter has been envisaged.

While sending the request letter to the SPCB or UTPCC for arranging the public hearing the applicant is required to enclose certain documents with the letter. These documents are ten hard copies and ten soft (electronic) copies of the draft EIA report along with summary of EIA report in English and in the official language of the state or local language. The EIA report should be prepared strictly in accordance with the terms of reference approved by the Expert Appraisal Committee (EAC). In addition to the concerned SPCB or UPTCC, the applicant is required to send one hard and one soft copy of each of the above documents to the concerned District Magistrate, Zila Parishad, Block (intermediate) Panchayat, Gram Panchayat, Municipality, District Industries Officer, Development

Authority, if any, and the Regional Office of the Ministry of Environment and Forests. It is not mandatory at this stage to enclose a copy of the EMP. But it is in the interest of the project proponent to enclose a copy of the EMP also, as the EIA report will only list the impact of mining activities on the environment including, inter alia, adverse impact on productivity of land, loss of grazing lands for the cattle, health of the people etc. If there is no mitigating steps mentioned anywhere in the document, the public shall raise lot of objections against the project. In order that the persons present in the meeting do not get agitated and become hostile to the project even at the initial stage it would be a practical approach if the proposed EMP is also presented before the audience. Since the project proponent is required to initiate the process with a presentation on the project and the summary of the EIA Report he should utilize the first opportunity to explain to the audience item-wise the impact and the corresponding proposed mitigating measure and financial outlay to undo the adverse impact. In fact, this will be the most ideal moment for the project proponent to highlight the steps he proposes to take with financial implications. For example, he can highlight the method of mining and the technology to be deployed to minimize the adverse impact of mining. This will create an instant favourable impression among the audience. Since it is a common demand of the local people for employment the project proponent can work in advance and include in the EMP the type of employment that would be available to the local people. He can also indicate the steps proposed to train local employable boys and girls in the relevant skills required for the project and to impart vocational trainings. He can also highlight the steps proposed to be taken to provide gainful economic activities like goat rearing, poultry farming etc. as per the traditional skills of the local people on a sustained basis. It is possible to convince the audience that scope for direct employment in the mining project being limited, vocational training and creation of gainful economic activities would be more beneficial to the people. Therefore, if the EMP is also ready the project proponent would be in a better position to convince the people who participate in the public hearing. As already indicated, since the proceedings will be initiated by the project proponent or his representative, such a golden opportunity to convince the public about the merit of the project should not be missed.

It is good, no doubt, to explain the mitigating measures proposed to be taken, in the public hearing. But people to be affected need to be satisfied about the bona fide of the promises made by the project proponent. Here comes the relevance of the pre-feasibility project report. As stated earlier, the pre-feasibility project report would show the financial investment and the project proponent can inform the people present in the public hearing about the provision of funds for various socio-economic activities like provision for drinking water facility, health and sanitation, provision for funds for training including vocational training, provision of funds for creating gainful economic activities, etc. He can also highlight the salient features of the proposed CSR activities.

The date, time and venue for the meeting shall be decided by the Member Secretary of the concerned State Pollution Control Board (SPCB) or Union Territory Pollution Control Board (UTPCC). He will also give wide publicity about the meeting through newspaper advertisement or radio or television as also through other means like beating of drums in remote areas which is the common practice adopted by the government machinery and with which the general public are familiar to ensure that there is no complaint. It would be in the interest of project proponent to ensure that maximum number of persons participate in the public hearing and that attendance of all those present in the public hearing is noted and the videography is done in a way that gives a clear impression that the process is transparent and that the persons present in the public hearing have been given reasonable opportunity to express their views on the project. It is not necessary for the project proponent to presume that the local people are opposed to the project.

The entire process of public hearing is to be completed within a period of 45 days from the date of receipt of the request letter from the applicant. The SPCB or UTPCC shall send the public hearing proceedings to the concerned Regulatory Authority, that is, the Ministry of Environment and Forest for "A" category project or the State Environment Impact Assessment Authority for category 'B' project within eight days of the completion of the public hearing. A copy of the proceedings shall also be sent to the project proponent. The project proponent shall ensure that the concerns expressed by the public and his response to address those concerns item wise with the financial commitments are prepared in a tabular form and the same becomes a part of the proceedings. It is quite possible that, as stated earlier, the EIA report and the EMP prepared before public hearing need modification in the light of the outcome of the public hearing. In such a situation the EIA report and the EMP should be modified after incorporating the concerns expressed in the public hearing along with action plan and financial allocation, item wise, to address those concerns. If this procedure is followed, the project proponent shall find it very easy to convince the members of the expert appraisal committee whose recommendations are essential for the project to get environmental clearance.

In the most unlikely situation when the SPCB or UTPCC fails to hold the public hearing within the stipulated 45 days, the appropriate authority at the central or at the state level may engage any other agency or authority to complete the process following the same procedure. This is only an enabling provision as in reality there will be no occasion when SPCB or UTPCC would fail to hold the public hearing in time. Since the district administration is directly involved in the process no District Magistrate shall allow such a contingency to happen.

Chapter – 5

Terms of Reference and Pre-Feasibility Project Report and Preparation of Environmental Impact Assessment Report and Environment Management Plan

Considering the importance of the pre-feasibility project report, Terms of Reference, the EIA Report and the EMP in the process of obtaining environmental clearance I have decided not to follow the conventional format of narrating the whole thing treating the miner in third person singular (or plural) form as such a format would create an artificial distance between the author and the miner. Hence, I have decided to directly address the miner in the second person singular form as if I am giving my advice and suggestion directly to some one sitting opposite me at the same pedestal with none in between in this Chapter and in the next seven chapters ending with Chapter-12 on Health Environment.

PART-A
PRE-FEASIBILITY PROJECT REPORT AND TERMS OF REFERENCE

Pre-feasibility Project Report

In terms of para 6 of the 14th September Notification the application for prior environmental clearance for a mining project must be accompanied by a copy of the pre-feasibility project report. This book is not the appropriate place for suggesting a model pre-feasibility project report. Nevertheless, I shall broadly give an idea about the purpose and contents of such a report. As the expression "pre-feasibility project report" would indicate, such a report would convince the EAC that the project is, prima facie, financially feasible. That is to say, the project operation would be a profitable one after meeting all operational expenses including the expenses on environmental concerns as also the expenses on socio-economic activities. You have to convince the EAC that you would have the required disposable income to take care of the environmental concerns. But since you are not ready as yet to prepare a final feasibility report as also the detailed project report you would only submit a pre-feasibility project report which shall contain relevant ingredients of the final feasibility report. Remember that there should not be any confusion, as it had been noted in few cases, between a pre-feasibility project report and a mining plan which is an essential prerequisite and to be approved by the Indian Bureau of Mines on behalf of the Central Government or by the State Government in some cases under Section 5(2) of the MMDR Act before a mining lease is granted.

Such a report (pre-feasibility project report) will indicate the mineable reserves of the minerals, future potentials after detailed exploration that you would undertake in due course, rated capacity as also the life of the project. Make sure that the rated capacity per annum, total mineable reserves at the current status and the life of the project are not out of sync. For example, if the mineable deposits are, say, one million tonnes and the project's rated capacity is, say, 500000 tonnes per annum, the normal life of the project shall be twenty years. An estimated cost of producing per tonne of the minerals, the cost will include the cost on salaries and wages of the employees, various consumables, cost apportioned to the machinery and equipment deployed (whether own or hired), bank interest if loan would be obtained from a bank or financial institution and the like, need be indicated. It is advisable you include the cost on protecting the environment and on socio-economic activities as per your Corporate Social Responsibility (CSR) policy as part of your project cost to convince the EAC that the project is financially viable to take care of the environmental concerns. Find out the market price for the minerals you would mine. In case the minerals would be transported to a different location for final disposal through sale add the cost of transportation of the minerals to the selling point. Suppose after all the above factors are taken into account while calculating the cost of production the total cost thus calculated comes to, say, Rs.500 per tonne and the selling price is Rs.650 per tonne, your project becomes viable and you have also met the concerns of the environment. There is no reason as to why the EAC should not appraise your case for prior environmental clearance as financially viable. So you have crossed the first hurdle to make a presentation before the EAC for prior environmental clearance.

You can engage a suitable expert to prepare the pre-feasibility project report which, as I have maintained, shall be a very brief one only to prove that even after meeting the requirement of environmental concerns the project is financially viable and this will also dispel the apprehension, if any, that any expert member of the EAC may have that you might be doing only mining without spending any money or spending very little on environmental concerns.

Terms of Reference (TOR)

Under stage (2) – scoping of para 7 of the 14th September Notification preparation of TOR and getting the same approved by the EAC is essential. Based on the information furnished by you in the application for environmental clearance the EAC on its own can frame comprehensive TOR for the preparation of EIA Report and the EMP. For your benefit only, the EAC has already prepared a Model TOR as at Appendix-B. You may save time if you yourself frame the required TOR for your project. Model TOR at Appendix-B is a useful guide for you in framing the TOR specific to your project.

PART-B
PREPARATION OF ENVIRONMENT IMPACT ASSESSMENT (EIA) REPORT AND ENVIRONMENT MANAGEMENT PLAN (EMP)

I have already stated elsewhere in this book that the Model Terms of Reference (TOR) prepared by the Committee as revised in April, 2008 is a fairly elaborate one which a miner can adopt in the preparation of the EIA Report and the EMP. I have followed the Model TOR in the write up of this Chapter and the related next eight chapters dealing with environment in all its ramifications. I have made an effort in presenting such a complex work as lucidly as I can, with my limited command over appropriate vocabulary, for a proper understanding even by the small mine owners scattered all over the country and in remote places who take up mining as a sheer economic need for the survival of their families.

Before I go into the specific work on the preparation of the EIA Report and the EMP I would first introduce the miner to certain basic concepts and few requirements while reserving my rights to deal with them in greater detail at the appropriate space.

The first and most essential requirement is that you (miner) must possess a valid mining lease over an area of land for which you intend to apply for prior environmental clearance. Remember that without a valid mining lease you have no *locus standi,* that is, legally identifiable status. Moreover, environmental clearance is given for doing certain activities over a piece of land only and not in the vacuum. Hence, a physically identifiable piece of land, i.e. the lease hold area and of course the surrounding land mass are to be there. If you are unable to appear before the EAC you may authorize some one else, who could be the consultant who has prepared the EIA Report and the EMP, in writing to present your case before the EAC. Make sure that unless you are physically incapacitated due to any reason such as illness or due to some other compelling reasons making your absence inescapable you must make it a point to be present in the meeting of EAC even if your authorized agent is to make the presentation on your behalf. Some of the expert members of the EAC and sometimes the Chairman himself may like to get an assurance from the mine owner on doing certain things which the EAC considers essential in recommending your case to the Competent Authority for grant of environmental clearance. You will yourself realize what difference does it make in the attitude of the EAC if the assurance comes from the owner himself as your assurance becomes a commitment that goes into the proceedings of the meeting of the EAC.

The requirement of a valid mining lease for a new mining project is an absolute necessity. For an existing mine, whether being operated or closed due to some unavoidable reasons, if the lease had already expired a renewed lease is essential.

While appearing before the EAC for grant of environmental clearance you must submit a copy of the duly approved mining plan alongwith your application for environmental clearance. Though a mining plan, duly approved by the Central Government (the Indian Bureau of Mines, a subordinate office of the Central Government authorized to exercise the power of approval on behalf of the Government) or by the State Government in some cases, is essential under Section 5(2) of the MMDR Act before grant of a lease, expert members may like to raise some question on the mining plan as well.

Related to the mining lease are two concepts which you need to be conversant with. One is *core* zone and the other is *buffer* zone. Core zone is the lease hold area as shown in the mining lease. It is desirable that you know the significance of the core zone which is the lease hold area. The lease hold area could be a larger area, say 60 hectares or even could be many times more, whereas the ore bodies could be situated only, say, in 5 hectares of the total 60 hectares. In the Committee a member, who was generally not taken seriously by the Committee, once asked a project proponent, who had, during presentation, indicated the area which was quite small that had the minerals, why he had taken such large area for which environmental clearance was being sought for. The project proponent was at a loss and obviously he did not have the answer. Now you can imagine his predicament in such a situation. I could only save the situation but it took a lot of time to explain the implications in detail more for the knowledge of the members of the EAC than for the miner.

When you apply for a mining lease you include the entire plot of the land that is identified by certain number besides the name of the village, etc. as per the revenue records. If occurrences of the minerals are in, say, three or more plots of lands and occurrences of the minerals may not always be contiguous, you have to include those plots in your application. So this becomes your compulsion. Moreover, you also need additional lands for your administrative requirements like a site office, sometimes even a small township for your employees besides the land required for a processing unit, if that is also part of your project activities.

Likewise, the State Government has its own reasons to determine the area. For example, as a lessee you would be in the occupation of the entire land area for the period of the lease unless you decide later to surrender part thereof and the State Government accepts the surrender. Due to your mining activities certain ancillary and other activities would come up in the area. Even local villagers would find it worthwhile to establish some tea shop or some small eateries. So the chances of unauthorized encroachment on the land including that (encroachment) on the nearby areas, not actually required for mining but included in the lease hold area, would be there. Once established, these small shops etc. would continue even after the closure of the mining activities. The Government, therefore, makes sure that as a lessee you do not allow any unauthorized encroachment on the land and if allowed you are held responsible for such encroachment removal of which generally becomes very difficult for the government. Besides, the State Government has the revenue earning interest that would not otherwise accrue to the exchequer from the lands having no commercial value.

Under Section 9 of the MMDR Act a lessee is required to pay royalty in respect of the minerals at a rate specified in the Second Schedule to the Act. You know that there is a gestation period that may run for some years depending on the complexity of the deposits. Hence, the mine development activities might take fairly long time before actual mining starts and royalty becomes payable only on the minerals mined. In the initial period the quantum of minerals removed may not be much giving less revenue to the Government in the form of royalty. So the Government would realize the revenue in the form of dead rent under Section 9A of the MMDR Act at the rate specified in the Third Schedule to the Act. Under the proviso to sub-section (1) of Section 9A the holder of such mining lease is liable to pay either such royalty or the dead rent, whichever is greater. The rate of dead rent is on a graduated scale per hectare which is at present Rs. 200 per hectare per annum from second year of lease, Rs.500 per hectare per annum from third year and fourth year and Rs. 1000 per hectare per annum from fifth year onwards if the minerals are low value. The above rate would go up to two times or three times or even four times depending on the nature of the minerals, i.e., medium value minerals or high value minerals or precious metals and stones respectively. The system also works as a disincentive for you to delay the start of the mining operation in full scale as you may consider it uneconomic to pay dead rent which in some cases could be quite unremunerative.

The *buffer* zone is a much larger area compared to the core zone. It comprises an area which falls within a ten kilometres radius of the core zone. A question may quite naturally arise in your mind as to why as a miner you should have to do anything with the area beyond the lease hold area. I appreciate that fact. But if you as a miner ponder a little you would take no time to realize that your mining operations would impact the areas much beyond the lease hold area—whether it is 10 kms radius or less than that is immaterial. You see it always in the normal day-to-day activities. For example, while drinking water if one small drop of water falls to the ground the water would spread to an area larger than the simple point on the ground that a drop of water would require if it falls on a tiny grain size container. But we never apply our mind to such happenings as there is no need for that because the tiny drop of water gets dried up in no time. But the adverse impact of mining operations both in the core zone and in the buffer zone is too serious to be ignored.

Now just imagine when you are winning minerals by breaking the lands, loading the same on the truck and transporting the loaded minerals to another site for final disposal, what would be the impact on the physical environment. Depending on the wind direction and its speed the dust so created during the course of the mining operations would travel a long distance adversely affecting the productivity of the lands on the way. Unfortunately, you cannot avoid generating dust while extracting minerals even if in small quantity. There would be other adverse impacts, health of the local people getting adversely affected being one of them. So it has been thought proper that the miner must take care of the area falling not only in the core zone but also the area falling within the buffer zone. So obvious a fact which we never take note of.

Before dealing with the preparation of the EIA Report and the EMP I would refer to a strange, even you can say funny, non-issue.

It seems you should also be conversant with the provisions of the Ceiling Act of the State as some expert members of the EAC might think so. A miner, who was also the legal owner of the lease hold area, while making a presentation before (my) Committee disclosed the total area which was more than 60 hectares. This was a case from Andhra Pradesh. The same member as referred to in one of the preceding paragraphs dealing with core zone and buffer zone almost charged the miner for violating the provisions of the Ceiling Act as possessing more area than permitted under ceiling laws. He went to the extent of suggesting that the Committee should recommend action against the miner under the ceiling laws. You can imagine my embarrassment as the Chairman, not due to any fault on the part of the miner but due to the fact that the member had gone beyond the mandate given to the Committee under the 14th September Notification. Much to the discomfiture of the member I had to tell him that the mandate of the EAC does not encompass the treatment of the offences under ceiling laws.

The Forest Rights Act dealt with in Chapter-3 has become an important piece of legislation with which you should be adequately conversant with. I would at this stage, refer to the expression "sustainable use" by giving an example with which you are so familiar. The tribal people and other traditional forest dwellers collect minor forest produce, say, non-timber dry branches of trees and other plants as fuel wood. A tribal will never fell even a small tree but its dry and dead branches. Why? Because he knows that if he fells the tree or even cut the branches which are raw and green he would only destroy the tree for ever and he would lose for good at least one source of his fuel wood which is almost a golden goose for him. Thus he will cut only that much portion which will allow the tree to grow more branches. So a tribal knows how much a tree can sustain as if after offering something to the forest dwellers for their sustenance. I feel compulsively inclined here to cite the wisdom of the saying of the ancient great Boeotian poet Hesiod who has given in his writings a picture of rural life in Greece at the time. The great philosopher Socrates in his dialogue on the virtues of an ideal Guardian (Ruler), while deprecating the fact "if any Guardian looks for happiness in a way unworthy of his status and is impelled by some senseless and extravagant idea of happiness", has also expressed his conviction that such a Guardian will ultimately learn the wisdom of Hesiod's saying that "the half is more than the whole". See how a tribal forest dweller, without knowing anything about the Boeotian poet, knows by heart that few dry branches of a standing tree are more than the whole tree and still we non-tribal consider ourselves more enlightened than a tribal, no doubt a sad commentary on our professed knowledge on sustainable use of the forest. Even a wild animal, say a predator like a lion, when hungry, preys on other animals. But if the lion catches one animal, say a deer, it knows that it (deer) is enough to satisfy its hunger. The lion does not go on killing animals when it is not hungry enough. So you see how even a predator follows the principle of sustainable use of its preys. In a lighter vein I would say that even if the forest officials provide a refrigerator, the lion would not unnecessarily kill an animal and store (in the refrigerator) it for future use. The forest dwellers, both human and animal, live in perfect harmony with the forest as if supporting each other. It is only man's insatiable hunger and sense of possessiveness, an irrational pride if I may say so, and the like, that are singularly responsible for polluting the forest cover. We humans really do not need any enemy. The new definition of the expression "bona fide livelihood needs" as reported by the *Times of India* referred to in Chapter-3 might appear to have diluted the meaning of the expression "sustainable use", while in reality it is not. In the above example, a tribal will never fell the tree for storage purpose as he knows it very well that storing the tree means losing the tree for good.

At this stage I will not go into further details on some preliminary points. However, I would advise you that while arguing your case before the EAC keep yourself to relevant facts and never try to give any misleading information as that may be counterproductive and at times may go against you. Remember that the members are distinguished experts and they are there only to guide you how to carry on the mining operations and protecting the environment. Humility does not cost anything to you but it pays and pays quite handsomely. Take the expert members as "*King can do wrong*", as after all, they have been given the mandate to appraise your proposal and to make appropriate suggestion to ensure that as a miner you discharge your responsibility of protecting the environment while exploiting the non-renewable natural resources minerals for the well-being of the society. If in the process of exploiting the mineral wealth a diseased society is born who will enjoy the benefits of mining operations?

Surely you do not want that, as being part of such unhealthy society, you are also not a less sufferer.

Preparation of EIA Report and the EMP, and for that matter writing any report, is an art. It is not simply putting certain things in black and white. Even using colour print so commonly used now a days does not help unless the whole thing is presented in a way that makes it easy to grasp and convincing as well, just like an object of art, say a picture does not, *ipso facto*, becomes an object of art unless different shades of various colours used are applied in proper places. To highlight the point I will give an illustration.

Suppose you have an iron ore mine and so does another miner and both of you make a presentation before the EAC for prior environmental clearance on the same day and may be in close succession in the same meeting. You claim that you will ensure zero-waste mining by taking out all the minerals out of the pit without telling the EAC as to how you achieve the goal of zero-waste mining. The other miner, on the other hand, tells the EAC that he will deploy a particular technology, perhaps indicating the name of the technology, and method of mining whereby he would be able to take out all the minerals that are geologically extractable and utilize the raw materials iron ore in his steel plant, if he has one, if necessary by beneficiating the low grade ore, so that the metal content is extracted to the extent technologically possible leaving the waste that would contain least metal thereby resultant waste is least pollutant. In case he does not have a steel plant he would sale the ore to other user(s) and if the ore is not of a uniform grade he would find market for different grades as there would be consumers who can utilize low grade ore as well. The thrust of his argument will be that he would not leave behind any extractable ore in the pit(s) on the ground that some grades may not have a ready market or may not fetch him an economic price. You can make your own conclusion as to whose presentation, yours or the other miner's, would be convincing to the EAC. Obviously, the other miner wins. I do not say that you would not do the same process as the other miner has presented before the EAC. It is quite possible that you have an equally, if not more, strong case. But your presentation lacks the appropriate art. So it is not the substance alone that counts, rather the art of presentation is equally, if not more, important.

When your paper, in official parlance it is called PUC (Paper Under Consideration), is put up in the government file your PUC becomes less convincing. So be sure that your Consultant prepares the report with cogent and realistic arguments.

I would now proceed to deal with the preparation of the EIA Report and the EMP. While doing so I would follow the Model TOR which is a fairly elaborate one and cover the major and relevant components of environment. I advise you that you follow the Chapters and the Sections in the same sequence as they appear in the Model TOR as that would give the baseline data, anticipated impacts and the proposed mitigating measures in respect of each component of the environment separately in one place and such a compact presentation would help the EAC to comprehend the entire gamut of the problem at that point of time and at the same time making the job easy for you to clarify any doubt as may be raised by the members of the EAC.

While preparing the EIA report and the EMP you will notice that the seven critical components of environment dealt with in the next seven chapters (Chapter-6 to Chapter-7) and the issue of risk assessment and disaster management plan dealt with in Chapter-13 are continuation of this chapter as being integral part of the EIA report and the EMP. It is only for easy comprehension that separate chapter has been allocated to each segment. Hence, Chapters-5 to 13 should be read as one composite chapter.

First start with an executive summary as:

> "**Executive Summary:** The executive summary shall consist of gist of all relevant details chapter-wise and section-wise of the EIA Report and the EMP. For example, if mining is intersecting groundwater or not and if yes, a brief mention of the studies carried out and environment management plan, i.e. mitigating measures to be mentioned. Further, the nature of possible impact on the socio-economic aspects of the people in the buffer zone with special emphasis on the people in the core zone shall be briefly mentioned alongwith proposed mitigating measures as a component of the Corporate Social Responsibility (CSR). Likewise, if the area is ecologically fragile with flora and fauna, a brief mention about the impact on flora and fauna and mitigating measures like conservation plan for wildlife to be mentioned. The executive summary shall give a prime facie idea about the objectives of the proposal, use of the minerals to be mined, justification, etc. and should be co-related to the details given in the EIA Report and the EMP. Post project plan in brief should also be included. In a nutshell, the executive summary shall be a miniature EIA Report and EMP."

Allot adequate number of pages to the executive summary so as not just to appear like a precis. The idea is that members of the EAC will first read the executive summary, each expert member would usually confine to his own area of concern and if necessary the member would refer to the main body of the EIA Report and the EMP for a more detailed information. It is quite possible that after reading the executive summary a particular expert member might not feel the necessity to refer to the details in the related Chapter and Sections of the main Report. So the executive summary should be compact but sufficiently informative. For example, the "zero-waste" mining, as referred to in a preceding paragraph, can be succinctly put as follows:

> "Zero-waste" mining would be ensured by extracting all the ore geologically extractable and eventually extracting the metal content to the extent technologically possible or alternatively selling the ore, both high grade and low grade, in the market.

Your Consultant would be able to put appropriate words and he would know how best it can be done.

The TOR at Annexure-B is only a model and when you prepare the EIA Report and the EMP for your project you include only those aspects which are relevant and specific to your project. In fact, as I have suggested in Part-A of this Chapter, the TOR that you have prepared in case you choose to do so, should be so framed as to take care of your own project requirement so that the EIA Report and the EMP does not include any irrelevant details, just like the pre-feasibility project report as explained in Part-A (ibid) gives the cost analysis and profitability relevant to the particular project. Nevertheless, the format of the EIA Report and the EMP would basically remain the same as the Model TOR in all mining projects.

After the executive summary part is completed you may now write the "Introduction" part. Your Consultant should be in a position to expand the various components of "Introduction" as given in the Model TOR.

The EAC has every right to know your credentials and ability to undertake the proposed activities, hence your profile is an important input. It is not your Bio-Data or Curriculum Vitae. Here you can give information like your professional background. For example, if you or your family is already engaged in mining activities or in any other business or trading activities that you may like to cite as grounds strong enough to convince the EAC that you know how to run a business and take risk in investing your money. You should by all means mention that. If you are already in some activities for which you had taken loan from a bank(s) or financial institution(s), you can prove that as well. If you are also the owner of the lease-hold area that can be an effective point in your favour as the question of payment of compensation to the land owner would not arise except, may be, you may need some extra land in the surrounding area, in case your own land is not sufficient for the purpose, for certain related activities and in such a contingency it is advisable to settle the question of compensation to such land owner(s) in advance which may be included in the "Introduction" part. Remember, your ownership of the lease-hold area does not, ipso facto, make you eligible to get environmental clearance just the same way your right to purchase a motor car with your money does not confer on you the right to drive the car unless you posses a motor vehicle driving licence to prove your fitness to drive the vehicle. If you posses professional qualifications like an engineering degree or an M.B.A. that becomes an easily acceptable eligibility criterion. So give as much information as you can justifiably give about your credentials to undertake the proposed activities.

Having introduced yourself, may be, established also, as a promising entrepreneur you may proceed to the genesis and objectives of the project. It is not enough to say that the objective of the project is to mine the minerals as that is obvious as nobody takes a mining lease over an area to keep the land idle. You say that there are some large or small steel mills in certain areas that either do not have any captive iron ore mine or have only small captive mines that cannot cater to full requirement of the raw materials iron ore and you would supply the ore from your mine to such steel mills or if your mine would produce small quantity of ore you would supply your ore to some other big suppliers of iron ore to the steel mills. If you also have or propose to set up a steel plant you may say so and state that the iron ore mined by you would be utilized in your plant. In short, you describe the mode of disposal of the ore either as R.O.M. or after beneficiation or in any other form to convince the EAC that the ore will be put to some productive use. Remember, iron ore, or for that matter any other mineral, is a non-renewable natural resources, need be put to its proper use and every grade of iron ore, whether low or medium or high, has a market and use. The idea is that you have to convince the EAC that ore mined by you would not be a waste. If you have already an agreement with a steel mill to which you want to supply your iron ore or if you have any document to show that you would yourself set up a steel mill do show such documents to the EAC to make your case convincing. Remember that documentary evidence has instant acceptance.

Then you give some idea about the project itself and its importance to the region and the country. Indicate the nature of the project, i.e. whether it is only mining activity and or processing activity. If it is also a processing activity give the exact activity, that is, whether it is only converting the R.O.M. to the ore of certain size through a crushing machine or also upgrading the ore through beneficiation or sintering or *pelletisation.* Remember, mining alongwith processing in any form is always welcome compared to simply disposing the R.O.M. without, of course, minimizing the importance of stand alone mining in any way. Size, i.e. the capacity of the project is an important and relevant aspect and so is its location from environmental point of view. If the capacity is small and the project is at a safe distance from inhabited areas it has less of environmental issues for the humans. Again if the project is in a remote but forest area, whether with good flora and fauna or not or with human habitation or not, the environmental ramifications are fraught with so much complex possibilities. Mention the details of the lease-hold area, total reserves and the mineable reserves, the rated capacity per day and per annum and the life of the project based on number of working days in a year clearly specifying the approximate period when mining is not possible due to, say, rain or extreme hot or cold weather. When there is marked difference between total reserves and the mineable reserves give reasons thereof, for example, it could be due some seismic consideration or it could be due to the fact that mining in certain spots would endanger the forest cover which is more valuable than winning the minerals. You can also mention the benefit that according to your perception would accrue to the surrounding areas and also to the country. The examples of the benefits to the surrounding areas would be in the form of employment opportunities both direct in the project and with the contractors and indirect employment opportunities like income through small and road side tea shops or other eateries, benefits like road connectivity, education, health, drinking water facilities, gainful economic activities based on traditional skill of the local people like goat rearing, poultry farming, etc. as a part of your corporate social responsibilities. You need not give all the details here, you can do so later in the component on Socio-Economic Environment as in Chapter-11.

As regards the benefit to the country you may say how your iron ore would make real contribution, even if small, to steel making which is so essential for the massive planned construction activities, be it road and bridge building or residential houses for the people and how such infrastructure construction project would generate employment opportunities for hundreds of skilled, semi-skilled and unskilled workers besides making contribution to the exchequer in the form of tax, both Central and State.

It is quite possible that the core zone and possibly the buffer zone fall in ecologically fragile area. You have to give convincing justification for mining in such area. Simply saying that mining can be done where minerals are found is not a correct stand to take. Such a view may find some acceptance, though not always, where the minerals are of strategic importance, say uranium, but even in such a situation it may not be easy to get clearance as it has happened in some cases where the State owned Uranium Corporation of India Ltd. could not succeed. So it is advisable to find alternative deposits where likely environmental concerns can be effectively tackled. Any serious miner, I am sure you are one, would always opt for a site with less of a problem. But if you are sure that you can effectively take care of protecting the ecology and the forest and wildlife conservation plan you have prepared is likely to be accepted by the EAC, there is no reason as to why you should not go ahead, after all you know that there is no gain without risk in business.

After you have established your bona fide and credentials as an eligible and serious entrepreneur with a project that is environmentally acceptable and is in the interest of country's economic development you are in a position to buttress your claim further by telling the EAC the status and stage of various regulatory clearances the foremost of which being, as stated earlier, that you are in possession of a valid mining lease or certain other documentary evidence that would lead the EAC to accept your claim to get a mining lease in due course.

There is requirement of certain regulatory and statutory clearances. In Chapter-1 on Introduction I have referred to the relevance and criticality of certain Acts, Rules and Notifications under which you are required to obtain clearances before starting mining operation. Of the Acts, the Forest (Conservation) Act, the Water Act and the Air Act are of special importance. If in the process of mining you would use forest land for non-forest purposes you would require permission under Section 2 of the Forest (Conservation) Act. Even though the permission is accorded by the same Ministry, i.e., MoEF which is competent to grant prior environmental clearance, there is a separate procedure prescribed for obtaining permission from the same Ministry for using forest land for non-forest purposes. At a later stage in Chapters-6 and 7 I would be dealing with air environment and water environment. At this stage it is enough to tell you that no living things including human beings and animals can survive without air and water and therefore, your proposed mining activities which are sure to pollute air environment and water environment must ensure that the level of pollution is maintained within the limit of tolerance for all living things. You can prove your credential to maintain the air and water quality by obtaining consent to do mining activities and if processing is also involved you have to obtain the consent to establish the plant from the State Pollution Control Board (SPCB). Without the consent of the State Pollution Control Board no mining activities or processing activities can be started. If the lease hold area falls within the CRZ notified area you need specific permission from the Coastal Zone Management Authority. As mining activities would involve disposal of hazardous waste you need authorization under the Hazardous Waste Management, Handling and Transboundary Movement Rules. In case you have all the clearances referred to above you may tell the EAC accordingly to strengthen your case. Since, however, the obtaining of the statutory clearances referred to above are parallel activities, it is quite possible that your applications for the required clearances, if not finally decided, would be at different stages under process. In such a scenario, you can inform the EAC of the status of various clearances and if it is practicable you can indicate the likely time schedule for getting the required clearances. In other words, if certain clearances could not be procured before applying for environmental clearance, you may indicate the action taken by you in that regards. Remember, even if you get environmental clearance you can start the project only after getting all the clearances which are, in fact, parallel and cannot be as such simultaneous. This you can very well understand by the fact that even if you get the environmental clearance for the project, you may not get forest clearance for utilizing forest land even if it is the same Ministry, i.e. Ministry of Environment and Forest (MoEF) administratively responsible and competent authority to grant both the clearances. Such is the government system. It would have been ideal if there could be one *Empowered Agency* with representatives from the concerned Ministries and Departments of the Government to take a composite and final view. But that is not practicable. Every related Agency has its own policy on its part of the various components of the environment. That is perhaps the reason that the MoEF could not itself constitute one single Committee that could make its recommendation covering both environmental clearance and diversion of forest land for non-forest purpose. So you have no option but to take parallel action to obtain all regulatory clearances.

It is an irony though, but you will realize that how certain negative facts can be positive factors in your favour. Few examples are given below.

- If mining is not intersecting groundwater at any stage you say so in the EIA report in greater detail.
- If there is no forest cover or wildlife within the core zone and the buffer zone mention that clearly in the EIA report and to buttress your claim the site map you have already prepared can be shown as a proof.
- If there is no human habitation or crop land within a certain kilometre radius of the core zone and the area where mining activities would be done at some point or other during the life of the project this should also be appropriately indicated.
- If the project does not attract the provisions of Coastal Regulation Zone Notification mention that in the EIA report also.

You will yourself realize that negative factors like the above are strong enough to make a positive impression in the EAC. Your consultant would be in a position to enumerate many such negative but at the same time very critical segments in any EIA report and the EMP.

Project Description

By now you have successfully introduced and established yourself as a promising and serious entrepreneur to undertake the proposed mining activities. What is now required of you is that you give as vivid and reasonably elaborate as practicable description of your project. A proper description of the project details would be instantly appreciated by the members of the EAC but while doing so don't overdo by going into irrelevant details as, more often than not, that may go against you. At the same time give all essential and critical details so that the members of the EAC could raise either no or very few questions for you and your consultant to clarify. You must keep it in mind that your clarifications after the presentation should be only supplemental in nature. If your clarifications take more time and space than the original details given in the EIA report and the EMP the obvious conclusion would be that the EIA report and the EMP submitted before the competent authority suffer from serious deficiencies.

You also know that the prior environmental clearance you have sought for, if granted, would be only in respect of a particular land-mass, i.e., the site on which the proposed activities would be carried on. Therefore, the most essential and basic component of your project description is to present the nature, i.e., the physical features of the site where mining and related activities would be carried on. It, therefore, becomes imperative for you to realise that the visual presentation is more effective than the audio one. No wonder the television has instant effect on the viewers than the audio mode, i.e., radio. Again, a clear visual is more effective. So you have to first prepare a site map encompassing both core zone and the buffer zone at a scale that gives a clear picture of the total area for which you have prepared the site map. The model TOR prepared by the EAC suggests 1:50,000 scale. The Model TOR was finalized in April 2008 and is being followed by the EAC. Thus it's time tested and the mining fraternity as also its consultants are broadly familiar with the Model TOR. It is because of the above facts I would advise you to adhere to the above scale 1:50,000 in the preparation of the site map. This will eliminate at least one possibility for the EAC to raise any question on the quality of the site map. Therefore, it is not worthwhile to deviate from the standard prescribed in the Model TOR.

Authenticity of the physical features depicted on the site map is equally, if not more, important. So while preparing the site map don't hesitate to take the help of satellite imagery prepared by the National Remote Sensing Agency (NRSA), Hyderabad. The NRSA's data are used by a number of agencies of the Government of India in the areas of groundwater targeting, flood mapping and damage assessment, soil mapping, watershed management, crop estimation, ocean studies, etc., to name just a few.

To procure the satellite imagery from NRSA you may make a formal request through a letter to NRSA. While requesting NRSA to supply the satellite imagery you attach a copy of the revenue map that is available either in the Survey and Settlement Office of the State Government or from the office of the District Collector in respect of the area of your operation that would include the buffer zone also. This will help the NRSA to find out from its record if it has got the satellite imagery for the particular area for which you want the satellite imagery. In case the NRSA does not have the satellite imagery of the particular area obtain a written communication from the NRSA to that effect. In that eventuality you can engage a competent person to prepare the site map and mention in your EIA report that NRSA has expressed its inability to supply the satellite imagery and as a proof a copy of the letter from the NRSA can be adduced.

The site map shall contain the details of the land mass which is likely to be impacted due to your proposed mining activities. It is most unlikely that the entire area that includes the core zone and the buffer zone would be plain in nature. Therefore, the site map should indicate the contour, i.e., the outline of a natural feature, i.e., a coast or mountain mass. In other words, the site map should represent the land mass with the elevation and depth as naturally existing. Again, the topography of the area should be distinctly shown in the map. It is quite possible that beside the natural features which are already there, there could be artificial features due to various construction activities if the area has also a township. In other words, a detailed description i.e., a representation on the site map of the natural and artificial features as prevailing when the site map was prepared should be distinctly indicated. The area would have both human and wildlife habitation, crop land, water bodies, drainage systems, *nallah,* river, water reservoir, forests, places of worship, historical places etc. If the area involves forest land there could be reserve forest, protected forest, national park, sanctuary, bio-sphere reserve, elephant reserve, tiger reserve etc. All these details as above should be shown in appropriate and acceptable colours. To make them easily understood and appreciated by the members of the EAC, appropriate and commonly used legends, i.e., wording on the site map explaining the symbols should be used. For example, if the area mapped has, say, a place of worship indicate that by a symbol with which the common people are familiar. Ours' is a multi-religion country and common people are quite familiar with the physical structure of a Hindu temple or a Muslim mosque or a Christian church and, therefore, there should not be any difficulty for you to prepare the symbol representing a particular place of worship. There could be avifauna, i.e., birds of different species of which some could spend lot of time in the water bodies. Again these birds could be local and found throughout the year and some birds could be migratory which usually fly to the region during winter. You may indicate such birds as standing on tree top or floating in the water bodies or indicating the birds flying in the air with their wings spread by using words like local and migratory birds as the case may be.

A question may arise in your mind as to why you must take the help of satellite imagery while preparing the site map. Not that the EAC would doubt your version of the site map without the help of the satellite imagery. But it is not worth it to give any scope for anybody to raise any doubt about the correctness of the map. Remember that the Chairman of the EAC is generally a retired government employee and some of the members are either retired government employees or working in some institutions which are generally funded by the government and, therefore, most of the members of the EAC including the Chairman have bureaucratic mind-set and naturally they would have more faith in any paper supplied by a government agency. A bureaucrat by training (or may be by long subjugation) tends to be inflexible reposing more faith in any government system. NRSA is an organization sponsored by the Department of Space, Government of India and is devoted to the acquisition, processing and dissemination of remote sensing data. I think I do not have to elaborate further as to why the satellite imagery procured from NRSA has instant acceptance. Now you can decide if it is worth it to have a meaningless and avoidable conflict with the EAC that is mandated to appraise your proposal and make appropriate recommendation for rejecting or granting environmental clearance.

Though the site map must necessarily encompass the core zone and the buffer zone, for your interest it is advisable that you prepare the site map for a larger area that would include the area outside the buffer zone to the extent possible. While the site map could be for a larger area you may indicate the core zone by drawing a boundary in a particular colour, say, red and boundary of the buffer zone may be indicated by a different colour, may be, black or any other colour which you have not used to represent the physical features like water bodies, forest, etc. as there could be a confusion. For example, if water bodies are shown by green colour, same colour should not be used in drawing the boundary of the buffer zone as it might give the impression to the EAC that there is a *nallah* or a rivulet bordering the buffer zone. The same logic would apply in respect of the colour used for showing the boundary of the core zone.

You may naturally be thinking as to why the site map should include the area beyond the buffer zone. Perhaps an example will make you realize the requirement of the site map covering a larger area. Suppose there is a *nallah* or a rivulet that is passing through the core zone and the buffer zone and going beyond the buffer zone to merge into a big river or a water body like a lake which is a place where various aquatic fauna like fish which are consumed by the local people are available. Therefore, soil erosion that would take place due to your mining activities especially during rainy season would flow to the *nallah* and rivulet and finally to the larger river or the water body and fishes will be contaminated and ultimately it will go in to the bio-system of the people who consume such contaminated fishes. Likewise, the small area of forest cover found in the buffer zone could be a continuation of the larger forest cover beyond the buffer zone. Therefore, movement of the fauna could be adversely impacted as the forest cover does not have any artificial boundary like that of the buffer zone.

The site map you have already prepared gives the physical features of the land. You have also shown the water bodies, crop land, forest etc. on the map. While making presentation before the EAC on your proposal you start with the site map reflected clearly on the video screen before you start with the executive summary, introduction, project description and the rest. This will help the members of the EAC to have a broad idea about the contour and other physical features not only of the core zone and buffer zone but also of the area beyond buffer zone already mapped by you. The members of the EAC would like to have certain other details that could be effectively displayed on the site map. As a serious miner you would, no doubt, give the details of the project as suggested in Chapter-2 of the Model TOR. While doing so indicate the location of the project, the lease hold area, clearly indicating the occurrences of the ore bodies and dump sites for the Overburden (OB) on the site map itself distinctly marked by different colours with appropriate legends. At the time of presentation these details should be projected separately for a wider view by the members of the EAC. Once you have done that the members will have a fairly good idea about the physical features of the core zone with the occurrences of the ore bodies and this will help the members also to take a composite view on the core zone and the buffer zone. You should also mention the latitude, longitude and elevation of the site, topography of the area, topo sheet number, geology of mining lease area and other details as mentioned in the second para of Chapter-2 of the Model TOR. The Indian Bureau of Mine (IBM) approves the mining plan for a period of 5 years at a time. Though the mining plan is approved by the IBM for a period of 5 years, you have to indicate by appropriate diagram year-wise mining plan and production of OB. It is therefore essential that the OB dump site(s) should have adequate capacity to store the OB. In case you have a plan to refill the exhausted mine pit(s) with the Overburden (OB) mention that also clearly. In such a scenario one dump site with the required capacity would be an option for you, may be more environment friendly, as you would degrade less land for dumping the OB.

The life of your project is, say, 23 years as per your annual production plan and mineable reserves. Since the IBM will approve the mining plan for the first 5 years, the members of the EAC would like to have an overall idea about your mining plan for the entire period of life of the mine which is, as indicated above, 23 years. Since, it is not possible for you to get the mining plan for the remaining (23-5) 18 years approved by the IBM at the moment, you may be in a dilemma as to how to satisfy the members of the EAC on your mining plan for the remaining 18 years also. Therefore, as suggested in the Model TOR, you have to prepare a conceptual mine plan for every 5 year period for the life of the mine which is now 23 years. The conceptual mining plan for every 5 year block would have the same essential ingredients of the first mining plan of 5 year period as approved by the IBM. Therefore, you have to prepare 3 conceptual mine plans for every 5 year period each and another conceptual mine plan for the last 3 year period. That means there will be 4 conceptual mine plans out of which 3 would be of 5 year period each and the last one would be of 3 year period. It is quite possible that initially conceived life of the mine for 23 years would undergo change either way (more or less than 23 years) depending on reserves estimation that you might have to do as the result of exploration activities that you may undertake. Depending on the increase or decrease in the quantum of deposits the 5 year conceptual mine plan would have to be revised. As a serious miner you would be doing exploration activities to upgrade the reserves and in the process the life of the mine gets extended by, say, another 10 years assuming that your annual production capacity will remain unchanged. So the life of the project becomes 33 (23 + 10) years and accordingly you would be required to prepare 5 conceptual mining plans of 5 year period each besides the last one for 3 years. Obviously you cannot project the additional conceptual mine plans covering 10 years more before the EAC at the time of first presentation. At the appropriate time and as required under the extant guidelines of the MOEF you may have to go back to the EAC for environmental clearance for the extended life of the mine. These conceptual mine plans would be converted into regular mine plans in due course, incorporating necessary modifications based on your experience while working the earlier approved mining plan(s), and the same would have to be approved by the IBM before you start mining subsequently. This process will continue till you have extracted all the minerals. There are also few more requirements that you must comply with. After a mine pit is completely exhausted you have to prepare a mine closure plan. This is an essential component of your mining project as you cannot leave the area in degraded condition. A scientific mining plan would mean that the mined out area has been so restored as to match with the surrounding areas to the extent feasible. The basic requirement is that after the closure of the mine the area should not be hostile to the smooth and free movement of humans and wildlife. It is also essential that you clearly indicate your production capacity as at present and also your planned production capacity for the future. If there is any increase or decrease that should be properly explained. To make immediate impact on the minds of the members of the EAC you indicate all these details with the help of appropriate drawings and diagrams using, if you so like, different colours for instant and better understanding. Remember that presentation is an art and it makes lot of difference in convincing the expert members of the EAC.

Project Details

While giving the project details include all that you will find in Chapter- 2 of the Model TOR. I will only explain the implications so that your consultant can present all those details in appropriate manner. You are already aware that visual presentation is an effective method of presenting your case. Therefore, you must use appropriate drawings showing the layout of the project, various components of the project, lease hold area and nature and extent of mineralisation. There are certain minerals which would have associated minerals. It is important to show with the help of different shades of colour to indicate the main mineral in your project as also occurrences of associated minerals, if any, using some symbols. It is part of the zero-waste mining that the associated minerals are also extracted and segregated and you must indicate how you propose to dispose of the associated minerals, i.e., whether by using the same in your plant, if any, or by selling the same to other consumers. It is not enough that you indicate the reserves and quality of the ore. You must also give mineralogical analysis of the ore and its elemental composition. Equally important is the fact that nature and behaviour of ore body is indicated as that would determine the method of your mining. Suppose the occurrences of the ore body do not follow a uniform pattern you have to ensure that there is no selective mining for the sake of convenience as that would mean that you might leave behind some deposits and such deposits would have no use in future because mining of such deposits would not be economical. Another important aspect is use of the minerals that would be extracted. While preparing the pre-feasibility project report you might have undertaken a market survey of the use of the minerals. In case the minerals to be extracted are not for your captive use you must either have a tie up with the user industry or it is possible that even without such a tie up disposal of your minerals would not create any problem as there are many user industries for the mienrals. All these facts should be clearly brought out in the EIA report.

The most critical requirement relevant in the mining activities is to study the nature of the soil and the physico-mechanical properties of rocks which could be simple rocks or host rocks. If there is a possibility of subsidence during extraction of the minerals you must indicate the proposed protective measures as it is important for the safety of the mine workers. Don't give vague and unspecified assurances that adequate protective measures, to either completely prevent or to ensure that the subsidence does not go beyond a point as to endanger the life of the mine workers and leave the land with dangerous degradation, would be taken. If the soil characteristics are such that there is no possibility of any occurrences of subsidence highlight this negative factor to create a strong positive impact in your favour.

There are certain other details like surface plan with every prominent surface feature which should be given as the mineral deposits are unlikely to be uniform in depth and spread. Therefore, you need to present the transverse sections of the deposits. The word "transverse" means the way in which the mineral deposits are situated. This would be possible only if you collect the relevant data through drilled bore holes with reasonable gap between two bore holes so that a clear picture of the occurrences of the ore bodies is available. Since an uneven land would interfere, with easy movement of men and machinery it is essential that you also prepare the contour maps, physiography and drainage pattern as this will help you making advance and appropriate planning to do your mining activities.

Details of Mining

If you go through this particular paragraph in Chapter-2 of the Model TOR you will take no time to appreciate that whatever have been suggested (*ibid*) are most essential and critical components of a scientific mining operation and also for the safety of the mine workers, prevention of land degradation to the extent possible and for the safety and well-being of the local populace. I will highlight this with few examples.

Any serious miner would have an idea about the exploration activities conducted in the area, characteristics of ore and host rocks and estimation of mineral reserves. It is also essential that you are reasonably sure about the mineable reserves as that determines your investment decision. Besides the mineable reserves there will be also some deposits which are proven and for which you need to carry out detailed exploration to find out if such proven reserves could also be categorized as mineable reserves, i.e., the deposits that can be exploited. Usually, Geological Survey carried out by the Geological Survey of India (GSI) and the State Directorate of Mines and Geology mention another category which is called inferred. The nature and direction of occurrences of the ore bodies and the characteristics of the soil and rocks of the area surveyed indicate that there is a possibility of existence of the deposits in a larger area. In other words, an inference is drawn on the basis of past experience that possibilities of existence of ore bodies can be reasonably predicted in the larger area necessitating further action. Such areas would need further detailed exploratory mining to determine the existence of mineral reserves. Thus the inferred category of the minerals is also potential reserves.

As you would be using explosives for blasting operation, if blasting becomes necessary, the frequency of blasting operation, blast hole design, types of explosives to be used and most importantly intensity of ground vibration due to blasting operation become very critical. You might be wondering as to why a simple blasting operation becomes so critical in a remote area. It is not that simple. If the houses constructed by the local people for their living are not at a safe distance from the blasting point, the intensity of ground vibration would determine if those houses would be damaged. Likewise, ground vibration caused due to blasting operation would have immediate impact on the standing trees and the birds sitting on the branches of the trees would be terrified. The blasting operation would also raise the level of sound and consequentially there would be high decibel (dB) which will affect the wildlife including the birds. If no blasting is involved mention that clearly explaining the method of mining without blasting as such an operation is noise environment friendly.

Locations for dumping the OB as also its dimension are relevant if the OB contains any traces of the minerals as such OB would be a pollution hazard. In such a scenario plantation of any tree on such permanently dumped OB site(s) would need special care. If, however, the OB is simple earth and rocks and the OB is not meant for subsequent refilling the exhausted mine pits the plantation work on such OB does not pose any pollution problem. If you propose to refill the exhausted mine pits with OB mention clearly that you can manage by having only one or two dumping site (s) for the OB thereby creating less land degradation.

You would also be deploying various mining equipments. Therefore, you need to clearly explain why you are using a particular equipment and also the technology that you propose to use in your mining operation. You must be absolutely sure that the technology you have adopted or propose to adopt for your mining operation is environmentally compatible and is also more relevant for your specific project compared to other technology. Since, the possibility of break-down of the equipment deployed by you cannot be altogether ruled out you need to be ready with a plan to rectify the breakdown as that is essential for scientific mining.

Any mining operation would have a perceptible impact on the hydrology of not only the core zone but also the buffer zone. If mining is intersecting groundwater you must have a hydrological study of the area to know different levels of groundwater and the nature of aquifer. An aquifer is basically a layer of rock or simple soil which is capable to hold and transmit water. We all talk of groundwater. These groundwater could be the rain water held by the aquifer or the soil of the area which we take out with the help of pump for drinking and for other purposes. The groundwater could also be the water flowing underground from a river or a large water body existing somewhere in the area. Let me now explain how the groundwater is impacted due to your mining operation.

If mining is intersecting groundwater it would mean that the metal content of the mineral, say, iron ore, would contaminate the groundwater. Depending on the length of the aquifer or the nature of the soil the impact of mining intersecting the groundwater would be felt over a larger area. If the hydrological study shows that the radius of influence from the point at which mining is intersecting groundwater would be, say, 200 metres and if there is no human habitation within this area and water of this area of influence is not being used for drinking purposes you should clearly mention that in your EIA Report. The basic idea is that mining intersecting groundwater should not be a hazard for the people who take groundwater for drinking purposes also. If mining is not intersecting groundwater at all during the life of the project never miss the opportunity to highlight that as, one area of environmental concerns is completely eliminated.

Even in an open cast mine after the minerals are extracted completely the place itself becomes an artificially created water body which would contain rain water and therefore, such water body could also become a source of hazard if the water is contaminated. Therefore, both pre- and post-monsoon groundwater survey becomes essential. What is important is to ensure that the nearby households closest to the mining operation are not adversely impacted and if such people are not using the groundwater of the impacted zone, you may straightaway tell the members of the EAC with the help of appropriate site map of the area showing the extreme outer boundary of the area of influence and the nearest village or hamlets. Be very careful to show the location of the revenue village which could be at a much longer distance. You must also clearly mention the location of any hamlet that could be located at a place away from the revenue village, which is quite common in rural India, inhabited by people for various reasons including protection of their nearby crop land from the animals.

Zero-Waste Mining

Zero-waste mining is not only scientific mining of the deposits it is also most environment friendly mining operation. Now a question will be asked as to what constitutes zero-waste mining? You should not get confused by thinking that zero-waste mining means no minerals should be left behind. Since zero means "nil" your perception that there will be nil waste is perfectly valid. But unfortunately there is no technology so far that would ensure extracting all the minerals from the mine. Assuming that in a distant future there could be a technology ensuring full extraction of the minerals, the prospect of extracting the total metal content from the ore remains an impossibility. Thus, a practical interpretation would be that if you can extract all the minerals from the mine that are geologically extractable you have crossed the first hurdle in reaching the state of zero-waste mining. It is to be kept in mind that the nature of the rocks may not permit full extraction of the minerals. It is quite possible that the seismic nature of the area could also be an impediment in mining in certain area if it is prone to earthquake. Further, the occurrences of the ore body could be in an ecologically fragile area where mining is not permitted.

After extracting the minerals that are geologically extractable your next step will be to utilize the same for which you might have already prepared a plan. If you are having a steel plant you are in a position to utilize the minerals (iron ore) in your own plant and in that case the mine is for your captive use. As the grade of ore is not likely to be uniform in nature, you would have to upgrade the low grade ore through beneficiation. Such beneficiation process could be sintering or pelletization. Supposing it is not possible technologically for your steel plant to utilize the ore below certain grade even after beneficiation, you must ensure that the balance ore is disposed of through sale to such consumers who could use these low grade ore. In other words, after the disposal of the minerals in the way suggested above the remaining waste would be least pollutant as you have taken adequate step to extract the technologically extractable metal content from the ore and disposing the low grade ore through sale to other consumers.

There are certain minerals which are called associated minerals that you get from direct mining or as by-products of your main mining operation. As in the case of low grade ore, such associated minerals, which could be often more valuable than the principal minerals, would also have use. For example, a copper mine would have associated minerals like gold, cobalt and or molybdenum.

You are definitely well aware that any mineral is a non-renewable natural resource. Our country might be having large quantity of iron ore reserves and of good quality. But even if you mine 1 (one) tonne of iron ore from a mine the country becomes short of the reserves of the iron ore by one tonne. Even the discovering of more reserves by the GSI and other exploration agencies would not change the fact that the mineral reserves would still be a non-renewable natural resources as mining any quantity of mineral reserves would mean corresponding depletion of the natural resources whether known or not. Likewise, associated minerals, though not part of your main mining operation, should not be treated as waste for dumping purposes as such associated minerals have use, may not be for you, for others. You can now understand that when you are ensuring zero-waste mining and utilizing associated minerals you are basically adding to the resource base of the minerals. I will give an example. Suppose you have two separate mines of iron ore in two different leasehold areas at different locations. Both the mines have high grade as well as low grade iron ore. The high grade iron ore is of 63 per cent fe content or more while the low grade iron ore has fe content below 60 per cent. Suppose you have a steel plant of your own which can utilize iron ore with fe content of 60 per cent or more you would prefer mining ore of higher grade from both mines for your steel plant. Alternatively, you have an agreement with the steel plant set up by someone else for supplying the iron ore mined by you and that particular steel plant can utilize only iron ore with fe content of 60 per cent or more, you may be tempted to extract only high grade iron ore with fe content of 60 per cent or more and leave out the low grade iron ore in both the mines. So if you are going to extract only the high grade iron ore you are not upgrading the reserves of iron ore in your mines. Rather, you are depleting the deposits. However, if you are extracting all the minerals including the low grade ones you are indirectly increasing your resource base because the same two mines would give you more output as mined iron ore.

I will give another example based on my personal experience as Joint Secretary to the Government of India, Ministry of Mines, during 1989-94. I was dealing with the public sector company Hindustan Copper Limited. As the copper ore in their existing mines at Mosabani and Khetri were fast depleting, the company was badly in need of new deposits which they found in Malanjkhand in Madhya Pradesh. The grade of the ore was fairly good with around 1.25 per cent Cu. It was noted that the company had been consistently producing high grade copper ore. Since, I had some doubt I enquired privately from the Chairman-cum-Managing Director

(CMD) of the company as to how there could be consistently only high grade ore. I was the dealing Joint Secretary and in that capacity a part time Non-Executive Director on the Board of Directors of the company, the CMD had to be frank enough to tell me that because of the pressure from the Ministry the company took recourse to selective mining, an euphemism for slaughter mining, and the overburden was being dumped on the area below which low grade copper deposits were in existence. Since it was a highly unscientific mining this practice was discontinued and it was decided that mining should start from one side and before a new mine pit is opened the extractable mineral reserves of the pit already opened should be exhausted. But there was the problem of removing the dumped overburden before mining out the lean grade ore which was, incidentally, either of the same or higher grade compared to the copper deposits in their existing mines in Mosabani and Khetri. In fact, the company had to spend large amount of money for removing the overburden which was dumped on the nearby vacant land beneath which low grade copper ore left unexploited. You can now imagine if the company would have extracted initially the left out low grade ore, its ore reserves would have increased besides saving avoidable expenditure on removing the overburden.

The point I am trying to make out is that scientific mining with zero-waste mining as the goal and utilization of associated minerals result in increasing the resource base of otherwise non-renewable natural resources. Abundance of minerals like good quality iron ore, bauxite, or for that matter any other minerals, whether in abundance ore not, should not be the reason for selective mining.

Environment

In the next seven chapters I would be dealing with the seven critical components of environmental issues that would arise due to mining activities. Before going into the components chapter-wise I consider it necessary to explain the import of certain expressions that would come up for detailed explanation. As an experienced and serious miner you may think that there is nothing new in whatever I would be narrating while dealing with the seven critical components of environmental issues. But there would be an unspecified number of new entrants in the field of mining and such new entities and perhaps including some non-miners who might have academic interest in the subject would need elaborate description about the ramifications of various components of environment. I have put a self-imposed onus on me to prove that mining and environment can go hand-in-hand and in fact they are bound to co-exist harmoniously in the interest of both physical and social environment. Therefore, I must give a reasonably elaborate description which even a complete novice would be in a position to appreciate. Even for an experienced miner this could be quite refreshing.

While going through the seven critical components of environment, i.e., air environment, noise environment, water environment, land environment, biological environment, socio-economic environment and, of course, the health environment for the mine workers and the populace of the area, as elaborated in the Model TOR you would notice that three expressions, baseline status, anticipated impacts and proposed mitigating measures, appear without any exception in each of the above seven components of environment dealt with in the seven chapters that follow in that order. It is, therefore, logical that I must give a brief idea about these three expressions.

Let us start with baseline *status* and I would be also using the expression baseline *data* and both the expressions carry the same meaning. Baseline status is the starting point. That is, the status of various inputs of a particular component of environment as are existing before the start of mining. For example, in respect of land environment we must know the existing, that is, prior to mining operations, nature of the soil, cropping pattern, vegetation cover, etc. While collecting these data you may notice that the land is fertile with good vegetation and crop productivity of the land is also quite good, say, 5 quintals of paddy per acre of land annually. Perhaps you would also be knowing the per acre production of any other crop. There are other baseline data that would have to be collected which I would be going into more details at the appropriate place.

Now you are ready with the baseline data of land environment. It is incumbent on you to anticipate the likely impact of your mining activities on the baseline conditions of the soil. It is definite that dust will be created during mining operation and depending on the speed and direction of the wind dust particles would travel certain distance before the same settle on the land that, for example, has the capacity to produce 5 quintals of paddy per acre per year. The dust created due to your mining operations and these dust particles settling on these paddy fields would reduce the productive capacity of the land. Similarly, there would be soil erosion on account of your mining activities and the seepage would adversely impact the otherwise fertile land. You, therefore, have fairly good idea about the adverse impact of your mining activities on the surrounding lands. As a man of sound common sense you would take no time to come to the conclusion that the same land is likely to give a yield of, say, 3 quintals of paddy, a reduction of two quintals compared to the pre-mining yield of 5 quintals, as a result of the adverse impact caused due to your mining activities on the productive capacity of the land.

Since there would be adverse impact on the soil characteristic and productivity of the land due to your mining activities it becomes your moral responsibility to prepare, may be in consultation with the local officers of the Agriculture Department as also with the local people, effective measures to mitigate the likely adverse impact on the land. Such mitigating measures could be by way of taking preventive measures ensuring that mine water does not spill over to the cropland and clearing dust through water sprinkling and if that do not yield the desired result you may have to pay adequate financial compensation so as to ensure that the loss in production due to your mining activities is taken care of.

With the above introduction to the subject I would now proceed to deal with the seven most critical components of environment in the related chapters. In this context I would advise you to go through Table 1 of Annexure-B on Details of Parameters, Procedures and Methods for Description of Environment for Mining Projects as indicated after Chapter 5 of the Model TOR. This table will give you an idea about the details to be collected on each of the seven critical components of environment.

Chapter – 6

Air Environment

Before I start with the three components of air environment, i.e. base line status, anticipated impacts and proposed mitigating measures, let us see the importance of air in our life as also in the life of animals, both domestic and wild. Just imagine you are in an air-tight room without any ventilation to circulate air inside, you would soon reach a state of breathlessness and if prolonged it may result in death due to suffocation.

What is this air? By definition air is an invisible gaseous substance surrounding the earth where we live. It is a mixture of mainly oxygen and nitrogen. For the sake of convenience I would use the word "air" and the word "wind" as synonyms. When air is in more or less rapid natural motion, i.e. moving from an area of high pressure to an area of low pressure we call it wind.

We know the value of oxygen, one of the two main ingredients of air, in our respiratory system. Let us start with a very common example. Nowadays it is quite common to see people, both young and old, going for morning walk as it is considered good for your health. Perhaps many of us would not be knowing that in the early morning hours the air is fresh and full of oxygen. This oxygenated air is inhaled while we breathe and this oxygenated air travels to our lung and it purifies our blood that goes to the heart. That means the heart is getting oxygenated blood which is good for our cardiovascular system.

Base Line Status

Details to be collected on Air Environment under different headings have been indicated at Item A-Air Environment in Table 1 at the end of the Model T.O.R. at Annexure-B. Your consultant would be in a position to collect the information and appropriately mention the same in tabular form.

Such detailed information in required number of statements form part of the EIA report to be submitted before the EAC for consideration at the time of appraisal of the project by the Committee. These are, no doubt, routine information but are very relevant and critical in appraising the impact of your project activities on the air environment and the adequacy of the proposed mitigating measures. It is, therefore, advisable that you collect as much information as are possible.

While preparing the baseline status in the context of air environment it is essential that you obtain the details of climate and meteorology from the nearest India Meteorological Department (IMD) station. Information supplied by the IMD would be most authentic and acceptable to the EAC. While doing so it is essential that you mention the approximate distance, as the crow flies, of the nearest IMD station from the project site. In the most unlikely event of the nearest IMD station, which could be at a fairly long distance, not having the required climate and meteorological data you could engage an expert to collect the information. But such a situation is not likely to happen.

Section 3.1.1 of Chapter-3 of the Model TOR at Annexure-B enumerates the relevant data to be collected. Levels of temperature, humidity and speed and direction of wind and rainfall are very important climatic data. These information should be representative in character for the area in different seasons of the year. It is, therefore, advisable that these information are collected before monsoon and after monsoon so as to have a clear idea about the impact of the mining throughout the year. An appropriate wind-rose should be prepared and shown on the video screen. This wind rose should reflect the direction of wind blowing in different major seasons. A wind-rose, a diagram of the relative frequency of wind directions at a place, is basically a drawing of the flower (rose) in such a way that its petals, i.e., different parts of the corolla of this rose (drawing) should indicate the direction of the wind during different seasons. It is, as if, a large size rose in full bloom with all its petals spread in different directions. Imagine a rose in your private garden and in full bloom as if to show you the direction of each petal as per the wind direction. In fact, the wind-rose would mirror the direction of the wind and the consequent route the dust will fly and the speed of the wind would broadly indicate the distance that are likely to be affected by the dust. If there are bushy and leafy vegetation and leafy trees of a particular height which may contain the flying dust within a limited sphere you should highlight that in your EIA report that the dust would not impact the agricultural and other productive lands. Make sure that the wind-rose represents the actual wind direction and properly shown on the map so that the members of the EAC can make an assessment of the extent of impact on the surrounding land mass. Remember, the members of the EAC would like to know the pre-dominant wind direction to assess the impact on the lands during larger part of the year. So it is advisable that you indicate that (pre-dominant wind direction) in your EIA report and the EMP.

Select appropriate location of monitoring stations that must conform to the wind-rose. Suppose the pre-dominant wind direction is from south to north the monitoring stations should be so located as to give you the data for the whole year as per the wind direction. That does not mean that you should not give the location of the monitoring stations for areas not covered by pre-dominant wind direction. The wind direction and its speed, whether pre-dominant or not, would determine the extent of adverse impact on the crop land. I am highlighting these facts as the Committee often comes across large number of cases where the project proponents prepare wind rose that would not conform to the wind direction of the particular area as per the data supplied by the nearest IMD station. The monitoring stations should be representative in character. Therefore, you should appreciate that all the data you present before the EAC should be representative in character, i.e., covering the entire area and during different seasons of the year so that a composite view can be taken by the committee.

Besides the air pollution caused due to your mining operation, there will be air pollution caused due to crushing operations, ore processing operation and ore beneficiation plant, if any, and the air pollution created on the routes through which you would be transporting the ore to the final destination for disposal. If you do not have any processing or beneficiation operation or even crushing operation and you propose to transport the minerals as R.O.M you don't have to give the data on these non-existing operations except the air pollution data on account of transportation. Since, however, dust will be created while extracting the minerals and their loading on the transport vehicles you have to collect such data.

When you give the baseline data on air pollution as per the Model TOR and as are applicable to your project make sure that the data reflect the actual status and are representative for the area throughout the year. Since, the baseline data, wind direction and speed, for example, would determine the likely impacts necessitating a particular type of mitigating measures it is very important that the baseline data are true to the ground reality.

Anticipated Impacts

Once you are ready with the baseline status of the components of air pollution, you can pause for a while and make an introspection how the different climatological data would affect the physical environment as also humans and other living things due to the pollution that would be created on account of your mining activities. Remember that there is no mining technology that can eliminate the possibility of air pollution. Such polluted air is bound to have an adverse impact. You may argue that even the natural events like forest fires or high speed storms would also create air pollution and, therefore, mining activities should not be singled out as the only source of air pollution. It is not my intention to pronounce that mining activities are solely responsible for polluting the air. The air pollution that takes place due to natural events like forest fires or storms are only occasional and even the most vocal cynic would not say that forest fires or high speed storms would occur throughout the year. The people living in the area as also wild animals get accustomed to the change in the air environment caused by natural processes. But as a miner, you are polluting the air environment by your mining activities and, therefore, such polluted environment is not natural but artificial, man made to which the local populace are not accustomed. Once you stop mining and other related activities it does not take much time for the air environment to come back to the original status. There could still be some air pockets in the degraded land. If you do not restore the land to match with the surrounding areas to the extent feasible making such land environment friendly for all living things, both human and animal, for free and smooth movement over the area that (degraded land) might make such polluted air take longer time to get back to the original status.

The Model TOR enumerates the anticipated impacts due to air pollution. You must co-relate these impacts to the baseline data that you have collected. Whatever, items are specific to your project you may accordingly list the anticipated impacts and explain to the EAC that your project would likely to create certain types of adverse impacts as listed.

I dare say that mining activities would not have any positive impact. For example, because of your mining activities, you would need and ensure reasonably good road connectivity for the movement of men and materials. Such road connectivity would also be enjoyed by the local population. I will separately indicate the positive impacts at appropriate places. But I can tell you with full confidence that the air pollution caused due to mining activities would have only negative environmental impacts. I will give few examples to prove the contention.

So long the people living in the areas as also the animals and birds and inhaling the air with whatever natural pollutions are there, their body system has survived and all living things have been existing in complete harmony with the nature. But due to your mining activities, as you would be using various mining equipments, the presence of gas and/or solids, the otherwise natural good quality air would get polluted. The health of the people living in the area becomes the first casualty and they would gradually start acquiring various diseases on account of the polluted air. In short, the exposure of the people to the polluted air could result in diseases like silicosis, lungs cancer, dust related pneumonias, to name only a few. Another very simple example would make the point very clear and I am sure as a good entrepreneur you would agree with me. You might be aware that the dust generated on account of the mining activities would travel as per the wind direction and speed till the dust settles on the leafy trees and other leafy plants and vegetation even assuming that the speed of the wind would not cover much area. Nevertheless, you have already admitted that dust will get deposited on the leaves of the standing trees and other vegetation. Assuming this happens during the months of, say, January and February, and rainfall would occur in the area sometimes in the months of May and June, this would result in the accumulated dust remaining on the leaves of the trees and other vegetation during the intervening period till rain water clears the dust. The photosynthesis, a process under which the leaves of the plants collect their energy from the sunlight, would not function or would function imperfectly till the rain clears the dust. If you have an ornamental plant in your own house and if you have also a small private garden in your house with lot of ornamental plants, you are experiencing everyday this phenomenon, perhaps without taking note of the changes as your domestic help has and may be you yourself as a garden lover have watered the plants to clear the accumulated dust. A spread of water over the plants, the plants would take no time to give you an eye pleasing lush green (fresh and natural and not necessarily green in colour as there are certain plants whose leaves may not be green in colour) and soothing experience.

I have given the two examples just to bring home to your sensitivity the damage that would be caused to the green surroundings on account of one single pollutant dust that is invariably caused due to any mining activities, as you simply can not avoid generation of dust. There are other adverse impacts on account of air pollution which you must list in your

EIA report and corresponding to the adverse impacts you prepare a plan for mitigating these adverse impacts which I will be dealing with in the next section.

Suggested Mitigating Measures

Once you have identified the adverse impacts due to air pollution you are in a position to prepare a scheme to mitigate those impacts. No doubt, it is not possible to completely contain the impact. But at the same time you should not be perceived as either doing nothing or doing very little to mitigate the adverse impacts to the extent possible.

The Model TOR at section 3.1.3 at Annexure-B has suggested certain broad steps which, I am sure, should be taken up seriously by you. There are many universally accepted measures to ensure that the emission of pollutants are kept to the minimum so that the quality of air is acceptable to the human and animal body system. The golden principle is "prevention is better than cure". It is always advisable to spend more money on limiting the pollutants rather than spending any money to minimize the impact of polluted air as the later course of action might not be as effective as the former which is designed to contain the emission of pollutants. This can be well appreciated by a very common example but still we do not take any notice thereof. Supposing you get pure potable water through the water supply pipe and if you drink that water it would not cause any health problem for you. This means that the local Municipal Body, to which you have been paying property tax and which is supplying drinking water to your house, would have water treatment system as it is the responsibility of the municipal body (part of your property tax has already been apportioned to the water treatment cost) to supply pure drinking water. Alternatively, if the municipal body supplies raw water without any treatment and you as a health conscious person would purify that water by installing a small RO plant or a water purifier in your house. Perhaps, still you may not be completely sure about the quality of the water even though you would be spending more. So let us control the source of pollutants rather than creating pollution and then spending money to minimize the impact which may not be still adequate because some of the adverse impacts may surface long after the start of emission of pollutants and, more often than not, it could happen long after the mining operation was finally closed.

I have given the example of the impact of air pollution on the flora and fauna of the area in the Section on Anticipated Impacts. Don't give s stereotype explanation that water sprinkling would be done to remove the dust and other pollutants settled on the flora unless you prove that the technique you propose to employ to mitigate the impact is the most commonly one used by a scientific miner. So don't hesitate to tell the EAC that the technique you propose to employ would be an effective one and if you can give an example of another mine of yours or some one else's employing the same technique with good results you should tell the EAC so.

Taking the stand that "prevention is better than cure", your effort should be to convince the members of the EAC that your methods of mining are scientific resulting in least dust pollution and if the methods are the most widely used ones by the miners in similar cases of mining you have a fairly reasonable chance to get the approval of the EAC. So you give details of the methods through appropriate drawings. It is not only the air environment that would be influenced by the methods of mining but the same (methods of mining) would also reduce the adverse impacts of other components of the environment like noise environment, land environment etc. which I would be dealing with at the appropriate place. But to bring the matter home to you I would give a simple example. Unless you are compelled to open two mine pits simultaneously in the same lease hold area, it could be due to your need to get a particular grade of ore as a sweetener and which is not conveniently available elsewhere, always confine your mining operation to one mine pit at a time and in no case you should open the second mine pit before exhausting the first mine pit following your principle of zero-waste mining. And simultaneously you should also start restoring the mined out area to match with the surrounding areas to the extent practicable as you might need some of the mined out areas for certain related activities connected to the subsequent stages of mining and if you start plantation work on the restored land at the earliest possible time you will notice that by the time your first mined pit is exhausted the lands will have fresh vegetation cover and standing trees. I have seen some areas in Goa where there has been good growth of plantation on the mined out land in about 3 to 4 years' period. If you can manage by breaking lands in one place at a time and with good plantation work as you do mining you would create less air pollution.

I would emphasise one of the most effective ways of containing emission of pollutants and more particularly spread of dusts while transporting the minerals. Here again don't try to over-emphasise the mode of your transportation in trucks covered with heavy-duty waterproof cloth commonly called tarpaulin as this may not be a very effective one compared to the transportation of minerals by conveyor system. You will be surprised to know that some of the project proponents who appeared before the EAC readily accepted the suggestion of the Committee to use conveyor belt as they realized that investment for installing the conveyor belt was worth it and they very frankly admitted that they had not applied their mind to this aspect. So, wherever the physical terrain permits and is cost effective (taking into account the post-mortem of spending more money to mitigate the adverse impacts) you must prepare a plan to install an aerial conveyor system. Such a conveyor system could be covered or open depending on the height and the wind speed. Perhaps you would yourself come to the conclusion that a covered conveyor belt or a covered container to move through aerial ropeway would be preferable. So you must specify the nature of the conveyor belt or the nature of the container to be moved through aerial ropeway indicating whether the same would be covered and in case it would be open you may give proper justification thereof. But a covered conveyer belt or an aerial ropeway container (preferably covered one) system is most environment friendly.

Chapter – 7

Noise Environment

Before I go into the details of noise environment I would first explain the relevance of noise in your day-to-day life. In the context of environment, noise is nothing but a sound specially a loud and unpleasant or undesired one. Take a common homely example. If a person enters your house and he closes the door with a bang that would create noise which you might consider unbecoming because the noise so created has caused some annoyance to you. I will explain this aspect while dealing with the question of noise pollution that is invariably created in the process of mining operations.

We all in our normal day-to-day living can make out which noise or sound (noise and sound have been used as synonyms) is pleasant and which sound is harmful. We would never call a loud sound a pleasing one even though many a time we make loud sound by shouting at others to get their attention. Thus a small child would cry loud when it is hungry just to draw the attention of the mother or any female member to satisfy its hunger. As opposed to such unpleasant sound we always welcome certain varieties of sound which are pleasing and soothing to our auditory organ i.e., ear. If you are living in a rural area with reasonably good flora including leafy trees you would invariably experience the beauty of the sound made by, say, a bird like *bulbul*, a song bird of the family of *Pycnonotidae*. Likewise, there is another type of bird called *cuckoo* of the family of *Cuculidae*. This particular bird though may not be, strictly speaking, a song bird, has a characteristic cry and it is usually seen during spring in certain parts of India. This bird is also nick named as bird of fair weather that appears only in the most pleasant season (spring) of the year and a person of that nature is derogatorily called as *cuckoo* of the fair weather (spring) at least in some of the eastern States of India. But still the sound it makes during its seasonal visit in spring is welcomed by the people and if in a particular spring this sound of *cuckoo* is not audible the people would feel that something is missing.

Another very common experience that any family man would, at sometimes or the other, have. A father or mother with a small baby knows very well the effect of a *lullaby.* What is this *lullaby* that has such a profound impact on a baby who would never fail to convey, by various means including cry or some annoying physical behaviour, to the mother that it is feeling sleepy? The mother through her experience would immediately take the baby in her lap or put the baby on the bed and starts singing some song to which the child has already been accustomed and the impact is instant as the child will be in deep sleep in no time. This we call a *lullaby,* i.e., a soothing song to send a child to sleep. In the present day technological development there could also be a musical *lullaby* without the words. Imagine, by contrast, the impact of the noise that is created by a crow. In fact, if a crow makes a sudden loud noise it would not only frighten a child but at times even an adult would find it extremely irritating.

Thus, we are sensitive to different types of sound and our response will vary depending on the nature of the noise. Even the sound of a *lullaby* could become highly annoying if the mother sings a *lullaby* with a loud sound. Again, the same *lullaby* sung by mother that would have created a pleasing and soothing effect on the baby would have a opposite effect if the *lullaby* is sung by any other person, both male or female, having a hoarse or a croaking voice.

It is, therefore, established that a noise or sound is an integral part of our living. The sound created by human or by a bird would have great impact on the quality of our life just like we humans need air to survive and the benevolent quality of the fresh air adds to the quality of our living. Even the same sound that we experience in our day to day living would have an irritating and annoying impact on the quality of our life depending on the particular pitch at which such sound is received by our auditory organ, i.e., ear. We often come across instances, though not taking note thereof, when sound would make some vibration. Unlike in the developed western countries where the houses are constructed in a way that when the doors and the windows are closed there is either nil or very little sound vibration, in our country (India) and in many other countries such sound-created vibration can not be avoided. For example, when we close a door or a window specially during winter when the gap in between the window frame or the door frame and the wall to which the frame is attached widens due to dryness, we will experience that the nearest door or the window is making some sound caused by vibration. Since such noise due to vibration is within a limit of tolerance and to which we are used such sound does not interfere with our normal way of life and we never apply our mind to the question if such noise is harmful or not. But supposing there is a big explosion in a nearby area the sound vibration would be so loud that it will frighten you and at times a weak structure of the house or even the entire building could be damaged. The impact is also clearly visible as some birds otherwise sitting on the branches of the trees in complete harmony with the nature would start flying away almost simultaneously with the loud sound caused by such explosion.

Thus noise or sound, per se, is not harmful and, if I may say so, has many positive effect and it improves the quality of our living and we can not imagine a life without sound. And if you are a man of poetic nature you would perhaps say that without sound a person will have a lifeless life. Only a man who is completely deaf from birth would have no idea about the value of noise. In fact, our knowledge of different nature of sound at times saves our life. Thus when we hear the hissing sound made by a poisonous snake or a particular sound made by a predator like lion or tiger we immediately make an assessment and run for safety cover either in our house if it is close by or in a place which we think is not likely to be visited by the snake or the predator. In contrast, a deaf person may not run for safety unless he has visual knowledge of such ferocious animals. So he runs the risk of being attacked and perhaps being killed by the predator for no fault of his.

Having given a brief description about the impact of sound on our life I would now proceed to deal with the noise environment caused due to your mining operation. In the context of mining we can not imagine any noise which can be termed soothing as mining operation is bound to create a series of loud sounds which are harmful and annoying. I will now take up the three components of noise environment starting with baseline status, anticipated impacts and mitigating measures in that sequence. We have accepted the position that baseline data are the starting point, i.e., the relevant data relating to noise pollution as obtaining in the area before you start your mining operations. It is also quite possible that there would be certain activities including, may be, some existing operating mines in the vicinity that have already adversely impacted the noise environment. So we must know the source of the noise as existing.

Any mining operation would involve removal of already existing vegetation, i.e., trees or plants. Even in a mine (bauxite for example) where the minerals may occur as outcrop you may have to remove certain quantity of surface soil including any vegetation before you remove the minerals.

In any opencast mine (iron ore) you have to remove the overburden as the ore bodies would be at a certain depth and such activities would create noise. Similarly, activities like drilling, blasting, loading, unloading and movement of vehicles would create noise. Therefore, if there are existing operating mines the level of noise would already be above the noise level in a virgin area. But if you are operating in an area where there is no mining or other industrial activities within a fairly long distance the noise level would be different and if there is no vehicular movement close to the area the noise level would be of the normal level. But still in such an area not affected by any mining and other industrial activities and vehicular movement there would be certain level of noise on account of occasional high velocity storm or sounds made by the wildlife including birds and due to other natural causes. In such a situation the people living there would not have any adverse impacts as they are used to the surroundings with natural level of noise. Therefore, depending on the existing noise level on account of some operating mines or industrial activities in the close vicinity and the natural causes without any influence by any existing mining or other industrial activities, you have to collect the baseline data as designed in section 3.2.1 of the Model TOR to the extent specific to the location of your project. If you are not required to collect the baseline data on certain component as enumerated in the Model TOR you may clearly mention that in your EIA report with justification so that the members of the EAC are sure that you have not missed any relevant data. With these preliminary comments I would now start with the baseline data to be collected. While doing so I would only give a broad idea which would help you and your consultant to complete the exercise with as elaborate details as possible and definitely relevant and specific to your project.

Baseline Status

Details to be collected on Noise Environment under different headings have been indicated at Item B-Noise Environment in Table 1 (Annexure B) referred to earlier. Your consultant would be in a position to collect the information and appropriately mention the same in tabular form. Such detailed information in required number of Statements form part of the EIA report submitted before the EAC for consideration at the time of appraisal of the project by the Committee. These are, no doubt, routine information but are very relevant and critical in appraising the impact of your project activities on the noise environment and the adequacy of the proposed mitigating measures. It is, therefore, advisable that you collect as much information as are possible.

In the preceding paragraphs what I have been trying to convey to you is that the area, that includes place of actual human habitation and the surrounding areas, has a particular decibel level (dB), that is, the noise levels that have been obtaining through out the year both during day time and night time. The noise that is created on account of various natural and human activities would not have any impact on the auditory system if it is in a vacuum without any mode of transportation, so to say. The noise once created needs a medium, which is provided by the air waves, to travel to reach the hearing organ, i.e., ear. That is, the noise would travel through the waves of the air before it has an impact on the auditory system. Therefore, one of the most essential ingredients of baseline data to be collected is the noise levels in different seasons of the year and accordingly you need to fix the monitoring stations. As the noise or sound moves along the air waves path it is necessary that locations of the monitoring stations are the same as the air quality monitoring stations so as to get an accurate reading to the extent possible. The wind-rose discussed in the preceding chapter on Air Environment becomes a practical guide to select the locations for monitoring stations for sound also.

Since the noise levels will vary during day time and night time it is necessary to monitor the noise levels during day time and night time. Even in day time or night time the noise levels could reach a peak level at a particular time and it could reach a very low level at a particular time during the day and during the night. For example, the noise level could be at the lowest level, almost reaching a pin drop silence, between, say, 12 midnight and 3 a.m. in the rural area in a calm atmosphere. Needless to say that the monitoring of the existing noise levels in day time and night time should be done as frequently as possible and indicating the time and date of such measurements of noise levels. You can make such measurements over a period of time which would be of representative nature. As the duration of noise at a particular level is an important factor to determine the intensity of the impact, it is necessary that duration of the noise levels specially at the peak level is monitored. For example, if peak level is 60 dB monitoring should be done to see the duration of the noise at that level (60 dB) and so should be the exercise for the other relevant levels. You will, no doubt, appreciate that if dB level of 60 lasts only for, say, two seconds, its impact would be momentary and marginal compared to the impact of the noise level if the duration of the dB of the noise at the same level is of, say, one minute or more. In India we experience this (impact) at least once a year during the Hindu festival of lights (Diwali) when the noise created by a particular cracker bursting continues at progressively ascending higher and deafening levels and there are also crackers whose noise impact is marginal as the levels last only for few seconds.

It is most unlikely that the area covered under your noise level monitoring exercise would be flat and undulated. In fact, the terrain features of the area could be such that it would be having both high and low lands or could have small hillocks besides standing leafy trees with branches spread in all directions. Such physical features of the area would also impact the noise quality and consequential selection of appropriate noise quality monitoring stations to assess the impact of noise quality in accordance with the terrain characteristics.

Section 3.2.1 of the Model TOR at Annexure B advises you to collect noise levels, i.e., Leq (day) and Leq (night) for each monitoring station in core zone and buffer zone along with the applicable standards. In simple language, which a layman can understand, the term Leq is *equivalent continuous noise level*, i.e., the normal noise levels to which the local people are used to in different times during day and night. In other words, the noise levels specially the peak noise level would be such that when the noise travels through air waves it would strike the ear drum of the person receiving the noise and the person would not have any undesired or annoying impact because he is used to it.

It is possible that existing mining activities or other industrial activities and movement of transport vehicles and possibly rail transport are also creating certain noise levels. It is, therefore, necessary that the noise monitoring stations should be so located as to cover the noise on account of these activities. If there are existing mining operations that involves blasting operation the level of vibrations caused due to blasting operation need to be monitored.

With the above exercise you are now fairly well-equipped with the two sets of baseline data of noise levels, one giving the baseline data of the noise levels that would normally exist as a consequence of various natural and human activities that I have briefly touched upon in some of the preceding paragraphs, and the other set of baseline data of noise levels due to any existing mining or industrial activities and movement of transport vehicles including rail movement. If the area of your study does not have any noise problem to be shown under the second set of data caused due to existing mining activities etc. you don't have to collect any baseline data caused by any non-existing industrial activities etc.

With the baseline data so collected you can now make an assessment and fairly reasonable prediction about the anticipated adverse impacts due to the increase in dB level on account of your mining and other related activities on the nature and quality of noise and impacts on the living things, both human and wildlife.

Anticipated Impacts

The noise created on account of your mining activities would have different impacts on the people and the wildlife including avifauna of the area and on the people in the workplace. It is, therefore, necessary you take the help of appropriate modelling for the prediction of noise levels at different and representative monitoring stations that you might have already selected while collecting the baseline data.

The most prominent and common harmful impact is on our auditory function. In fact, in case of a severe impact there could be partial or complete loss of hearing. Though noise induced loss of hearing might not be a common happening in so far as it relates to the people living in the surrounding areas, it (loss of hearing) could be quite common in the case of mine workers and other staff working in the mine and otherwise engaged in mine related activities. Again, the impact on hearing could vary from person to person depending on the sensitivity of a particular person to different levels of noise. For the mine workers and other staff the impact would be slow and the persons being affected might not be conscious of such impact immediately. Such inconspicuous but progressive exposure to noise pollution might appear to be inconsequential to the mine workers or any staff working in the project but after a lapse of time such exposed person(s) would come to realize that there has been loss of hearing which could not be noticed by him as the noise pollution worked like slow poisoning.

Though auditory impact is the most prominent one, noise level has other harmful impacts like noise induced fatigue, breathing trouble adversely affecting the respiratory functions and heartbeat, adverse impact on the efficiency of the workers, disturbed sleep, to name a few. As a miner you must therefore be very particular that you make an accurate assessment about the harmful impacts that the noise pollution, caused due to your mining activities, would have on the mine workers and other employees.

Besides, the adverse impacts on the mine workers and other employees you must also make a fairly and reasonably accurate assessment of the adverse impacts that are likely to be caused to the living things, both human and wildlife including *avifauna*, as a result of the noise pollution due to your mining activities as the noise levels so created would be of a much higher level than the ambient noise level to which the people and the wildlife including the avifauna have been used to so far. If there are already other existing mining and other industrial activities in the area you have to assess the additional adverse impacts that will be generated on account of your mining activities and to what extent the human environment and wildlife including *avifauna* would be further adversely affected. It is quite possible that as a result of the additional noise levels to be created by your activities which could be beyond the level of tolerance the wildlife including the avifauna might be forced to flee the area they have been used to live for years and there might not be any other suitable habitation for such wildlife at reasonable distance. In such a scenario the wildlife get exposed to immediate danger to their life.

If there are water bodies in the core zone or in the buffer zone, there would be fishes and birds. There are certain birds which also spend lots of time floating in the water and intermittently would fly and sit on the branches of any nearby trees. Such birds follow a more or less fixed time schedule. The noise created on account of your mining operations would have adverse impacts on the birds as at times they may be frustrated for the simple reason that some times as per their daily routine they would be at the point of touching the water body and may be, being frightened by the noise at that particular moment, unprepared to fly back. Perhaps, you may not be knowing that the noise has also an adverse impacts on the fishes. You might have yourself enjoyed the spectacular scene when different types of fishes float keeping half of their bodies and specially the mouths above the water level to get fresh air and during certain seasons of the year it is not quite infrequent that fishes in small groups would be found flying in the air above the water level, not necessarily always to catch hold of a flying insect as the feed, as if taking part in a sport in playful mood. The noise created on account of your mining operation would not allow the fishes to behave the way they would be otherwise behaving depriving the local populace of a most common and spontaneous eye pleasing scene created by the fishes on their own oblivious of the fact that the humans enjoy it.

The noise created due to your mining activities that would involve noise due to the use of various mining machinery and equipment would have adverse impact on the mine workers and other employees. The vibration caused due to the blasting operations, if blasting is involved, would damage the residential houses of the people if the structures are unable to stand the impact of the vibration. Depending on the impact the whole house might collapse causing injuries (including fatal ones) to the people living inside at that moment.

When you assess the likely impacts due to your mining operations, you must make an assessment about the likely impacts also due to existing and future surface transportation activities by road and rail. If you are an environment friendly miner you may like to transport your mined minerals by conveyor belt or by aerial ropeway carriages (covered or open). There would be some noise even in such transportation as the conveyor belt or aerial ropeway carriages might create air pollution but such pollution would be insignificant compared to the huge positive achievement in controlling dust pollution as you have seen while dealing with Air Environment in the preceding chapter.

Suggested Mitigating Measures

Once you have identified the likely adverse impacts on account of noise you are in a position to prepare an action plan that you, in the best of your judgment, consider adequate to mitigate the adverse impacts. It is a fact that as of now no technology can offer you the method of mining to completely negate the noise related adverse impacts. If the mineral wealth of the country is necessarily to be exploited for the economic development of the country, the accompanying negative impacts are bound to be there. But our effort should be to ensure that noise pollution is kept at a level which the humans, wildlife and avifauna can sustain. To achieve this objective you need to adopt effective noise control measure which I would briefly mention in the sequel.

You know by now that there is source of noise. These sources could be blasting operations, operation of various mining equipments, transportation etc. It is, therefore, advisable that latest available technology is adopted to reduce the noise level at the source itself and by far this is the most effective and desirable noise control measure. But at the same time you have to also consider the cost and the operational requirement as with the adoption of a modern technology your mining operations should not be a non-economic option. However, whatever suggestion I am giving here is with the assumption that as a miner you are in a position to adopt modern technology to keep the noise level lower at the source itself.

Once the noise is created at source and even if such noise is at a reduced level on account of your adoption of various steps, the available noise would not remain confined to the source just like the noise created by a baby while crying for feed would not remain confined to the room where the baby is stationed. As already explained earlier, the noise would travel through air waves to reach its target, i.e., the receiver of the noise. I will give a very homely example here. The grown-up children in your house are watching the TV programmes with a loud noise which is affecting your conversation, in the adjoining room, with a friend of yours who has come to your house to discuss certain important things. Your immediate response would be to control the source of noise by forcing the children to reduce the volume. If the children are reluctant to do so, which is not uncommon, you would prefer to close the door of the room where the TV is installed so that the noise does not travel to the place where you are in discussion with your visiting friend. In the above example, by closing the door of the TV room you have created an obstruction or a barrier for the air waves to travel to the adjoining room where you are sitting with your friend. But even if the door of the TV room is closed it is not possible to completely eliminate the possibility of some noise travelling to reach you but such noise level will be acceptable as it would not create any perceptible impediment in your normal activities including talking to somebody or reading some books or newspapers or even talking on telephone to some one else. In the case of mining operation you can design a suitable enclosure or errect barriers to ensure that the air waves, carrying the noise created on account of various operations, are, after hitting the barriers or the sides of the enclosure so put in place, transmitted back to the source. In the process of such forward and backward movement within the controlled area the noise, obviously a reduced one, that would travel through the air waves above the level of the barriers or the enclosure would be tolerable. There are a number of noise quieting techniques which you can adopt as per the requirement of your specific projects.

In the preceding two paragraphs you have seen that by adopting suitable techniques you can reduce the noise level at source and also in the transmission path. But still there would be noise level that would have harmful effect on the receivers. You have two distinct groups of receivers, one group is your mine workers and other employees including the labourers of the contractor, if you have engaged one, and the other group will be local population and the fauna including avifauna. So you have to take protective measures for these two groups of receivers. We can discuss this as follows.

I would first take up the protective measures for the mine workers and other workers and employees engaged in activities related to your mining operations. The common and most acceptable protective measure is to provide earplugs or earmuffs and make it sure that the workers who are exposed to harmful noise level use the earplugs or earmuffs properly. During presentation made by some project authorities before the EAC it was revealed that in many cases the workers would either refuse to wear earplugs or the earmuffs or they would use the equipment but after sometime those earplugs or earmuffs will be removed. The advice to such project authorities would be that the Mines Manager or any other supervisory category officer would explain to the workers the harmful effect of noise which may result in complete loss of hearing in the long run so that the workers understand the criticality of the matter. There would still be some recalcitrant workers who would not readily agree to wear the earplugs or earmuffs. In such cases the advice would be punitive action like "no wage" for workers not using the earplugs or earmuffs. It is essential to periodically check the level of effect of noise on the auditory organ of the workers and if there is any deterioration the workers could be told in clear terms that such deterioration has occurred due to non-adherence to the essentiality of using the earplugs or earmuffs properly.

Normally the local population might not be affected by the noise to the extent of hearing loss either partially or completely. So if you can control the noise level at source and also in the transmission path in such a way that the ultimate receiver of the noise is least affected. There are various techniques in quieting the noise impact of vibration. The most prominent adverse impact due to vibration would be felt in the damage that would be caused to the houses if such houses are close by. There are various vibration dampening techniques that can be adopted. Since vibration would not perhaps be a continuous one, you may have to compensate the house owners by reconstructing the damaged structures.

Existence of green belt has been found to be an effective tool to control noise while in transmission. But it is not practicable that you can grow plants in a barren land which would grow overnight. However, if you are continuing your mining operation in the area for a fairly long period you may plant some fast growing species of trees which would increase the green cover and would work as a sound absorbers.

Chapter – 8

Water Environment

So long you have been dealing with two of the seven critical ingredients of environment, i.e., air environment and noise environment. It is a strange coincidence that neither of these two components, i.e., air and noise, is visible as we cannot see them with our eyes. But we can always feel their presence in our day to day living. We feel the presence of air with the help of our touch sensation. For example, when the air blows it strikes our body gently or otherwise depending on the wind speed and we get the sensation and consequent knowledge of the existence of the air with our faculty of perception through physical contacts with the air even though we cannot see the air with our eyes. Likewise, we get to know the existence of noise, whether loud or otherwise, with the help of our auditory organ, i.e., ear. But we cannot see noise with the help of our eyes. While in the case of air we even do not see the source of the air, an all-pervasive and existing eternally an invisible gaseous substance surrounding the earth, in the case of noise we can see the source, a flute, for example, from which emanates a particular sound which our auditory organ receives. Comparison with a ceiling or table fan as source of air may not be quite appropriate.

As against air and noise, water is something which we can see with our eyes and feel with our touch sensation. Therefore, water as a physical entity is visible on the earth and without water no living things can survive. Therefore, before I deal with the need for collecting baseline data on water it is necessary that we have some brief idea about the importance of water for the survival of all living things including flora and fauna.

We need water for our survival and we experience this every moment of our life. When you are thirsty you can feel it immediately and will drink water at the earliest opportunity. No industrial activities are possible without water. Historically you will notice that all industrial activities and human residential houses have come up near the water bodies, be they rivers or sea or other water bodies. Water is also essential for maintaining the climate balance. In our houses you will find it quite common during summer in urban areas like Delhi when the day time temperature goes very high that people will be using air-cooler which is nothing but a simple device to circulate air mixed with water. Again, if fire breaks out in a house the fire brigade people would use water with great force to prevent spread of fire.

Another characteristic quality of water which we experience in any house universally without being aware thereof, it is a great solvent. It has the ability to dissolve and form something new. For example, if you want to drink milk in a thinner form you put water in the milk and it gets immediately dissolved in the milk to get you the desired level of milk. The same water (may be few litres) can dissolve even one small drop of poison or any other harmful objects in it in no time and make it unacceptable to our body system and at times may be a cause of serious health problem. Water comes from various sources. Since about 70 per cent of the earth's surface consists of water, it is but natural that we find water almost everywhere in varying quantities except in a desert where surface water could be very scarce. We have various sources of water, i.e; ocean, ground water, fresh water lakes and other water bodies, rain water, atmospheric vapour etc.

In remote rural areas or in the forest areas not contaminated by any mining or other industrial activities the water that is available through various sources are taken as pollution free. The people and the animals living there use the water for all purposes including direct drinking and their body systems have got used to the water with whatever natural impurities contained in the water from various sources. It is only the rain water, not the first quantity of rain water as that might still contain some atmospheric dusts in it, but the subsequent quantity of rain water deposited in a tank or any other container, would be most pure water. I had this experience when as a short term consultant to the Commonwealth Secretariat, London, I spent about two weeks in an island of the South Pacific country Tonga, north east of New Zealand. Though the island is surrounded by sea water, there is no treatment of sea water for human consumption. I was staying in a government house which had an overhead water tank in which the rain water gets deposited. There is also an undergroundwater tank in which rain water gets deposited which is lifted through a hand-pump to the overhead tank from which the water goes to the kitchen and the bathroom through normal pipeline which we see in Indian urban areas. I was quite surprised that I had no health problem due to the consumption of the rain water. Of course, the local people would have no problem as they are used to it. I am giving this example just to emphasize the effect of pure water and polluted water on our bio-system.

Water as it exists in its natural form would be pollution free but not necessarily fit for drinking. For example, sea water would not be fit for drinking as it is full of salinity. So the question is how the water gets polluted. Like air and noise, water also gets polluted in normal natural processes and as also by human activities.

Take the case of a water body like a big pond in a village which is quite common throughout India. People living in the village would utilize the water of the pond for various purposes including drinking purpose. People also take bath in the same water and scouring is a common practice in a village water body where people will be cleansing their body with the help of soap and in the process they are polluting the water of the pond. If the area is low land and is flooded during rainy season this polluted water gets automatically cleansed and the water of the pond also gets purified. But if the pond is in a high land and is not flooded the pollutants would remain there except that the fresh rain water deposited in the pond could make the water less polluted. I am not particularly referring to the act of defecation indulged in by the rural people who are not aware of the polluting effect. In the process the water of the aquifer would ultimately get polluted.

The most dangerous source of pollution is discharges from the industrial units set up on the river bank as also near any other water bodies. As per the Hindu mythology the water of the river Ganga (the *Ganges*) is capable of purifying not only our body but also our soul. But it is a tragic irony that the Government is now seriously concerned about the pollution of the water of this sacred river and so now we hear of the plan government makes to cleanse the watei of the Ganges. Now we have reached a situation where the water of the Ganges believed to possess the natural potential to purify our souls and bodies needs to be cleansed and purified.

Another example is the polluted water that is deposited in the aquifers due to mining activities. The minerals pollute the water which gets deposited in the aquifers and if people are using this undergroundwater they will be afflicted with various diseases. It is a common complaint in Delhi that the undergroundwater is full of salinity and other impurities and is not fit for direct use.

You can now appreciate the importance of water environment in the core zone and the buffer zone of your mining activities as your project activities are bound to pollute the water. So long you had no idea about the quality of water of the area. Therefore, you are not in a position to envisage the impact that would be there as a result of your mining operations. So you must know the baseline status, that is, *in situ* characteristics, i.e., the quality of water in the core zone and the buffer zone as obtaining before mining starts so that you may periodically review the change in the quality of water as a result of your mining activities. This will lead you to anticipate the impacts of your mining activities on the quality of existing water resources and to plan corresponding mitigating measures to contain the adverse impacts.

With this introduction I will now give you a brief idea about the baseline data in respect of water to be collected. While collecting the baseline data the details given in Section 3.3.1 in the Model TOR at Annexure-B would be a valuable guide and you collect the data which are specific to your project.

Your consultant should be in a position to answer any question that may be raised by the expert members of the EAC on any data relating to water environment even if the particular data are not relevant to your project. The EAC members could raise questions which are generally applicable in mining areas. They are not expected to know before hand that some of the baseline data are not specific and relevant to your project. In such a situation you and your consultant could tell the EAC that the particular question is not applicable as the ground reality is different.

Baseline Status

Details to be collected on Water Environment under different headings have been indicated at Item C-Water Environment in Table 1 (Annexure B) referred to earlier. Your consultant would be in a position to collect the information and appropriately mention the same in tabular form. Such detailed information in required number of Statements form part of the EIA report submitted before the EAC for consideration at the time of appraisal of the project by the Committee. These are, no doubt, routine information but are very relevant and critical in appraising the impact of your project activities on the water environment and the adequacy of the proposed mitigating measures. It is, therefore, advisable that you collect as much information as are possible.

The baseline data should cover the existing status of rainfall data, run off and sediment data preferably to be obtained from the nearest IMD station and if such information could not be supplied by the IMD station the same could be obtained from a reputed institution in the absence of which you can engage an expert to collect the data.

Mining will affect the water bodies, more proximate ones would be more vulnerable. Water of such proximate water bodies will have adverse impact not only on the human population but also on wildlife and flora besides adverse impact on your workers. It is necessary that details of existing springs, lakes, reservoirs, rivers and other water bodies like drain etc. within core zone and buffer zone indicating the distance from the mine site are collected.

Water in various water bodies, undergroundwater and natural surface water, would have some physico-chemical properties including toxic/trace/heavy metals/elements besides bacteriological and radiological characteristics. The living beings, both humans and wildlife, as also the vegetation get their sustenance from the existing water from different sources. Their body systems have become used to the existing water from such sources. Therefore, once you know the status and quality of the water through sample testing it would help you to monitor the quality of the water from time to time to see if there is any adverse impact on the quality of water due to your mining activities. Accordingly you can plan appropriate measures to contain the mitigating factors at source and if necessary treating the water so as to maintain the quality of water at acceptable level. Select the locations of the monitoring stations in different directions from the core zone and indicate the distance and make sure that the locations of the monitoring stations take care of the sources of water so as to become representative of the core zone and the buffer zone.

The water bodies would normally have certain variety of biological species which are essential to maintain the water quality at acceptable level. Therefore, while collecting the baseline data, you must get the details of the algae population, a particular type of non-flowering stemless water plant.

Water will be used by the local population for various purposes and wildlife would also need water. As a miner, you would also utilise water for your mining activities besides providing drinking water to your workers and if you have a township for your employees, water would be required for various purposes in the township. Therefore, the baseline data should include water balance and approximate quantity of water to be withdrawn for various uses by the local population to which you have to add the quantity of water that is likely to be withdrawn by you for mining activities and the township, if any. To know the impact of withdrawal of water for various purposes on the water balance, you must also collect the data on water recharge facility like rainfall and perennial water bodies like rivers and rivulets. This will give you an idea about the shortfall in the availability of water over a period of time and accordingly you would have to take mitigating measures to ensure that the water balance does not become too low.

Aquifer characteristics are important baseline data. If the aquifers do not have adequate water absorbing and transmitting capacity the problem of water shortage would continue as even if the area gets fairly good rainfall the aquifer(s) would not be able to absorb such water. Perhaps you have to undertake a hydro-geological study if the ground reality so demands.

If your mining activities are likely to intersect groundwater at any time during the life of the mine indicate the radius of influence from the mine pit(s). If there is human habitation within this radius of influence that may be indicated.

It is quite likely that certain new water bodies would be created as a result of your mining activities. You may indicate the locations where such new water bodies are likely to be created on account of your mining activities.

If any water course like rivers or *nallahs* (drains) are passing through the core zone and depending on the existence of the ore bodies it may be necessary to shift the water course as without such shifting of water course mining activities would not be possible. In such a situation the meandering effect of any change due to the shifting of water course would be important baseline data to be collected as it would be relevant for you to anticipate the adverse impact and to adopt corresponding mitigating measures.

Another important baseline data would have to be collected if the mineral bearing areas are close to sea and there is possibility of sea water incursion which would pollute the underground water. Besides you have to indicate if the leasehold area attracts the provisions of the CRZ Regulation. These data would be relevant not only for predicting anticipated impacts but also for taking appropriate mitigating measures.

Once you are ready with a fairly accurate baseline data, you should be in a position to anticipate the impacts on account of your mining activities. You have already seen the use of water by the local people and the wildlife and you have also estimated the requirement of water for your workers, for the mining activities and possibly for the township, if you would establish one. Therefore, you are now in a position to list the anticipated impacts.

Anticipated Impacts

I will start with the two most common harmful impacts, one due to mining intersecting groundwater and other due to shifting of water course.

If mining, both opencast as well as underground, intersects ground water, minerals and many other harmful elements in the earth would get into the underground natural water which was otherwise of good quality. In the example I have given in some of the preceding paragraphs it has been assumed that the radius of influence is 200 metres. Therefore, the undergroundwater contaminated with harmful elements due to your mining activities would travel within this radius of 200 metres and if the area is inhabited by human population and if they use this water for drinking purpose it will have adverse impact on their health. If the mining operation continues for a longer period the contamination would only aggravate as more the people withdraw this contaminated water more will be the inflow of these harmful elements.

If mining necessitates shifting of water course and if the shifted path of the water course is in a sinuous, i.e., in a serpentine way the new water course could have adverse impacts on the lands through which the water course would pass. Such impacts could be many. The new water course could flood the low lying lands making the same inaccessible to the living things, both humans and wildlife, besides changing the nature of the lands that might result in loss of crop production either permanently or temporarily. The owner of the lands would lose the benefits of growing good crop specially if such lands are fertile.

It is also quite possible that the core zone where the ore bodies exist would have shallow surface water bodies here and there and once mining activities are undertaken in such area this water would get contaminated and might adversely impact the undergroundwater including the aquifers.

As explained earlier in the context of collection of baseline data, you may have to withdraw the required quantity of surface water and if the surface water is inadequate you would have to withdraw the groundwater for your project activities as also for the township for your employees, if you have one. Such withdrawal of water might create shortage in the water balance. If the replenishment of such loss of water does not take place due to normal natural process like rainfall or supply of water from any perennial water bodies the local people would experience serious problem in getting adequate water for various purposes including drinking purpose as also water for crop fields.

Thus mining would have an adverse impact on the hydrogeology of the area and in the absence of any effective natural replenishment, over exploitation of water, both surface and underground, would have permanent adverse impacts. f mining continues for fairly long period such impacts would only increase as the time passes. Thus there would be impact on surface and undergroundwater and if you are also having a processing plant the tailing pond would also be a source of adverse impact.

Suggested Mitigating Measures

You have already assessed the likely impacts due to your mining operations as explained in the preceding section. Now it is your duty to prepare a plan of action to mitigate the likely adverse impacts. Section 3.3.3 in the Model TOR at Annexure-B lists the possible mitigating measures and these are valuable guide for you. You may draw up a plan of mitigating measures on the lines suggested in the Model TOR which are specific to your project. For example, if the project is not located in the coastal zone or near the sea the question of incursion of sea water would not be relevant for your project and this will also be clear from the site map that you have prepared and presented before the EAC. I would not elaborate the mitigating measures suggested in the Model TOR. However, I would give a brief reasonings as to why and how the mitigating measures are an absolute necessity.

But for your mining activities the existing available water in the core zone and in the buffer zone would be of acceptable quality for the local populace and the flora and fauna. As a natural process there would be number of factors that could pollute the water to a certain extent. Such polluted water has not been a problem of any serious magnitude as the body systems of the humans as well as wildlife are used to such water with whatever pollutants it has. For example, if a pond or any other water body has fishes in it, some of the fishes would die as a natural process and fleshes of such dead fishes would add to the pollution of the water. But it is only in extreme cases that treatment of such polluted water becomes essential. Usually in a village pond such polluted water is pumped out and later the pond is filled with rain water or by transporting water from elsewhere. But your mining activities would definitely pollute the existing water, whether it is surface water or underground water, unless no such water source exists in the area which is most unlikely.

Before starting mining operation or even before mine development activities you may have to remove the surface water and store it in a different location. Therefore, you must select the location in such a way that your mining activities do not contaminate such water. Such location could be an existing low land or some other water bodies which are at a safe distance.

If mining is intersecting groundwater it would have adverse impact on the human population using the water available within the radius of influence from the mine pit. Such water is bound to be contaminated and would travel in all directions within the radius of influence. Such contaminated water would have certain physical, chemical and biological pollutants. The existing water table would be having physical elements like a particular odour, certain level of suspended solids, taste or temperature, etc. which are acceptable to the body system of the population. Likewise, there are certain chemical elements like fluoride, certain amount of TDS (Total Dissolved Solids), hardness, metals, both toxic and non-toxic etc. which are also acceptable to the population using such water. There would be also some biological elements, i.e., bacteria and viruses which might cause some water borne diseases but the people living in the area also know that there is a cure for such water borne diseases. Now if your mining operation is intersecting groundwater you are definitely enhancing the existing pollutants and perhaps adding certain new categories of pollutants which would further pollute the water. Therefore, you would be required to ensure that the people get quality water to which they are used to so far. While doing so you have to assess the cost of treating the water at source, i.e., in the mine pit itself in a way the treated water gets mixed with the existing undergroundwater and the cost of transporting water from another source which is not polluted by any mining or other industrial activities. If the cost of treatment at source is cheaper you definitely opt for this method failing which alternative source of quality water has to be arranged by you.

If withdrawal of water for your mining activities and also for the township, if you have set up one for your employees, results in chronic shortage of water even after the replenishment by natural process like rain water, the mitigating measure that would be required is to transport quality water from the nearest available source which could be any water bodies like river, rivulets, big pond or lake which have perennial water supply.

If mining results in the shifting of water courses, say, river(s) or nallah(s), and if the meandering effects of such shifting are likely to have adverse impacts on the lands and living things, both human and wildlife, you have to select the new course for the river(s) or the nallah(s), to the extent the terrain of the area permits, in such a way that the adverse impacts are minimal. For example, if by taking a circuitous course the adverse impacts could be completely avoided or the impacts are least it is worth doing it rather than adding to your financial burden, i.e. the cost of compensation on account of loss of production that might necessarily have to be paid to the affected people. Since, the people are used to the existing water course the same should be restored to the original position after mining is over unless the new water course is considered by the people acceptable.

If there is sea water incursion in the core zone action to stop that would be essential failing which the authority might be forced to stop your mining activities. Even if there is no sea water incursion, but your core zone falls within a costal area, plantation of mangrove and other trees over a certain area in between the mine pits and the sea shore should be done to prevent sea erosion.

If you adopt scientific mining method that ensures OB dumps with the standard slopes and use of appropriate geo-textile liner and proper plantations it would be an effective way of preventing water pollution due to accumulation of rain water over the OB dumps. Slope stabilization with retaining walls, vegetation, construction of gully checks, check dams, settling tanks etc. are standard methods of water management to prevent contamination.

When the mining activities take place on the hill top the need for effective mitigating measures is all the more essential. Unless you create appropriate garland type check dams encircling your mine pits the polluted water as also the rain water would flow down adversely impacting the foot hill lands which could be otherwise fertile land for crop production. Therefore, filtering mechanism should be in place in a way that whatever water flows down has pollutants which could be called minimal.

Settling tank(s) could be an effective mitigating measure. If you are not living in an urban area with underground or surface sewage system you would construct a septic tank with three chambers connected to the toilet. Of the three chambers, the first chamber which is closest to the toilet would receive the refuse as it comes in and this first chamber and the next, i.e., second chamber would be connected at the top level so that the second chamber gets only the water. The second and the third chambers are connected at the bottom through proper hole and the third chamber thus gets more or less semi-clean water which is discharged, through a hole fitted with a pipe at the top of the third tank, to a make shift surface drain and this water is used as some sort of manure and perhaps you would be growing some vegetables there. You might have also noticed the automatic generation of a type of white coloured insects in the first chamber which consume the refuse in the original form and you would also ensure that nobody uses any detergent which goes into the first chamber as that would kill the insects.

If you extend the above concept of septic tanks to the concept of settling tanks in the context of mining activities on hill top, you can develop the concept in the following manner. After you have exhausted a particular mine pit you can, in the exhausted mine pit or alternatively in the area where there are no ore bodies, construct not three but two big tanks in such a way that natural water and the water discharged from your mine pit could be diverted to the first tank where the solid particles could settle at the bottom and the water with least pollutants can overflow to the second tank and this water can be very easily and conveniently pumped out of this tank and discharged outside. Periodical de-silting of the first tank would be required to maintain its projected storing capacity. You would perhaps like to experiment such settling tanks system to see for yourself if such a primitive method can be very usefully utilized.

If you develop the items in Section 3.3.3 of the Model TOR at Annexure-B you would notice that whatever has been suggested therein is only for ensuring that the contaminated water does not get entry in to the existing water system. In case of an unavoidable need for treating the contaminated water or getting the supply of water from elsewhere, may be at a longer distance, you would always make an assessment of the cost involved in either of the methods and accordingly you would opt for the method that you would consider most convenient as also cost effective. Since it will be part of your project cost even if a particular method is expensive it is worth adopting and perhaps there would be small reduction in your profitability but as an imaginative and environment friendly miner you could take it that you are making your own small contribution to creating a healthy environment and I am sure you would feel that it is worth doing.

Depending on the volume of your operation two activities which are universally recognized as very cost effective way of meeting the water balance could be part of your project activities. These are rain water harvesting and construction of water harvesting structures. If the area has good rainfall, it (rain water harvesting) would be an useful method to maintain the water balance and assuming that the area has low and scanty rainfall it is still worth it as in a scantily rain fed area even a small drop of water becomes useful. Don't forget that in India our common belief is that, at least the author of this book has got the lesson from his teacher in a village school, a sea or a river or any water body is nothing but accumulated individual drops of water. One can try it at home in a small container, it could be a tea cup, and see how many drops of water makes a cup full of water. Construction of water harvesting structures at appropriate locations to retain surplus surface water is another way of maintaining water balance. The point I am trying to make is that saving even one drop of water amounts to adding one more drop of water to the water balance.

There could be existing water bodies in the core zone and also in the buffer zone and new water bodies are likely to be created as a result of your mining activities. Since, it would not be perhaps feasible to fill all the exhausted mine pits which could become new water bodies and these new water bodies along with the existing water bodies could be developed as fisheries and also for irrigation purposes which I would be dealing with under proposed mitigating measures under socio-economic environment later in Chapter-11. Thus these water bodies could be a source of providing economic activities to the villagers on a sustained basis. And if you are fond of certain water related recreational activities and you have the resources you would perhaps think of making any of such water bodies as recreational centre for boating, for example.

Make sure that you do the plantation work in such a way that there is wide enough space between the boundary where the ore bodies ends and the nearest water bodies so that the plantation becomes an effective barrier between the mine and the source of water.

It is a fact that water, critical for the very survival of all living things, when contaminated, could also be the single largest contributor to many of our health problems, be it direct or indirect. Therefore, availability of quality water needs be ensured. So you have no right to contaminate the water which is not acceptable to the living things, both humans and wildlife. Since your mining activities are responsible or creating some of the water pollutants it becomes your moral responsibility to take appropriate mitigating measures as a part of your normal project activities.

Chapter – 9

Land Environment

By now you have got a fairly good idea about three of the seven important components of environment starting with air environment, followed by noise environment and water environment. Air is a gaseous substance which is invisible and cannot be seen by our eyes but which is most essential for our life and its presence can be felt only when it comes in contact with our body. Noise is also, like air, an invisible entity which can be perceived through our auditory organ, that is, the ears. It adds quality to our life. For example, we enjoy the pleasure of listening to good music. As against the invisible nature of air and noise, water is something which we can see with our eyes and we can also feel it with our body parts and we can also perceive the sound water creates while falling from the high places with great force. Water is in the liquid form and to that extent it has a form as compared to air and noise which are formless. We have also seen in the preceding chapter how water is essential for all living things, both humans and wildlife.

Let us see the significance of land in our life. We cannot, in fact, no living thing can, exist without land. Just imagine a situation that there is no land, where do we stand? Obviously we cannot live in the vacuum. Even if you are flying in an aircraft high in the sky you are still standing or sitting on something which is solid. When a sportsman takes a long jump to reach his destination, he would be, no doubt, in the air only for few seconds as it is not possible to hang in the air. Likewise, we hear someone telling that his lands have grown certain quantity of crop, say, paddy and wheat, which is adequate for meeting his requirements of foodgrains. Thus, land is the most essential thing which provides content to all, as if, we have realized our full potential as human being. What is this land on which all living things, both human and wildlife, also trees and other vegetation stand and depend? Land is the solid part of the earth's surface as opposed to water. Land constitutes about 30 per cent of the earth's surface and the rest is water. For the purpose of this book I have taken only the land part of the earth's surface and how to deal with the question of land environment in the context of mining of the minerals which exist only in land whether as outcrop or underground. I have the mining in the land in mind and not the mineral wealth under the sea. In the context of your mining project I will deal with lands in the core zone and in the buffer zone. I have already dealt with the air environment, noise environment and water environment affecting all living things in the core zone and buffer zone. With the above introduction I would now proceed to give an idea about the baseline data that you need to collect. While collecting the baseline data on land environment you follow the guidelines in Section 3.4.1 of the Model TOR at Annexure-B. I will only highlight why collection of baseline data about the land is so relevant for you as a miner.

Baseline Status

Details to be collected on Land Environment under different headings have been indicated at Item D-Land Environment in the Table 1 (Annexure B) referred to earlier. Your consultant would be in a position to collect the information and appropriately mention the same in tabular form. Such detailed information in required number of Statements form part of the EIA report submitted before the EAC for consideration at the time of appraisal of the project by the Committee. These are, no doubt, routine information but are very relevant and critical in appraising the impact of your project activities on the land environment and the adequacy of the proposed mitigating measures. It is, therefore, advisable that you collect as much information as are possible.

Since your mining activities would impact the nature and quality of land in the core zone and in the buffer zone it is important that you select the location of the monitoring stations in such a way that these stations are of representative nature, that is, these stations cover all lands falling in the core zone and the buffer zone. The purpose of these monitoring stations is to see the changes that are constantly taking place in the nature and the quality of land on account of your mining activities compared to the pre-mining state of the lands. Since your response in the form of mitigating measures would vary from area to area you would appreciate that unless the monitoring stations are of representative character you might not be in a position to anticipate correct adverse impact on the lands in different locations and to adopt corresponding mitigating measures.

As the fertility of the land and consequent productive capacity of the land in growing crop of various types including foodgrains are critical elements that determine the quality of life of the people living in the area, it is essential that you collect the baseline data as in the sequel.

To know the characteristics of the lands in the core zone and in the buffer zone you need to collect soil samples from near the monitoring stations in such a way that the samples become of representative character. Testing of these soil samples would give you an idea about the physico-chemical and micro-biological characters of the land. It will also give an idea about the water holding capacity and porosity of the land. For example, even if the area has fairly good rainfall it would be of no practical use to the owners of the lands if the lands do not have the capacity to hold the water. Again, even if the water holding capacity of the lands is adequate but it does not have the porosity to allow the water held by the lands to move to other adjoining areas in all directions, the particular piece of land would become muddy which would mean that even with the adequate water the particular area of land becomes unfit for crop production. Sample testing would also give an idea about the toxic contaminants of the land which would help you in determining the impact of your mining activities on such pre-existing toxic contaminants and this will be relevant for you to prepare appropriate mitigating measures.

As no human being can survive without foodgrains and vegetables the soil samples collected by you and tested would give you an idea about the fertility status of the samples tested and if the samples have been collected from different locations the result of the testing would give you a fairly good idea about the fertility status of the area. The standing crop and vegetation would also give you an idea about the fertility status of the lands. Once you know the status of fertility of the lands it would help you to anticipate the impact on the fertility of the lands on account of your mining activities. Therefore, fertility status becomes an essential baseline data on land environment.

You would, no doubt, be knowing the land use pattern, cropping pattern, vegetation cover, etc. before you start mining operation. The relevant data could be collected from the local revenue office and office(s) of the Department of Agriculture of the State Government. These data would help you in detecting if your mining activities are changing the existing pattern of land use, crop production etc which would help you in planning appropriate mitigating measures.

Siltation and sedimentation are critical factors on the fertility of the land. If due to siltation and sedimentation predominantly harmful elements get consolidated and settled on the lands, productivity of the soils gets affected. To highlight the importance of siltation and sedimentation I would give an example with which the entire population living in the Gangetic belt are familiar. The entire belt on either side of the river Ganges have alluvial soil. These lands are nothing but deposit of fine fertile soil as a result of flood or normal flow of water. The taste of vegetables grown in this belt is commonly appreciated and accepted by the consuming people as most likeable. The river Ganges end at Bengal before merging into the sea. And being at the tail end of the river the soils of Bengal are known to be highly fertile and productive. It is no wonder that the first Asian Nobel Laureate and the universally applauded poet Rabindranath Tagore had alluded to Bengal as *Sonar Bangla* (Golden Bengal). Likewise, other river belts would have varying effect on the productivity of the lands. Therefore, the nature of run off water, siltation and sedimentation are very relevant baseline data on the nature and quality of the lands.

While collecting the baseline data and the land use pattern you may come across the fact that over a period of, say 10 to 20 years, there have been changes in the land use pattern. For example, due to rise in population there might be need for constructing additional dwelling units and this may result in dwelling units coming up on otherwise hitherto fertile agricultural lands. Similarly, Government might acquire crop growing lands for certain common welfare activities like construction of roads to improve rural connectivity, establishment of electric sub-station, etc. Even the landowners on their own might change the cropping pattern. For example, due to availability of water throughout the year the lands which were earlier single crop lands might change into multi-crop lands. Even the produce may also change. For example, the landowner might come to the conclusion that it is better to switch over to the production of cash crop like potatoes, pulses, etc. from the existing non-cash crops as his economy would be to earn more money which would allow him to purchase foodgrains from elsewhere and the landowners would still get surplus cash. Thus, such data are essential as it is quite possible that your mining activities might result in the land use pattern.

While mining, OB will be generated and these OB would be dumped at a particular location and depending on the volume of overburden that would be generated on account of your mining activities you might be dumping such overburden at more than one location. You can not stop the leaching effect of the dumped overburden as the overburden would have pollutants including heavy metal pollutants as it is not physically and technologically possible to separate the overburden without any metal trace or other impurities. And due to rainfall and also in normal natural process these pollutants would percolate and would get merged in run-off water which would affect the nature and quality of the lands around the overburden dumps. Therefore, you must collect the overburden samples from different points which would be of representative character and through testing of such samples you would have the data on leaching properties of the overburden and the likely impact of such pollutants.

Anticipated Impacts

In the preceding paragraphs I have given a brief idea about the critical items on which you would collect the baseline data on lands. As the mining activities are bound to have adverse impacts on the lands and such impacts would be more on the lands proximate to the mine pits, you must be in a position to list the anticipated impacts on the land environment.

If applicable in your case you can mention the positive impact like how after the removal of the minerals bauxite and limestone (as outcrop) the lands can become fertile as mentioned in Chapter-11 on socio-economic environment later in this book.

Agricultural activities, forestry and fisheries are some of the main occupations of the local people. Dust generated on account of your mining activities, seepage of water contaminated by heavy metals and other pollutants, etc. would adversely affect the productive capacity of lands and it will also pollute the water of the nearest water bodies. And fishes grown in such water bodies would be contaminated and ultimately it will go into the bio-system of the people who consume such fishes.

While collecting the baseline data of leaching effect on the water flowing from overburden you must have made an assessment about the lands around the overburden and vulnerability of the lands to the adverse impact of leaching effects. So by testing such water you would be able to know the nature and extent of leaching effect on the quality of surface water and groundwater. If you are mining on lands which are at an elevated level there would be land slide and soil erosion and these will affect the adjoining lands and if such lands are fertile there will be loss of production and you have to quantify the loss of production on such agricultural lands. Even if the lease hold area specially the area that is of the same level as the adjoining lands there would be adverse impacts on such lands on account of your mining activities and, therefore, you have to assess the impact on the quality of the lands. You have already collected the baseline data on the fertility status of the soil through testing of soil samples gathered from different points all over the area. You would also be knowing the quantum of OB to be generated on account of your mining activities and therefore you can assess the nature and extent of all adverse impacts on the fertility of the soil. You cannot completely prevent the seepage of mine water and needless to say that mine water would have various pollutants. Therefore, seepage of such water with the pollutants would pollute the groundwater. You have also collected the baseline data on the quality of groundwater. So you are in a position now to assess the impact on groundwater caused due to seepage of mine water with pollutants. Obviously, if a polluted groundwater is used as drinking water by the local people it would have immediate adverse impacts on their health. So you must make appropriate prediction of the impacts on groundwater.

Top soil of any land has special characteristics. There are certain types of vegetation that grow on the top soil. In fact, in forest areas it is not uncommon that top soil cover has many medicinal plants. When you are given permission to divert certain forest land for non-forest purposes the MOEF invariably puts a condition making it obligatory for you to remove such fertile top soil over which medicinal plants grow to some other safe location so that the medicinal plants growing potentiality of the soil does not get permanently destroyed. Since, it is top soil, it becomes an easy and immediate victim of your mining activities. So you must make an accurate assessment about the impact of your mining activities on the top fertile soil cover of the area irrespective of the fact weather such top fertile soil grows medicinal plants or other rare vegetation.

Since I have taken iron ore mining in the forest lands for the purpose of this book I would advise you to assess the impact of your mining activities on the bio-diversity of the area.

There would be wildlife including avifauna besides fishes in the water bodies. There would be forests of varying thickness with fixed corridors for animals to move around. Your mining activities would interfere with normal movement of the animals who were hitherto used to the calmness and serenity of the forests cover. So you must make an assessment of the adverse impacts due to your mining activities on the bio-diversity of the forest cover.

I have given a brief idea as to the nature of impacts that are bound to be caused due to your mining activities and it is up to you to assess the nature and extent of adverse impacts. While doing so you may follow the guidelines in Section 3.4.2 of the Model TOR.

Suggested Mitigating Measures

In the preceding paragraphs I have given a brief idea about the nature of adverse impacts that would be caused to lands in the core zone and in the buffer zone. As these impacts are due to your mining activities it becomes your responsibility to prepare in advance a plan of action to mitigate the likely impacts. It is advisable that you proceed with the worst scenario on the nature of impacts and accordingly you prepare the mitigating measures so that you remain ready to tackle any adverse impacts.

In Section 3.4.3 of the Model TOR at Annexure-B certain mitigating measures have been suggested. While these suggested measures are applicable in all cases of land environment you may make an assessment about the specific types of mitigating measures that would be relevant for your project.

There is no substitute for scientific mining methods that would automatically take care of mitigating the adverse impacts due to mining activities on the lands as a scientific method of mining would result in minimal degradation of the lands in the core zone and to some extent in the buffer zone. In other words, since degradation of lands specially in the core zone is inescapable as no minerals can be extracted without breaking or damaging the lands, scientific mining method would ensure that such degradation is kept to the minimum to the extent practicable. It is, therefore, clear that the investment that you would make in adopting a modern and scientific method of mining would give you more benefit as lesser degradation of lands would mean less expenditure in mitigating the adverse impacts which could be minimized by adopting scientific mining method. This can best be understood if I give a very simple example on deciding the number of OB dumping sites that cause many adverse impacts. If it is possible to fill the exhausted mine pit with the OB you could manage by having only one OB dumping site at any given point of time and at the end of the project you could perhaps leave the place without any OB dumping site by filling the last mined out pit. Not a bad idea to think about, is not it so?

As degradation of lands in any mining project is inevitable, such degradation being different in degree, I would give few examples on the mitigating measures that you could consider as specific to your project.

Earlier I have said about the importance of mine closure plan. At a given point of time in future your project would be closed depending on the extent of mineral reserves. Would you then wait for the final stoppage of the mining activities to implement the mine closure plan? If you do that you would only add to the enormous complexity as you would find it not only frustrating but also almost an impossible task to implement your own mine closure plan. It is, therefore, not only essential but a practical course of action for you to implement the mine closure plan as and when you close your mining activity in a particular mine pit. Unless it is essential, for example, you need minerals of a particular grade to mix with minerals of certain grade, generally lower grade, do not open a new mine pit before the earlier pit is exhausted and also do not open pits in different locations simultaneously as that would create widespread land degradation over a large area.

Let me briefly explain the significance of the expression "a progressive mine closure plan". There is a wrong impression, may be confusion, that the word "close" and the word "closure" have the same connotation while in reality it is not so. When somebody says that the mine is closed he only means that the working of the mine is closed, i.e., no mining is presently going on. But when it is said that a miner must ensure that a mine closure is planned and implemented it means that after the particular mine pit is fully worked and no further extraction of minerals would take place, the miner is to implement the mine closure plan. Such a mine closure activity would mean that the mined out area should be broad back, to the extent feasible, to match with the surrounding areas and the implementation of the mine closure plan should not wait till the next or subsequent mine pits are exhausted. Such a mine closure activity should be progressive, that is, implementation of the mine closure plan would be a continuous and ongoing process for the mine pits as and when such pits are mined out and the process would not wait for the last mine pit to be exhausted. It is not only scientific method of mining but also is in the interest of the lessee himself. For example, if mine closure is completed along with the complete extraction of the minerals from a mine pit, it would not put any extra burden on the miner compared to the difficult task and more expenses on completing the mine closure after all the mine pits are exhausted. That is why mine plan emphasizes progressive mine closure activities as otherwise the miner may be tempted to neglect mine closure activity completely or he might do the mine closure which is not acceptable. One of the common conditions prescribed under the sanction letter granting prior environmental clearance is to do plantation work. Here also if the miner starts planting trees as and when a particular mine pit is exhausted and mine closure has been achieved it becomes a very simple operation and if a miner goes on planting trees as and when the subsequent mine pits are exhausted he would be surprised to realize that at the end of the life of the mine the plantation work done by him has resulted in creating an eye soothing green environment.

As a scientific miner you must have already made a progressive mine closure plan and a final mine closure plan an integral part of you project activities. This is also your statutory responsibility under the Mineral Conservation and Development Rules, 1988 (MCDR) and accordingly the Indian Bureau of Mines has the statutory power to take action against you for not complying with this statutory responsibility. You can best understand the relevance and importance of the mine closure plan if I may draw your attention to the most common activity in your own residential house. In your house besides bed rooms you would have a sitting room where as a man of taste you might have placed sofa set, central table, side tables and may be some stands to keep some decorative items on to make the sitting room which you consider to be tastefully decorated. You have a part time housemaid who works for, say, two hours daily to clean your house by sweeping the floor and dusting the furniture. Suppose while sweeping the floor of the sitting room and dusting the furniture the housemaid has shifted the furniture for her convenience and she leaves your house keeping the furniture in the sitting room in a state of chaos scattered here and there. Would you appreciate the work of the maid? The answer is obviously "no". You would like that the placement of the furniture etc. in the sitting room should be restored to the original places that you have already designed. Perhaps the society would expect you to bring in the concept of restoration of the land to match with its surroundings after mining is over as you would expect your house maid to do the same in respect of your sitting room in the example above.

A piece of land has many uses and if the land has minerals, mining is only one use of the land for extracting the minerals and thereafter, the land is of no use to you as a miner as was the case before you got the lease and started mining activities on the piece of land just like the housemaid has no work to do for the sitting room before and after cleaning and dusting the same. Suppose there are green vegetation and standing trees on the land and the land is also fertile and the local people have been cultivating that land for growing agricultural crop and perhaps using the land for their residential purpose also. So when your mining operation is over, the land is in a state of degradation as you could not escape degrading the land in the course of your mining activities. Therefore, it becomes your responsibility to restore the land so as to match with the surroundings to the extent possible.

While restoring the land to its pre-mining state, the most critical aspect is that the land should not be left unsafe for the people and their domestic animals as also the wildlife, if any, for going over the land to which they had a free and unfettered access before you started the mining activities. Even if the land could not be made plain it could be so restored that it does not become hostile to the people and the animals. In other words, you should not leave the land as a source of safety hazards that the damaged land otherwise is bound to be.

Remember that if the land was being used by the local people for growing agricultural crop they would always prefer to grow crop on the same land to which they have been used for years. In case some people had their residential houses but had to be shifted elsewhere so as to enable you to extract the minerals it becomes all the more important that the post-mining land should be made suitable for such willing persons who would like to have their residential houses back on the same land.

In a country like India where there is too much pressure on land if your mining activities result in permanent degradation of the land and the land being of no value to the people you are only enhancing the already acute pressure on land.

I have already explained the advantage of progressive mine closure plan in some of the preceding paragraphs. Once you implement the plan you have prepared for mine closure for the last mined out pit you would notice that something more is to be done for the final mine closure for the entire area as, for operating the last pit you had to keep certain lands for the movement of mining equipments and your workers. Now is the time for you to complete your mine closure plan for the left over part of the land and if you have done that you would be making the entire area liveable by the local people the way they have used the land prior to your mining activities. As mining is only one of the so many uses of the land, your mining activities should not make the land unfit for other uses.

Mine closure plan thus basically means that you take steps to rehabilitate the mined out lands to match with its surrounding land use. Supposing, the lands had a particular vegetation cover which have been destroyed due to your mining activities as you had no option but to remove the top soil to extract the minerals. As an imaginative miner, you must have studied the productive nature of the top soil and might have also removed such top soil before starting mining operations and stored by spreading such top soil in another location for reuse at the time of implementing the mine closure plan that you have already prepared, needless to say, taking into account the productive nature of the lands. You need to ensure that the lands are brought back to the original position to the extent practicable and the top soil is spread back over the rehabilitated lands so as to enable the land to grow the vegetation that was there earlier.

One very effective way of rehabilitating the degraded lands is to make such lands for forestry cover using local species. So development of green belt with suitable local plant species is strongly suggested. In fact, such green belt should be developed in all sides of the mine pits, around ore processing and beneficiation plant, if you have one, and on the dump sites besides avenue plantation including such plantation in the workers' colony, if you have established one. Development of such green belt and plantation activities should go along with your mining activities so that the residual work of land restoration in the mined out areas after the closure of a particular mine pit becomes less burdensome.

As lands will be destroyed due to extraction of minerals, the lands become vulnerable to soil erosion specially during rainy season. So you must prepare in advance a technological package of practices for the prevention of soil erosion and consequent soil loss both in the core zone and may be in the buffer zone. There are available models for preparing such packages and you may adopt the model that is suitable for your project.

In a nutshell, the mitigating measures should be aimed at restoring the lands degraded on account of your mining activities to match with the surrounding areas to the extent practicable. After the removal of the minerals it may not be practicably feasible to fill up the degraded low lands to its original position. But you can always make the lands so as to become friendly for the animals and the humans to move over such lands without any risk to their safety. Don't keep the degraded lands in a way to endanger the life of the human as well as animal population. It is more so important if the lands are productive as keeping such productive lands in a state of degraded condition so as to make it inaccessible for any productive purposes is not a desired course of action as it would mean that certain productive lands would be of no value to the community.

In this chapter I have only highlighted the rationale and importance of adopting appropriate mitigating measures beneficial to the society in so may ways. It is up to you to think and to take a view if you really owe something to the society by doing something to negate the adverse impacts that would not have been there but for your mining activities.

Chapter – 10

Biological Environment

In this chapter I shall try to familiarize you with the environment relating to living organisms. These living organisms would cover the vegetation, plant species, wildlife including avifauna. You might be surprised as to why the most visible living things, i.e., human beings, are getting excluded. As a separate Chapter-11 under the caption "socio-economic environment" has been allotted on the impact of mining activities on human beings as also the impact on the social fabric I would not be dealing with the living organisms in the shape of human beings here though there could be some references to the impact of the changing biological environment on the life of the humans as well.

Out of the seven important segments of environment I have dealt with four, namely, air environment, noise environment, water environment and land environment in the preceding chapters. You have seen the impact of air environment, noise environment, water environment and land environment on all living things, both humans and wildlife including avifauna. Now is the time for you to appreciate the relevance of biological environment to the very survival of not only human beings but also all animals, whether domestic or wild, as also avifauna. And it would be useful to know the relevance of the above four segments of the environment in appreciating the significance of biological environment.

Air can exist in the vacuum on its own without any contact with any material objects including living things, both humans and animals. Likewise, there would be noise, may be, in a subdued form depending on the speed of the air. Without the existence of water or land there would be nobody to perceive such noise just in the same way in the absence of living things there would be none to feel (through touch sensation) the existence of air. Thus, in a way both air and noise can exist only in form without any content. Since, nature abhors vacuum, air and noise are the most elementary substances that occupy the vacuum or empty space. When you get to know water environment for the first time you come across something which you can feel with your body parts and which you can taste also. So there is a completely different scenario compared to air environment and noise environment. You also know that about 70 per cent of the earth's surface is water and this makes it clear as to why water is so important for the very survival of all living things, both humans and animals including avifauna as also for all living organisms which is the subject of this section, i.e., biological environment. Just as nature abhors vacuum, likewise water can not, as if, be satisfied unless it creates an environment which necessarily gives birth to large number of aqua-fauna starting with the most common and perhaps friendly varieties of fishes as also the hostile variety of crocodiles with every variety having tremendous impact on human life, by providing nutritious food (fleshes of fish) for example, the other satisfying our aesthetic sense when we enjoy the presence of playful crocodiles and other water animals in an artificial aquarium as also in some other natural water bodies. You have also realized the contribution made by air, noise and water together to the quality of our life which is not only eating, drinking and perhaps going into a state of sleeping. Just imagine how excited you would be to see a beginningless and endless and perhaps timeless series of waves on a wide perennial river and on the sea as also the small ripple created by a falling object even in a small water body near your home. All these beautiful experiences you would have never got but for the existence of air. Thus if nature abhors vacuum it also makes your life enjoyable.

Like air, noise also adds to the quality of your life and sound is a source for providing a pleasing impact on your auditory organ, i.e., the ears. The waves in the water created by air gives you a pleasing scene perceived by your eyes. For example, when you watch a waterfall, not only you see the water falling with high speed from mountain top you also enjoy the noise (sound) made by such waterfall. If you are living in the forest area with a good wildlife and there is a water body near your home you would never miss the opportunity of the sound being created when a wild animal drinks water from such a water body and perhaps you would ensure that the animal drinks water without any disturbance for the simple reason that you enjoy such sound.

You also know that there would be plants growing in the water bodies around your home and the *algae* population would provide fodder for the aqua-fauna. You have also seen that a fish does not remain under the water all the while and occasionally it will fly in the air to get oxygen provided by air. If there is a sudden sound you would have noticed that the fishes which are always on the move would all of a sudden become motionless due to the impact of the noise. If you are living in a village in low lying areas which are visited by flood every year you would have noticed that a fisherman would throw from a certain distance a piece of bamboo about two feet in length closed from both sides but empty inside, like an empty drum of around two inches diameter, thereby making it float in the water. The impact is immediate as due to the noise caused by the piece of bamboo thrown on the water by the fisherman the fishes would be motionless for a few seconds, may be, a minute or so, giving enough time to the expert fisherman to throw his net or other fish catching devices to catch those fishes leaving some lucky ones to escape. So, you can see the close and interlinked relationship among the three segments of the environment, i.e., air environment, noise environment and water environment.

Let us now see the relationship of the above three segments of environment. i.e., air, noise and water to land environment. Imagine a situation when there is no air or noise or water and only land without any vegetation, i.e., barren lands all around. No living things can survive even for a moment in such a situation. In fact, if the entire surface of the earth is devoid of air, noise and water there will be no vegetation and no living organisms. So water has helped lands to produce various types of crops on which humans and many animals survive. Depending on the availability of water whether on account of natural stored water in various water bodies, water reservoirs, rivers etc. as also water due to seasonal rainfall crops of various kinds grow. We have also forest cover. Therefore, water is a very critical element in the survival of all living things both human and animals and as also flora and fauna.

I will give two examples of how air and noise also help us in our attempt to survive and survive well.

You can imagine a situation when there are vegetations and plants of different kinds but there is no insect like bee to carry pollen from one plant to another plant to help reproduction process. In such a situation pollen is carried by air from the male part of a flower to fertilize the female ovule resulting in the production of crop or fruits of different kinds. At the same time a very strong and stormy wind could completely damage the productive capacity of a plant or even a tree. It is not uncommon to hear that because of untimely stormy wind condition a particular area which is otherwise known for growing bumper mango crop could not produce enough mango crop in that particular year.

You, no doubt, know that forest dwelling tribal people and other non-tribal traditional forest dwellers collect various minor forest produce like wax and honey which are some of the stable sources of their livelihood without knowing the intricate process of how a honey-bee collects nectar and pollen to produce wax and honey. The honey-bees move in a group and the group would collect nectar and pollen and get them deposited in an aesthetic structure hanging from the branch of a tree that creates a beautiful shape of a beehive leading to the creation of a delicate honey-comb that becomes a store for honey. The humming sound of the bees as they move their wings attracts the notice of the forest dwellers who can immediately get to know that there is a honey-comb close by and they would wait for the proper time to extract the honey and also the wax. Here, is a case where water has helped the land to grow a tree with branches and other flowering plants and trees to attract the honey-bee to produce wax and honey. So noise (sound) becomes an essential element in helping the forest dwellers to know the existence of wax and honey.

In the preceding paragraphs you have seen how air environment, noise environment, water environment and land environment have together, as if in a co-ordinated effort so to say, created the wonderful biological environment with rich flora and fauna including avifauna and aquatic fauna which have made the human life a most exciting one. As we can not imagine a life without air, noise (sound), water, lands and flora and fauna it becomes imperative for us to know what a biological environment is like and what impact it has on our life. It should make you pause for a while and think about the adverse impact that your proposed mining activity would cause to the biological environment with the accompanying adverse impact on the living things, human, animals including avifauna, aquatic fauna and the forest cover and consequent planning of appropriate mitigating measures to negate the adverse impacts due to your mining activities. So you must know the baseline status of biological environment of the study area, the anticipated impacts due to your mining activities and plan corresponding mitigating measures. I would be dealing with these three aspects in the sequel.

Baseline Status

Details to be collected on Biological Environment under different headings have been indicated at Item E-Biological Environment in Table 1 (Annexure-B) referred to earlier. Your consultant would be in a position to collect the information and appropriately mention the same in tabular form. Such detailed information in required number of Statements form part of the EIA report submitted before the Expert Appraisal Committee (EAC) for consideration at the time of appraisal of the project by the Committee. These are, no doubt, routine information but are very relevant and critical in appraising the impact of your project activities on the biological environment and the adequacy of the proposed mitigating measures. It is, therefore, advisable that you collect as much information as are possible.

As in the case of other segments of the environment, my advice here is that you follow the details given in Section 3.5.1 of the Model TOR at Annexure-B and collect the baseline data relevant for your projects. To appreciate the importance and relevance of certain aspects of biological environment I would give briefly the rationale as to why certain baseline data are so critical to know the consequences of the adverse impacts caused due to your mining activities. Remember, that your mining activity would have only adverse impacts on the biological environment except in some rare cases, which I have cited in some of the preceding paragraphs, when mining of bauxite or limestone as outcrop might result in the lands beneath the ore bodies turning into fertile agricultural lands. Let me now proceed to give some examples only to make you realize the importance of the baseline status.

Biological environment covers every living organism that germinates on the soil, grows and flourishes contributing to the unique and exciting nature of the earth. The core zone and the buffer zone of your project would have a biological environment which could be of a kind of its own and could perhaps be different from the biological environment of the surrounding areas. It is, therefore, essential that you collect the baseline data through field survey as also with the help of the secondary data authenticated by the forest and wildlife protection authorities. The significance of such data can best be appreciated if I give you few examples.

Take the case of forest litter fauna. It is a common scene in a forest area to see dry tree leaves and other loose vegetation spread over a large area. After sometimes there would be living organisms growing automatically under such litter. Many people perhaps do not know that such litter faunae, i.e., faunae grown under the litter, are also responsible for mineralization of the soil beneath such litter and such soils could become fertile and such fertility is due to the contribution of the litter fauna. You could yourself notice that while starting your mine development activities leading to mining activities the movement of vehicles and machinery would damage the litter fauna as either you would remove the litter spread over the land to make road for moving the vehicles and machinery and if such litter is thin you would perhaps allow the vehicles and machinery to role over such litter. If you come across very rich litter fauna and if you know the characteristics of such litter fauna and if the litter fauna has a positive impact on the productive capacity of the land you would perhaps on your own ensure that the damage to the litter fauna is kept to the minimum and if you are doing that you would virtually be taking mitigating measures even at the beginning of your project activities. Therefore, it is essential that you get the primary data about the characterization of forest litter fauna.

The baseline data would include the details of fauna including avi-fauna indicating the endangered and endemic species. When we talk of wildlife usually we think of wild animals like lion, tiger and other predators, deer, etc. and domestic animals besides birds. But in reality such faunae are a very small segment compared to the larger animal world. I will quote one paragraph from *Animal Encyclopedia* (Kingfisher Publications Plc) below:

> "Mammals and birds make up only a small proportion of this huge figure. Although they are spread all over the globe and are often large and conspicuous, they are outnumbered many times by much smaller animals, such as insects, spiders and worms. One bucketful of garden soil can contain more than a million tiny roundworms and, throughout the world, the total number of these animals runs into thousands of billions. However, because animals like these are small and difficult to see, we hardly notice that they are there."

Thus, you can imagine that animal habitats dominate the entire surface of the earth and it would not be an exaggeration to say that but for the existence of such rich wildlife the earth perhaps would not have been worth living. It is not only the animals but their habitats are also different and the animals have the amazing capacity to survive in any habitat by adapting to the terrain and turbulence (*ibid*).

I need not over emphasize here that the vegetation, flora and the general forest cover and the water bodies of the core zone and the buffer zone of your project could be the habitats for the wildlife including the avi fauna and the aqua-fauna specially suited for the prevailing biological environment. Once you start your project activities, it would interfere with the hitherto free and unfettered movement of the animals and avi fauna. Your activity would also interfere with the right of the cattle over the grazing lands. It is, therefore, necessary that you have the baseline data per centabout the flora and the general forest cover and the names of the animals and birds. If the study area has any endangered and endemic species it becomes all the more necessary for you to identify them as specific mitigating measures would be required for such animals. As these animals and birds would need water to slake their thirst there would be water holes which could be various water bodies, big and small, as also any river. Surprisingly predators like lion and tiger would be frequenting such water holes to pounce on their objects of prey. For example, if a lion knows that a deer would be drinking water from a particular water hole it would, when hungry, look for its victim. Since wildlife makes the forest rich, the presence of water holes is an integral part of the forest life as otherwise the animals might migrate to another area that would have water holes and in the process it could make the existing forest full of vegetation and trees but devoid of life in the form of wildlife including avi-fauna in the absence of any water holes for the wildlife to slake its thirst. The baseline data, therefore, must include the details of water bodies.

As you have seen in one of the preceding paragraphs that there are large number of smaller animals such as insects, spiders and worms. Therefore, you are required to collect the details of such smaller animals. You have already known how a small insect like honey-bee provides a valuable source of livelihood to the forest dwellers. If you are of a poetic mind you would definitely appreciate the multi-coloured bright butterflies. If I ask you this question as to if you would like to see that your mining activities result in the killing of such beautiful eye-pleasing butterflies, your answer would, no doubt, be in the negative.

You would no doubt appreciate that the baseline data about the animals and birds including smaller animals are necessarily to be collected and listed indicating the Schedule to the Wildlife (Protection) Act under which various species fall. Since, the secondary data authenticated by the forest authorities may not be up to date it is essential that you engage a professional to make a field survey to collect the up to date data.

While collecting the baseline data you would also identify the usual route of movement of wildlife. You can do so through the survey to be conducted by a Forest and Wildlife expert. In fact, the forest dwelling tribal people and other traditional forest dwellers would be a very reliable source of information on the movement of wildlife. In their normal vocation such forest dwellers traverse across the forest lands and in the process they would, may be for their safety from the attack of the predators like lion, tiger, cheetah, etc., invariably watch the movement of the wildlife.

These are important and relevant primary data as, in case your mining activities would interfere with the movement of the wildlife you would have to take appropriate mitigating measures.

Even without being a bird lover you would never miss the beauty of the birds returning at the end of the day in group with an artistic formation to their night resting shelters which are nothing but the branches of an imposing tree. It is, therefore, essential that you collect the data on avifauna and its usual flying zone and the night resting locations as the noise created on account of mining activities would adversely impact their free flying.

In the Model TOR you have been advised to collect details of forest and fishery resources in the study area. The importance of these information is not difficult to appreciate. Once you are in possession of such data it becomes easier for you to plan, and prepare in advance, relevant economic packages for the local people. In the absence of such information you would be greatly handicapped. It is quite likely that you might have to repent later that you have missed a great opportunity to prepare an appropriate economic package for providing gainful economic activities to the affected people, as also to other people who might not be directly affected on account of your project activities, on sustained basis.

While collecting the data on forest and non-forest flora you are required to give emphasis on the rare and endangered species, endemic species, medicinal plants, major and minor forest produce and social forest trees, all these information are relevant as some of these plants and other species have medicinal and other value.

As cattle grazing is a common practice among the forest dwellers and in fact the cattle population would on its own move around and would be visiting the grazing lands even without any human guide. Such grazing rights are traditionally enjoyed not only by the permanent traditional forest dwellers, both tribal and non-tribal, but also by nomadic people, i.e., a particular tribe who would be roaming from place to place for pasture. Such a tribe also enjoys the traditional rights for grazing its animals specially cows or sheep. Even among the resident traditional forest dwellers there would be scheduled tribe pastoralist communities to enjoy the cattle grazing rights. Since, it is very important from economic point of view and for the very survival of certain groups of people primary data on cattle grazing rights enjoyed by the scheduled tribes and other traditional forest dwellers including nomadic and pastoralist communities as also the locations of the grazing lands are essential.

As mining activity is likely to impact agricultural activity, crop production and productivity of the lands you must collect the primary data on these items. Since water is important for agricultural activities, information on existing irrigation facilities should form part of the primary data. Such data would be available in the offices of the Revenue and Agriculture Departments of the State Government.

It is quite possible that your project is located not far away from national park, sanctuary, tiger reserves, elephant reserve, etc. and in case if any national park, etc. exist within, say, 10 km. radial distance from the outer boundary of the lease hold area you must prepare a location map on a scale 1:50,000 for consideration of the members of the EAC.

While preparing the list of animals, both wild and domestic, and avifauna, it is essential that you indicate the scientific name of each species as also the names by which the local people know such animals and avifauna giving the names in English also for easy understanding by the EAC. In case certain animals and birds are shown in different schedules to the Wildlife (Protection) Act indicate that also.

In case your project involves felling of trees and clearing other vegetation/shrubs you need to prepare an estimate of the number and types of trees and shrubs that would have to be cut/removed as a part of the deforestation for project activities.

Anticipated Impacts

While dealing with the need for collecting baseline data in the preceding paragraphs I have briefly given the rationale of collecting such data and if you think for a while you would, in no time, be in a position to anticipate the impacts of your mining activities on the biological environment. Such impacts would generally be adverse except in very few instances of positive impacts.

Section 3.5.2 of the Model TOR at Annexure-B lists possible impacts of your mining activities on biological environment. I am giving few examples for your benefits so that you can yourself prepare a list of likely impacts.

If the lease-hold area has good forest resources, economically important plants, medicinal plants and also rare and endemic species it is most likely such forest resources would be adversely impacted. Even if the forest resources are outside the lease-hold area the adverse impact would not get automatically eliminated as depending on the speed and direction of wind as also the route for the transportation of the mined minerals dust will fly in various directions impacting the forest resources. So you have to estimate the magnitude of adverse impacts.

Likewise, there will be impact on the wildlife including avifauna as mining activities which might include blasting operations also would interfere with the movement of wildlife including avifauna. Under the law you are empowered to protect the lease-hold area from possible encroachment by the local people with visible demarcation and possibly by erecting barbed wire fencing or some such devices. If the lease-hold area was earlier regularly frequented by wild animals it would interfere with the hitherto free and unfettered movement of the wild animals. The likely injuries to be inflicted on the animals coming in contact with the barbed wire fencing and the noise created by blasting operations or other activities scaring away the birds are distinct possibilities. In case there are cattle grazing lands in the core zone and if there is opportunity for collecting minor forest produce by the local people your fencing the lease-hold area would adversely impact the cattle grazing rights and minor forest produce collection rights of the traditional forest dwellers.

Another important adverse impact would be on bio-diversity, wildlife habitats and migratory corridors for the wild animals. It is quite possible that there would be rich bio-diversity, habitats for the wildlife as also corridors passing through the lease-hold area for the migratory wildlife. Needless to say that your project activities would interfere with the usual movement of the wildlife.

There would be adverse impacts on various gainful economic activities as mining is bound to have adverse impacts on fishery resources and productive capacity of the lands for agricultural crops.

Not only movement of the wild animals but also the usual route of movement of the local people would be affected if the lease-hold area creates an artificial division of the human habitations in case there are human habitations around lease-hold area.

There could be other impacts which you are in a better position to anticipate.

As I have said earlier, there would be some positive impacts which you must, without overdoing, project before the EAC. Some of the positive impacts would be as follows.

If the minerals are outcrop and after the removal of the minerals the lands beneath the ore bodies are found fertile you could indicate the prospect of creating fertile agricultural land.

Beside, the existing water bodies it is quite possible that some new water bodies would be created on account of your mining activities and if such water bodies would have perennial water you could project before the EAC that pisciculture in such water bodies would be a beneficial impact besides irrigation facilities.

Apart from the employment potential for the local people in your organization, there would be possibility of the contractor, if you have appointed one, employing some of the local people. The project will also create some opportunity for setting up small tea shop or other road side eateries which will give the local people to earn some extra income as there would be lot of people to enjoy the services of such tea shop or road side small eateries.

You can also project before the EAC that the medical facilities that you would provide to your employees could also be enjoyed by the local people. In case you are also establishing any educational institution it would also provide an opportunity to the local children to get admission atleast at the primary level.

Suggested Mitigating Measures

Having listed the anticipated impacts you would be in a position to plan and prepare the mitigating measures to take care of the adverse impacts. Such mitigating measure would also include certain socially beneficial measures like setting up a new educational institution and if there are already existing educational institution such measures can include improvement of the facilities in such educational institution. If, for example, there was no educational facilities for the local boys and girls, nobody can hold you responsible and say that your mining activities had resulted in the lack of educational facilities. But if you set up an educational institution it would be a mitigating measure of a different kind as the educational institution you would be setting up would remove the lack of educational facilities and such step would be a socially positive and beneficial one.

If your project is an existing activity you might have already taken some photographs of the vegetation cover before mining and after mining to project before the EAC the contribution you have made to the forest cover. In case it is a new project it would be advisable to take some photographs of existing vegetation cover and you can make an appropriate submission to the EAC that you would take necessary steps to protect the existing vegetation cover and that in case some areas with good vegetation are to be destroyed for carrying on the mining activities you would grow alternative vegetation cover and if possible on the same lands after mining activities are over. If yours is an existing mining company you might be operating a mining project in a different place which could be in a different district or even in a different state you may like to highlight your achievement in conserving the forest cover and to prove your credential you might like to show some of the photographs of your other projects indicating the nature of forest cover before mining and after mining.

With this introduction I would now proceed to suggest the likely mitigating measures in the sequel.

Section 3.5.3 in the Model TOR at Annexure-B gives a general frame of the mitigating measures. It is possible that all the items suggested there might not be relevant in respect of your project. In fact, there could be certain other steps outside the suggested mitigating measures relevant for your project. You would, no doubt, generally follow the guidelines in Section 3.5.3 as the EAC, after due deliberation, has considered that the suggested mitigating measures would, by and large, apply to all mining projects. I would not go into explaining the individual items as your consultant would be doing the needful. I will only briefly highlight the rationale behind the proposed mitigating measures.

Just like other segments of the environment, there is no substitute for adopting scientific mining methods which would automatically take care of protecting the bio-diversity, wildlife and forest cover. I would give a simple example to make the point clear. Suppose there is a standing tree right at the point you plan to open the mine pit as the occurrences of the ore bodies are such that the proposed mine pit site would be logistically more convenient. In the process you decide to cut the standing tree for which you might have got the permission of the competent authority. Accordingly you cut the tree and to compensate the loss of one standing tree you might decide to plant more than one tree sapling at different locations. So one standing tree goes and it will take years for the newly planted tree saplings to grow up to the height of the tree you have already felled. So the area would remain without any tree for many years. Now suppose I give an alternative proposal like this. You don't cut the standing tree but the entry route to the mine pit could be designed in such a way that the standing tree remains as it is. You might have to spend some extra money for the new entry route to the mine pit. In the process you would conserve a standing tree and it is no mean contribution you are making to the biological environment of the area. I have no doubt that you would give serious consideration to the alternative I have suggested. The same rationale will apply to the route for movement of men and machinery.

Depending on the extent of ore reserves you may have to open more than one mine pit, say, five mine pits in different locations in the lease hold area during the life of the mine which could be, say, fifteen years. If the grade of the ore is more or less same you must prepare a plan to start your mining activities from one mine pit only at a time. You have to transport the mined minerals to the crushing plant, if any, otherwise to the storing point for final disposal. It would be necessary for you to decide the route of transportation. Accordingly, you have to decide the particular location at which you want first to extract the minerals. Once you decide to open the first mine pit at a particular location you should not open the second mine pit before the first mine pit is completely exhausted following your principle of "*zero-waste mining*". If you also carry on the land restoration works and plantation of trees as and when the lands are free from mining activities you would realize at the end that by the time you take up the next mine pit for extracting the minerals the lands affected by your mining activities in the first pit have been restored to the original state to the extent practicable and the plantation work you have done has started showing visible growth. I had the occasion to see some mines in Goa where the exhausted mine pits have full forest cover within a period of five years. You would no doubt realize now that at the end of fifteen years of the life of your mine most of the areas except perhaps the area around the last mine pit would have good green cover and depending on the plant species the trees could be quite high as fifteen years are a long period for the planted species to grow.

During the collection of baseline data you might have listed rare plants of economic significance and also medicinal plants. If your mining activities are likely to result in the loss of such plants you would, no doubt, as a prudent miner, remove the top soils containing such rare plants including medicinal plants and spread such top soils in a different location and nurture the area so that such rare plants do not vanish permanently. At the end of your mining operations and as a part of your mine closure plan you might like to bring back part of the top soils spread elsewhere as suggested above to the original location as a part of your land and vegetation restoration work.

The suggested mitigating measures in the Model TOR list compensatory afforestation and I am sure you will do that with all seriousness. I will, however, deal with the need for development of green belt between the outer boundary of the lease-hold area and the nearest water bodies including a river or any other natural water course. As a result of your mining activities there would be destruction of lands and during rainy season various pollutants would flow over to the water bodies. The best and effective way of preventing such pollutants from going into the water bodies is to develop thick green belt between the outer boundary of the lease hold area and the nearby natural water bodies including water course. The Model TOR suggests atleast 50 metres wide area between the lease boundary and the water course. The EAC has arrived at this width as it was considered quite safe as the thick green belt would completely block the pollutants getting mixed with the water.

There would be some water bodies with perennial water sources besides seasonal water bodies on account of rainfall. These water bodies would have various water plants besides aquatic fauna. In fact, the local people might be using this water for drinking purposes also. Therefore, it becomes incumbent on you to ensure that your mining activities do not pollute the water of these water bodies as the polluted water would ultimately affect the health of the people and since such water could be used for agricultural purposes the productive capacity of the land would be adversely impacted. Fishes grown in such water bodies would be infected by the pollutants and since the tribal and non-tribal traditional forest dwellers would also consume such fishes the pollutants would eventually go into the bio-system of such people. While dealing with the air environment, water environment and land environment I have also dealt with such issues. In the chapter on 'socio-economic' environment after this chapter various mitigating measures have been suggested. You may, while presenting your proposal before the EAC, refer to those mitigating measures as are relevant in respect of biological environment.

I have in one of the preceding paragraphs dealt with the importance of forest litter fauna. If the litter fauna is beneficial for the soil you can very well appreciate that such litter fauna need be protected and since the litter fauna is on the surface, movement of man and machinery can be so regulated as to avoid such litter fauna. But never burn with fire such beneficial litter fauna. It is quite possible that such beneficial litter fauna might not grow in all the areas. It is, therefore, advisable that you develop the forest floor by litter fauna in the reclaimed areas after mining is over.

Cattle grazing rights are traditionally enjoyed by the forest dwellers besides their right to collect minor forest produce and if your mining activities would result in the denial of such traditional rights to the forest dwellers you have to develop alternative cattle grazing areas as also making it convenient for the people to collect the minor forest produce in some other area or, may be, within the lease hold area in consultation with the local people as provided for under Forest Rights Act dealt with in Chapter-3.

There are restrictive provisions for mining in areas either close to the national park, sanctuary, etc. or even within such national park or sanctuary as also in the costal zone. Make sure that you have got the necessary permission from the concerned authorities for mining in such areas as mitigating measures for any adverse impact in such areas are very difficult and complex ones.

On the required mitigating measures relating to wildlife including avifauna I am giving below the importance of such mitigating measures.

You have already realized that the wildlife including avifauna add to the quality of forest life just like the quality of water bodies gets enhanced with the presence of water plants, fish population and in some cases flowers like water lilies and lotus. The animals, both predators like lion, cheetah, etc. as also their easy victims like deer, have the unfettered rights to move freely within the forest areas with occasional straying in the areas outside the forest cover. The following are critical in the conservation of forest fauna including avifauna.

The animals as also the birds need water to slake their thirst. Prior to your mining activities the animals and the birds used to drink water from various water holes notwithstanding the fact that the victim like a deer knows it very well that such water holes are regularly frequented by the predators who would visit such water holes both for drinking water as also for pouncing on their preys when hungry. If your mining activities are interfering with the hitherto free rights of the animals to drink water from their usual water holes it becomes essential that you create alternative water holes that would the acceptable substitute.

Animals develop, over years, certain routes for movement within the forest area. Selection of such routes might have been done on various consideration like easy movement within the forest area both for self protection specially for the preys or due to the existence of water holes and good open grassland for rest purposes. There could be more than one forest area which are continuous and the animals would be moving from one forest area to another forest area. In the process such animals develop a more or less fixed route commonly known as animal corridor. The forest could fall in more than one state and in some cases the same forest could run into the jurisdiction of some other country. Africa is an example, where the animals, say, elephant would move in herd from the forests of Kenya to the forests of another country, say, Zambia. These wild animals do not need any permit from the concerned country government for their movement. If your mining activities are interfering with the routes of movement of the wildlife you have to develop an appropriate corridor for the migratory animals much before your mining activities start. This can be done only with the help of an expert on wildlife. We can not apply human standard like construction of a bypass for the motorists to avoid a congested and thickly populated area with appropriate sign boards and road direction before the bypass starts. An expert on wildlife would advise you the appropriate alternative route for the wildlife and how to make the animals follow the route. So when you create new water holes for the animals the same should be falling in the areas through which the new route will be available for the animals. When it comes to slaking their thirst the wild animals do not believe in any segregation, an egalitarian system under which the *King* (lion) of the forest and his *subjects* (the preys or victims) drink water from the same water hole. So no extra cost to create two sets of water holes—it makes your job that much simple. New water holes could be an attraction for the wild animals to follow the new corridor. Should you decide to erect physical barrier fencing to protect the lease hold area from encroachment, do not use barbed wire as that would cause unintended injuries to the likely encroachers including the animals. It is advisable to use chain links or some other harmless (not likely to cause injury to the body parts) device.

As for the birds the same wildlife expert would advise you how to protect the usual resting places of the avifauna. He would also suggest the required mitigating measures for the scheduled fauna as special measures are essential for the protection of the scheduled fauna.

I would be dealing with the question of administrative and technical set-up for monitoring and guiding the implementation of various mitigating measures in Chapter-13. I would briefly mention here that unlike other segments of the environment excluding occupational health environment there has to be an exclusive institutional mechanism to supervise and monitor various mitigating measures in respect of biological environment. Make sure that the person concerned is a technically qualified one who should be made exclusively responsible for protecting the biological environment. I will go into further details later in the appropriate place in Chapter-13.

Chapter – 11

Socio-Economic Environment

As a miner you must be extremely careful and sensitive to the impacts that your proposed mining activities would have on the society. The term society is an abstract concept that stands for the people living in the area, their sources of livelihood, their cultural life, health and education status of the people, use of land by the people, etc. So when you collect the baseline data on socio-economic environment you must collect those essential data that pertain to all aspects of the social life and the economic activities. Section 3.6.1 in the Model TOR at Annexure-B would give you an idea about the relevant baseline data to be collected. I would not be dealing with these details as your consultant would guide you appropriately. But I will give a brief idea about the significance of certain data, which are relevant to the socio-economic environment, to be collected.

The first and foremost details to be collected pertain to lands and land uses which are an essential source of livelihood for the local populace. Mining is a site specific activity as mining can be done only where minerals exist. But, as stated earlier in the context of mine closure, mining is only one of the so many uses of the same land. Needless to say that minerals exist only in land, whether as outcrop or underground. Therefore, you cannot avoid acquiring the land where ore bodies occur and also certain other lands which would be required for carrying out certain related activities like crushing, loading, unloading, etc. In the process of mining lands will be broken which can be more in case of opencast mines and would be less for an underground mine. Therefore, data on land are an essential pre-requisite in the process of collecting baseline data.

Because of your mining and related activities perhaps certain ancillary activities would come up besides road-side small eateries, tea shops, etc. This would result in the emission of pollution which will add to the existing pollution of the area with its accompanying other issues on cost of living, impact on hitherto uncontaminated drinking water, pressure on the existing infrastructural facilities like roads, etc. Though certain restrictive measures would affect the local people both in the core zone and buffer zone, it will have greater impact on the people and their life style who have been enjoying free access over the lands falling in the core zone and it is quite possible that certain areas in core zone are of greater economic significance to the local people. As the lease-hold area (core zone) can be demarcated erecting some barrier at times with barbed wire fencing preventing entry of local people and the animals citing reasons of safety as mining activities could cause injury to the living things, both human and wildlife, it would, nevertheless, interfere with free movement of the people and their domestic cattle population.

While collecting baseline data you would be required to collect details of the private lands with ownership and the annual income of the land owners from the lands. It would also be essential to collect the data on the right of the local people on the government lands and forest lands including their right to use certain lands for grazing their cattle. So you have realized that your proposed mining activities would impact the social and economic life of the local people both in the core zone and in the buffer zone. Therefore, you must collect the baseline data on the line suggested in Section 3.6.1 of the Model TOR. I am mentioning below a general framework for collecting the baseline data.

Baseline status

Details to be collected on Socio-Economic Environment under different headings have been indicated at Item F-Socio-Economic Environment in the Table 1 (Annexure-B) referred to earlier. Your consultant would be in a position to collect the information and appropriately mention the same in tabular form. Such detailed information in required number of Statements form part of the EIA report submitted before the EAC for consideration at the time of appraisal of the project by the Committee. These are, no doubt, routine information but are very relevant and critical in appraising the impact of your project activities on the socio-economic environment and the adequacy of the proposed mitigating measures. It is, therefore, advisable that you collect as much information as are possible.

While collecting the relevant information on socio-economic environment, you must carefully go through the contents of Table–1 (Annexure-B) (Demographic Profiles of the Villages in the Core Zone and the Buffer Zone), Table–2 (Annexure-B) (Occupation of Population and Work Forces of the Buffer Zone), Table–3 (Annexure-B) (Land use and Cropping Patterns of the Core Zone and the Buffer Zone), Table–4 (Annexure-B) (Educational Facilities and Community Based Organizations within the Study Area) and Table–6 (Annexure-B) (Other Infrastructural Facilities Available in the Study Area) as indicated at the Annexure attached to the Model TOR. You would take no time to realize the importance of these information while preparing the economic package as part of your CSR Policy.

The people have been living in the area for generations and they have certain types of residential houses, healthcare facilities, existing infrastructure facilities for the society, sources of livelihood of the local people and if it is a forest land the sources of livelihood for the forest dwellers, their forest rights, etc., etc. and therefore, all such details should be important components of the baseline data.

Details of the land holding pattern in the core zone should be collected indicating the nature of ownership that would be very vital when the question of payment of compensation is considered. The tribal families and other permanent forest dwellers would be having usufructuary rights over the lands without owning the lands. Therefore, such details should be clearly indicated as suggested in the Model TOR. The proposed project activities would impact areas outside the core zone, might be in the radius of 3 km area. So baseline data to be collected should cover all the villages falling within the radius of 3 kms with information for the villages within 1 km radius and villages within 2 kms radius and 3 kms radius separately as the impact would vary depending on the distance of the villages from the core zone. While collecting such information you might be giving the names of the revenue villages. This may not be the present actual status with human settlement. It is a common practice in rural areas that there are small hamlets in different locations at a certain distance within the revenue village where many people reside. So when you give the names of the revenue villages without the locations of the human settlements in various small hamlets, the information would be misleading. The main revenue village could be situated at a distance of more than 1 km while these human settlements in hamlets could be closer to your mine site. You cannot dismantle these hamlets without proper resettlement sites at convenient locations as the people have been living there for various purposes like guarding their lands, standing crops and their cattle grazing fields etc.

There is one common feature in the rural areas and more so in tribal and forest dwellers dominated forest land on the use of public lands including common property resources. In rural areas every village would have cattle grazing lands either in one big plot of land or in different plots located at different convenient places and the society takes a view on the use of such common lands by the people as convenient depending on the places of their residence. These are important baseline data to be collected.

Certain information relating to the sources of livelihood of the household as distinguished from sources of livelihood of individuals, traditional skills like poultry farming, piggery, goat/sheep rearing, basket making, floriculture, pisciculture, collection of minor forest produce, etc. should be collected through a household field survey as it may not be possible to get all such information in the office of the local village panchayat or the revenue office of the state government. Such a survey would give the latest information. There will be clamour for employment in your project. You know for certainty that it may not be possible to give employment to every one including the owners of the lands which you would be acquiring for the project. But to have an idea about the magnitude of the problem it is necessary that while doing the household field survey you must collect the accurate information about the employable young boys and girls with their educational status. I would give the reason why such details are required while dealing with the proposed mitigating measures. It is advisable that information on this item is collected covering all the houses falling within the radius of 3 kms (as the crow flies). Since, it would not be practical for you to give employment to every eligible person it is necessary that information about the available natural resources which could be put to productive purposes for providing gainful employment to the local people are collected. Such natural resources could be water bodies for pisciculture and other lands where fruit-bearing trees can be grown. Even the information about the routes of communication by the local tribals and other forest dwellers in their daily pursuit of various activities like collection of minor forest produce, etc. as source of livelihood would be relevant as you might have to take certain steps to minimize the hardship experienced by these people which will be a part of your proposed mitigating measures.

Socio-economic profile of the people within 2,5 and 10 kms radius of the core zone including buffer zone in the prescribed proforma at the end of the Model TOR would be required for undertaking certain socio-economic activities with reference to the existing facilities such as education facilities, health facilities, etc.

Even in rural areas and forest areas there would be certain places which are of historical importance and information on such places should be collected. Needless to say that all these information might have already been shown by you in the site map referred to earlier. A separate site map for the area of which you have collected the baseline data should be shown for a better understanding by the members of the Expert Appraisal Committee (EAC).

Anticipated Impacts

Once you are armed with the relevant baseline data affecting all essential aspects of the socio-economic environment you are in a position to anticipate the impacts that are likely to visit the people, productivity of the land, the normal vocation of the people, etc. It is not necessary that the impacts would be only negative. There will be some positive impacts also due to any industrial activity and more so in case of mining activity. Many people do not know that mining activities, though apparently would be associated with degradation of lands, generate considerable gainful economic activities. As a single industrial activity mining perhaps creates maximum employment opportunities, both direct and indirect, for skilled and unskilled jobs, as also self-employment opportunities. Don't give the impression that you are overdoing the positive benefits that would be generated on account of your proposed mining activities. I am mentioning below a very few of such positive impacts and I am sure you are in a better position to add many more positive impacts.

Before you will start actual mining operations you will be doing mine development activities and that could last for one year to five years depending on the extent and complexity of the ore and the terrain of the area. So you will be mobilizing your human resources as also certain machinery in constructing a link road from your mine site to the nearest existing road which could be a district road, state high way or national high way. Once this road is ready the same will be available to the local people without any cost on their part.

You will notice that in no time some small eateries and tea shops would come up in the area and this will be set up only by the local people or even if they are set up by outsiders, young boys and girls of the locality will be employed in such small eateries or tea shops and this will give an income to these people which was not there earlier.

If you would also set-up small temporary residential area for your employees you would make arrangements for supply of electricity and drinking water. The local people will also be benefitted directly or indirectly.

Likewise, you would set-up medical facilities for your employees and you would feel morally obliged to provide some medical services to the local people.

Another positive impact would be how you intend to train the local employable young boys and girls as such training would enable them to get employment in your project or get self-employment elsewhere in motor mechanism, motor vehicle driving, etc. At the end you can give a brief details about the revenue, both Central and State, that would accrue to the government on account of payment of sales tax, income tax, excise duty, etc. by you. But such positive impact like revenue accrual would not be of much significance to the local people and therefore, there is no need to over emphasize this positive impact on account of revenue accrual. Your emphasis should be on the positive impacts that you anticipate for the local people some of which I have briefly explained above.

I will give you one practical experience gathered in a meeting of the Expert Appraisal Committee (EAC) on the presentation on limestone and bauxite mines. In this case both bauxite and limestone were outcrop beneath which the soil was reported to be soft. The project proponent informed the Committee that in one such mine after the minerals limestone were removed the resultant soils turned out to be very fertile for agricultural purposes. I am citing this example so that if your mining operations would give similar results you must present that also before the EAC.

As against the anticipated positive impact(s), the adverse impacts on account of your mining activities would be quite significant and that would determine your commitment to adopting practical and pragmatic mitigating measures. It is not my intention to create a fear complex in your mind but you must accept the reality that would prompt you to adopt adequate mitigating measures and a Corporate Social Responsibility (CSR) policy that would have an immediate appeal to the local populace.

The lands both in the core zone and in the buffer zone would have particular level of fertility and cropping pattern with certain amount of productivity. There could be some barren land also. Once you have collected the baseline data about the cropping pattern and crop productivity, you are in a position to assess the likely loss of crop production due to accumulated dust that would settle on these lands as also due to the water contaminated by your mining activity. You would yourself be in a position to assess the loss of crop from the lands falling within a distance of 2 kms or so of the core zone. For example, if the land has a capacity to produce, say, 10 quintals of paddy a year per hectare, you would be in a position to assess the likely impact on account of your mining at the end of the year. And if the land gives crop twice a year you can yourself make an assessment at the end of each year. If you find that the production capacity of the land has gone down to, say, 8 quintals a year, you would agree that the loss of 2 quintals per hectare of land is due to your mining operations. So you have arrived at an approximate quantity of loss and depending on the volume of your mining activities and the magnitude of the pollutant effects you can work out the loss in productivity for the remaining years of your project activities.

Another significant adverse impact would be on the sources of livelihood of the people, i.e., tribals and other forest dwellers. If you travel in a tribal dominated forest area anywhere in the country the common feature that would never fail to attract your attention is that the tribal people especially the women would be travelling long distance on foot to collect minor forest produce including the fuel-wood. And these women would be found moving with big head load of the minor forest produce and would go to the local weekly market place to sell these forest produce after retaining some quantity for their own consumption at home. Once you start the mining operations or even from the start of mine development activities you would prohibit these tribal and other forest dwellers to go over the core zone to which earlier they had free access. Therefore, these tribal women and other forest dwellers would have to travel longer distance and might be in a different and possibly in a difficult terrain adversely affecting their health which in any case even otherwise may not be in a good shape. Among all the people most vulnerable section would be affected severely.

While collecting baseline data you might have also got the details of the people with small land holdings as also people who work as share croppers. It is but natural that any adverse impact on the cropping pattern and productivity of the land would have severe adverse impact on such marginal or small land holders and the share croppers.

Another common feature besides collection of Minor Forest Produce (MFP) in the tribal areas is that most of the households have cows, goats or sheep. So it is a common phenomenon in the tribal areas that these cattle have free access to the grazing lands or to any land where they can get feed, may be, green leaves of the trees, etc. It is also possible that the core zone would be near and convenient to the households for grazing their cattle. Therefore, any mining activity would interfere with the free movement of these cattle.

If mining activity would involve, which is not uncommon, displacement of human settlements during the life of the project the impact on such displaced persons would be enormous. Therefore, you must assess the nature of impact on such displacements that might involve, besides loss of residential houses, loss of sources of livelihood of such displaced persons. While new residential houses can be constructed by you in a different location, it may be difficult to identify sources of livelihood in the immediate aftermath causing great hardship to the affected people.

There will be certain other adverse impacts on land due to your mining activities. For example, the topography of the land would undergo sea change due to opening of mine pits, causing damage to the lands etc. and, therefore, land use pattern would change perceptively. Land subsidence would be quite common though many not be as severe as in coal mine areas.

Societal impact, which might not be visible immediately, would be quite harmful to the ethnic culture of the people. Increasing outside population in the area would mean that the local tribals and traditional forest dwellers would get exposed to the behavioural norms of outsiders which might have undesirable impacts on their traditional social norms under the watchful eye of the community. These are changes which become visible over a period.

Adverse impacts on the health of the local populace due to the pollution created by the mining activity would be a serious concern. I am not going into details here as there is a separate chapter on health environment, both occupational and other, where the matter will be discussed in greater details.

I have only given a brief idea about the likely impacts. But you have to assess the impacts that are specific to your project and it is quite possible that impacts may not be severe in your project affected area and if it is so I only wish good luck to you.

Suggested mitigating measures

Once you have made an assessment about the adverse impacts due to your mining activities you are in a position to prepare a plan of action to mitigate these adverse impacts to the extent that is feasible. These mitigating measures would be an integral part of your Corporate Social Responsibility (CSR) Policy and the expenditure to be incurred on these mitigating measures as also the expenditure on various mitigating measures relevant to all the seven segments of the environment would be a part of your project cost. In fact, some of the cost on mitigating measures you have to incur would be part of your mine development activities before actual mining activities start. How and when such expenses are to be incurred on certain mitigating measures would be explained at the end of the suggested mitigating measures to prove that it is not the amount of money but the time when such money is spent is more important.

Before I go into the details of the suggested mitigating measures, and you are free to select those mitigating measures as are specific to your project, I would explain the ethical aspect of your CSR Policy. I have in an earlier occasion in this book have emphasized that but for your mining activities there would have been no additional and specific adverse impacts on the environment of the area. Whatever, be the compulsion for you, be it your active involvement in the economic development of the country by exploiting the mineral resources or for any other reasons, there would be adverse impacts on the environment already anticipated based on the baseline data that you have collected. Therefore, it becomes your moral responsibility to take effective mitigating measures specific to the requirement of the people living in the core zone and the buffer zone. So it is not a charity or philanthropy that you are doing to mitigate adverse impacts. Once you accept this moral responsibility, you are automatically led to the irresistible conclusion that your CSR Policy is not a mere policy frame work of your organization but it is a corporate mission that you have taken up. If you accept this as a corporate mission and implement the mitigating measures that have been suggested in Section 3.6.3 of the Model TOR at Annexure-B you will realize in no time that you have created an asset of good will of the local people, whether adversely affected or not. This good will is much more valuable and paying than the amount that you would be called upon to expend on mitigating measures. In the subsequent paragraphs I will give some examples as to how a very insignificant amount of money and most importantly the time of spending this amount on the proposed mitigating measures really does not cost much to you but it pays and pays handsomely.

The suggested socio-economic activities to mitigate the adverse impacts get divided into three categories for the purpose of better understanding. You might have a CSR Policy for establishing an educational institution of excellence, a super speciality hospital and perhaps an impressive temple for worship. Such activities would benefit the larger community much beyond the area of core zone and the buffer zone and possibly of the country as a whole, and more so in case of a place of worship depending on the perception of the devotees about the Presiding Deity of the temple. When you set-up an educational institution of excellence like an engineering college or any other technical institute at the state capital or at the district headquarters, it is undoubtedly a laudable activity you have taken up. The benefits would, however, go to the people who are not likely to be the only people in the remote and forest land included in the core zone and the buffer zone of your project unless by act of providence there are some local boys or girls who are eligible and you make special quota for such socially and economically disadvantaged people. So these socio-economic activities are meant for the larger community.

Your mission to set-up an educational institution of excellence or a super speciality medical institution or a place of worship would bring name and fame to you and it will be highly appreciated and perhaps you may get wide publicity through media. You must make an introspection to find out the source of your surplus wealth which you could utilize in establishing such institutions of excellence as referred to above. Since yours is a mining company, so has been assumed by me for the purpose of this book, whatever income you have generated has come out of your mining activities. Therefore, while acquiring this wealth through mining activities you have also generated lot of adverse impacts on the socio-economic environment of the area of your operations. If you think deeply you would yourself realize that you owe something to the area and the people that have been the source of your wealth. I therefore, assume for certainty that whatever suggestions I have advocated in this book for mitigating the adverse impacts are exclusively meant for the area of your operations, i.e. the core zone and the buffer zone and the inhabitants, both human and wildlife as also the flora. In the process the people living in the surrounding areas outside the buffer zone would also be benefited.

Coming to the socio-economic activities in the core zone and the buffer zone there are two categories of socio-economic activities. One would relate to the activities that would benefit the entire population of the core zone and the buffer zone as also the people outside but in the vicinity of the buffer zone. If the tribals and other forest dwellers are socially and economically very weak, which is generally the case, such activities may not be of much relevance to them. For example, if you are constructing roads in the area or constructing a place of worship or establishing a school, the benefits will go to everybody and perhaps mostly to the well off section of the populace unless you take specific measures to ensure that vulnerable section of the tribal and other forest dwellers of the core zone and the buffer zone get a chance to use these roads or to visit the place of worship or to get education in the school established by you. By all means you will take such activities which would benefit the community as a whole and it is a welcome step as the benefit will be enjoyed by the local populace who could be the affected people in the core zone and the buffer zone as also the people who are not affected due to mining activities. This would also create a good will among the community as a whole and perhaps such activities would have a positive and benevolent impact on the community who would appreciate if you do something for the people who are affected, both directly and indirectly, by your mining activities.

In the succeeding paragraphs the mitigating measures that I would be suggesting would be applicable to the affected people in the core zone and the buffer zone without, of course, excluding the possibility that the people outside the buffer zone would also get your benevolent support as there could still be people outside the buffer zone some of whom may be equally deserving as the people in the core zone and the buffer zone.

With this brief introduction I would now suggest certain specific mitigating measures which as a miner you can adopt as per the specific requirements of the people in the core zone and the buffer zone of your project. While giving these examples I have assumed that these are generally applicable in all mining affected areas and more so in the tribal and forest areas.

You must keep in mind that your proposed mitigating measures should take into account the needs of the people which you might have already ascertained through the household survey. In short, such mitigating measures should be need based.

In case you are acquiring private land whether as a part of your lease-hold area and lands outside the lease-hold area for carrying out certain project related activities your priority should be to prepare a Rehabilitation Action Plan for land oustees especially such land owners who would not have any other lands. For such people a Rehabilitation Action Plan has to be implemented during the period of mine development activities and definitely before the mining operations actually start. There could be some land owners whose lands you have acquired as would be having other landed properties and in such cases the nature of Rehabilitation Action Plan would be different. Again, if the lands you would be acquiring are the only homestead lands with residential houses any rehabilitation action plan must be such as are acceptable to such land oustees.

Compensation for the lands acquired by you including lands that are part of the lease-hold area and land outside the core zone would have to be calculated with lot of care. I would cite some practical examples from my experience as the Chairman of Expert Appraisal Committee (EAC). Quite a good number of project proponents took the plea in the meeting of the EAC that the lands which they had purchased as also the lands over which they would have surface rights are barren lands without any productive capacity. Perhaps there would be such barren lands even without any tree or vegetation over such lands. Assuming that the lands are barren as claimed by the project proponents but if the land owner refuses to give his consent to the project proponent to enjoy the surface right for the simple and essential requirement of going over to the mine site what would the option left to the project proponent? It is quite possible that from the nearest road you need some passage to go over to the mine site and private land falls in between the mine site and the road. In such a case it becomes imperative for you to get unhindered access over such private land. So the lands could be, as claimed by the project proponent, barren without any income to the land owner, but for the mine owner the land is not barren and in fact it is quite valuable as without any access over such land the proposed mining activity could not be started. Even if you take a detour to go over to the mine site you are not sure if in the alternative route you would not face similar problem. I would, therefore, suggest that when you calculate the amount of compensation it would always be advisable to consult the land owner and reason with him how a particular sum of money would be adequate compensation. If such lands are also crop lands you have to take into account the loss of income to the owners during the period the lands will be under your occupation. In fact, loss of income on account of crop loss would perhaps continue for some time even after the closure of mining operations. So you have to work out separate compensation amount for the lands which you would be permanently acquiring with the legal title and the lands that you would be taking over for a fixed period depending on the life of the project for surface rights. Even for the lands which you take over for surface rights the amount of compensation would vary if the lands are barren or if the lands are productive. Therefore, you work out the amount of compensation taking into account the advantage that you would gain and the extra amount that you would have to otherwise expend if you have to take a detour for going over to the mine site. Once you have assessed the compensation that is accepted by the land owners the question of modality of payment would come. There would be many assessees who would like to take the money as lump sum payment as they are otherwise well to do people and they could invest this extra money in some gainful activities. But there would be one category of people who might be tempted to spend such ready cash on non-productive hedonic activities being totally oblivious of their own practised abstemiousness with bitter realization and repentance in no time soon. So it would be advisable to give an option to such people that the amount of compensation would be paid on annual basis or the payment can be made either on quarterly basis or half yearly basis depending on the convenience of the land owners. This will have a great and abiding positive impact on such people who would be temporarily out of possession of the lands but still getting regular and periodical income as a compensation. If they accept your proposal to collect the compensation money from your office periodically there will be a reminder to such people every time they get the money that you are doing something for their welfare. The good will thus created would be permanent between you and the land owners. While making payment, make sure that the amount is paid directly to the beneficiary and if practicable it can be paid through an account opened in the name of the beneficiary either in a local bank or in the post office as convenient to the beneficiary.

At times the miner might allow certain activities believing that such activities are beneficial to the affected people whose productive agricultural lands get adversely impacted as a result of his mining operations. It is not necessarily the case that the miner would indulge in such activities deliberately. I would narrate such incidents in the next paragraph as presented by some project proponents before the EAC.

You (miner) are operating the iron ore mine on the hilltop or on the hillock. During the course of mining you would be breaking the lands while extracting the minerals and in the usual course due to rain water or the water that you would be using while mining, some quantity of the minerals would flow down the hill or the hillock, as the case may be, and these minerals would get deposited on the fertile agricultural lands down hill. As per the agreement with the land owners you would be paying compensation money to the land owners for the loss in the productive capacity of the lands. You would be surprised also that the land owners will be collecting those accumulated minerals in the form of sludge, that is, something like a thick watery mud. You may or may not be knowing that these land owners will collect bucket full of these sludge containing iron ore and sell the same to some traders who would be supplying such materials to many unauthorized small smelters to convert the sludge into iron slabs which would ultimately find its way into the plant of some steel maker. The land owners would be getting some extra income through such operation in addition to the monetary compensation that you would be paying. You would also feel happy thinking that people are happy with you and that you don't have to yourself remove these accumulated sludge. But you have not appreciated the serious implications as over time the productivity of the land would be either completely ruined or greatly reduced and once you leave the area after the mining operation is over the land owner would shockingly realize the damage caused to his otherwise productive land. This would be the consequence unless you are conscious of the damage and accordingly implement a well conceived land restoration plan whereby the productive capacity of these lands could be restored to the pre-mining stage.

While on the question of compensation for loss of lands, the question of cattle grazing rights and other rights on any public or private lands would be an important factor. If your project activities have resulted in loss of cattle grazing rights or other rights you have to allocate alternative lands for cattle grazing purposes and other rights following the procedure prescribed in the Forest Rights Act dealt with in Chapter-3 of this book. This should be done during mine development activities and much before actual mining starts. If you do not do that in advance as suggested you are likely to face resistance from the local people and you might suffer on account of delay. I will narrate a real story to make my point clear to you. Bhilai Steel Plant (BSP), a unit of the Steel Authority of India Ltd. (SAIL) in the State of Chattisgarh has a mining lease in Rowghat region which is an ecologically fragile area. The Company got in-principle environmental clearance. However, BSP took more than 10 years to approach the MoEF for final environmental clearance on a regular basis. BSP presented their case before the EAC. Though the Committee recommended grant of environmental clearance with certain conditions, a very casual approach of the Company got the attention of the EAC. Bhilai Steel Plant (BSP) had identified lands in almost every village where cattle grazing ground would be established. When the Committee wanted to know when actual lands had been identified what prevented the company from making the cattle grazing lands ready, the Company had no answer although a senior officer present in the meeting frankly admitted that this should have been done long back. I am giving this example just to impress upon you the need for doing certain things in advance so as to give an unmistakable impression to the local people that you have been doing things quite seriously and that you care for them.

Though it is not exactly a mitigating measure, but is an essential and highly paying proposition to impart vocational training in advance to the eligible local boys and girls. I would briefly explain this. When you start mining operations local people especially the young employable boys and girls would see an opportunity to get job in your organization and obviously they would be frustrated if they find that outside people have been brought by you to work in the mines and other related areas. Common argument put forward by the project proponent in the meeting of EAC is that skilled people are not locally available. If you think a little you will find such an argument totally hollow. It will be impractical to think that local employable boys and girls would have got themselves trained to be categorized as skilled workers if they had no idea about the future after getting training in any particular skill much less in a mining project of which they had no idea beforehand. As a miner you would definitely know that you are unlikely to get skilled man power in the locality. At the same time it is not possible for you to give employment to each and every eligible employable boys and girls and perhaps it may not be possible for you to give employment to even one member of each of the families of land oustees. So you have to prepare a list of required skills for your activities and arrange for training the local eligible boys and girls who could be ultimately engaged in your project. Again, it is agreed that your requirement would be limited and therefore it would be unwise to train large number of people that could not be gainfully engaged in your activities. So you have the option to arrange for vocational training for the local eligible boys and girls and you select the particular vocation as per the temperament and aptitude of the boys and girls. For example, motor vehicle driving, motor repair works etc. training can be selected as vocational training for eligible boys and perhaps girls also. Likewise, vocational training in tailoring, etc. could be given to the girls. If such boys and girls have got required minimum educational qualification they could be trained in typing or computer operation, etc. The question will come when and where such training should be imparted. Here again I will give an example of Andhra Pradesh Mineral Development Corporation Ltd. (APMDC). Though I had no occasion to see it personally, the Managing Director of APMDC who was also a senior State Government official told me that he had already spent lot of money in training large number of boys and girls who could be employed in the project after getting environmental clearance. After getting proper training including vocational training such trained persons as could not be employed in your project would find job elsewhere or they would have self-employment with initial financial assistance by your company or through the bank with your support. There are facilities available now a days for such training in many industries and also in the Industrial Training Institutes (ITIs) run by the State Governments. Such training in advance would create a friendly environment and would be a valuable asset for you. You know the skills required in your project and you also know that vocational training in certain skills would ensure fair chance of employment in certain industries or in self-employment to such trained persons and therefore spending some money in advance for such purpose would not go in vain.

In the preceding paragraph I have given a brief idea about the need for proper training in skills relevant for the project as also vocational training. The boys and girls once employed may like to shift to urban areas for better prospects. If you look at the family life in the remote especially in the forest areas you would in no time notice that the family consisting of parents and their children and some times grand parents and other blood relations would be staying in the same household sharing common source of livelihood. If trained boys or girls get employment either in your company or self-employment it cannot be presumed for certainty that he or she would continue to live in the same household as he or she might have to shift elsewhere for better prospects or on transfer. The family, therefore, as such may not get any exclusive relief. Your project activities have already generated lot of hopes and aspirations in the minds of the local people as they envisage a better future for the locality. In the absence of any improvement in their living condition they would naturally get frustrated. At the same time you would expect that there should be a friendly environment around so that your business pursuit can be carried on without any tensions or without any resistance by the local people. To take care of the genuine aspirations of the local people certain gainful economic activities to be pursued by them can be thought of. To start with, you may like to confine your activities to the areas falling within 1 km of the core zone followed by areas falling within 3 kms gradually. As a demonstration case you would like to take the nearest village, not a bad idea to adopt such village for all round socio-economic development, and once you succeed in your effort in the village, the people living beyond the nearest village would themselves come forward and they would like to have some economic package. I would give some examples of gainful economic activities as part of your economic package. While doing the house to house survey at the time of collecting the baseline date you have listed the traditional skills of the people as also the opportunity to develop additional skill(s) for exploiting the existing natural resources. Section 3.6.3 of the Model TOR at Annexure-B enumerates certain activities which are only illustrative and cannot be exhaustive. It is also quite possible that of the activities mentioned in the Model TOR very few could be relevant to the area of your operation. I will explain only a few of them in the succeeding paragraphs.

Poultry farming is a very common practice among the tribal family and traditional forest dwellers. This is also not uncommon among the non-tribal and non-traditional forest dwellers. When I talk of poultry farming, do not get confused with a poultry farm of the modern variety as I am talking in the context of making poultry farming as a gainful economic activity for the project affected people. The tribal families maintain such poultry farm outside their house or in the backyard of their house. They would also be eating the flesh and eggs of the birds selling the surplus in the local market at a price. Since, the tribals do not count any wages for their labour, any price they get is acceptable. If you think of helping an existing poultry farm activity of a particular house-hold, the first requirement will be to ensure that birds are protected especially during night time from the attack of predator like hyena, even dogs, etc. A tribal family would be very happy if you provide a metal wire netted enclosure at a convenient location in the house-hold area where the birds can be kept during night time. If you want to increase the family income you can provide financial assistance so that the poultry owner can purchase chicks and also some feed for the birds. You would perhaps have a small township or some make shift accommodation for your employees some of whom would also like to have the eggs and flesh of the birds. You would also be giving food subsidy to your employees. Imagine these poultry farm owners whom you have given small financial assistance supplying eggs and flesh to your employees, you would immediately realize the benefit both to your employees and to the tribals who would be more than happy with this additional income and perhaps you know the art of expanding his poultry farming activities and sale of the products in the nearest weekly market. Similarly, there are many such activities like piggery, goat/sheep rearing, coir making, mushroom cultivation or any other activities that you might have already identified during the field survey. As the nature of assistance from you would be more or less on the same line as for poultry farming I am not going into further details.

There are certain activities which could be organised on cooperative basis as individual initiative may not be feasible and perhaps in some cases may not be possible also. India is quite organised in the cooperative sector. You might have heard of the institutions like Credit Cooperative Societies, Consumers Cooperative Societies, etc. The most well-known cooperative society is, of course, Amul, whose milk products are widely known throughout the country. We have also seen how Cooperative Group Housing Societies have been a great success in providing residential accommodation to many people especially in the middle and low income groups in even expensive urban areas like Delhi and Mumbai. As a part of group activity, I will first give a brief description about the Fisherman Cooperative Society. There will be water bodies in the core zone as also in the buffer zone. In many villages the existence of big ponds is not uncommon. Fishes grow in such water bodies. So pisciculture on cooperative basis would be a viable economic activity and could provide steady income on sustained basis. Formation of a cooperative society is a very simple act under the State Cooperative Societies Act. Normal requirement is that 8 or 10 persons would form a society. The number could be more depending on the volume of activities. There are model bye laws that are available in the office of the Registrar of Cooperative Societies and his field offices which are generally at the district level as also at sub-divisional level and headed by either a district cooperative officer or an assistant registrar of cooperative society. With necessary changes in the model bye laws a society, say, of 10 persons as members can be registered. To become a member of this society one has to pay Rs. 10 as membership fee and to purchase its shares usually of the value of Rs. 100 per member. If there are 10 members Rs.1000 would be required for the purchase of shares for the members. Once it becomes a society there will be a Managing Committee consisting of an honorary President, honorary Secretary and some members which would be elected by the members themselves. There will be need for maintaining certain records for the society and needs for some managerial assistance. Earlier, government used to provide financial help as managerial assistance. Once the society is formed one of your office staff can initially do the book keeping work and simultaneously train one of the members who is educated enough to maintain certain registers failing which one of your staff can do this job till the society is in a position to have one. If you calculate the amount of money to be paid for the part-time work to be performed by one of your staff it would not be perhaps more than Rs. 50 a month i.e. Rs. 600 a year. So with your initial one time payment of Rs. 1000 as share money and another Rs. 100 as membership fee @ Rs. 10 per member making a total of Rs. 1100 and payment of Rs. 600 only per annum for the book keeping work you have created a legal entity. You can now locate a suitable water body within the jurisdiction of a particular revenue village and explain to the villagers the benefit of doing pisiculture through this cooperative society. At the beginning of the rainy season purchase the fish seedlings and release them in the water. The pond would be having enough algae, i.e. non-flowering water plants as feed for the fish seedlings and the fish seedlings may not need any additional feed and in a few days the fish seedlings will grow and certain varieties grow very fast and become ready for sale. This financial assistance for purchase of seedlings for the society would be required, may be, for 2 to 3 years whereafter, the members themselves would be able to save enough money to procure the seedlings.

Just imagine that with little financial help you have provided an economic package to the people for a steady income. There is another type of cooperative society, namely, Industrial Cooperative Society. Basket making, coir making or even floriculture are common activities pursued by the tribals and other traditional forest dwellers. These activities can also be organised on cooperative basis as I have suggested in the case of piscicultre. Here, the financial assistance will be very nominal but the benefit would be enormous.

I have earlier talked about the common vocation of the forest dwellers relating to collection of minor forest produce. What the people need is that collection centre close to the area of their activity is established and minor forest produce collected by the forest dwellers could be marketed by some one engaged by you paying them a price which should be better than the price they would have got in the weekly market. This will give much needed financial relief by ensuring a remunerative prices for their produce. This will also give a much needed relief to the tribals and other traditional forest dwellers, specially the women, from the grueling long distance walk with headload of minor forest produce in an unfriendly terrain.

Therefore, besides some financial assistance your main focus should be on proper market tie-up for the products of the local people so that they are not exploited by any middleman.

There are certain other land based activities which can be organised both on individual house-hold basis as also on community basis. I would suggest that you plant fruit-bearing trees in the homestead land especially of the poor people and tell such people that these trees belong to them and provide them initial help in growing the tree even though such people already know by tradition the art and they would take all possible care to protect the trees. In the community land you can set up orchards with fruit-bearing trees and plants and this would be a source of regular work to the poor wage earners and the income out of the proceeds of the fruits could also be shared by the community. Similarly, you would also be doing avenue plantation and you can handover its maintenance to the local community who would also be entitled to collect the fruit if the trees are for the use of the community. Local students could be motivated in the tree plantation work with good success.

Earlier, I have talked about skill development. The reason is that there could be certain natural resources which could be put to productive use if required skill is available. For example, there could be good bamboo crop in a particular area but the villagers do not possess the required skill to make use of the bamboo crop for productive purpose even though they might possess some other skills. Since, bamboo could be converted into basket and many useful house-hold furniture and decorative products, you may arrange appropriate training for the local villagers to develop the required skill to make use of the bamboo crop and thereby giving an economic package for earning a reasonably good income on sustained basis if you also help marketing the products.

To make all these economic packages viable you must involve the local people especially the women self-held group as well as others who can communicate with the local people and motivate them.

Another area where you could help is in providing at least primary education to the children of the local people. Besides constructing school building you can provide financial assistance for books and stationery, school uniform and tution fees. If it is possible to have higher secondary school, may be at a different location, you should do that and make sure that the students coming from the primary schools established by you for the affected people get priority in admission and introduce monetary scholarship for few select meritorious students.

If you work out the financial commitments that you have to make for the activities that have been suggested you will be surprised that the amount involved is really not significant and this can be taken as a part of your project cost and therefore you don't have to link such funds to your profit only as these activities would be treated like any other activities. In other words, if this payment is a part of the project cost, it would not make any difference whether you make profit or loss in a particular year as the loss on account of the expenditure for such socio-economic activities would be insignificant compared to the loss on account of the cost on the wages of your employees and other activities including cost on consumables. I will strongly advocate that expenditure on socio-economic activity should not be linked to either the profit or loss of the organization as exploiting the minerals is your activity, may be, many other activities, assisting socio-economic activities on the lines I have suggested should also be taken as one of the so many other activities that would be carried on while doing the main activity of mining.

I would end with a reference to Rehabilitation Action Plan for the displaced human settlements. Please make sure that the new settlements are at a place where the settlers would not find themselves out of place. And also remember that they have been used to living in an area for generations and separation would always hurt them as unwanted refugees. The new settlements should be completed and people settled there during the mine development activities and much before the actual mining starts.

While on the issue of settlement of the displaced persons elsewhere I will narrate a real proposal put before the EAC by a major aluminium producer. This company has a bauxite mine whose life is for five years and the minerals bauxite cannot be mined without shifting about 230 families living there for generations. The company very proudly announced that these families would be shifted elsewhere for five years and after the mining operations are closed they would be brought back. That the families left to themselves would not like to leave their dwelling places for good and live elsewhere was confirmed by a Sub-group of the EAC which made a site inspection. I am giving this example just to impress upon you the need for a very human approach in shifting any person elsewhere. Such people should not be treated as a flock of sheep to be tossed around and be kept as if in a state of peripatetic existence.

Besides providing new settlements to the displaced persons the question of compensation for the lands would arise if the proposed mining activities would deprive the land owners of their right to cultivate the lands. While calculating the amount of compensation for any land required for mining activities you would, no doubt, consult the local Revenue and Agriculture Department Officials and also take into account the productivity of the land. While doing the calculation you would come across some ticklish issues about the legal ownership of the persons who were cultivating these lands. I have referred to the cases of about 230 families in the preceding paragraph. In this particular case the company took the plea that as per the Rehabilitation and Sesettlement Plan of the State Government compensation for loss of land is admissible only in favour of persons who have legal rights over the lands and not otherwise. Of the 230 families about 75 per cent families do not have any legal documents in their favour. Such families are called BEJA-KABJA occupants, that is, unauthorized occupants of the lands. Whatever, be the reason, such BEJA-KABJA families have usufructuary right over these lands meaning thereby that such people have their right of enjoying the use and advantages of such lands, may be, belonging to the State Government. This is a common feature in tribal areas where without being legal owners of the lands the tribal families can cultivate the land and enjoy the crops grown on such lands and do everything that a legal owner is entitled to except to legally transfer the ownership of such lands. As a progressive miner you should only consider the lands the usufractuary right over which would be lost as a result of your project activities and fix the compensation which is acceptable to the land users without going into the legal ownership of the land. For you it is not mandatory that you should follow the guidelines of the State Government as this might result in denial of compensation to the land users who do not have any legal documents to prove that they are the owners of the land. Further, the fact of your paying any compensation to such land losers would not confer any legal ownership of the lands on such land users. It is part of your CSR Policy and if you leave aside the issue of legal right you would yourself realize that you are paying compensation for certain loss, i.e., the loss of usufructuary rights on the land, caused to a particular person because of your mining activities. If you pay the amount at a rate higher than the rate of compensation as per the State Government guidelines you are not committing any illegality. Why I am emphasizing the fact that usufructuary right should be accepted as a valid ground for calculating the amount of compensation is that the stand taken by the company I have referred to in the preceding paragraph was that it would be illegal to pay any compensation to the BEJA-KABJA families. For you as a miner what is relevant is that these families have been living there for generations and your mining activities would deny their usurfructuary rights on the lands. Therefore, you should have a compensation package for such people also for the loss of their usufractuary rights over the lands due to your project activities and not for loss of legal ownership over the lands as without adequate compensation these families would be totally destitute which surely you don't want. Moreover, it is your money and you are the best person to decide if such expenses would be in the interest of your project.

While dealing with the suggested mitigating measures I have also emphasized that it is not the amount of money spent on various socio-economic activities but what is more important is the time when such expenses are incurred. I will try to explain the relevance of the time for doing certain things by giving an example. By now you have come to realise that grazing land is very critical for the tribal people and other traditional forest dwellers who maintain their domestic cattle. Suppose your mining activities would interfere with the cattle grazing rights of the tribals and other traditional forest dwellers what would be the consequences? Obviously these people would be denied their traditional rights to graze their cattle and they would be forced to find out an alternative grazing land. As a part of your socio-economic activity you have already accepted the immediate need for developing an alternative grazing land for the cattle. That being so you should not wait for the completion of the mine development activities leading to actual mining operation. If you do that it would mean that these forest dwellers would be put to lot of hardship in locating an alternative grazing area for their cattle for the intervening period. Therefore, what is important is that before you start your mine development activities you must identify, with the approval of the Gram Sabha or the Gram Panchyat as provided for under the Forest Rights Act, the land and develop the same for cattle grazing purposes. If you do that the people would highly appreciate your gesture and it makes lot of difference if you would have done the same thing after mining operation starts. Though it is an inalienable right of the forest dwellers to have grazing land for the cattle the forest dwellers would be very happy not because you have restored their cattle grazing rights but because you have done so without their asking for that and in advance. There are many such activities including gainful economic activities on sustained basis like helping the forest dwellers in goat or sheep rearing which can be implemented along with mine development activities so that by the time you start your mining operation these affected people would already start enjoying the benefits of your economic package. You have the option to do such activities after your mining operation starts. But the impact will be different and definitely the affected people would not be that appreciative of your activities as they would have been if such socio-economic activities could have started along with or before mine development activities. You can take your decision but you must consider whether you would like to have a friendly population around by spending the same amount of money in advance or at a later stage. The choice is yours.

Proposed Mines and Minerals (Development and Regulation) Bill, 2011—Implications of Certain Provisions

The above Bill envisages creation of a Mineral Development Fund to which every lease holder would be required to contribute certain amount @ 26 per cent of the profit after tax in respect of coal mines and in respect of other major minerals such sum would be equal and in addition to the amount of royalty payable on any mineral while the state government will decide the quantum of the amount in respect of minor minerals.

The ostensible purpose behind the above provisions is to improve the socio-economic conditions of the area affected by any mining project. Apparently, it would appear that after making his contribution to the proposed Fund the lessee would not be required to execute any socio-economic activities for the affected people. But the question will remain whether the local people would allow a lessee to operate the mine if they find that no socio-economic developmental activities are visible. In the absence of any prompt socio-economic developmental activities the local people would always blame the lessee as what they would see is that the mining activities are destroying their lands and polluting the area. The net result will be that the project proponent would be under tremendous pressure due to resistance from the local people against the project activities. The only tangible thing the project proponent can do and by all means should do is to train the local employable boys and girls for the skills relevant for the project besides engagement of local people in the unskilled operations.

If the proposed Bill is enacted by the Parliament as an Act the above contingencies are a distinct possibility. The net result will be that in addition to the contribution to the proposed Fund a lessee would be forced to spend additionally large amount of money for meeting the aspirations of the local people and this may result in the mining specially that of small lease holders becoming uneconomic.

Chapter – 12

Health Environment

The caption used at Section 3.7 in the Model TOR at Annexure-B tells you "Occupational Health Environment". However, I have used the caption "Health Environment", the reason being that in this section the EAC deals with the health of not only the mine workers and other employees working in your project but also the health of the local people as local people also become vulnerable to various diseases that are caused due to mining activities and also the activities carried on in the processing plants, if any.

While dealing with the critical segments of the environment like air environment, noise environment, water environment and biological environment I have referred to various health related issues. Therefore, health environment becomes the most critical segment as, if a diseased population is created due to your mining activities it becomes a tragic irony that the very purpose of exploiting the mineral resources for providing a quality life to the people gets defeated. Therefore, health environment should get its prime of place in any industrial activities. If health environment is so critical a segment one might wonder as to why this has not been dealt with in the beginning itself as the first segment of environment. I think it is appropriate that one first gets familiar with the health hazard on account of mining activities which would have adverse impact on air environment, noise environment, water environment and biological environment. Therefore, having realized the impact of these segments of the environment on the health of the people the importance of health environment becomes obvious.

With the above introduction I would proceed to deal with the baseline status, anticipated impacts and proposed mitigating measures. In every item of health environment I would divide the subject into two parts, one relating to the health issues of the local population and the other relating to the health issues of the mine workers and other employees who are directly or indirectly exposed to various occupational health hazard. Thus, while dealing with the baseline data I would do that in two different segments giving first place to the health of the local people and the next segment to the health of the employees without minimizing the importance of the risk of occupational health hazard. I have done this deliberately as when you collect the baseline data relating to health environment of the local people, work out the anticipated impacts of mining activities on the health of the local people and prepare the mitigating measures, the local people get an immediate impression that you have shown great concern for their health. As regards the occupational health of your employees the problem would appear much later when you start mining operation. You are giving a message to the local people that you care for them. The local people specially the forest dwelling people would appreciate your gesture and this is no mean achievement as the goodwill of the people would be already with you.

Let me now deal with the baseline status, anticipated impacts and proposed mitigating measures, just the way the same have been done in respect of other segments in the preceding six Chapters.

Baseline Status

Details to be collected on Health Environment under different headings have been indicated at Item F-Health Environment in the Table 1 (Annexure-B) referred to earlier. Your consultant would be in a position to collect the information and appropriately mention the same in tabular form. Such detailed information in required number of Statements form part of the EIA report submitted before the EAC for consideration at the time of appraisal of the project by the Committee. These are, no doubt, routine information but are very relevant and critical in appraising the impact of your project activities on the health environment and the adequacy of the proposed mitigating measures. It is, therefore, advisable that you collect as much information as are possible.

The Model TOR specifically suggests collection of certain information on medical facilities within the study area at Table 5 (Annexure-B) as indicated in the Annexure attached to the Model TOR. These information would be very helpful for you to adopt the required mitigating measures.

Health of the Local People

The first and the foremost primary data to be collected should be in respect of certain diseases the local people suffer from and the existing health care facilities for treatment of such endemic diseases as also other ailments the local people suffer from. It is a common phenomenon that in certain locality or region certain diseases occur regularly. Also certain diseases are found in a particular locality or region which may or may not be found elsewhere. Such diseases are called endemic and therefore, it must have already got the attention of the State Government which provides treatments for such diseases through the existing primary health centres. For the purpose of our consideration let us take the case of malaria. If you find, through field survey, that malaria is an endemic disease in the core zone and in the buffer zone of your project you ought to mention that in your primary data as also the facilities for the treatment of the disease malaria. Such information can also be obtained from the local health functionaries of the Government.

Along with the primary data on the medical facilities already existing you must also collect the information if there is any pathological facility to test the blood of any suspected malaria patient and if so the existing facility for treating the affected patient. Let us take the worst scenario that there is no primary health centre of the State Government and there is no pathological facility to test blood within the easy reach of the people.

As the core zone and the buffer zone of your project have the endemic disease malaria you must, while collecting the baseline data, ascertain from the local people if any government health staff or any employee of non-government organization, if any, make regular visit for providing medical assistance to the affected people. For the purpose of this book I would assume that no such visit by any health staff takes place.

Occupational Health Environment

Having collected the primary data in respect of the local people you are required to collect the primary data on occupational health environment of your workers including the workers of the contractor, if any, engaged by you in carrying out any project related activities specially the post mine development activities, i.e., actual mining activities. The primary data should be *inter alia*, as under.

You must have already categorized the project activities which are hazardous and which are either not hazardous or only partially hazardous as also the number of workers with the duration of the day who are likely to be exposed to various health hazards. Such information are necessary as these will enable you to anticipate the magnitude of impacts on such workers and employees.

If you are already an existing miner you may list the practices followed by you in your existing projects for assessment of the impact of occupational health and also the medical facilities including the facility for conducting various medical tests. If you are a new miner you would have to find out from other mining projects the practices being followed.

Not that all occupational health ailments are very severe. Section 3.7.2 of the Model TOR at Annexure-B lists certain diseases likely to inflict any person engaged in mining activities. You are required to make a risk assessment to rank the risk to health and list the diseases in order of severity as specific to your project. Therefore, the methodology to be adopted by you in doing this job need to be explained in detail so that the EAC is satisfied that you have done a proper assessment on occupational health related issues.

In case you do not have your own pathological laboratory to conduct various tests, you would like to tie up with some reputed hospital within a reasonable distance for the treatment of your employees including required pathological tests and if so you may indicate the name(s) of such institution(s).

Remember, the well-known cliché that prevention is better than cure. While it may not be possible to prevent completely the occurrences of the occupational health related diseases, you can always make an honest effort to minimize the impact of the diseases that would occur because of the occupation of the mining activities. Therefore, education and training in occupational health and safety are a *sine qua non,* i.e., a binding requirement for you with a view to making the workers and other employees to be fully aware of the consequences of working in a mine. As proper education and related training would result in the workers and other employees adopting various preventive measures it is necessary that you clearly spell out the authority to impart proper education and to conduct the required training.

While a general medical practitioner could be adequate for taking care of the usual health related problems of the local people, for the occupational health related treatment you need a medical doctor who is trained in occupational health related diseases. If your project justifies a full time doctor trained in health related diseases you should appoint a full time doctor who is trained in occupational health related diseases. But if you consider that a full time expert doctor is not necessary in that case you may like tie up with a trained doctor for providing the required medical services. Whatever arrangement you would like to make needs to be clearly spelt out.

Anticipated Impacts

Section 3.7.2 of the Model TOR at Annexure-B gives an illustrative lists of possible diseases to which anybody working in mining activities is likely to be exposed. You would have noticed that occurrences of certain diseases are quite common occupational illness in a mining project. So you would think that such diseases would take place and therefore required treatment to be provided. However, it is not so simple as it might appear to be. Let us take two scenarios based on the life of your mining project.

Suppose your mining project has a life of, say, fifteen years. During this period some of the workers might develop hearing defect. If such hearing defect is not so acute as resulting in complete loss of hearing the affected person might get back his normal hearing power in due course. But there are certain diseases like lung cancer, tuberculosis or some other diseases as mentioned in Section 3.7.2 (*ibid*) the occurrences of which might be detected long after the concerned worker has left your organization. It would not be humane to think that you are not responsible for the disease as it was not detected during the period when the concerned person was your employee. Therefore, only an expert doctor trained in occupational health related issues would be in a position to list the adverse impacts due to mining activities. The list of adverse impacts should be as exhaustive as practicable and obviously as specific to your project.

Once your are ready with the likely adverse impacts on your workers you would be in a position to plan and execute the required mitigating measures.

Likewise, you need to anticipate the impacts of your mining activities on the health of the local people. If there would be human habitation close by you can not avoid flying dust, either from the mine or from the mined minerals while under transport in trucks, falling on such inhabited areas. Therefore, depending on the speed and direction of wind the local people getting affected by dust related health problems can not be ruled out.

If there is a water body close to your core zone and if during rainy season various pollutants as a result of your mining activities flow down and get mixed with the water, the aqua-fauna, if any, would get impacted. If the local people eats such contaminated fish the pollutants get into the bio-system of such people which would have adverse impact on their health.

Once you have listed the anticipated impacts on the health of your workers and other employees as also on the health of the local people you would be in a position to prepare the required mitigating measures. In the following paragraphs I would explain the likely mitigating measures both for the local people and for your employees.

Suggested Mitigating Measures

In Section 3.7.3 of the Model TOR at Annexure-B you would no doubt notice the suggested mitigating measures. As these suggested mitigating measures are not specific to any particular project, you would have to select those measures relevant for your project. It is quite possible that you may have to, using your imaginative power, take certain mitigating measures which do not find a mention in the suggested list (*ibid*). I would broadly give a brief idea about some of the mitigating measures and a rationale thereof. I would start with the mitigating measures for the local people followed by such measures for your workers and employees.

I have already taken that malaria is the endemic disease in the area. Once a person is inflicted with the disease the only option left is to provide the medicine which is supplied free by the government. You can as well take the responsibility of supplying the medicine to the affected people. As prevention is always better than cure you may adopt the preventive measures so that the people are not affected by this disease. As mosquito is the carrier of the germ of malaria the preventive step would include use of such devices which protect the humans from mosquito bite. While in the urban area the municipal bodies resort to fumigation periodically to kill the mosquito and to ensure that there are no mosquito breeding grounds, the same (fumigation) is not a practicable and feasible solution in the forest areas as also in the rural areas in general. Therefore, use of mosquito net while sleeping is the most effective preventive measure. Nowadays good quality and user friendly mosquito nets are available. Unlike in the past when the mosquito net used to have a netted cloth on the four sides with the ceiling cloth consisting of a non-netted loin cloth like fabric which did not allow air circulation making the sleeper under such a mosquito net uncomfortable specially in the summer time, the present day mosquito net which is a mixture of synthetic and cotton fabric, if not fully synthetic, is more comfortable as the sides as also the ceiling are fully netted making it comfortable to use. You can supply such mosquito nets to the people residing in areas which have shown more incidence of malaria cases, to start with, followed by similar action in other areas. If the expenditure of mosquito nets is taken as a part of your project cost you would never feel that you are incurring huge expenditure while the people would remain grateful to you for such a benevolent gesture. The people can also be advised not to allow any space in the vicinity of their houses to have accumulated stagnant water which is a very ideal breeding ground for the mosquito just like the municipal bodies would advise the residents not to allow the ornamental plants and flower pots in their houses to breed mosquito. You can exercise the option also to periodically fumigate the likely breeding grounds of mosquito.

Before the start of the mining operation you must have made a survey of the health status of the people listing various diseases. This will be the baseline status of the health of the people. Accordingly, you may take the preventive and curative measures for such diseases. A periodical survey in three years or so period can be conducted to see the impact of the mitigating measures you have taken. For example, if the incidence of the cases of malaria shows a downward trend, if not completely eliminated, you would be justified to conclude that the mitigating measures taken by you (supply of mosquito nets) have started showing results. It may also happen that some new diseases might have occurred in the meantime. This need to be investigated and a trained doctor would be in a position to tell you the reason for such new diseases, if any. For example, if the pollutants of your mining activities have flowed into the water body close by and if the people use such water for drinking purposes they would develop stomach ailments besides other ailments. Likewise, contaminated fish, if consumed, could result in some other disease. Even there could be dust related disease. In such a situation you have to take preventive measures besides curative measures once some diseases have occurred. The preventive measure could be provision for safe drinking water.

There are certain Public Health Programmes and government machinery is involved in implementing such programme. Eradication of polio is a national programme and by now, thanks to coverage by Television and newspapers, the phrase "Polio Sunday" is quite well-known and government fixes every month a particular Sunday throughout the nation for administrating polio vaccine (drop) to the children of certain age group. Likewise, there are some other preventive action like vaccination of children against certain diseases in future. You can be an active partner in implementing such national programmes in your project area.

To make your effort visible to the local people, providing medical facilities to such people through a mobile van would be an effective method to gain instant goodwill of the local people. This mobile van can be used for collecting blood sample for pathological test to identify the cases of malaria or other diseases.

While dealing with the mitigating measures for your workers it is important that you communicate to the workers and other employees the risk of various diseases to which they would be exposed unless preventive measures are taken. I will give some examples to highlight the need for such communication, induction training for workers, education and training for the workers and the steps to enforce the various preventive measures so as to minimize the impact of occupational health issues.

When a mine worker goes inside the mine pit use of helmet is made compulsory. Even for other activities use of helmet is made compulsory. You should not assume that every worker you have engaged is aware of the risk of not using a helmet. A particular person might be using helmet because he finds that his co-workers are also using helmets. At the induction training stage the workers would be explained in a straight language that if someone does not wear a helmet and if some stone piece or some other hard material falls on his head what would be the nature of injury to his head. The workers will immediately realize the implication and your job becomes that much easier.

Education about the occupational health risk can be an effective mitigating measures to prevent the occurrences of such health risks and even if such risks occur the impact could be kept to the minimum and manageable level with medical treatment. For example, to avoid the impact of noise and air pollution use of personal protective measures for the ear and the nose must be made compulsory and the workers can be explained that if one does not use a ear plug he might lose his capacity of hearing completely. Likewise, if nose mask is not used there would be certain diseases like silicosis caused due to inhalation of dust and may be you have to tell the worker that this is a disease of your lungs so that he understands the seriousness of the disease.

There is another risk of inhaling radon gas specially in a uranium mine perhaps without the knowledge of the worker. There could be other health risks also. For example, in an underground mine a worker would feel thirsty and unless he carries safe drinking water in a container he would be tempted to drink any water that would be coming through the earth thinking that this is pure water without any contamination. In a case of uranium mine such water could contain radon gas and, therefore, unknowingly he might be affected by radium related complications. Therefore, it becomes your responsibility to ensure that the underground mine workers carry required quantity of safe drinking water.

Another common adverse impact caused by noise you might be routinely ignoring because you never perhaps thought that the efficiency of your workers including those in the supposedly safe office building would get affected. Noise beyond a certain level will adversely affect the efficiency of even an office worker. This can be appreciated if I ask you to provide a small cabin which is reasonably unaffected by the surrounding noise and another cabin which is not so protected from the noise you would notice that over a period of time the efficiency of the person working in the cabin which is not affected by the surrounding noise is better than that of his counterpart in the other cabin. Therefore, ergonomic study is important to know if the noise is continuous and is at a high level. Basically, it (ergonomic study) means a study of the impact of noise on the efficiency of your workers and employees in an environment with high noise level. So it is more to your advantage as you can take adequate preventive measures to ensure that the efficiency of your workers and other employees does not fall below the expected level.

At the cost of repetition I would advise you to appreciate the fact that the time tested maxim *prevention is better than cure* is more relevant in case of occupational health risks which are a certainty and more so in a mining project where the workers are constantly exposed to the possibility of getting infected with serious diseases some of which might occur later and, may be, several years after they have left your organization.

You should not think that by taking adequate preventive measures that include use of personal protective equipment like ear plug or helmet things will move smoothly. It may not be so always. As there could be some recalcitrant workers who might use the personal protective equipments you have provided while entering the mine pit but later on he might remove some equipment like ear plug while using the helmet thereby deceiving even his supervisor as it might not occur to him (supervisor) that a particular worker has removed the ear plugs subsequently because absence of the helmet is detected in no time while the absence of a tiny equipment like an earplug is not easily noticed. Therefore, constant check is essential. Likewise, a worker might not take the water you have supplied while going underground. For such a recalcitrant worker punitive action like denial of wages for not wearing personal protective equipment could be effective.

Another most important step is to maintain the health record of each and every worker and employee and specially the persons who are directly engaged in mining and related activities. Some of the diseases might become manifest in future and it could manifest many years after the person has left your organization. Since, the diseases are on account of exposure to the hazardous activities in your mine it becomes your moral responsibility to maintain the record for future reference. Such health record must contain the findings of periodical health check up which should also be part of the mitigating measures in providing appropriate treatment in future when the disease surfaces.

There are certain financial involvement which, as an employer, you can not escape. You would yourself appreciate that apart from the financial compensation under the various labour laws for injuries or casualties etc. there are certain other expenses involved in the payment for conducting various tests and for providing treatment and such expenses need be borne by your organization.

There has to be a safety committee and its function should be properly demarcated and any recommendations by this committee for the safety of the workers and for the health of the worker must be given due consideration. A medical doctor trained in occupational health must be member of this committee.

As it may not be possible for you to provide medical treatment for all diseases caused due to mining activities as not being financially feasible to establish and maintain a hospital, you may have to have an arrangement with a nearby reputed hospital for providing medical assistance in deserving cases.

All the mitigating measures including those for providing medical assistance would have financial implications. Therefore, there should be adequate budget provisions for taking mitigating measures relating to occupational health issues which would be part of the total budget for all environmental issues. If you take such budget provisions as a part of your total budget provisions for your project activities you would never feel that the expenses on health environment have become a burden on your project. It is only when you consider the expenses on health and other environmental issues in isolation of the cost incurred on wages of the workers, cost of fuel, cost of repair and maintenance of equipment and machinery etc you feel that this is an additional burden without realizing that the expenditure on health and other environmental related issues is insignificant compared to the total cost of the project including the annual expenditure that you would be incurring on your project.

I would think that with an imaginative approach and a human face you can always find finances for such mitigating measures without feeling the pinch thereof.

Chapter – 13

Miscellaneous Addenda

In this chapter I will be dealing with certain aspects of environmental issues which, though dealt with in different chapters of this book specially the immediately preceding seven chapters, require special emphasis as, if certain critical requirements are not taken care of adequately all mitigating measures taken by a miner could prove to be disastrous. Chapters 4 and 5 of the Model TOR have highlighted the requirement of certain activities which a miner would necessarily comply with. I would only very briefly explain why such activities are so essential while leaving it to the judgment of the miner to take the required course of action as specific to his project area. But I would definitely utter a word of caution that the steps suggested in the above two chapters in the Model TOR should be given utmost consideration. In the following paragraphs I would explain the justification for the suggested course of action.

Risk Assessment and Disaster Management Plan

Any mining activity, whether underground or opencast, involves risk of various types that warrant appropriate disaster management plan. Take the case of an underground mine. With all available geological knowledge about the composition and structure of the rocks and the soils as also the seismic knowledge about the area the possibility of roof-fall inside the mine can not be completely ruled out. In the same way, surface subsidence and inundation of the area are a distinct possibility. The disaster in the Chas Nala Coal Mine in the district of Dhanbad of Jharkhand State in late 1970s is a glaring example of the likely disaster of high magnitude. The latest case, similar to the Chas Nala Coal Mine disaster, is in Chile where 33 miners remained trapped underground for more than two months in San Jose copper and gold mine in the Atacama desert region of Chile during August–October 2010. The effort by the Chilean Government could, no doubt, result in saving the precious life of the miners. I would not hazard a definitive guess that such a disaster could take place in any mine in India. Nevertheless, such incidents are facts of life.

There is a lesson or two that could be learnt by any miner in India. Why I am referring to the accident that occurred in the Chilean mine is that many of the miners specially the younger ones might not have heard about the tragic accident that took place in Chas Nala coal mine more than 30 years back. I presume that all miners might not have read the media coverage with same interest about the episode of the San Jose copper and gold mine in Chile. I have, therefore, decided to quote three news items published in *The Statesman* dated 15th October, 2010 and 18th October, 2010 and the paper's editorial dated 15th October, 2010, all in its Delhi edition below for the benefit of all miners. While two news items have emanated from the globally well-known News Agency Reuters, the third news item has been provided by the Press Trust of India (PTI).

"CHILLING RESCUE

Chile's Stark Message to the World

YES, indeed. Chile "is capable of doing great things," as its President, Sebastian Pinera, proudly boasted to the world on Wednesday. Never was Barack Obama's chant—"it can be done"—made in a different context, more resonant. The rescue of the trapped miners is a great moment in the country's history, a profound chapter in man's struggle for survival. As the 33 miners reunite with their families, one must marvel at the wonders that technology can achieve as the story evolved from despair to hope to the eventual rescue. The operation, that could have dragged for weeks, was largely accomplished in a matter of days. Yet amidst the overwhelming national optimism and the emotional outpourings, the cause of he disaster ~ which mercifully didn't lead to a tragedy ~ ought not to be overshadowed. As a nerve-racking drama comes to a merciful end, the owners of San Jose copper mine in the Atacama region must bear responsibility for the nightmare of the trapped. So too must the government for its failure to regulate activity in a mine with successively adverse records of safety. No fewer than 180 miners were injured in 2006. Between 2004 and 2006, the mine was fined on 42 occasions for violating safety regulations. And the government had ordered its temporary closure in 2007 in the face of miners' complains about inadequate safety. Both the company and the government had let the miners down, and literally so. Mining is a lucrative enterprise for companies but an extremely perilous profession for miners. This is the stark dichotomy of the industry across the world. And in the anxiety to thrive as a corporate enterprise, safety rules are either given the short shrift or breached. All or most of the 33 Chilean miners will in all likelihood get back to the grind; a livelihood is as much a part of one's struggle for survival. Yet as they savour the renewed lease of life as it were, the country must now take a call on the inherent dangers under the ground. And 35 years after Chas Nala, there is a message for India as well. And not least because of the renewed thirst for natural resources. The perils beneath have been beamed into drawing rooms the world over.

(Editorial, The Statesman, Delhi Edition dated 15.10.2010)

CHILE MINERS GO BACK TO THEIR 'TOMBS'

COPIAPO (CHILE), 17 OCT: Some of the 33 miners in northern Chile who were rescued last week after 69 days trapped underground will return on Sunday to the mine that almost became their tomb.

The mines, their families and friends are set to attend a morning religious ceremony at the mouth of the San Jose copper and gold mine from which they were rescued on Wednesday in a painstakingly planned and perfectly executed operation that was watched live on television around the world.

The men were trapped for more than two months at 2,050 feet underground before being rescued. The ceremony, expected to trigger strong emotions, will seek to honour the miners' solidarity and determination to survive. "It's going to be difficult, but we know we can take it,"Omer Reygadas, a widower who was the 17th miner to be rescued, said of the planned service.

Another rescued worker, Jose Henriquez, the group's prayer leader who asked for 33 bibles to be sent down while they awaited rescue, became the first to go back and visit the mine on Saturday. He said he wanted to get to know the area near the mine known as "Camp Hope", where family members gathered to pray and await news about their husbands, sons and fathers.

"I came to look in my locker to make sure I didn't leave anything behind," he joked.

Ending what many felt was a spiritual mission, families of the miners on Thursday packed up the tents they had lived in for the previous two months and prepared for life outside the intense fellowship that the camp provided.

They descended on the barren land around the San Jose mine after the collapse on August 5, fearful that all the miners were dead but refusing to give up. Many of the relatives are deeply religious and some prayed almost around the clock. On Saturday, three days after being pulled from the depths, the 33 started removing the sunglasses provided to protect their eyes after so much time in near darkness.

REUTERS *(Statesman, 18 October, 2010)*

RECOVERY AN INSPIRATIONAL STORY: OBAMA

WASHINGTON, 14 OCT: President Barack Obama has said that the Chilean mine rescue operation is a tremendous inspirational story as he watched live the great human rescue mission to evacuate 33 works trapped 2,041-foot underearth.

"This is obviously something that's captivated the world's attention and this rescue is a tribute not only to the determination of the rescue workers and the Chilean government, but also the unity and resolve of the Chilean people who have inspired the world," Obama told reporters at the White House.

PTI *(The Statesman, Delhi edition dated 15.10.2010)*

FREE MINERS ARE FLOODED WITH VARIOUS JOB OFFERS, ADVERTISING DEALS, BOOK AND FILM CONTRACTS

Rescued Miners Recover, Bask in New Celeb Status

REUTERS

COPIAPO (Chile) 14 OCT: Chile's 33 newly rescued miners recovered from their ordeal on Thursday while also pondering the celebrity status they have gained following a more than two-month entrapment deep under a remote desert.

Most of the miners were found in surprisingly good health considering that they had been stuck in a wet, hot, collapsed mine tunnel since August 5.

The men were resting in a hospital after being hoisted to the surface in a rescue operation watched by hundreds of millions worldwide. One of the miners had pneumonia and was being treated with antibiotics.

In a complicated but flawless operation under the South American nation's far northern Atacama desert, the miners were hauled out one-by-one through 2,050 feet of rock in a metal capsule little wider than a man's shoulders.

With much of the world transfixed by the rescue, celebrations erupted in Chile. The miners set a world record for survival underground and were welcomed as national heroes.

It took less than 22 hours from the time the first miner was brought to the surface until the last one was pulled to freedom late on Wednesday. Abut 2-1/2 hours later, the last of six rescuers who had gone down the shaft to help the miners get out also emerged from the gold and copper mine, and the operation was complete.

"It's so incredible that they all made it out alive" said 51-year-old Luis Pina, a miner, hugging a perfet stranger as he celebrated in the main square in Copiapo where thousands of people danced into the early hours, cheering and waiving red, white and blue Chilean flags.

"We hope that some of them, two or three, can be released this afternoon," said Jorge Montes, an official at the hospital in Copiapo, where the miners were being treated and where President Sebastian Pinera visited them on Thursday.

"They've been in a situation of stress for two months... Nonetheless, most of them are coming along perfectly well," Montes said. Families were being allowed to visit in shifts.

Still wearing dark glasses to protect their eyes from glare after being trapped so long in near darkness, the miners received an invitation from Pinera to visit the presidential palace towards the end of the month. Pinera, a soccer fan who also plays the game, challenged the miners to a match against a team made up of his cabinet.

"The team that wins will stay in La Moneda (presidential palace). The team that loses goes back to the mine," he joked. Despite the suffering they went through, and the emotional stress some will still face, the previously unknown miners could now have plenty to look forward to if they take up the offers open to them. Among a flood of invitations and gifts, Real Madrid and Manchester United have invited the miners – many of whom are avid soccer fans - to watch them play in Europe. A flamboyant local singer-turned-businessman has given them $10,000 each, while Apple boss Steve Jobs has sent them all a latest iPod and a Greek firm has offered an islands tour.

Most of the miners are unlikely to return to their old employment, with various job offers, advertising deals, and book and film contracts coming their way. Pinera, whose popularity has risen over his handling of the crisis, was at the San Jose mine in the Atacama desert to greet each man as he emerged and plans to host them at his palace in the capital Santiago. "I hand the shift over to you and hope this never happens again," the last miner out, Luis Urzua, 54, told Pinera.

Having suffered a massive earth-quake in February that killed more than 500 people, Chileans were euphoric about the happy ending to their latest challenge and proud of the technology that went into the successful rescue.

Church bells and car horns sounded across Chile in celebration, while family members and well-wishers both wept and laughed for joy outside the mine.

When the mine caved in on August 5, the men were all thought dead in yet another of Latin America's litany of mining accidents. But rescuers found them 17 days later with a bore hole the width of a grapefruit. That tiny hole became an umbilical cord used to pass hydration gels, water and food to keep them alive until a bigger space could be bore to bring them up."

There is lot to be learnt from the Chilean experience. That the instincts for survival are common and strong in not only humans but also in animals is well known. But it was an astonishing surprise that 33 miners could survive one of the most severe ordeals for more than two months after remaining trapped more than 2000 feet underground. The saying "survival of the fittest" has once been proved beyond doubt.

The question is whether man's inherent desire to survive could have saved the miners. Had it been so, the trapped miners in the Chas Nala coal mine would have also survived even though at the time the newspapers had reported that some of the trapped miners were alive for few days and that assumption was made on the basis that some of the miners could grow beard which testified beyond doubt that some of them were alive for few days as no hair could grow on a dead person. It is the technology marvel that saved the 33 Chilean miners. After the accident that took place on 5th August, 2010 a belief was gaining ground that the miners might be dead but to the great relief of the Chilean people, their Government and specially the families of the trapped miners the "rescuers found them 17 days later with a bore hole the width of a grape fruit. That tiny hole became an umbilical cord used to pass hydration gels, water and food to keep them alive until a bigger space could be bored to bring them up." The successful effort in Chile to bring back the miners alive more than two months after being trapped underground only underscores that there is no substitute for employing state-of-the-art technology that would ensure scientific mining and which would also eliminate any chance of serious accident though there could be unforeseen circumstances due to the nature of underground rocks and soils that might still result in serious accidents.

Another lesson the Indian miners could learn and that is, to make any accident victim miner to keep up his spirit. The newspaper reports hint at the possibility that some of the trapped miners might go back to the same mine for their livelihood as they know it very well that with all such possible hazards, still working in a mine would ensure sufficient financial compensation for a reasonably comfortable life. So the spirit of the miners was no doubt up and here I would refer to two humorous comments, one by the Chilean President Mr. Pinera and the other by the last miner out Mr. Luis Urzua.

While inviting the miners to play a soccer game the President joked "the team that wins will stay in La Moneda (Presidential Palace). The team that loses goes back to the mine." One can very appreciatively enjoy the humorous comment of Luis Urzua when he told the President "I hand over the shift over to you and hope this never happens again". The hidden message in the utterances of Mr. Louis Urzua is that let not such deadly happenings repeat and this is a clear and loud message for the mine owner and also the country's Government that nobody should play with the life of an innocent miner whose only fault, if it could be called a fault, was that he had taken such risk in working underground so that he might be in a position to see cheerful smile on the faces of his near and dear ones.

A miner in India could pause for a moment and visualize what would have been the consequences of such a tragic happenings in his mine. It needs no emphasis that the miner must prepare the disaster management plan keeping in mind the age old maxim that *"hope for the best but be prepared for the worst"*.

It would be relevant in this context if I could narrate my personal experience of visiting underground mines during the last about 30 years or so.

I visited three underground mines of Bharat Gold Mines Limited (BGML) a Government of India undertaking (since closed), situated in Kolar Gold Field (KGF), in the State of Karnataka, the West Bokaro Colliery of TISCO and one underground mine of Uranium Corporation of India Limited, a Government of India undertaking, both in the State of Jharkhand. While I never felt scared visiting the underground mines travelling through the narrow tunnel and witnessing the mine workers working in the colliery as also in the uranium mine, I could not but be quite nervous initially while I was at the depth of 2 km. in the BGML mine and I preferred not to go further down as at that point of time the mine was the deepest in the world. Since, I was comparatively young at that time and with the helmet on and senior officers of BGML accompanying me I was psychologically assured that I would not face any mishap. But the tunnel that could run several kilometres had a steel structure supporting the roof rocks and in many places we had to almost bow down as the steel structure was in a bending position because of the heavy loads of the rocks. But since as a dealing Director and subsequently Joint Secretary to the Ministry I had made it a point to see the working conditions in underground mine and therefore I took all the visits as a part of my official duty. The visit to the underground uranium mine was during 2006-07, and long after my retirement from service, as an independent Director on the Board of Directors of the company.

Perhaps there would be no parallel in any mine in India to the underground tunnel of several kilometres like that of BGML, but the fact is that the possibility of land slide or the overhead rock and soil collapsing can not be totally eliminated. Hence, my considered view is that the disaster management plan in respect of any mine, whether opencast or underground, is essential so that the miner is not faced with a situation which he is unable to tackle.

If mining involves blasting operations, storage of explosives in a well protected magazine is essential. Even then such well protected explosives could, at times, result in dangerous explosion either through sabotage or even in a natural way. Surface fire specially during summer season is a common phenomenon in certain areas. If somebody wants to have a glimpse of fire in a coal mine one can pay a visit to a certain colliery in Dhanbad district during night time. A miner would be using fuel oil for running the vehicles and machinery besides storing engine oil, etc. and occurrences of fire caused by such materials can not be completely ruled out.

A miner must, therefore, make an assessment of the likely risks. Having made such an assessment he must be ready in advance with a plan to manage such disaster. It is, in a way, a mitigating measure, a preventive one at that, but in mining industry this is called Disaster Management Plan. It means that a miner would adopt scientific mining method so that the mine benches do not fail. Construction of mine benches as per the standard practices specific to the particular deposits would avoid disaster like surface subsidence or roof-fall. So it does not need any emphasis that a miner should adopt scientific mining method so as to ensure that certain disasters do not occur. As I have said earlier, with all due precaution the possibility of any natural calamity can not be totally eliminated. But such a possibility should not deter the miner in preparing an appropriate disaster management plan.

While making presentation before the EAC as a part of the procedure for obtaining prior environmental clearance it is advisable that the miner lists the likely risks and the corresponding disaster management plan. If the miner has any such plan in operation in any of his operating mining projects he could highlight those measures to convince the EAC that the miner has, indeed, applied his mind to such critical and distinct possibilities.

Environment Management Plan and Post-Project Monitoring Programme

I am sure the miner has taken note of what have been explained in this chapter. If he has done so I am confident that the members of the EAC would have no occasion to take a negative view on his proposal. I also assume that the consultant has prepared a reasonably well EIA Report and the EMP. What is now required is to have an institutional mechanism to implement various mitigating measures including risk assessment and disaster management plan. Assuming that the miner has an institutional mechanism in place that is carrying on its assigned duties or managing the environmental plan, he must also have a system of monitoring the implementation programme which would necessarily cover the post-project monitoring activities. I would, in the sequel, explain various activities that a miner would take so as to ensure that the EMP does not remain only on paper.

Irrespective of the size of the organization there has to be a designated administrative set up and a technical set-up. Whether the manpower of such a unit should be whole time employees exclusively for the unit or employees who, in the best judgment of the project proponent, would be competent to do the job in addition to their normal duties, is to be decided by the project proponent. Having regards to the importance of protecting the biological environment it would be advisable to have an expert on forest and wildlife to be made solely responsible for protecting the biological environment. Perhaps it may not be required to have a full time young employee. But should the project proponent require a full time expert on forest and wildlife the possibility of appointing somebody on deputation from the State or Central Forest authority should be explored as such an arrangement is ideal as the project proponent could extend the period of deputation if required or taking a new expert on deputation if the existing expert is found not upto the mark. But taking a serving government officer on deputation may not be financially desirable. Apart from the salary and other allowances that would be payable to such a deputationist officer there could be some unreasonable demands from such deputationist government officer. I would strongly suggest that the project proponent should not put himself to the most likely undue demands of such a deputationist. By my own experience of working under the State Government and the Central Government and dealing with State and Central Public Sector Undertakings I would not advocate engagement of a serving Government servant on deputation as the preferred option. It is, therefore, advisable to appoint some expert who has worked under the government and who has either retired or is prepared to take voluntary retirement before actual superannuation. Such an employee would be a valuable asset for the project proponent as with his past experience he would be in a better position to plan and implement various measures to protect the biological environment. Wherever, assistance from the government is required it would be easier for him as he would be fully conversant with the government system and working. Thus what I am suggesting is that this particular unit should be headed either by a full time person or a part time person who could be an outsider or one of the serving officers of the project proponent depending on his assessment except that the person to be made accountable for protecting biological environment must necessarily be an expert on forest and wildlife as I have emphasized above.

Needless to say that the officer as Head of the unit must have a complete picture of the area where you have to implement various mitigating measures. The reason is that unless the head of the unit referred to in the preceding paragraph knows the details of the mitigating measures and the particular areas where such mitigating measures would have to be implemented it would not be possible for him to effectively monitor the progress of the work. Therefore, the project proponent must have an environment map of 1:50,000 scale (as suggested in the Model TOR). Such a map would indicate all surface features showing mine workings, de-forested area (if any), dump sites (with height) and other relevant details. For example, if land restoration works are to be executed after a particular mine pit is exhausted the officer concerned must know the locations of various mine pits and the sequence in which the mine pits are to be worked as also the contour of the surrounding areas so that he can plan in advance the land restoration works. Likewise, if afforestation and development of green belt are to be executed the area should be properly indicated on the map. If things are done without any properly drawn up plan there would be lot of confusion and in the process he would find it very difficult to implement various mitigating measures and it is quite possible that the project proponent might have to stay in the area for a longer period beyond the life of the project to execute the mitigating measures and the project proponent would, no doubt, agree that in the process he would be creating avoidable complications entailing unjustified additional expenses.

Another important critical element is that the mitigating measures the project proponent has planned in advance for certain anticipated adverse impacts might not be adequate. Some of the mitigating measures might need mid-course correction to suit the situation which even with due diligence exercise the project proponent might not have anticipated while planning the mitigating measures. I will give one example to make it easy for the project proponent to understand. It is quite common that mining activities are likely to interfere with an existing water course and the project proponent has to divert the water course in a way that the water course avoids mining area while ultimately merging in the same water course at a different point or in a different water body, if any. While preparing the new water course he might have thought that it would not inundate the areas on either side of the new water course creating difficulties for the land owners in cultivating such land for growing agricultural crops. Normally he would not think that at a certain point the soil is so soft that the water course would find it easy to go downward and make a hole, may be, a small size water body, which would interfere with the normal flow of water, i.e., the accumulated water might not follow the previously planned water course. If the water level goes up the surrounding areas would be inundated and may be completely submerged making the same unfit for cultivation purpose. In such a situation he has to plan an alternative water course to regulate the water flow. Thus, in such an eventuality the project proponent has to make some mid-course correction. It is not his fault as he could not anticipate such a contingency in normal circumstances.

While doing plantation work in different areas including development of green belt between the outer boundary of the lease hold area and the nearest water bodies the project proponent might have projected survival rate, for example, of 75 per cent of the planted species. While monitoring the growth rate of plantations specially in the reclaimed areas he might notice that the survival rate is only 50 per cent. Therefore, he has to find out the reason for lower survival rates and accordingly take corrective measures to ensure that the survival rate does not fall below the anticipated 75 per cent.

I am not elaborating other suggestions given in Chapter 5 of the Model TOR. If certain things are relevant for his project the project proponent has to take action accordingly. For example, mining in the State of Goa generally intersects groundwater and therefore hydrological monitoring becomes essential.

For implementing any mitigating measures provision of funds becomes an important element. It is possible that the anticipated expenditure could exceed the original budget provision while implementing various measures including modified measures in certain areas where mid-course correction warrants such modifications. Therefore, appropriate budget provisions should be made through replenishment.

There are some tables added at the end of the Model TOR at Annexure-B for submitting certain information as a part of the EIA Report and the EMP. If the project proponent studies these tables carefully he would find that these are routine but essential information which would help the members of EAC to assess the magnitude of the environmental problems of his project and while recommending his proposal for grant of prior environmental clearance the EAC would suggest certain mitigating measures besides putting some restrictive specific conditions. My advice is that the project proponent should try to give as much information as feasible and possible to collect. In the absence of adequate information the expert members may ask for certain clarifications which the project proponent might find difficult to give.

Chapter – 14

Role of the Stakeholders

Environment in its wider ramifications encompasses not only the physical and social environment in which we and all living things reside but also the day-to-day existence of any living being including human being and the animal. Therefore, it is difficult to pinpoint any one particular agency to be the stakeholder in maintaining a healthy and clean physical environment. Without perhaps being aware every individual member of a household is doing his part to keep the house environment neat and clean. Thus, one of the daily chores is to sweep the floor of the house and keep it clean and dry, to keep all the water outlets including the washbasins and sinks clean and germ-free, so that we can effectively eliminate the possibilities of any contamination. We never forget to keep the daily generated household waste in the garbage bag in a closed bin and get it deposited in the nearby municipal bin with the belief that the municipal agency will remove such accumulated waste for final disposal. Even a child is told how not to make the house dirty thereby a child as it grows up learns the need for and the art of keeping the house clean for a healthy atmosphere in the house. If we extend this concept of healthy and clean environment in a household to the area outside, we would like to have the roads and other land areas to be clean as well. It is a different matter altogether that our role as a member of a particular household changes completely as the responsibility for keeping the roads and the outside lands clean becomes a collective one. Here, the society, of which every individual is a part, is collectively responsible for ensuring that everybody makes his own contribution in keeping the physical environment healthy and clean (for example, by not spitting, urinating or otherwise defecating here and there) as he would have done in keeping his own household healthy and clean to live in.

In this book, I have been dealing with the environmental issues thrown up due to mining activities in remote areas, usually forest area, inhabited generally by a section of the people who have been traditional forest dwellers for their sustenance for generations. As I have earlier mentioned, I would be referring to only the mineral iron ore which generally occurs in remote forest areas which are also the dwelling places of the tribal people and certain other traditional forest dwellers and therefore, we must divert our attention from the traditional habitations of people other than the tribals and the traditional forest dwellers.

The forest area in which mineral occurs is also the habitation of the animals, birds besides the forest dwellers. The tribals and other forest dwellers have been living there for generations in complete harmony with the nature. The animals and the birds and other fauna have been equally freely living in such forest areas. Thus, two sets of living beings, the tribals and other traditional forest dwellers, and the animals, birds and other fauna, have their independent ways of surviving without interfering with each others' style of living. In such a scenario, the men and the animals are the only stakeholders and they know how to maintain the environment for their own sustenance. They do not require the help of any external agency to provide them a liveable physical environment. Thus the co-existence of the humans and the animals is perfect.

The whole scenario gets a sea change after the miner encroaches upon the so far unfettered right of a particular lifestyle and movement of the forest dwellers, both human and animals. Therefore, the responsibility of maintaining the environment of the area, where mining activities can continue with nil or least interference with the normal life style of the forest dwellers and the wildlife, would devolve naturally on the miner as, but for his mining activities, there would have been no environmental problems. This brings in the question of the paramount responsibility of some authority who can guide and regulate the mining activities and the related other activities like transportation of the mined minerals etc. It goes without saying that state is the most competent authority to ensure that ecological balance is maintained by effectively regulating the mining and related activities. Therefore, the Government, both Central and State, becomes the natural choice for the job. In a federal country like ours, the Central Government in the Ministry of Environment and Forests (MoEF) thus becomes the most important stakeholder in maintaining the environment. Without minimizing their importance and role, the miner himself, various Non-Governmental Organizations (NGOs), and the local people are no mean stakeholders in keeping the environment healthy and clean. In the following sections starting with the role of the MoEF, I have made an attempt to critically and objectively examine the role played by the stakeholders. While doing so, I would also suggest as to how the stakeholders can make positive contribution with a view to ensuring a healthy and clean physical environment for all living things.

Ministry of Environment and Forests (MoEF)

The MoEF is the competent authority to grant prior environmental clearance for any mining project. The Ministry is also responsible for grant of permission for utilizing forest land for non-forest purposes. A miner must get these two clearances, i.e., prior environmental clearance and permission for use of forest land for non-forest purposes, if any (commonly known as forestry clearance), which are also the obligatory statutory requirements without which no mining activities can be executed. The MoEF on its part, after due deliberation and following a transparent procedure, while sanctioning the two clearances (prior environmental and forestry clearances), puts number of conditions with a view to ensuring that the environment of the area in all its ramifications are protected. The MoEF thus, as the most important stakeholder, discharges its primary statutory obligations in so far as grant or rejection of any application (s) for prior environmental clearance and permission for use of forest land for non-forest purposes, if any. Since the minerals would be located in remote forest areas, the MoEF has the dual responsibility to conserve the forest while granting prior environmental clearance for mining projects. The ministry exercises the power of granting prior environmental clearance under the provisions of the Environment (Protection) Act, 1986 and the Rules framed thereunder. In order that a transparent process which is subject to judicial scrutiny is followed in the grant of environmental clearance for mining projects, the Ministry has issued a Notification vide Notification No. S.O. 1533 (E) dated 14.09.2006 the implications of which have been explained in Chapter 2. For the benefit of the miners and a convenient and instant reading the following part of the Notification in the beginning is extracted below:

> "S.O. 1533(E) Whereas, a draft notification under sub-rule (3) of Rule 5 of the Environment (Protection) Rules, 1986 for imposing certain restrictions and prohibitions on new projects or activities, or on the expansion or modernization of existing projects or activities based on their potential environmental impacts as indicated in the Schedule to the notification, being

undertaken in any part of India, unless prior environmental clearance has been accorded in accordance with the objectives of National Environment Policy as approved by the Union Cabinet on 18th May, 2006 and the procedure specified in the notification, by the Central Government or the State or Union territory Level Environment Impact Assessment Authority (SEIAA), to be constituted by the Central Government in consultation with the State Government or the Union territory Administration concerned under sub-section (3) of Section 3 of the Environment (Protection) Act, 1986 for the purpose of this notification, was published in the Gazette of India, Extraordinary, Part II, section 3, sub-section (ii) vide number S.O. 1324 (E) dated the 15th September, 2005 inviting objections and suggestions from all persons likely to be affected thereby within a period of sixty days from the date on which copies of Gazette containing the said notification were made available to the public;

And whereas, copies of the said notification were made available to the public on 15th September, 2005;

And whereas, all objections and suggestions received in response to the above mentioned draft notification have been duly considered by the Central Government;

Now, therefore, in exercise of the powers conferred by sub-section (1) and clause (v) of sub-section (2) of Section 3 of the Environment (Protection) Act, 1986, read with clause (d) of sub-rule (3) of rule 5 of the Environment (Protection) Rules, 1986 and in supersession of the notification number S.O. 60 (E) dated the 27th January, 1994, except in respect of things done or omitted to be done before such supersession, the Central Government hereby directs that on and from the date of its publication the required construction of new projects or activities or the expansion or modernization of existing projects or activities listed in the Schedule to this notification entailing capacity addition with change in process and or technology shall be undertaken in any part of India only after the prior environmental clearance from the Central Government or as the case may be, by the State Level Environment Impact Assessment Authority, duly constituted by the Central Government under sub-section (3) of Section 3 of the said Act, in accordance with the procedure specified hereinafter in this notification."

The above extract makes it abundantly clear that the MoEF is very serious in the matter and at the same time has made its intention clear by making the whole process transparent so that nobody can doubt the decision taken by the Ministry in the grant or rejection of any application for environmental clearance. The Notification itself is quite elaborate and easy to understand by any project proponent without any scope for any confusion. Nevertheless, there are certain deficiencies which I will highlight as we proceed and which have introduced certain amount of arbitrariness in the process of appraisal of any proposal by the Expert Appraisal Committee (EAC) both at the Central level and more so at the State level at least in certain aspects.

The Notification itself is now more than eight years old. It would have been proper for the Ministry to get a feedback from the Chairman and Members of the Expert Appraisal Committee about the working of various provisions of the Notification either formally or informally, and accordingly required amendments carried out. I was appointed Chairman of Expert Appraisal Committee on Mining on 23rd August, 2006 for appraising the proposals for grant of environmental clearance relating to seven states. There was another Expert Appraisal Committee for the remaining states. Since the pendency of cases was very large, the Ministry was under compulsion to constitute an additional Committee so as to clear large number of pending cases as the Notification made it mandatory for the Government to decide the cases within a fixed time frame. Thus, my tenure as Chairman of the Committee started almost simultaneously with the issue of the above Notification. I understand there is only one Committee now on mining projects for the entire country.

Within a few months of my working as a Chairman of the Committee, I could realize that even though the Notification itself is quite elaborate it requires amendments in certain critical provisions besides issue of detailed guidelines. My assessment was that after the issue of the Notification, the Ministry thought its responsibility was over. I would not have the temerity to say that it was deliberate but circumstances would show that the Ministry exhibited an attitude of indifference and left it to the Committee and its Chairman to deal with any unforeseen complexity that would invariably come up before the Committee while appraising any particular proposal. It was impossible to get an audience with the Administrative Head of the Ministry. While I personally did not have any problem because of my personal acquaintance with the Secretary of the Ministry during whose tenure the above Notification was issued as also with the next Secretary whom I knew very closely as she had worked, though for a brief period, under me more than twenty years back. Thus I had the occasion to discuss with both of them briefly the need for carrying out certain amendments in the Notification as also for taking certain administrative action. However, they did not have enough time left to do much except issuing two amending Notifications, one dated 11.10.2007 and other dated 01.12.2009, the last one being issued after my tenure was over. These two amending Notifications do not take care of some of the more critical aspects except adding certain routine provisions which were earlier missing. Besides, the two Committees on mining projects, the Ministry had constituted certain other Committees for dealing with industry, thermal power etc. sectors. I have no idea if Chairman of any other Committee had made any attempt to interact with the Secretary of the Ministry. But apart from my brief interaction with the first two Secretaries, I made an attempt to meet the next Secretary but unfortunately his personal staff could not give me any appointment which is quite unusual as the tradition in the Central Secretariat is that the Administrative Head of the Ministry and even the Minister In-charge always find some time to spare for a meeting with the Chairman of an important Committee constituted by the Ministry to assist itself in the discharge of a statutory responsibility under a Central Act. I was feeling frustrated due to such indifference on the part of the Ministry and some of the members of my Committee were quite upset. Finally, I tendered my resignation from the post of the Chairman of the Committee much ahead of the end of my tenure as per the above Notification though I cited an administratively minor issue for my premature resignation. However, the then Minister (Mr. Namonarayan Meena) called me to his office and told me plainly that he would not accept my resignation but he also conveyed his unhappiness about the inaction on the part of the Ministry on such a very routine administrative matter. In deference to the Minister's desire I withdrew my resignation letter. The Ministry officials did not take any action on my request as desired by the Minister. Since general election to the Parliament was announced the bureaucracy delayed any action on my request thinking perhaps that the Minister might not be there in the new Government which, to the liking of the bureaucracy, did really materialize as the Minister, though elected to the Parliament, got a different portfolio. I had no option but to continue as Chairman of the Committee till its tenure was over in the 3rd week of August, 2009.

It is clear that the responsibility for keeping the environment clean and pollution free evolves on the MoEF. Hence, the approach and attitude of the MoEF are the guiding factors in the entire process. The MoEF, like any other ministry in the Government, has, besides the Minister in-charge, a permanent bureaucracy headed by the Secretary as the administrative head who is assisted by other officers and staff under him. As per the established practice, the bureaucracy tends to play safe and usually goes by rule book even if the officer has the discretion to interpret a particular rule or instructions in any specific manner depending on merits unless the officer is otherwise motivated due to any reason whatsoever to help a particular applicant for grant of environmental clearance, and to put it bluntly, in such a case the officer concerned knows which side of the bread is buttered. The reader is free to have his own interpretation about what I intend to tell but not telling exactly. I will give some examples in appropriate context. As the bureaucracy is not expected to make any significant impact it is the Minister in charge who can play the role of a genuine friend, philosopher and guide in the exploitation of the mineral resources while effectively containing the ecological balance that will ensure that the benefits of economic development are enjoyed by the people in a healthy and clean environment. With a polluted environment what is the purpose of exploitation of the natural resources? In this background, I will briefly discuss the role played by the three different Ministers in as many years.

The Committee under my Chairmanship was constituted in August 2006 when Mr. A. Raja was the Minister followed by Mr. Namonarayan Meena and Mr. Jairam Ramesh. While Mr. Raja is a political person, Mr. Mèena is a retired I.P.S officer and the status of Mr. Ramesh is not clear to me. The Committee had no occasion to have any interaction with them, nor is it the normal practice except one particular member, by way of name drop, never missed any opportunity to inform the Committee in its meeting that he had met or he would meet the Minister and also occasionally same name dropping about his access to two very senior bureaucrats was resorted to. I had enjoyed this (name dropping) as a source of good amusement in an otherwise stressful meeting of the Committee that at times would run for more than eight hours continuously.

The Committee followed the procedure under the 14th September Notification and made its recommendations either rejecting or allowing applications for grant of prior environmental clearance for any mining project. Both the above first two ministers as the Central Regulator had accepted the recommendations of the Committee without any exception. It is also understood that the conditions prescribed by the Committee while making its recommendations had also been accepted by the ministry. It was but natural for the Committee to presume that it had been following the proper procedure and making recommendations which the MoEF had found in order as per extant policies of the Government. My Committee had always been of the view that non-renewable natural resources like minerals should be optimally exploited and exploited scientifically in an environment-friendly manner causing 'Nil' or least pollution and without endangering the health of the populace and with sustainable physical degradation affecting land, water, air, flora, fauna, etc. In fact, the Committee had prescribed the conditions specific to a particular project keeping the above in mind. Here, I will refer to a particular, and the only one, interaction of mine with one of the two Ministers (Mr. Meena) which might appear a bit of self satisfying, but nevertheless informative about the approach of the MoEF on the larger issue of environmental clearance for mining projects and it is significant in the context of certain observations reportedly made by his successor Mr. Jairam Ramesh as published in some newspapers.

Due to some reasons, I submitted my resignation before my tenure was to be over. The Minister (Mr. Meena) called me to his office and wanted to know the reason for such drastic action (resignation). When I explained the circumstances leading to the submission of my letter of resignation he just laughed and asked me to withdraw the letter of my resignation. The Minister also told me that he would like that the mineral resources of the country be exploited for accelerated economic development and he expressed his satisfaction with the way the Committee had been appraising the proposals for prior environmental clearance and the specific conditions being prescribed on case to case basis. But he did not forget to remind me about my reluctance to accept his very rare and the only request for a reconsideration of Committees' recommendations in a particular case which the Committee finally agreed to as the suggestions of the Minister, if accepted, were found to be less polluting than the original proposal of the project authority which was not highlighted by the party at the time of appraisal. Here, the difference between the opinion of the Committee and that of the Minister was purely technical on procedural requirement. But I felt humbled by the courtesy shown by the Minister to me.

The Committee had never been told by the Ministry that its recommendations were not upto the mark. The MoEF had never rejected any of the recommendations of the Committee though it has the power to do so as per the provisions of the 14th September Notification except that in the event of disagreement between the Committee and the Ministry, the only requirement is that the matter is to be reverted back to the Committee for reconsiderations. That being so let me refer to certain observations attributed to the minister as reported in a section of the print media with wide circulation throughout the country. Sometimes after his induction in the Cabinet, the Minister (Mr. Ramesh) made the observations that his Ministry had an *unnatural* number of grant of prior environmental clearance in ninety per cent of the cases. I was amused to see such a statement not because of the number but because of the fact that the Ministry had never indicated to the Committee or its Chairman the *natural* percentage to be followed. By the time he became Minister of MoEF, the EACs had been in operation for almost three years and I think it was long enough a period for the MoEF to fix a so-called *natural* percentage for grant of environmental clearance. No guidelines have been issued to my knowledge even after four years since the 14th September Notification was issued. I will go into further details on this point little later. When one of his senior cabinet colleagues in-charge of some other Ministry aired his grievance publicly against unhelpful attitude of the MoEF adversely impacting the execution of various road construction projects of his Ministry, he (Minister, MoEF) became defensive and as reported by the same print media attributing to him the observation that in last three years or so the MoEF had rejected only 30 of the 300 cases considered for environmental clearance. The figure of 30, which is 10 per cent of 300, is significant as the Minister had taken credit that his Ministry had in fact accepted record number of 90 per cent (100%–10%), *the so-called unnatural percentage*, of the proposals received by his Ministry. We Indians are quite apt in utilising our knowledge of a language and if the language is that of the Empire we claim to be more English than perhaps the English people. Thus a particular figure can be utilized as an effective tool in an offensive way to denigrate some one of lesser value or in a defensive way to placate some one creating an uncomfortable situation. But in the process a lot of confusion has been created in the minds of the miners, both existing and prospective. When an observation or even an apparently innocuous statement emanates from a person in high and final authority in the government it carries lot of weight and meaning. I would not like to comment further except referring to a comment made by a more than 100 years old *English Daily*, *The Statesman*, known for its responsible journalism, that talking or *tongue wagging* (the expression used by the Daily) does not clean the atmosphere rather it might cloud the whole environment.

The 14th September Notification is silent, it is not feasible also as the Notification is a statutory one, about the specific number of proposals to be cleared over a period of time. The established practice followed by the Government is that detailed guidelines are issued subsequent to the issue of any statutory Notification. Such guidelines generally contain provisions like creation of certain desired capacity in any industry as per the policy of the Government. For example, if the country is to achieve a planned growth in, say, infrastructure like roads, bridges, residential buildings, etc., additional capacity for production of minerals like iron ore (for steel), limestone (for cement) etc. need to be created within a specified period of time. Such additional capacity can be by way of new mining projects and or expansion of existing projects if that is feasible based on the available mineral reserves with the existing players. In a liberal economy where competition is the key to survival such quantitative regulation is not the accepted norm. This was the practice in pre-liberalization Licence Raj when licensed capacity without reference to the actual production capacity used to determine the fate of any new entrant. In the absence of any specific or even general guidelines, it is not possible for the EACs to determine in how many cases with desired capacity grant of prior environmental clearance should be recommended.

Even the Minister, at least till the expiry of three year tenure of my Committee in August, 2009, did not give any indication about the so-called natural percentage to be followed in the grant of environmental clearance. He (Mr. Ramesh), no doubt, referred back three cases for the re-consideration by the Committee which did not find those three cases worth reconsidering as having any issues left unscrutinized earlier by the Committee. The MoEF has the informal option to convey to the members or at least to the Chairman its policy on grant of environmental clearances only in certain special circumstances. This can be done only through periodical interaction with the Chairpersons of various Committees. In fact, during my tenure of three years no such interaction could take place and I have reason to believe no such interaction had taken place thereafter also. The only known interaction that took place between the Secretary of the MoEF and three Chairpersons of the six Committees (Chairman of the Committee on mining could not take part due to his other pressing engagements) was in a meeting on 4th July, 2006, more than two months before the issue of the 14th September Notification. The problems discussed in this meeting were basically the ones concerning disposal of cases which was getting delayed due to certain grounds not quite justified. The consensus, *inter alia,* that emerged in the meeting is extracted below:

> "....... it was decided that similar meetings will be held periodically in order to facilitate regular exchange of views between the Expert Committee and the Ministry."

No such meeting had ever taken place thereafter at least till August 2009 though the 14th September Notification more than justifies similar periodical meetings. I am perhaps not wrong in my assessment that the attitude of the Ministry has been one of total indifference. The subordinate functionaries had shown scant respect for a decision taken by the Secretary of the Ministry with the Chairpersons who are generally senior retired bureaucrats and some of them were retired Secretaries to the Government of India and much senior to the Ministry's Secretary and the Ministry officials never thought it proper to take time and date from the Secretary to arrange such periodical meetings in future.

Before I proceed further on the issue, I would like to observe here that the Ministry washed off its hands after the issue of the14th September Notification and left everything to the respective Committees to fend for themselves. The MoEF, besides issuing the prior environmental clearance letter for a particular mining project, for that matter any project requiring prior environmental clearance, did precious little to review the status of compliance with the conditions, both general and specific, relevant to a particular project, imposed by the Ministry. The MoEF has its own field formations throughout the country headed by senior experienced officers with supporting manpower located at convenient centres to monitor the status of compliance with the terms and conditions prescribed in the clearance letter besides compliance with the relevant legal provisions. That an inspection mechanism essential for assessing the compliance status is a matter of priority for the Ministry was reiterated in 4th July, 2006 meeting (*ibid*) taken by the Secretary with the Chairpersons of some Committees. The specific decision (consensus) is extracted below:

> "Ministry would evolve a system for the random inspection of the projects, which have been granted environmental clearance for assessing the compliance status."

That because such an inspection mechanism, like any Inspection Raj, might open the flood gate of corruption, the government cannot evade its primary responsibility in enforcing its conditionalities to ensure that a miner must fall in line. In this context a reference can be made to the kneejerk reaction of the MoEF to revoke the environmental clearance earlier granted to M/s. Vedanta Resources Plc for its bauxite and aluminium project in Orissa. I am well aware that this book is not the place for criticizing any particular project authority nor do I intend to make any comment on the case of Vedanta or on such drastic action on the part of the Ministry revoking the environmental clearance as reported in both print and electronic media. The tested lesson is that prevention is better than cure. In fact, the MoEF could have avoided the unintended embarrassment both for the Central Government and the State Government and also the likely protracted litigation that any such affected party would like to take recourse to dragging the Government to the court if its own field officers would have kept a watchful eye on such projects in a tribal and ecologically fragile area. It is only after media reports that the Ministry swung into action. The NGOs are working there and it is inconceivable that the MoEF was unaware of their concerns. Can the Government constitute a special committee in every such case of violation of environmental norms to initiate corrective actions? While nobody, much less the author of this book who has worked under Mr. N.C. Saxena, I.A.S. (Retd.), would doubt the conclusions arrived at by a Committee headed by him, it is a case of simple abdication of the Ministry's primary responsibility. There are many such areas where tribal and other traditional forest dwelling people have been exploited and exploited very badly. Obviously you cannot have a "Saxena Committee" for each and every such area. An embroidery can not and does not add any additional strength to a piece of cloth if otherwise of weak texture to sustain on its own. I had no occasion to see the particular project in Orissa and therefore, have no personal knowledge. But after viewing, by sheer chance, a documentary on the Vedanta project in Orissa televised by the well-known T.V. channel Al Jazeera during the later part of the second week of September, 2010, I could make out the huge expenditure the company would have incurred in various construction activities. These are physical activities involving construction of massive plant buildings, roads etc. How can one believe that the Ministry officials were not aware of such visible physical activities on massive scale that involved movement of heavy duty vehicles with huge quantity of construction materials for fairy long duration as the T.V. footages would give the unmistakable impression that the construction activities might be going on for at least three years or even more?

The Ministry of Environment and Forest (MoEF) is expected to have a list of places in the country which are tribal dominated and ecologically fragile. It is not as if the Ministry came to know this particular region in Orissa only after the media highlighted the alleged seriousness of the matter. If the Ministry was not aware of the area, it is unfortunate and otherwise the inaction on the part of the Ministry's field officers is clearly an act of criminal negligence and not a simple dereliction of duty.

Newspaper reports suggest that the company has violated the terms and conditions of grant of environmental clearance by the MoEF and grant of permission by the State Pollution Control Board. If it is so the violation was not a one time one but continued violation for a fairly long period. It is time for the Ministry to examine why no follow up action was taken for random inspection for assessing the compliance status as per decision in a meeting taken by the administrative head, the Secretary of the Ministry on 4th July 2006 (*ibid*). It is equally important that the Ministry prepares a list of ecologically sensitive areas based on its own criteria and make it mandatory for the Ministry officials to inspect such areas as frequently as feasible and at least once every quarter to see the state of affairs and take remedial action. Post mortem does not help. It makes no sense if Ministry's inaction results in infructuous expenditure of large amount of money by any project authority. A situation of fait accompli should not be allowed to happen. The illegal activities of any project authority and the negligent inaction of the Ministry are always subject to strict judicial scrutiny and to think that the Court will take a lenient view on the default of the Ministry is too naïve a mindset. Rather, it is most likely that the Court will come to the irresistible conclusion that the government officials have simply acquiesced in the wrong doings of the project authority short of telling that there is active connivance between the officials and the project authority. If the protector becomes the destroyer no amount of loud talking and any post mortem would save the environment. To put the entire blame on the miner is erroneous. Assuming that a miner, in his anxiety to make more profit, will always neglect the environmental aspects, one can make an introspection and looks for the reasons. The reasons are obvious to any discerning mind. Getting a mining lease and all statutory clearances including the prior environmental clearance is not only a strenuous time consuming process, it also involves considerable expenditure under the table to manage a favourable recommendation of the entire hierarchy and notings in the relevant file before the final authority gives its approval. Unfortunately, mining is an activity which, some how or the other, shall continue to be under the control regime and so long discretion is to be exercised by the authority at different levels in the process of granting permission, the evil of corruption can not be eliminated altogether. It will be too simple to assume that a miner will not make good the loss already incurred in obtaining various statutory clearances that too before any return that would accrue to him long after. A large unit may not feel the effect as its capital investment is also large and for such a unit time is money and therefore earlier it gets the required clearances better for it and it will not mind if the *speed* money, an euphemism for *greed* money, is to be paid. Smaller lessees, whose number is fairly large, face genuine financial hardship that may deter such lessees from spending enough money for protecting the environment. So the temptation grows and grows faster than expected with concomitant growth in the desire to make money on both sides of the divide resulting in only a semblance of inspection to stop illegal activities.

In many cases delays and indecisions on the part of the Ministry creates lot of confusion resulting in the scope for discretion in the process of grant of environmental clearance. In some cases the MoEF notifies certain areas to be eventually declared as Wildlife Sanctuaries. Most of the areas are also rich in mineral reserves. As per the procedure there is a statutory time gap between the initial date of issue of the Notification and the actual date of declaration of an area as a Wildlife Sanctuary. In such an area there are pre-existing mining activities and road communication. New mining leases are being granted in areas falling within the notified area either partly or fully. MoEF has been granting prior environmental clearances for such activities subject to, of course, the rituals of conditions which become impossible to comply with due to various pressures. Then there is pressure for excluding certain areas from the areas to be declared as Wildlife Sanctuary. If the authority is hither and thither or in a confused state of dilemma the cause of the conservation of flora and fauna suffers and subsequently crying hoarse or making loud and shrill noise does not, *ipso facto*, cure the damage except that some higher level of dB is emitted in the atmosphere. As I have said earlier, the age old and tested principle i.e., *prevention is better than cure*, is the only option.

I had no intention to make this digression into the act of referring to the three Ministers in a preceding paragraph. But I have done so with a view to impressing upon the Ministry the need for a clarity in its thinking and to convey to the Chairpersons of the EACs so as to avoid any confusion. The Expert Appraisal Committee (EAC) is not an external or alien body. It is a statutory committee constituted by the Ministry to assist the Central Regulator (presently the Ministry). Since, the recommendations of the EAC are part of the process influencing the decision of the Ministry in the grant or otherwise of environmental clearance any misunderstanding between the Ministry and the EAC could create unintended complications. Further, as per the provisions of the 14th September Notification the proceedings of the EAC are to be put in the website of the Ministry and hence the same become a public document in the eye of law and which everybody has access to and is subject to judicial scrutiny. If this position is accepted, I see no reason to think otherwise, the distinction between the Ministry and the EAC, though not blurred, becomes thin but clearly distinct by the independent status of the EAC. The Member Secretary of the EAC is a senior officer of the Ministry who also processes the proposals in the file and therefore he/she is an effective link between the Ministry and the Committee. But for certain observations of the Minister discussed hereinbefore the Committee never felt that the working of the Committee had been expressly in discord with the general approach of the Ministry.

I would not comment further on the matter and I leave it to the Ministry to decide if clarity on such an important and critical issue is called for as this concerns the style of working of the Ministry which is not the avowed subject of this book. In the sequel I would deal with the palpable lack of seriousness on the part of the Ministry in so far as it relates to the 14th September Notification.

As stated earlier, no guidelines have been issued by the MoEF elaborating and clarifying the implications of certain specific provisions of the 14th September Notification for a clear understanding by the project authority. I am citing few such instances just to highlight the casual attitude of the Ministry giving a clear an unambiguous impression that role of the MoEF ended with the issue of the Notification.

This book is not a text-book grammar for a learner of English as a language. But surely it was possible for the Ministry officials to let the world know that Indian bureaucracy can produce a quasi-legal document without any such glaring mistakes except clerical or typing errors. Few examples:

Look at the last line of sub-para (iii) of para 7(i) 111. stage (3) – Public Consultation—in page 40 of the Notification. The completed clause should be *"within 45 (forty five) days"*, but the printed clause is *"within 45 (forty five)"*—the word *"days"* missing.

Again in the same place in first line in sub-para (v), the alternate public agency or authority is nominated under *sub-para (iv)* and not *sub-para (iii)* as printed as would appear from a reading of the sub-para.

Look at the first four lines of para 9 of the Notification on the validity of environmental clearance in page 43 of the Notificaton. What the Ministry intends to convey is that the validity of environmental clearance is for the period from etc. etc.... to the start of production operations *of* (not *by* as printed in the beginning of the fourth line). The wordings in the beginning of the sentence do not convey a completed sense as the correct clause should be "Validity of Environmental Clearance" *means* and not *is meant* as printed. In the same place in the third line the reference should be to sub paragraph (iii) of *para 8* of the Notification and not to *sub paragraph (iv) of para 7* as printed.

The above deficiencies are purely syntactical in nature and perhaps can be totally ignored. But there are substantive provisions that need special attention. In the subsequent paragraphs I have made an attempt to briefly discuss some of the substantive issues.

Para 6 of the Notification deals with the procedure for filing an application for prior environmental clearance and also the documents to be furnished along with the application. For mining project a copy of the pre-feasibility project report needs be furnished along with the application. In the absence of any guidelines on the subject there is lot of confusion in the mind of the applicant and the consultant who prepares the EIA Report and the EMP. In fact, some project authorities have, in the beginning, confused the pre-feasibility project report with the mining plan referred to in sub-section (2) (b) of Section 5 of the Mines and Minerals (Development and Regulation) Act, 1957 (MMDR Act). A mining plan as approved by the Central Government [Indian Bureau of Mines, (IBM)] is essential before any mining lease is granted. Such a mining plan will deal with method of mining, formation of benches and other technical details that go with scientific mining. A pre-feasibility project report, on the other hand, deals with cost of mining, selling price of the mined minerals etc. to prove that the project is financially viable to generate reasonable profit so as to enable the project authority to incur the required expenditure to control the environmental pollution as a result of the proposed activities besides enough surplus fund to spend on the steps to mitigate the adverse impacts on the socio-economic front as a part of Corporate Social Responsibility (CSR) policy as otherwise it is quite possible that the project proponent might do only the mining, either doing nothing or very little in taking the required mitigating measures. Since, the proposals for environmental clearance are referred to the EAC for appraisal without any even preliminary examination to see if the required documents are there or not it is doubted if the Section in the Ministry dealing with the subject are conversant with the contents of a pre-feasibility project report. It is a genuine and real problem for smaller miners who may find it very difficult to hire a financial expert in preparing a pre-feasibility project report even though such miners know very well the cost of mining and sales realization without knowing the nuances of cash flow statement, internal rate of return and other parameters of financial calculation to decide if the project is financially viable or not.

Screening is an essential stage in appraising category 'B' projects and activities inasmuch as it entails scrutiny by the state level committee for determining whether or not a particular project or activity requires further environmental studies for preparation of an EIA report for its appraisal as the nature and location of the project will determine such further studies. The SEAC shall accordingly classify the projects as Category 'B1' that require EIA report prior to the appraisal and as Category 'B2' projects that shall not require EIA report. One can imagine the importance of this classification for the purpose of a proper appraisal of a particular project as any improper classification is fraught with serious environmental implications and it is more so as the project will not be subject to the generally detailed scrutiny at the level of the Ministry as such a project will be decided by the State Level Impact Assessment Authority lacking an independent office establishment of a government department. Not that the MoEF was not seized of the criticality of the matter as will be clear from the last sentence of the particular para i.e., para 7(i), I Stage (1) – screening—which enjoins upon the MoEF the responsibility of issuing appropriate guidelines from time to time for categorization of projects into category 'B1' and 'B2'. To the knowledge of the author no such guidelines have been issued. Hence, I will not be far off as I have earlier commented, after the issue of the 14th September Notification the MoEF has shown an attitude of indifference. I wish if I could be wrong.

While on the subject of category 'B' projects there still remains some confusion. By the Ist December 2009 amending Notification a provision has been made that in case there is a difference of opinion among the members of SEAC, the details of the views, for and against, shall have to be clearly recorded in the minutes and a copy thereof sent to the MoEF. Unless the MoEF has the authority to overrule the majority opinion, the purpose of the exercise is not clear as the aggrieved party would not know what to do. I think this needs clarification by the Ministry.

For a meaningful appraisal of any mining project the EAC is required to determine Terms of Reference (TOR) addressing all relevant environmental concerns for the preparation of an Environment Impact Assessment (EIA) report in respect of the project for which prior environmental clearance is sought. The Ministry itself has highlighted the importance in para 7(i) – II Stage (2) - Scoping - (i) and (ii) of the 14th September Notification. Since it is not practical to determine TOR separately for each project as it would require enormous time, it would have been ideal if the Ministry could have made an attempt to prepare a model TOR that could be modified keeping in mind the specific circumstances of a particular project. The Ministry did not make any attempt in that direction. My Committee nevertheless prepared a Model

TOR within six months of its existence. Dr. S.R. Wate, a member of my Committee, did an excellent job in preparing the initial draft based on the generic structure of environment impact assessment document in Appendix-III and Appendix-III A to the 14th September Notification. The draft Model TOR was circulated among all the members of the committee for their comments and suggestions. The members took no time in giving their suggestions which resulted in the birth of the first Model TOR that was followed by all the applicants for grant of prior environmental clearance. The EAC would invariably add new points in this TOR as the Committee also learned many aspects of the environmental issues not covered in the original TOR partly based on the facts disclosed by the project authority and partly on the basis of the new ideas emanating from the members themselves as a natural process of evolution. A need was felt by the EAC that the Model TOR needed modifications incorporating additional TORs that were being prescribed by the EAC subsequent to the original TOR. The result was the re-birth of the Model TOR (revised) in April 2008 which is at Annexure-B. I will very briefly describe the salient features of the latest Model TOR in the sequel.

The salient features of the revised TOR have been indicated in the beginning of the TOR itself and are extracted below:

> "The revised TOR has been devised to facilitate the project proponents and their consultants to prepare the EIA Report and the EMP which are informative, compact and easy to comprehend. In short, the revised TOR is expected to be user friendly for all concerned. Its salient feature are as under:
>
> – EIA Report and the EMP shall contain in the beginning an Exclusive Summary which shall be a miniature EIA Report and EMP.
> – It has five chapters as against six in the earlier TOR.
> – One chapter (Chapter-3) has been exclusively allotted to environmental issues with a separate section for each component of the environmental issues.
> – Each component of environmental issues has been dealt with in all its ramifications such as baseline status, anticipated impacts due to mining activities and proposed mitigating measures to contain the adverse impact, in that sequence, in one section assigning sub-section 1 to baseline status, sub-section 2 to anticipated impacts and sub-section 3 to proposed mitigating measures.

2. Even if different chapters/sections are prepared by separate experts with separate page numbers for individual chapter/section, the consolidated and composite EIA Report and the EMP shall have consecutive page numbers beginning with Executive Summary using automatic numerator (English Numbering Machine), if necessary.
3. In the beginning of the EIA Report and the EMP, proper and correct reference to the page numbers of various chapters, sections and sub-section with the appropriate title/sub-title of the subject shall be clearly indicated under the heading CONTENTS. The pages of the CONTENTS shall be numbered in numerals like 1, 2 etc.
4. The project proponents and their consultants must adhere to the framework of the revised TOR in the preparation of the EIA Report and the EMP as also in the presentation to be made to the Expert Appraisal Committee (EAC) in its meetings failing which the proposal shall be treated as incomplete and hence liable to be rejected outright."

Though this is not the space to deal with the salient features of the TOR but I could not but be compulsive to do so if only to show the casual way the MoEF, belated no doubt but as the well-known cliché, better late than never, took up the job of preparing a Model TOR more than two and a half years after the 14th September Notification. The Committee came to know this as the Ministry sought for its comments after consideration by the Committee in the already fixed meeting allowing no time to the members to make a proper study. The MoEF had entrusted the work to the Administrative Staff College of India (ASCI), a Hyderabad based reputed Institute to impart training in various disciplines of the administration. The Central Government routinely send civil servants in batches for training to ASCI for duration of one week to four weeks as scheduled in advance. Frankly speaking, it was a revelation to me that ASCI has also the expertise (so perceived by the MoEF) on such an important document like preparation of environment impact assessment report and environment management plan. I would very briefly go into the draft TOR prepared by the ASCI as presented to the Committee for comments. Model TOR drafted by ASCI is also (if not entirely) for mining sector and it (TOR) did not have any section on *occupational health environment*. I leave it to the readers to ponder if there can be any mining activity or any other industrial activity that does not throw up environmental issues on occupational health for the workers or health issues for the people living in the surrounding areas. So the only comment the Committee could give was to suggest to the MoEF that the revised (April 2008) Model TOR as adopted by the Committee be treated as the base paper on which ASCI could make its own model TOR by making the required modifications, by way of deletion, alternation, elaboration, etc. as appropriate. I have no knowledge about further progress in the matter. But I believe that the reconstituted EAC, there is now only one committee on mining for the entire country, has been following the Model TOR prepared by my Committee, in appraising the proposals for environmental clearance.

I shall now refer to certain guidelines issued by the MoEF ostensibly for the guidance of the EAC. One such circular is on operational guidelines for observance of good practices in environmental regulation. These guidelines deal with the timely processing of cases for environmental clearance already in practice as circulated under MoEF's letter No. 20011/3/200-GC dated 26th July, 2004. The EAC has been following the time schedule in deciding the cases. But it Expert Appraisal Committee (EAC) is handicapped by the absence of any scrutiny at Ministry level to ensure that a proposal to be considered by the EAC in its pre-fixed monthly meeting is complete with all the essential documents. In fact, there is no scrutiny at all in the Ministry and it is left to the EAC to see if the proposals are complete. One can imagine the harassment caused to the applicant if he has to be told in the meeting that certain documents are not there as he may not be in a position to make the documents available then and there. If the consideration of such an incomplete proposal is to be deferred to the next meeting, it would put extra cost on the project proponent on travel etc. Thus the so-called good practices have been followed more in breach than in observance.

Another circular was issued on 13th October, 2006 that deals with the treatment of cases pending disposal under EIA 1994. It never occurred to the Ministry that it is also under obligation to issue certain operational guidelines in respect of the 14th September Notification.

Yet another circular was issued by the MoEF on 8th December, 2006 specifying only the nature of recommendation to be made by the Committee, i.e. recommended, or deferred or rejected, of course with reasons thereof. The immediate provocation to issue the above missive was the uncomfortable situation the Ministry found itself in as a result of certain recommendations purportedly made by one EAC with the conditions that the recommendation to grant environmental clearance would be subject to submission of additional information and its examination by the Ministry. It (examination) was too much for the Ministry to digest. But the Ministry apparently was oblivious of the fact that its own guidelines on *Good Practices*, referred to earlier, enjoin upon itself the task of scrutiny to ensure that the required relevant information and documents are available before the case is remitted to the EAC for its consideration. So the Ministry very conveniently shifted the responsibility of collecting the information from the project authority to the EAC which the EAC had to do time and again by deferring the consideration of the case but not before some wasteful expenditure incurred by the applicant in presenting his appearance with the consultant. If there is a proper checklist the Ministry could itself do the scrutiny and a simple communication to the applicant telling him that his case would be considered only after receipt of the information would evoke instant response with least expenses.

At times, the Ministry in its over anxiety to decide an application for prior environmental clearance within the prescribed time schedule ends up in issuing guidelines that create more confusion. The Special Secretary of the Ministry, through a demi-official letter addressed to the Chairman of the EAC, requested that the minutes of the meetings of the EAC should be finalized within five working days after the meetings are over failing which the draft minutes (without the approval of the Chairman) shall be deemed to be the final minutes. The provocation for such letter was not clear to me but it betrayed the total ignorance of the procedure that goes into the preparation of the minutes of any meeting of the Committee. In the course of the meeting the Member Secretary who is generally a Senior Director level officer of the Ministry assisted by another junior officer notes the salient points and the final recommendation. In the next two to three working days, the Member Secretary is ready with the draft minutes that are sent to the Chairman for his approval. In my case, since I was a local man, a simple telephone call was enough for the Chairman to come to the Ministry to peruse the draft minutes and approve the same with modifications as necessary. In cases of rejection as also in complex cases I myself prepared the minutes which were seen by the Member Secretary to ensure that there were no factual error. It was a miracle that the Member Secretary, at least the Member Secretary of my Committee, with whom I had close interaction and at times advising her on telephone as to how the draft minutes relating to a particular case should be worded, never failed to complete the job within the stipulated time. The EAC related work is a very small part of the total work allocated to the Member Secretary who, as Senior Director in the Ministry, has to deal with so much other work. In fact, initially for more than two years I could see her face to face while seated on a chair across the table in her office chamber on the 10th floor of Paryavaran Bhawan where the MoEF is located after removing piles of files on her table surrounding her to make space for a clearer view of the person on the other side of the table. I doubt if any senior officer ever visits the working condition of the officers at lower level. The threat that *failing which* the draft minutes as prepared shall be deemed to be final minutes becomes relevant if the Member Secretary prepares the first draft of the minutes within the stipulated time but the Chairman fails to finalise the same. If, however, the Member Secretary, due to any reason, fails to prepare the draft minutes, the question will arise as to why there has been delay. Since no Secretariat assistance is provided to the Chairman he is handicapped and consequently helpless.

I have earlier referred to the Office Memorandum (OM) dated 2nd December, 2009 of the MoEF at Annexure-C. This was long overdue. The Ministry has ultimately realized that quality Consultants are essential to have quality EIA Report and EMP. By the above OM, the Ministry has designated the National Accreditation Board of Education and Training (NABET) and the Quality Council of India (QCI) to certify the Consultants to be competent to prepare the EIA/EMP Report. It has been made clear that no EIA/EMP Reports prepared by any Consultants who are not registered with NABET/QCI shall be considered by the Ministry after 30th June, 2010. This is undoubtedly a step in the right direction. But considering the fact that a large number of lessees engaged in mining activities are living in different places through out the country it would be very difficult for them to contact a particular Consultant. It would be ideal if the names and addresses of the Consultants for mining projects with their registration numbers and validity period are made available through a well-known website periodically so that the small lessees specially those living in the remote areas can conveniently get in touch with the appropriate Consultants. In fact, it should be made incumbent on the licencing authority, i.e., the State Government, to ensure that a valid list of such registered Consultants are available in the Office of the District Mining Officers. A consultant fleecing the miner specially the small lessees not conversant with the process, by charging exorbitant fees for the job remains a distinct possibility. A possible remedy could be to relate the fees to be charged by the Consultant to the scale of operation and in addition the cost on travel etc. for making the presentation before the EAC on actual basis. The Indian Bureau of Mines, Ministry of Mines could be declared as the competent authority to decide the rate of fees etc. for the consultant. The Indian

Bureau of Mines has the requisite expertise to decide the ceiling rate beyond which the consultant should not charge any extra cost from the lessee.

The Ministry visualized a situation when views of an expert in a relevant field for a particular meeting of the EAC would be required. In order that the EAC can make proper appraisal of a particular project in all aspects, a specific provision has been made in the 14th September Notification that the Chairperson may co-opt an expert (para-3 of Appendix-VI) as a member in a relevant field for a particular meeting of the committee. The total number of regular members of the EAC shall not exceed 15 (fifteen) and it is quite possible that the required number of experts cannot be accommodated as regular members in a particular EAC, specially in mining sector. My Committee did not have groundwater expert and that became a genuine handicap in appraising such cases (specially cases of the State of Goa) where mining would in some cases intersect groundwater at certain depth. The Notification empowers the Chairperson to co-opt a groundwater expert for a particular meeting where such an expertise is called for. But such co-option has to be confirmed by the Ministry before such a co-opted person is invited for the meeting. This is a dichotomy as the statutory power under the Notification has been either neutralized or negated due to the administrative hurdle. No Chairperson would like to have his discretion under a statutory Notification subject to such avoidable administrative procedure. Assuming that such administrative approval is required for accounting purpose as it involves payment of sitting fee and travel etc. costs to a co-opted member the issue can be resolved by issuing a general order, with the concurrence of the Integrated Finance (IF) Division of the Ministry, as per extant practice, that a co-opted member will be entitled to the payment of sitting fee, travel cost, daily allowance etc. as are admissible to a regular member of the Committee and the concerned Member Secretary would be the competent authority to issue such a sanction letter or to countersign the T.A. Bill of a co-opted member. There is no harm if the Ministry takes the view that the Chairperson of the EAC would exercise his discretion to co-opt a particular expert only if it is essential. The Ministry has the option to prepare a list of such experts from time to time and convey its advice to the Chairperson to co-opt the expert only out of the list so prepared. The Ministry can at least facilitate the smooth working of the Committee as per the express and not implied provisions of the Notification.

There is a provision in the Notification under which a sub-group of the EAC can make a site visit only if considered necessary. My Committee has always been circumspect in deciding a site visit. In this case also approval of the Ministry is required before the sub-group could make a site visit. As my analysis and comments would be same as in the preceding paragraph on co-opted member, I do not think there is any need for allocating additional space for repeating the same here.

The situation was no better in a very critical and relevant area. My Committee came to the conclusion that there was a need to asses carrying capacity in areas like Bellary Hospet and Goa where intensive mining activities were going on and to see if any further capacity in mining activities in these areas could be allowed or not. The need for such an assessment arose as some expert members and many of the lessees were of the view that due to the adoption of modern and environment friendly technology in mining the ground situation might have improved. If that is so it would be a fit case when environmental clearance for a mining project can be granted if the lessee adopts such technology as would ensure least or tolerable level of pollution rather than imposing a blanket ban on mining. Hence, it was felt desirable to make such a study. Till the expiry of my Committee's tenure in August 2009 the Ministry could not take a view.

I cannot help referring here to a somewhat casual decision of the MoEF allocating the work of appraisal of a mining project where the mine (say limestone mine) is captive source of raw materials to the plant (cement plant) to the EAC (Industry). The environmental issues that crop up in the case of a mining project are both qualitatively and quantitatively much complex and different compared to that of a processing plant. Even if the mine is within the radius of same distance (say 10 kms) the environmental issues thrown up by the mining activities are different.The Ministry, as if by way of a favour, also decided that an expert member of the EAC (Mining) would be invited to attend the related appraisal meeting of the EAC (Industry). There was no provision to consult the Chairperson of the EAC (Mining) for suggesting a suitable expert member for the meeting. One of the members of my Committee was approached directly for taking part in a meeting scheduled the next day and he bluntly refused to oblige. Note the sheer casual way of treating a serious matter. A mining operation will have environmental issue like groundwater intersection, soil erosion, conservation of flora and fauna, occupational health problem much more complex than that arising out of (cement) plant operation, safety standard of different nature, socio-economic issues of more complex and wide nature over a huge area and population and much more. How does the Chairperson select an expert member who can raise such wide range of environmental concern? The only inference any person can make would be that some plant owner must have faced an uncomfortable experience of facing the

EAC (Mining) and might have used his good contact to manage such a decision as above. The consequence would be disastrous. In fact, one expert member of my Committee who once held a very high position on environment in the Central Government told me that one of his friends, a member in the EAC (Industry), told him that on a proposal for prior environmental clearance on cement plant and its captive mine no discussion took place on the environmental issue on mining activities and it was a smooth disposal and, of course, timely disposal at that.

I have in a previous context referred to the 2nd Amending Environment Notification dated 1st December, 2009. These amendments to the original Notification dated 14th September, 2006 were carried out after a gap of more than three years and it was expected that this would have taken care of the deficiencies of the previous and the original ones or at least the so called clerical errors through a commonly known and followed practice of issuing a corrigendum i.e., correction slip. But that was not to be. Rather, it has created some confusion, one specific case is cited below:

> In the amended (substituted) Appendix-IV at Annexure-A on the procedure for conduct of public hearing certain expressions were used which should have been done with clarity.
>
> Expressions like official language of the state, local language or vernacular are likely to create confusion besides raising the question of legal validity of a particular report or proceedings. Some states have more than one official language. Likewise, the purpose of using expressions like local language or vernacular is not clear.
>
> Part-IX and IX-A have been inserted by the Constitution (73rd Amendment) Act, 1991 with effect from 24.4.1993 and the Constitution (74th Amendment) Act, 1992, effective from 1.6.1993 in the Constitution of India creating the Rural and Urban Local Bodies respectively. These two are landmark Amendments and of which the bureaucrats both at State level and Central level are well aware. For the benefit of the readers the relevant inserted articles of the Constitution are reproduced below:
>
> "Article 243. In this Part, unless the context otherwise requires,—
>
> (a) "district" means a district in a State;
>
> (b) "Gram Sabha" means a body consisting of persons registered in the electoral rolls relating to a village comprised within the area of Panchayat at the village level;
>
> (c) "intermediate level" means a level between the village and

district levels specified by the Governor of a State by public notification to be the intermediate level for the purposes of this Part;

(d) "Panchayat" means an institution (by whatever name called) of self-government constituted under Article 243 B, for the rural areas;

(e) "Panchayat area" means the territorial area of a Panchayat;

(f) "population means the population as ascertained at the last preceding census of which the relevant figures have been published;

(g) "village" means a village specified by the Governor by public notification to be a village for the purposes of this Part and includes a group of villages so specified.

Article 243 P. In this Part, unless the context otherwise requires, —

(a) "Committee" means a Committee constituted under Article 243S;

(b) "district" means a district in a State;

(c) "Metropolitan area" means an area having a population of ten lakhs or more, comprised in one or more districts and consisting of two or more Municipalities or Panchayats or other contiguous areas, specified by the Governor by public notification to be a Metropolitan area for the purposes of this Part;

(d) "Municipal area" means the territorial area of a Municipality as is notified by the Governor;

(e) "Municipality" means an institution of self-government constituted under Article 243Q;

(f) "Panchayat" means a Panchayat constituted under Article 243B;

(g) "population" means the population as ascertained at the last preceding census of which the relevant figures have been published.

Article 243Q. (1) There shall be constituted in every State, —

(a) a Nagar Panchayat (by whatever name called) for a transitional area, that is to say, an area in transition from a rural area to an urban area;

(b) a Municipal Council for a smaller urban area; and

(c) a Municipal Corporation for a larger urban area,

in accordance with the provisions of this Part:

> Provided that a Municipality under this clause may not be constituted in such urban area or part thereof as the Governor may, having regard to the size of the area and the municipal services being provided or proposed to be provided by an industrial establishment in that area and such other factors as he may deem fit, by public notification, specify to be an industrial township.

(2) In this article, "a transitional area", "a smaller urban area" or "a larger urban area" means such area as the Governor may, having regard to the population of the area, the density of the population therein, the revenue generated for local administration, the percentage of employment in non-agricultural activities, the economic importance or such other factors as he may deem fit, specify by public notification for the purposes of this Part."

Under the provisions of the Constitution, the Panchayati Raj Institutions (PRIs) shall be three-tier institutions at village level, intermediate level (except in some smaller States) and at district level with different nomenclature in different states such as Gram Panchayat, Panchayat Samiti (intermediate level) and Zila Parishad, all known as PRIs. Likewise, Urban Local Bodies (ULBs) will have different nomenclature such as Municipal Corporation, Municipal Council, Notified area besides Nagar Panchayat (by whatever name called). as the name suggests, which is no longer a village Panchayat but yet to be a full Municipal Body, i.e. in a stage of transition from a rural area to an urban area.

The above will make it clear that three simple and distinct expressions like Panchayati Raj Institutions (PRIs), Nagar Panchayats and Urban Local Bodies (ULBs) would take care of all the institutions of local self governments both in rural and urban areas. While there is no mention of Nagar Panchayat as a separate entity, the use of the expression like Panchayat Union in the amending Notificaton (ibid) will baffle the lessees. Para 2.2 of the substituted *Appendix-IV* is not happily worded.

This book is not intended to be a critique on the role of the MoEF. But it is definitely a critical but objective analysis of the role of the MoEF that plays the pivotal role in maintaining the environment in all its ramifications. What I have observed in the preceding paragraphs are based on my practical experience that I have gathered as Chairman of the EAC (Mining) for three years, definitely a period long enough to form an objective view.

Even at the risk of repetition I would have no hesitation to say that the Ministry did not do much after the issue of the 14th September Notification. In a nutshell, the approach of the MoEF has been one of indifference. The Ministry never considered it necessary to get a feedback from the Chairpersons of various EACs while spending so much money of the taxpayers on sitting fees, travel and other costs for the Committee Members. The only interaction between the Secretary of the Ministry and the Chairpersons (some of them could not attend the meeting) took place last on 4th July, 2006, more than two months before the elaborate Notification was issued on 14th September, 2006. There was an agreement between the Chairpersons and the Secretary of the Ministry that an inspection mechanism to assess the status of compliance with terms and conditions subject to which the Ministry had been granting prior environmental clearance need to be evolved. Another decision taken in the same meeting was that similar meetings would be held periodically in order to facilitate regular exchange of views between the Expert Committee and the Ministry. The subordinate officers of the Ministry had, almost with a sense of impunity, ignored the existence of such decisions taken in a meeting presided over by the Ministry's Secretary. The fact that no follow up action could be taken even after the minutes of the 4th July, 2006 meeting were circulated among the members of the Committees is a pointer to the apathy of the concerned division in the Ministry.

The Ministry has its own field offices in various regions of the country. The recent media report has plunged the MoEF into almost convulsive kneejerk action against some influential entities in the mining sector in Orissa. What role the Ministry played in ensuring that its own field functionaries at least do their routine inspection work and report any wrong-doings by the miners to the Ministry? The Vedanta case in Orissa proves that the field officers of the Ministry have completely failed in their duty. That the Minister himself had to intervene, that too propelled by the media reports, while the proper basis should have been the report submitted by the Ministry's field officers, proves the gravity of the matter. If the Minister was forced to make shrill noise, his officers might also claim that they also did make some noise and if so, such noises did not appear to be in sync with the prompt action taken by their political master.

Expert Appraisal Committee (EAC)

The EAC in a broader sense is almost like an extended arm of the MoEF in the sense that its recommendations form an integral part of the process in the grant of prior environmental clearance for any project, mining or others. But it has its own distinct identity and its functioning is independent of the Ministry. Even the Central Regulator, presently the Minister in-charge of the MoEF, cannot reject the recommendation of the EAC at the first instance. Should he disagree with the views of the EAC, he can do so only after reconsideration by the EAC of its earlier recommendations on the basis of the grounds adduced by the Minister for his disagreement with the EAC. It is, therefore, essential that one becomes familiar with the functioning of the EAC and its Constitution that involves selection of members of integrity and reputation.

Appendix-VI to the 14th September Notification read with para 5 of the Notification deals with the constitution of the EAC. The members of the Committee are experienced persons in the relevant field. The 11th October, 2007 amending Notification keeps the post of the Chairperson of the EAC open to a person who has the expertise in the relevant field as indicated in the Appendix. Usually a retired bureaucrat or a mining expert holds the post of Chairperson.

The Ministry of Environment and Forests (MoEF) is the competent authority to constitute the EAC. It is presumed that the Ministry would consider the curricula vitae of the persons to be appointed as members of the Committee. Once appointed, there should normally not arise any occasion to make any aspersion on the credentials of the incumbent members. The Appendix-VI is silent on the question of conflict of interest on the part of any member or the Chairperson of the Committee. The standard practice followed by a Government servant, whether retired or working, is that if any item of work comes before him and he has conflict of interest he withdraws himself from that particular work. Media reports suggested that Judges of the Apex Court had declined to hear certain cases in similar circumstances. If this is the case, the observations of the Minister on the credential of a particular Chairperson, not related to the EAC on Mining, as reported by the print media are unfortunate. His penchant for media coverage is well known but as a Minister in-charge of the Ministry that had constituted the EAC he needs to show certain degree of circumspection. The particular Chairman was to quit and the Minister made it public the reasons for his quitting. The particular Chairman was Secretary to the Government of India and also he was Member of Union Public Service Commission (UPSC). I had no occasion to know him closely but in official circle he is treated with respect and is considered to be a thorough gentleman and being a member of the Indian Administrative Service with stringent Service Conduct Rules to follow he perhaps knows and surely not in need of any lessons from others after retirement how to behave in a case where conflict of interest may vitiate his opinion or decision. A simple hint to the person that he was not wanted by the Minister to continue on the post would have been more than enough for him to tender his resignation forthwith. If such humiliation was to be inflicted publicly the demoralizing effect on the other Chairpersons or members is not in the best interest of the functioning of the Committees. Has the Minister taken so much pain in constituting the EACs after verifying the fact if any member would have some conflict of interest or otherwise not fit? The author is in the know of at least one member re-appointed to the new EAC (Mining) who had claimed and also received sitting fee for a particular meeting without being present in the meeting. His absence was recorded in the days' proceedings. In fact, the author, who happened to be the Chairman of the previous EAC, had reported the case, through a D.O. letter addressed to the Secretary of the Ministry. The Ministry did not take any action against the particular member even when the Chairman recommended his removal. He was only rewarded by another tenure of three years as member of the EAC (Mining). The age old dictum that while sitting in a glass house one should not throw stones at others continues to be relevant even in a free and democratic society. Holier than thou attitude and selective action raises doubt about the bona fide of an action even if it is otherwise justified.

In a way the stake of the EAC is more than that of the Ministry. The recommendations of the EAC are put in the website of the Ministry and are instantly in public domain and are subject to scrutiny by every other stake holder besides the media. Thus the Committee can ill afford to appraise a proposal in a casual manner. In fact, the reputation of the EAC is constantly vulnerable to an ever watchful media and various activist groups. It is but desirable that the EAC, once constituted, be allowed to function. The Ministry is free to take proper precaution and to verify the antecedents and general reputation about the integrity of the persons before appointment as members of a Committee.

Under the 14th September Notification the Chairperson of the EAC has a unique role and is not merely a *primus inter pares*, the first among equals, inasmuch as it is his duty to ensure a consensus in each case failing which the views of the majority shall prevail. One can imagine the herculean task of taking a composite view accommodating the views of so many experts more often than not pulling in different and opposite directions. This underscores the fact that the Chairperson shall be someone who commands respect of all the expert members and whose objectivity and integrity are above board. It is perhaps not for nothing that most of the Chairpersons of the various EACs in the past had been retired Secretaries to Government of India with good reputation and varied experience, with the experience of working in mining, industrial and environmental sectors as added advantage.

Para 8 of Appendix-VI reads "The Chairman/members may not be removed prior to expiry of the tenure without cause and proper enquiry." The idea behind such a provision is, no doubt, loudable but its practical implications are complicated. The above provision is intended to ensure that the Chairman and the members shall function freely without any fear of getting removed at the whims of the Ministry, be it the Minister which is often the case or the Secretary of the Ministry. My Committee had a name dropper as an expert member who never missed an opportunity to mention his closeness to the power, both political and bureaucratic, and who thought that there was nothing under the sun which he would not know. He had proved that name dropping is an effective tool in getting re-appointed in the reconstituted EAC with the full knowledge of the Secretary of the Ministry that there is a report against the integrity of the individual if, of course, defrauding the government is taken as lack of integrity.

The wordings of para 8 of Appendix-VI needs a review to take care of some genuine cases of delinquency. One can understand that a person, once appointed, should not be removed without *cause* but to add that he can be removed only after *proper enquiry* is of a different dimension. The notification is a statutory one and so is Appendix-VI. Thus the mandated enquiry is not a simple one as it has to be a proper enquiry meaning thereby that the results of the enquiry would be subject to judicial scrutiny. After all, the Chairpersons or the members are not regular appointees with monthly salary. They are entitled to sitting fees and travel costs for attending the meetings of the EAC and not otherwise. The normal procedure should have been that the Chairperson makes a report on the performance of a member with reasons to justify removal of any member and the Ministry can take a view on such a report if necessary after a thorough discussion with the Chairperson. In the case of removal of the Chairperson the quality of the minutes of the meetings and the final recommendations in different and specially complicated cases should be the guiding materials based on which the Secretary of the Ministry is competent enough to take a view and obtain approval of the Minister for removal of the Chairperson. It is up to him to decide whether it is necessary to talk to the Chairperson before taking a final view on his removal. As stated earlier, a simple hint to that effect is enough for the Chairperson to tender his resignation without any embarrassment to either party.

I dare make a comparison between the stake of the Ministry and that of the EAC. But I cannot help taking the view that the EAC is at a greater risk than the Ministry in the entire process of examining a proposal for the grant of environmental clearance. When everything goes well and there is no controversy on any environmental clearance, the credit can always be legitimately claimed by the Ministry which is primarily responsible for grant of environmental clearance. But if something goes amiss, the Ministry would be perfectly justified to shift the blame to the EAC which is admittedly an expert body to judge if a particular proposal is a fit case for the Central Regulator to grant environmental clearance. This could perhaps be one of the reasons as to why the MoEF circular dated 8th December, 2006 enjoins upon the Committee to give categorical and unambiguous recommendations that a particular proposal referred by the Ministry to the EAC is either recommended or rejected or deferred, the three categories being mutually exclusive. My Committee, and so is the case with other EACs, was conscious of the special responsibility and had discussed the issue threadbare in the beginning so that the members, while expressing their views, would keep the critical importance of the recommendations of the EAC which are, so to say, *sine qua non* for the Ministry to take a final decision, in mind. One can look at the criticality of the recommendations of the EAC which may, at times, create a predicament for the Ministry. For example, the EAC may recommend a case for grant of environmental clearance, but it is the prerogative of the Ministry to take a different view on valid grounds and nobody can question the power of the Ministry to take a certain decision. But where the EAC recommends a case for rejection it becomes very difficult, nay impossible, for the Ministry to take an opposite view. The EAC, therefore, can ill-afford to appraise a case except with due circumspection and giving justified grounds either for rejection or for grant of environmental clearance.

As mentioned earlier, the proceedings of the EAC are put in the website of the Ministry and the same are instantly in the public domain and are vulnerable to the watchful eye of the media and other environmental activists even without taking any recourse to the provisions of the Right To Information Act (RTI Act).

From whatever have been stated hereinbefore I am inclined to come to the conclusion that the reputation of the EAC is at far more greater risk than that of any other stakeholders in the grant or otherwise of environmental clearance for any mining project. Therefore, the EAC is no less a stakeholder in the whole process and hence the integrity and reputation of the members of the EAC become critical.

The Miner

During the long years of my experience in and association with mining industry I could appreciate the role played by the mine owner in the economic development of the country. But he is more often than not a maligned entity in the eye of even a person enjoining the luxury of living in comfortably weather conditioned house or moving in an air-conditioned limousine, a large luxurious car, giving sermon to others as to how a miner is responsible for polluting the environment without even realizing and taking note of the fact that his air-conditioned house or the limousine is the result of the hard work of the miner who supplies the raw materials limestone or iron ore or bauxite or copper ore, name any mineral, to make cement, steel, aluminium, electric wire etc. that go into the making of a house or a motor vehicle. Still such people try to project the miner as the main polluter of the environment. But with his contribution to the nation's economy how come the miner is so much criticized?

The system of control and the accompanying corruption have created a vicious circle so much so that nothing moves in the corridors of power unless the greed of the bureaucracy at various levels is satisfied. Had it been an one time affair perhaps a miner could happily live with the system. But that is not the case. I have experience for fairly long period in this sector. Corruption is quite transparent, perhaps involving a reasonably manageable amount of money without much dent on the profitability of the operation, at the state level with easy access to the top political executive against the Minister-In-Charge (Mining). At the Central level, the operation is unhindered and smooth all in the name of mineral development and an honest Secretary has no option but to live with the corrupt practices at the political level. Any attempt to devise a system, where corruption could be contained, is always met with sometimes subtle and sometimes open resistance, again all in the name of mineral development. I would mention few instances based on my personal experience as to how a situation is created in which a miner does certain things just for sheer survival in the industry. This will also underscore the fact that the miner need not feel frustrated and he should rather take the reality of corruption as one of the hazards in operating a mine and in a lighter vein, I would say it (corruption) is less of a hazard than a fatal accident not uncommon in a mining project.

Immediately on joining as Secretary (Mines & Geology) in a large and major mineral-rich State I was confronted with a somewhat unusual and unsolicited advice through a formal letter written by a Mining Inspector in a district where there is no scope for any mining activity except brick- kiln. There were two sanctioned posts of Mining Inspector in the district and one post was vacant. So in the usual course, one person was notified to be posted against the vacant post. The advice of the existing Inspector was that there was no need for one more Inspector in the district and that he was competent to handle the entire work and of course he did not forget to remind me the laudable reason for economy in administrative expenditure on an additional post. With further probe, I got to know something which prompted me to amend the State Minor Mineral Concession Rules to tackle and permanently block the scope for making money by the corrupt field functionaries at least from the brick-kiln owners.

The State had at that time (1986) about 4000 brick-kilns and this particular district had about 100 or so brick-kilns. Under the extant Rules a brick-kiln owner was required to take a permit to operate the brick-kiln and he was to pay to the government royalty at fixed rate per 100,000 pieces of bricks and the Inspector is the competent authority to count the number of bricks in the kiln operated by the permit holder. I leave it to the imagination of the readers the extent of ingenuity that a Mining Inspector is capable of inventing while ostensibly making count of bricks in a particular kiln.

I proposed an amendment to the existing Rules under which the State was to be divided into four categories. In each category area a minimum number of bricks per kiln would be assumed for the purpose of payment of royalty. The lowest category would have the rate of royalty per kiln of certain capacity which would be higher than the existing rate with graduated higher rates for the next three higher categories. Any brick-kiln owner would deposit the amount of royalty per kiln as applicable in the particular category area through a Challan, the prescribed form for such deposit of money, in the government treasury and start operating the kiln. The proposal was called compounding rate of royalty on brick-kiln and it was submitted to the State Cabinet for approval. The officers of the Department of Mines and Geology through political support put pressure on the Chief Minister not to accept the proposal. I was summoned by the Chief Minister (CM). Minister (Mines & Geology), who was politically very close to the CM, was also present. The CM in his inimitable way (usually closing both the eyes) straightway put to me this question: "Commissioner Sahib (Mr. Commissioner as my statutory designation was so called), why do you want this arrangement, what is the provocation?" I answered by citing the above instance of the advice given by a Mining Inspector against the posting of a second Inspector. The Chief Minister smiled, paused for a while and gave his decision thus: "Commissioner Sahib, you have understood the working of the Department too early and in recognition thereof I support your proposal." Just imagine one simple amendment was enough to eradicate completely the scope for any chance for the field functionaries to harass at least a section of the miners (brick-kiln owners). In the process the government was the gainer as the four categories of areas were selected in a way that the lowest category area would have brick-kiln for which the rate of royalty was more than the rate of royalty being paid hitherto by the brick-kiln owners.

I will cite one instance where a miner could be held responsible for corruption at the level of Minister in the government only to highlight the fact that it is not always the bureaucracy that encourages corruption rather at times a miner is also responsible for the current state of affairs. While corruption at official level may affect few lessees, the corruption at the level of political executive pervades all mining activities as the system provides a fertile ground for corruption. I will go back to early 1990's to cite the instance hinted at the start of this paragraph.

If I remember correctly till sometime in 1992 the question of granting prior approval of the Central Government under Section 5(1) of the MMDR Act, 1957 in respect of any mineral specified in the First Schedule to the Act was being decided at the level of Joint Secretary before any lease etc. could be granted by the State Government. I do not think there was any complaint of corruption against any dealing hands and the officers, and even if any, it would involve very small amount of money in getting a copy of the typed (computer and word processing were not still common) sanction letter. No body could imagine that Ministers like Mr. N.D. Tiwari or Mr. Pranab Mukherjee or Mr. M.L. Foteder who had headed the Ministry of Mines and under whom the author had the opportunity to work would ever like to take over the power of granting prior approval of the government. But this was what happened and how it happened is briefly mentioned below.

There was a case for grant of prior approval in respect of renewal of mining lease for limestone mine of a large cement industrial house. The owner met the Minister and casually mentioned the case to the Minister perhaps without meaning anything. What a golden opportunity! The result was the suo motu direction of the Minister to put up all cases, not any particular case, of prior approval before the Minister. The rest is history and higher the authority means befitting consideration to minimize delay in getting the approval. Unlike in the State government where the Secretary of the Department has the option to take up the matter with the Chief Secretary who, in his discretion, may seek intervention of the C.M. and in at least one State under the Rules of Executive Business the Secretary of the Department can formally refer the matter to the C.M. through the Chief Secretary, the Secretary to a Ministry in the Central Government is helpless even if the concerned Minister takes blatantly wrong decision and at times decisions which are not legal. Even the Cabinet Secretary who is head of the bureaucracy in the Central Government cannot be of any help not because he doesn't want to do something but the system is such that he just plays safe by remaining indifferent.

The situation is no better, in fact could be worse, in the effort of a miner to get clearance under Forest (Conservation) Act if mining is to be in forest land in addition to environmental clearance. I had the experience about the working in the State Government and also in the Ministry of Mines, Government of India and what I have said above is based on my experience. Since I was not a part of the bureaucracy in the MoEF, though I worked as Chairman, EAC (Mining) for three years, but what I have heard from officers who are privy to the wrong doings at the political level and I have no reason to disbelieve the officers, it is clear that except very few honourable exceptions, it is much worse compared to the doings in the process of getting a mining lease. Once a mining lease is sanctioned the lessee also has motivation strong enough to go extra mile to get the required forest and or environmental clearance. For him starting the mining operation at the earliest is more pressing and he perhaps has no time to think about the corrupt practices so embedded in the system.

Thus a miner becomes a victim of and a party to the corrupt practices due to the bureaucratic hurdle in getting all the required permissions in time and for any business enterprise, mining is no exception, time is money. Thus unless money changes hand, call it *speed money* for the miner or *greed money* for the official machinery to do their allotted work for which the Government pays them salary etc. nothing moves. Unfortunately, a compounding system of fixing royalty as I had introduced for brick-kiln and referred to earlier does not apply and cannot be experimented in respect of major minerals except perhaps for sand for stowing. So no way out at the end of the tunnel so long discretionary power in the grant of permission exists.

We must find some way out to ensure that a miner is not necessarily to be always at the receiving end to bear the brunt of the vicious attack as the only target. I have in Chapters-5 to 8 elaborated the procedure and contents of EIA Report and the EMP. I am quite sure that if a miner follows my prescription for the preparation of the EIA Report and the EMP and with an attractive CSR Policy and pragmatic socio-economic package the chances of getting support of the local community are bright. Since time is essence, certain pre-project activities well in advance as I have emphasized (*ibid*) would create a very favourable impact among the locals who are likely to be impacted due to the proposed mining activities, the asset of goodwill of the local people thus created remains forever. This, along with compliance with the terms and conditions of a mining lease and the environmental clearance and forestry clearance, if any, in letter and in spirit would, I am sure, eliminate the chances of the corrupt officials harassing the miner to a great extent. So even if *greed money* is to be paid for securing all the clearances, it becomes an one time exercise.

Along with the suggested option as mentioned in the preceding paragraph, there is an urgent need to have a group of lobbyists (not the 2 G Spectrum variety) who are well conversant with the complete procedure in obtaining various statutory clearances, permits, etc. and who can effectively impress upon the authorities the paramount need for developing mining as an industry, that is, development of minerals as the resource base for industrial growth rather than simply winning the minerals and routinely disposing the same like a tradeable commodity. Ministry of Mines or the Department of Mines at the State level may be the parent body, but without the active support of other Ministries like Commerce, Industry, Finance etc. and of course, the Planning Commission any effort to develop the mineral resources the way it should be would not fructify. A miner should not feel shy of the "lobbying culture", as opposed to the "broker or middleman" culture pursuing a particular case for a favourable order by the competent authority, as this (lobbying) is not only an accepted system but is also a very effective system even in highly developed countries like the USA and the UK. I still remember a particular MP in the Rajya Sabha raising the issues of saving the dying mica industries in Bihar (now Jharkhand) in every session of the House and the Government used to give almost a stereotyped, the expression "cut and paste" was not in vogue at that time, reply. But simply raising the matter in the Parliament or drawing attention of the Government through letters written by the MPs or raising the issue in the form of question would not do. When the lobbying culture degenerates into a middleman culture it would automatically create a fertile ground for bribery.

The mining fraternity should rise and make their presence felt and felt pronouncedly so as to activate and motivate the policy makers to declare development of minerals a national priority. There is the in-house indifference also. I will cite three instances of large industrial Houses, two in steel sector and one in cement industry. Both SAIL and TISCO are large steel makers and look at their advertisements through attractive Bill Board across the country or through electronic and print media. There is bit of SAIL in everybody's life and TATA also makes steel. Same is the case with Ambuja Cement telling that how can a wall erected with Ambuja Cement give way and break down. But none of the above three big players even thinks of telling the nation anything about the minerals iron ore or limestone with slogan like, say, how can steel made of iron ore mined by SAIL/TATA or a concrete wall erected with cement made of limestone mined by Ambuja break? At least these companies can proudly say they also mine iron ore and limestone minerals for the nation. The mining fraternity had a bitter experience how the steel lobby almost hijacked the Hoda Committee on mining constituted by the Planning Commission few years back by orchestrating the virtue of captive mine and the banning of the export of iron ore rather than arguing the case for mining as an industry for the development of the mineral resources as a solid resource base for the steel, cement etc. industries. Mining fraternity should come out of the self-created shell and should not silently bear the brunt of unjustified attack.

As the stake of a miner is very critical the EIA Report and the EMP, the preparation of which has been elaborated in Chapters-5 to 13, can be made an effective instrument to prove to the Society that he (miner) is no less concerned about a clean environment and that he cares for the society.

Non-Governmental Organisations (NGOs)

During the three years of my tenure as Chairman of the EAC (Mining), I could come across only one NGO that operates in one of the States under the charge of the Committee and the main minerals in the State are iron ore and manganese ore. Before I go into the working of NGOs in mining area it will be worthwhile to have an idea about the general role that NGOs are found playing. I must frankly admit that I have no personal knowledge about the working of NGOs or any activist group or individual activist. Only once I had occasion to see reaction of the people who have been tremendously benefited by the work done by the Ram Krishna Mission (R.K. Mission). But nobody can imagine a Swamiji in saffron robe appearing before the electronic media and loudly criticizing the apathy of the government towards the problems of the poor and disadvantaged section of the society and inciting such people to take agitational route, more often than not, violent agitational route. But the good work being done by the R.K. Mission in the field of education and other social welfare activities is universally appreciated by one and all.

Now we have the film personalities and other celebrities visiting some troubled spots to exploit the situation and they are always accompanied by the media people, both print and electronic and as a source of entertainment people will remain glued to electronic media as the private T.V. channels will repeat the same news and footages round the clock. I am yet to see any news item either in the print media or electronic media on any concrete proposal that the NGOs or the activists think would ameliorate the sufferings of the poor people except the routine and general criticism of exploitation of the poor tribals.

As regards the socio-economic problems in the mining areas which also happen to be mostly the forest area in remote places and inhabited by the tribal people and other traditional forest dwellers, the Committee did not receive any proposal from any NGO about the actions to be taken by the concerned lessee to benefit the local people. Even in the public hearing which is an elaborate process as explained in Chapter-4 the local people mostly ask for employment and the so called environmentalist activists would argue only against the proposed mining operation.

A particular NGO that operates in one of the States under the charge of my Committee did once sent an attractively printed booklet giving photographs of certain areas allegedly damaged by mining activists. A sub-group of the Committee headed by me visited the State for two days in some other context. Nobody from the NGO appeared before the sub-group. One of the members of the sub-group was keen to visit some areas indicated by the NGO in the booklet circulated among the members. I agreed and asked the member to locate the spots which the entire sub-group could visit. He was quite excited but to his surprise he could not identify the area as no details like mining lease number, name of the village, plot number or other identification details were available in the booklet. In the absence of the required details about the location how does one know the veracity of the photograph? One NGO wanted to make a presentation before the Committee which did not agree as the Committee could not be an alternative forum for public consultation. The NGO would not take part in the public hearing which is a mandatory one. My own assessment is that the affected villagers would not accept any negative protest, rather they would generally like the mining operation but they want employment and economic benefits of the projects and protection of the environment including the flora and fauna.

I am doubtful if the NGOs or the social activists, as they operate now, are at all of any use to the areas affected by mining activities. The terrain and the populace of the area are not familiar with the NGOs etc. Unless someone knows the requirement of the local people and is ready with some implementable economic packages that would give result in visible economic growth as I have indicated in Chapter-11 on socio-economic environment the so-called activists would do no good to the affected people except that they would gain some brownie point which would have good publicity value. The NGOs and the activists would, no doubt, do well in certain areas closer to the mainstream habitation. Mineral rich remote areas need NGO like the R.K. Mission that works silently among the poor and the disadvantaged and does not need any publicity. I doubt if any newspaper or TV channel would get time to publicise the good work done by any reputed NGOs which perhaps also avoid such publicity.

The NGOs could do wonder in the optimal exploitation of the mineral resources and improving the living conditions of the tribals and other disadvantaged section of the people through gainful economic activities by the local people on a sustained basis. Orchestrated protests and loud voices can not be the substitute for some implementable economic packages for the locals. Further, if the NGOs are so emotionally addicted to the cause of the poor tribals they can prove their sincerity by boycotting the consumer products made out of the minerals which they allege, may be rightly so in some cases, have been mined by exploiting the local people with scanty regards for their well-being. It will perhaps be relevant here to refer to the essence of the comments made by the well-known London based Daily, *The Guardian*, in an editorial dated 28th August, 2010 (see the importance the Daily attaches to the subject so as to write an editorial) under the caption–Congo rapes–Scramble for Africa, the first two paragraphs of which run as follows:

> "Cassiterite, wolframite, coltan: they mjght be the spoiled offspring of celebrity parents, or characters from an unfamiliar fairytale. The truth is much more prosaic. They are the minerals on which laptops and mobiles and even the tin of tomatoes in the cupboard depend. Cassiterite is the main component of tin oxide. Wolframite is a source of tungsten, used in many electrical applications. Coltan makes mobile phones work.
>
> There are two reasons why it is necessary to know about these otherwise apparently esoteric minerals. First, the rich world has a capacious appetite for them and second, it is fueling conflict in the eastern part of the Democratic Republic of Congo (DRC). The rape of more than 150 women and children earlier this month in Luvungi, North Kivu, in the DRC's mineral heartland is

> probably (it is not yet proven) directly connected with the exploitation of the mines from which these minerals come."

The editorial also refers to more optimistic developments elsewhere and the global technology companies waking up to their vulnerability to consumer pressure and the Finland based Nokia banning the use of minerals from Congo in its phones.

What lesson can our NGOs learn from the episode in Congo? Do they have the courage to practise, rather than preach, the virtue of boycotting the journey from, say, Kolkata to Jangal Mahal in West Bengal, by rail if the railway track was built with the steel made out of the minerals iron ore mined from the mines falling within the now well known red corridor on the ground which the NGOs never forget to loudly announce that the minerals represent the exploitation of the local tribals? The truth is that it has become a vested interest of the so-called NGOs and other activists to keep the issue alive rather than offering a viable solution to the problem so that they remain busy in the their profession obviously being financed by some well-wishers in their own interest.

It would but be natural only that a reference is made to the fact that the Right To Information Act (RTI Act) has given a golden opportunity to many NGOs and the so-called social activists to make easy money by abusing the provisions of the RTI Act. There is no denying the fact that the government system functions with such absurd secrecy that more often than not its most sincere effort to do something for the welfare of the public is misunderstood due to lack of transparency. The RTI Act is intended to be an instrument to bring in total transparency in the working of the government and a well-informed citizenry would be an asset for the government. But some unscrupulous NGOs and social activists with the connivance of some equally unscrupulous legal practitioners have been using the provisions of the otherwise most liberal legislation guaranteeing easy access to the wrong doings of the bureaucratic system for unholy purposes by blackmailing certain officials to take revenge for some personal grievances. Recently, there was a news item in a national *English Daily* with large publication throughout the country on the naked abuse of the power given under the RTI Act. It pertains to the effort of an individual making application under the RTI Act to the Municipal Corporation of Delhi (MCD) for certain information on the sexual behaviour of certain officers of the MCD posted in South Delhi with their DNA report. It was so malicious in nature that on a petition filed by the MCD before the Delhi High Court, the Court could not help expressing its indignation by not only dismissing the plea of the information seeker but also imposing a hefty exemplary penalty on him. Some times a party with malicious personal grudge can effectively mislead the judiciary also to get a favourable order.

The role of the NGOs or the so-called social activities, if anything, has been negative as if stopping mining activities is the only panacea for all the problems that the tribals and other traditional forest dwellers are facing. With some imaginative approach the NGOs and other groups could do wonder in improving the living conditions of the people and there is no reason as to why a miner should not respond positively to any proposals for the benefit of the very people among whom the miner is to work and who knows it better than him (miner) that working among a hostile people will do him more harm while a friendly people is always a valuable asset?

The local people

The local populace being the immediate victims of the polluted environment caused due to mining activities, their collective resolve can be a very effective tool to ensure that the miner falls in line to ensure a healthy and a clean environment. They can do so by using the statutorily mandated public consultation elaborated in Chapter-4 of this book and I believe there is no need to repeat the same here on the role of the local people.

Chapter – 15

ILLS and the Panacea

Due to one sided propaganda against mining activities and names of certain influential personalities with lot of social and political clout getting involved an impression has been created that mining activities are singularly responsible for polluting the environment. I am not going into the debate on the veracity of such arguments as such a debate would lead us nowhere besides being not the purpose of this book. Before I proceed to deal with the three divisions of this chapter, i.e., policy prescription, the all pervading corruption and the governance, it would be pertinent to know if mining does only harm to the environment without any good.

The government of the country and the governments of various states very proudly and articulately pronounce that it would provide houses, road connectivity, electricity, safe drinking water, food, education, employment, etc. to the people. There is none in the country and perhaps anywhere in the world who would find any fault with the declared policy of the Government to provide basic requirements of a reasonably decent living to the people specially the weaker segment of the society. Even the so called environmentalists and the NGOs would dare to utter a single word against such a policy of the Government. Let us now consider the contribution of mining activities to the fulfilment of the policy of the Government.

Take the case of provision of residential houses for the people and road connectivity specially for the people living in the remote areas for easy access to the nearest state or national highway. What are the basic raw materials for constructing houses whether residential or commercial? One needs steel and cement besides bricks to construct a house. Likewise, stone chips and cement are basic raw materials for constructing a road. So cement is required for the construction of any road or house. Such a road on the way would cross a river or a canal and therefore, bridges are to be constructed to allow the road to go further till it reaches its pre-fixed point of getting connected with another road and thereby becoming a part of the network of road connectivity. To construct such bridges steel and cement would be required. If this is the scenario there is no escape from mining iron ore for the steel mills to produce steel of various categories and working a limestone mine to supply the raw materials to a cement plant. It is inconceivable to import the entire requirement of iron ore for the steel mills and that of limestone for the cement plants. If the country has sufficient iron ore reserves and also limestone reserves it makes sense to exploit these minerals. Mining activities have great potential for creating employment opportunities which is one of the declared priorities of the Government and the country's Five Year Plan invariably emphasises generation of employment opportunities. If the minerals are imported the employment opportunities becomes insignificant as the only visible employment in case of import would be in loading and unloading the imported minerals.

We may now take up the cases of copper and aluminium, the two most important non-ferrous metals. Copper wire is an essential ingredient in electrical industry. Earlier copper wire was used for transmission of power. Since copper has become a scarce commodity with high cost, aluminium wire has replaced the use of copper wire in many areas. Aluminium is also used in transport vehicles including aircrafts. There are many electrical appliances where copper is an essential ingredient. Extruded aluminium products are being extensively used as window frames and door frames in many commercial as also residential buildings. For such essential utilities for our day to day life there has to be adequate supply of these two non-ferrous metals. India is endowed with huge bauxite deposits of good quality in the East Coast in the states of Orissa and Andhra Pradesh. As in the case of iron ore it makes economic sense to exploit such good quality bauxite ore for the aluminium plants to produce the metal. India has got efficiently run aluminum smelters and their products are of good quality. In fact the National Aluminum Company (NALCO) has good export markets for its alumina which is the immediate raw materials for producing aluminium metal. India is a net importer of copper as the known deposits are limited and are located in only three states, namely, Jharkhand, Rajasthan and Madhya Pradesh. All these mines are being operated by the Central PSU, namely, Hindustan Copper Limited. The other copper smelters are based on imported copper concentrates. The units producing down stream items like copper wire, sheets etc are based largely on imported cathode or copper bar as the raw materials since the domestic availability is not adequate. Thus, import of copper in the form of concentrates or cathodes or bar would continue to be unavoidable till additional deposits are found through exploration. Therefore, mining of bauxite ore and copper ore becomes inescapable. Like in other mining activities, copper and bauxite mining would create considerable employment opportunities. Import of copper ore is not a viable proposition as even with a high grade of 2 to 3 per cent copper a large quantity of copper ore need be imported that would create unmanageable level of pollution. So if copper ore is to be imported the country would be inviting more environmental pollutants which is not worth it compared to the amount of metal that could be recovered.

What has been said in the preceding paragraphs about iron ore, limestone, bauxite and copper would equally apply to the mining of other minerals and I do not think that there is any need to deal with other minerals separately.

Let us stop for a while and assume that in order to avoid any environmental problems on account of mining activities, no mining would be allowed. Since, pollution would be caused due to other activities like generation of electric power, river valley projects etc. the logical corollary would be to stop not only mining activities but all other activities that cause environmental pollution as it would not be fair to single out mining as the only source of pollution. So, no electricity, no modern day residential house and we go back to the *ashram* stage, that is, the stage of hermitage, the final abode of religious leaders preferably in the Himalayas. Since so much economic development has taken place over the years which has resulted in a different type of lifestyle with many modern amenities it would be nothing short of insanity if one has to propagate the theory that all developmental activities that are accompanied with environmental pollution should be stopped forthwith. Obviously, a medical practitioner, while treating a person for stomach ailments caused by either food poisoning or overeating, does not prescribe that the patient after treatment should stop taking food altogether.

I can not help commenting on the views expressed by certain intellectuals, social activists and NGOs who, in the full glare of electronic media, very loudly criticize mining activities and more often than not propagating stoppage of any mining activities in the tribal dominated and other forest areas. First thing to understand is that mining can take place only where minerals exist. And it is a coincidence that occurrences of most of the major minerals like iron ore, bauxite etc. are generally only in forest land and this is also an area inhabited by the tribal people and other traditional forest dwellers for generations. Some of these activists would travel by air or by train or by road in air-conditioned vehicles with media crew specially the electronic media to a place nearer the on-going mining activities they are up in arms against, without appreciating, much realising, the fact that but for the mining of iron ore there would have been no railway track for them to travel or, but for bauxite and copper mining there would have been no aircraft or motor vehicle to take them in luxury. If such activists are made to travel on foot without using any of the modern means of transportation which are standing contribution of the mining activities they would not have perhaps survived the ordeal to show their presence on the electronic media. To me there seems to be an element of hypocrisy if we criticize mining of iron ore, bauxite or copper or limestone and at the same time lead a comfortable life in an air-conditioned house. Some of the activists and so called exponents of eco-friendly environment must make an introspection to see the disconnect between what they preach and what they actually enjoy. If such people are asked to abstain from indulging in material comforts or to become abstemious and to practise even moderate self-indulgment in eating and drinking (alcohol) and living in air-conditioned houses they would react with horror with the expression like how can a man live like that in modern times?

The fact is that human civilization throughout the world has reached a stage where going back to the age of hermitage to live in the serenity of nature is not simply possible. This leads us to the inescapable conclusion that mining activities, or for that matter, any other industrial activities, which are essential for the all-round economic development of the nation must go hand in hand with stringent anti-pollution measure so that such activities become sustainable. That is, the society for the benefit of which such activities are destined does not become a diseased one as, otherwise the very purpose of any mining or other industrial activities would get defeated. I dare say that post-mining and other industrial activities, environment could be brought to a level the living things can sustain as was the case prior to mining and other industrial activities. Complete restoration of lands and other environments is not practicable. But with effective mitigating measures the environment can be made to sustain living things including humans and wildlife and the forest cover. Here comes the relevance of the three divisions of this chapter referred to earlier, that is, Policy Prescription, Corruption and Governance, which I would be dealing with henceforth, the first two being relevant for the ills while the last providing the panacea.

POLICY PRESCRIPTION

No government can undertake or encourage any developmental activities without having a policy for different segments of the economy, education, health and other socio-economic development activities. For the purpose of this book I would only deal with the policy aspect relating to mining activities and controlling environmental pollution as a result of mining activities. I would not go into the merits or otherwise of the policy adopted and announced by the Ministry of Mines or by the Ministry of Environment and Forests (MoEF).

It is well-known to everybody that the Ministry of Mines has formulated a National Mineral Policy that gives an idea about how to exploit the known mineral deposits. The policy also highlights the importance of exploratory works to know the potential mineral deposits. As I have mentioned earlier, for the purpose of this book I would mainly refer to the mineral iron ore as iron ore are in abundance and the minerals occur mostly in the forest areas which are also the habitation of the tribal people and other traditional forest dwellers. The known deposits of iron ore as on 01.4.2005 are 252.49 billion tonnes (*Source*: *Indian Minerals Year Book* published by the Indian Bureau of Mines, a subordinate office of the Ministry of Mines, Government of India). These are the deposits of which we have the knowledge and the full potentials of the country in so far as existence of the minerals iron ore are not known to us as only further exploration would give us an idea about the likely deposits. However, it is believed that India is specially endowed with good quality iron ore for which both extensive and intensive exploratory works are called for. Even the known reserves are considered quite large and are capable of catering to the requirement of steel industry for many years. That being so there has to be a clearer and unambiguous policy prescription for exploiting the huge iron ore deposits of the country to meet the growing requirement of construction activities like residential and commercial houses, roads and bridges etc. The Planning Commission of which the Prime Minister is the Chairman determines, after detailed consultation with the consuming industries, State governments and related Ministries of the Government of India like Ministry of Mines, MoEF, Commerce, etc., the likely domestic availability of steel, cement, aluminium, copper, etc. that go into providing basic physical infrastructure. The Planning Commission prepares Five Year Plan as also the Annual Plan under Five Year Plan. While planning construction of residential houses for the people with special emphasis on the weaker segments of the society and road connectivity the Planning

Commission projects requirement of certain quantities of steel, cement, aluminium, etc. Since, export and import of various raw materials are an integral part of the economic activities, the Ministry of Commerce announces export-import (EXIM) Policy for the year. As export of iron ore is an important item of export projected by the Government the exploitation of country's iron ore deposits is automatically assumed as an essential industrial activities to meet the export target. The country also imports certain category of steel products. That being so the debate whether iron ore should be exported or not or whether export of iron ore should be controlled with high export duty becomes a frustrating one for the miners. Likewise, whether mining lease for iron ore should be granted only as captive to the steel makers or as stand alone mining activities are totally meaningless debate that has been going on now for a pretty long time creating a sense of frustration in the mining industry. Therefore, any policy on the exploitation of the mineral resources of the country should make it unambiguously clear that steel making or mining of iron ore or aluminium making or mining of, bauxite ore, etc. are independent industrial activities. Once such a clear policy prescription is made and implemented the entrepreneurs involved in these industrial activities would, in the best of their wisdom, take a view whether as a steel maker or an aluminium producer he would necessarily have captive iron ore mines or bauxite mines. Definitely mining of iron ore involves more complex issues to be tackled compared to simple steel making. Normally any wise steel maker should like to have a long term agreement with a stand alone mining company for supply of iron ore to his steel plant. Alternatively, the steel maker can form a separate and independent mining company to supply iron ore to the parent steel company with the liberty to sell the surplus ore in the open market. In such a scenario both the steel company and the mining company would function more efficiently and exploitation of the minerals would be optimal as the mining company would have the option to sell the surplus iron ore either in the domestic market or in the export market. Therefore, absence of a clear cut policy has caused more harm than good to both iron ore mining industry and steel industry. There is a joke going around that if a steel maker is to be granted on priority basis iron ore mines as captive source of raw materials for his steel mill, a rice mill-owner can, with the same logic, demand that certain paddy growing lands should be allotted to him as the captive source of paddy for his rice mill. In the absence of any clear cut policy prescription the discretionary power of the Government (read Political Executives) is bound to create havoc as without even directly regulating the mining of iron ore the

Government can effectively force the stand alone mining companies to restrict production by imposing high export duty and thereby helping the steel mills with captive mines and also helping such steel mills as are not having captive mines to enjoy the benefit of getting iron ore from the stand alone mining companies that, in the face of unviable export markets because of high export duty, is left with no option but to supply iron ore to such steel mills. This may at times, when there is less demand for iron ore from the steel mills due to any reason including recession, compel the mining industry to either stop production or producing lesser quantities as their export route is unviable due to higher export duty.

I would not go into further details as there are so many areas where the policy itself has allowed lot of discretionary power with the authorities. Even for grant of Prospecting Licences or Mining Leases or for grant of prior approval of the Central Government in respect of certain minerals (iron ore is one of such minerals) the discretionary power of the State Government and the Central Government has become a source of many unethical practices that I will deal with in the section on corruption.

In this context I would briefly refer to the regulatory regime in respect of mining activities. There is a Central Act under the title Mines and Minerals (Development and Regulation) Act, two rules under the title Minerals Concessions Rules and Mineral Conservation and Development Rules that regulate the grant and working of Prospecting Licence or Mining Lease. At the state level, every state has its own Minor Mineral Concessions Rules for grant of licences for mining various minor minerals. The title of the original Central Act was earlier Mines and Minerals (Regulation and Development) Act. On the recommendations of an Expert Committee of which I, as Additional-Secretary to the Government in the Ministry of Mines, was the Chairman, the title of the Act was amended as Mines and Minerals (*Development* and Regulation) Act with the idea that the Government of the day would give more emphasise on *development* and less on regulation except grant of licence or lease. This was done keeping in mind the title of the Act regulating grant of industrial licence in the light of the Industrial Policy Resoultion, 1956. I have seen the heyday of Inspector Raj when there was a committee headed by the Secretary, Department of Industry that used to meet every month for the consideration of applications for industrial licences. I used to attend the meeting of that committee on behalf of the Ministry of Mines. Gradually it became clear that the then IDR (Industrial Development and Regulation) Act, popularly known as IDR Act was being used by some big industrial houses as a pre-emptive Act by blocking the entry of any new entrepreneur in an area with most flimsy ground that adequate capacity had already been created in a certain area and hence there was no scope for further capacity to be licensed. The Directorate General, Technical Development (DGTD), more commonly known as DGTD, was almost the final authority, an arbiter of the sort, to declare if any more capacity should be created in a particular segment. There was a catch here. First a Letter of Intent (LOI) was granted to a particular entrepreneur for producing, say, some aluminium downstream products like extruded section etc. followed by the grant of an Industrial Licence. DGTD would keep the record of how many LOI's and industrial licences had been granted with what capacity. Since, the LOI holder was being given liberal extension there was no compulsion for him to convert the LOI into an Industrial Licence and to start production by a fixed time. But the system was good enough to pre-empt the arrival of any new entrepreneur who could be quite serious to implement any project but could not do so on the ground that there was already enough capacity (it was only capacity created on paper) existing and hence no scope for additional capacity.

The liberalization of the economy in early 1990's was expected to allow the industry to develop without much regulatory control. But in effect the provisions of the Act and the discretionary power available with the Government in the garb of Rules are working as a serious impediment in developing the mining industry. But even within the present legal frame it is possible to allow the mining industry to develop if there is a will to do so. I would give some suggestions on this subject in the last section of this chapter, that is, governance. I would now deal with somewhat similar issues in the procedure for grant of prior environmental clearance under the provisions of 14th September Notification.

Like the Ministry of Mines, the Ministry of Environment and Forest (MoEF) has its own policy to protect the environment and the ecology. This is a regulatory function of the MoEF exercised under the provisions of the Environment (Protection) Act, 1986 and the Rules framed thereunder. We have seen that mining of certain minerals, iron ore is one of them, would involve diversion of forest lands for non-forest purposes. In such a case the MoEF is the final authority to allow diversion of forest lands for non-forest purposes under the Forest (Conservation) Act, 1982. The MoEF has, for the purpose of granting prior environmental clearance for all industrial activities including mining projects, issued guidelines in the form of a Notification issued on 14th September, 2006 which is popularly known as 14th September Notification. The Ministry has tried its best to prescribe a transparent procedure for grant of prior environmental clearance for mining projects, both expansion of the existing projects as also new projects. I have dealt with this Notification in Chapter-2 of this book. A copy of this Notification incorporating the three amendments to the above Notification is Annexure-A. I am not repeating certain critical observations made in Chapter-2 which are only with a view to impressing upon the MoEF the need to take some corrective actions. I would only highlight here that having introduced a transparent system for grant of prior environmental clearance it would be a short sighted attitude if the Notification is allowed to create avoidable confusion.

The Expert Appraisal Committee (EAC) might appear to be a routine Administrative Committee whereas it is not so if one looks at the responsibility cast on it under 14th September Notification. The recommendations of the Committee become part of the process followed by the Ministry in the grant or rejection of prior environmental clearance. The proceedings are put on the website of the Ministry and, therefore, are in public domain and subject to judicial scrutiny. That being so an impression should not be allowed to be created that the EAC has been too liberal or too rigid in its consideration of any application for grant of prior environmental clearance. Such a comment is warranted on account of certain observations made by the previous Minister in charge as reported in the print media that the Ministry had, in an oblique reference to the cases of approval immediately preceding the start of his tenure as the Minister, unusual record of giving prior environmental clearances in 90 per cent of the cases. This has been dealt with in the preceding chapter, i.e., Chapter-14 on the role of MoEF as one of the stakeholders. Hence, no further elaboration is called for. The EAC, at least during the period of three years from September, 2006 to August, 2009 when I was the Chairman had never, either formally or informally, been told that the Government weren't in favour of granting prior environment clearance in large number of cases. In the absence of any clarity it becomes difficult for the EAC to process the cases for prior environmental clearance that would have been in conformity with the extant view of the MoEF.

Recent print media reports have dealt with the coinage of a new phrase, *no-go-zone*, similar to the concept of no-fly-zone during certain military operations. This *no-go-zone* is in respect of allotment of certain coal blocks in some states. MoEF is not in favour of allowing mining of coal in certain areas because of the fragile nature of the ecology. If one had any experience of visiting any of the worked out collieries in the state of Jharkhand it would appear that the MoEF can not be faulted if certain coal bearing areas are declared as *no-go-zone*, that is, no one should go to certain coal bearing areas for mining purposes. But the same print media also highlighted the resolution of the issues after the Minister of Coal took up the matter with the Minister of MoEF. It is beyond the comprehension of the author of this book as to how a fragile ecology categorized as no-go-zone could be converted into a *do-go-zone* after the meeting of two Ministers pulling the other day on opposite directions. This is bound to create confusion in the mind of an entrepreneur who is serious in investing his resources in a coal mine either for the supply of coal to his own consuming unit or to other consuming units like steel mill, power plant etc. that might consider mining not as their preferred option but are serious to have a long-term agreement with the coal mine owner(s) for supply of coal on regular and steady basis. Even if the two Ministries have resolved the dispute the confusion and uncertainty would continue to persist till this resolution is given practical effect and the related EAC under the MoEF considers such proposal for the grant of prior environmental clearance in the so called no-go-zone in the light of the changed views of MoEF. It is also not clear why such a controversy was to be created and in an open democracy like ours the media would be too happy to exaggerate such differences among the Ministries of the Government of India. No doubt the two political executives had resolved the issue as reported by the print media but the above episode compels me to refer to the most enjoyable humorous comments made by a very senior Union Cabinet Minister under whom the author had the good opportunity to work. This was a comment made by the Minister before television crew at Chennai in the context of the problems that arose in the division of Assembly seats to be contested by two major political parties in the last Assembly Election in TamilNadu. The comments of the Minister were like "we politicians do create problems but we have also the capacity to solve such problems". But in a serious matter like mining in the face of most likely environmental hazards any artificially created controversy is bound to dampen the spirit of even the most optimistic entrepreneur.

Another controversy that has erupted quite recently, and as reported by the print media, is on the status of bamboo. As per the reports in the print media the MoEF is of the view that bamboo is a tree and obviously with timber value. This will be clear if I quote from the *Oxford English Dictionary* the meaning of tree and that of timber. Tree has been defined as a perennial plant with a woody self-supporting main stem or trunk when mature and usually unbranched for some distance above the ground. And timber has been defined as wood prepared for building, carpentry, etc. The meaning of the word "wood" in this context is also relevant. Wood has been defined as a hard fibrous material that forms the main substance of the trunk or branches of a tree or shrub (*ibid*). Perhaps the word "shrub" also needs some elaboration. The word shrub has been defined as a woody plant smaller than a tree and having a very short stem with branches near the ground (*ibid*).

To appreciate the controversy between the claim and counter-claim about the status of bamboo I am tempted to quote from the same dictionary the meaning of bamboo. A bamboo, as the Dictionary defines, is mainly a tropical giant woody grass of the sub-family Bambusidae and its hollow jointed stem is used as a stick or for making furniture.

The use of bamboo and a tree (read timber) might justify in categorizing a bamboo as a tree. There are many such uses which have perhaps given rise, or created an opportunity for the two opposing groups to create the controversy about the status of a bamboo as a grass or as a tree, to the view that bamboo is also a tree. Household furniture are generally made of wood and so are office furniture. Even a partition wall in many office building as also in large houses is made of wood. It is not uncommon to see bamboo furniture nowadays in many houses and in fact the basic structural frame of many residential houses specially in the North Eastern States of India is made of bamboos which are properly seasoned to make it last for longer period and also termite proof.

Now the question is whether commonality of use should make bamboo a tree? If that is so many aquatic species of plant usually grown in marshy land in many of the Eastern States of India would have to be categorized as tree and in the process the marshy water bodies would have to be declared as a forest. In the absence of a universally and commonly known word or phrase the author is aware of (due to his limited command on English vocabulary) I would cite one species of aquatic plants grown quite extensively in the marshy lands of some of the Eastern States of India. Such a species of aquatic grass is locally known as *Hogla. Hogla*, dried and seasoned, is chiefly used in building the walls of cottage, that is, small and simple residential huts (houses) in the eastern part of India just like a wealthy person would use wood (timber) as walls with proper painting outside to protect against rain water. If one has to go by the views reportedly of the MoEF, *Hogla* would be treated as tree. Such a view would, no doubt, provide a legitimate source of amusement.

To determine if bamboo is a tree or grass one has to see the basic difference between a bamboo stem and the stem of a tree. A bamboo consists of a hollow jointed stem, that is, empty inside with a thick exterior (varying between 1 and 3 cm.) while a tree is a plant consisting of a thick and solid wooden stem. Thus, it would be totally erroneous to categorize bamboo as a tree. If one look at the provision of Section 2 of the Forest Rights Act it becomes clear that bamboo is a non-timber forest produce of plant origin. Section 2 (i) defines "minor forest produce" as all non-timber forest produce of plant origin including bamboo, cane etc. This is a Central Act passed by the Parliament and it is taken to be an epoch-making Act for recording the rights of the scheduled tribes and other traditional forest dwellers. I have dealt with this Act in Chapter-3 of the book and therefore there is no need for going into further details here. Therefore, no Central Ministry can take a view contrary to the definition of bamboo given in the above Act. Incidentally, no controversy, as far as my knowledge goes, has been raised about the status of cane, a fairly long climbing or creeping plant, which is more strong besides being solid compared to bamboo for making household furniture.

Trees grow on the land and individual trees would grow generally with adequate space in between, excluding the natural forests that have come up without any effort on the part of any human being. The afforestation and plantation work carried on by the MoEF or by any other entities to increase the forest cover has ensured that saplings are planted with adequate space so that each individual tree can grow in full form without any obstruction from the nearest tree. The growth pattern of bamboo which also, like a tree, grows on land, is completely different. One would rarely find one single individual bamboo growing at a particular point. Bamboos grow always in cluster form. If you make a measurement of the circumference, that is, the outer boundary of four adjoining and closest standing trees you would be astonished to see that an equivalent space would be enough to accommodate few hundred standing bamboos. Further, the diameter of a tree can be as long as one meter or more, that of a bamboo would rarely be more than ten centimeter.

It is not my intention to give a verdict that bamboo is not a tree as I am not the competent person to pronounce a definitive conclusion. I am only raising this issue as needless controversy has been created about the status of a bamboo *vis-à-vis* a tree. If the MoEF insists that bamboo is a tree the impact would be enormous as the moment bamboo is taken as a tree the provisions of the Environment (Protection) Act and the Forest (Conservation) Act and the Rules framed thereunder would be applicable and may be the MoEF and EAC would be flooded with proposals for cutting bamboos for different purposes. This is a meaningless controversy and it has already created lot of confusion in the minds of the people though many of us would be inclined to enjoy the controversy as a source for providing free entertainment.

I would not give any more example as I think the point I am trying to highlight is clear now. The need for a clear and unambiguous policy prescription with detailed guidelines both for mining as also for protection of environment can hardly be over-emphasised.

CORRUPTION

The word corruption needs no elaboration as it has become widely known to the public due to the recent cases of alleged corruption and bribery in the allotment of 2G Spectrum by the Ministry of Telecommunication as widely published and in fact there is not a single day for quite some times when newspaper does not come up with almost endless series of alleged corrupt practices. The veracity or otherwise of the alleged bribery is not the subject of this book. But speed money, an euphemism for bribe money, has been part of life for any miner in the long drawn process for obtaining a Prospecting Licence or a Mining Lease and for obtaining prior environmental clearance in starting mining operation. The practice of bribing government servants at various levels has become rampant as it has become difficult, nay impossible, to eradicate the virus of corruption from the system. One can only perhaps control it. In this context, the observations of the Minister in charge, MoEF as reported in the *Times of India* in its Delhi Edition dated 19th January, 2011 are quite meaningful. I quote his observations below as published by the above newspaper:

> "I can control the demand for corruption but someone has to control the supply of corruption too. I can not stop that".

The Minister was so right and candid that even though he is the Central Regulator with the final authority to grant or reject any application for prior environmental clearance he is totally helpless in eliminating any demand for corruption practised by the officials of the MoEF as he can only control it. I would deal with these observations at a later stage in this section.

Before I deal with the virus of corruption and the modus operandi followed by the government servants at various levels starting from the field level and going up to the Ministry level, I will introduce the readers to a simile, though of a different and, may be, reversed kind but quite effective to make the comparison, as simile has been found in ancient Greek society in the discourse of the great philosopher Socrates as also in our Hindu society in ancient times to effectively illustrate certain views. If we make a comparison between a predator like lion, its hunger and its behaviour when hungry and the greed of a government servant and the behaviour of a greedy government servant we would, without any hesitation, come to the irresistible conclusion that the behaviour of the most dangerous predator is more restrained than that of even a not so greedy government official. This can be elaborated further at a later stage in this section.

As mining and environmental pollution are the subjects of this book I would confine to the corrupt practices that have become an integral part of the system. In this section I would not deal with the ways for eliminating the scope for corrupt practices as the matter will be dealt with in the next section on governance as only good governance can eliminate corrupt practices to a great extent.

The day a prospective miner files an application under the relevant provisions of the MMDR Act for grant of a Prospecting Licence or a Mining Lease it does not take time for him to realize that nothing moves in the government system unless money is paid to all and sundry government functionaries. If we proceed step by step the following picture would emerge.

Though Mines and Minerals (Development and Regulation) Act (MMDR) Act is a Central Act it is administered by the State and State is the owner of the minerals existing within the geographical boundary of the state concerned. Every State Government has a department of mines and geology and many major mineral bearing states have independent department of mines and geology headed by a senior IAS officer as Secretary of the Department and he is also designated as Commissioner under the provisions of the State Minor Mineral Concessions Rules to exercise the powers under the above Rules and this power of the Commissioner is more or less similar to the revisional power of the Central Government under Section 30 of the MMDR Act. Besides the Secretariat set up some of the States have Directorate of Mines and Directorate of Geology headed by the senior most Mining Engineer and Geologist respectively. While some states have independent Directorate, in many states the Secretariat Department and the Directorate are amalgamated. There are field officers like District Mining Officer and in some states there are senior officers in between the State/Directorate Headquarters and the District Mining Officer at convenient locations who are designated as Deputy Directors to supervise the work of the District Mining Officers. The District Mining Officer is assisted by certain field officers who are designated as Mining Inspector(s). The District Mining Officer works under the District Collector. With this usual office set up I would now proceed to deal with the process followed by the Government in granting a Prospecting Licence or a Mining Lease and renewal thereof.

There is a prescribed form in which an application is to be filed before the District Mining Officer in charge of the District in which the particular mineral occurs. For the sake of convenience I would deal with only an application for Mining Lease for iron ore. I am not familiar with the present system of on line filing of such application. The application is filed before the District Mining Officer who does not personally receive the application. There is a clerk working in the Office of the District Mining Officer who receives the application and a receipt thereof is granted to the applicant. Unless the applicant has got any prior knowledge about the prevailing corrupt practice he would be surprised to see that the concerned receiving clerk is not showing any inclination to receive the application on some pretext or other. He would find out deficiencies in the application form by pointing out that certain columns have been left blank knowing well that there are certain columns in the form which in a particular case do not have to be filled in. A clever and practical applicant would hand over a small open envelope containing some currency notes whose number and denomination would be visible to the clerk who would be instantly polite and receive the application and he would also take the trouble of correcting minor errors in the application, if any. A file is opened and it has to go to the District Mining Officer through the designated route and there would be one Section Officer and probably a dealing hand and the file with this application would not move up to the District Mining Officer unless a similar exercise as was followed in filing the application before the clerk is repeated. So the applicant satisfies the dealing hand and the Section Officer and the file is put up before the District Mining Officer who would normally exercise his privilege to be satisfied at a later stage when the application is ready to be put up before the District Collector for forwarding the same to the Director of Mines for obtaining approval of the Government. The District Mining Officer would order in the file that the application may be given to the designated Mining Inspector for enquiry and report. If the applicant is not approaching the Mining Inspector he would get a message and the applicant would meet the Mining Inspector and since the report and recommendations of the Mining Inspector are vital the amount of bribe money also goes up. If the Inspector is satisfied he would submit a report to the District Mining Officer and it will be processed in the same file and if the District Mining Officer is convinced that it is a fit case for grant of Mining Lease he would put up the matter before the District Collector for his approval. There would be cases where even the District

Collector might not be free of the corrupt practices. After the approval of the District Collector is obtained the District Mining Officer is to be satisfied by the applicant and satisfaction has to be commensurate with the expectation of the Officer and once he is satisfied the application is forwarded by the District Mining Officer to the Director of Mines and if there is another layer of supervisory officer in between the Director of Mines and the District Mining Officer the same practice is to be repeated for the in between officer.

A file would be opened in the Office of the Director of Mines and the proposal submitted by the District Mining Officer would be examined in the concerned section headed by a Section Officer with a dealing Assistant and the file will move if the section staff are satisfied and the file would move through at least one senior Mining Engineer before it lands on the table of the Director of Mines. If the Directorate is not amalgamated with the Secretariat Department, the Director of Mines would send the proposal in the form of a letter to the Secretary of the Department in whose Office a file will be opened and the same process of satisfaction is to be ensured before the file is put up to the Secretary through at least one senior Officer who could be a Joint Secretary or even an Additional Secretary. If, however, the Directorate of Mines is amalgamated with the Secretariat Department the file that is opened in the Office of the Director of Mines would be submitted by the Director of Mines to the Secretary and usually through a Deputy Secretary or Joint Secretary. Depending on the inclination of the Deputy Secretary or the Joint Secretary or the Director of Mines the applicant is to satisfy all of them in varying degrees. Since the minerals occur in a piece of land the State Government considers any grant of Mining Lease as leasing out the related land and as per the practice followed, the proposal, once approved by the Minister in charge of the Department, would be submitted to the Council of Ministers headed by the Chief Minister, commonly known as the Cabinet, for approval. Before the proposal is placed for consideration by the Cabinet, it is examined in a different department attached to the Cabinet which is known as Cabinet Secretariat or some such Secretariat and depending on the inclination of the concerned Officer dealing with this subject something is to be done there also to ensure that the proposal is placed before the Cabinet for consideration. I had a bitter experience and had to directly confront a particular officer in the Cabinet Secretariat on account of my suspicion that something wrong was being done with the result that consideration of the proposal was getting delayed though ultimately it had to be placed before the Cabinet for consideration. While obtaining approval of the

Cabinet would not usually be difficult as the proposal is submitted with adequate justification, it is the approval of the Minister in charge of the Department that becomes very critical. The common knowledge in a major mineral bearing state is that Minister in charge, if so inclined, can mint a fortune. While it would be hazardous to guess the amount of money that has to be paid to the Minister, the fact that money is to be paid is never in doubt. The ordeal of the applicant does not end with the payment of bribe money at various level as the office in the Department of Mines would have to be satisfied so that a draft letter of recommendation is approved by the Secretary before it is forwarded to the Central Government for prior approval under the provision of the MMDR Act as such approval is mandatory in respect of any mineral included in the First Schedule to the Act, iron ore being one such mineral. As the applicant comes to know that the State Cabinet has approved the proposal he would be very keen to see that the proposal is submitted to the Central Government at the earliest and, therefore he would not mind paying some extra money as for him time is more important than money at that particular point because he has successfully crossed all the hurdles. The proposal forwarded by the State Government is received in the Ministry of Mines, Government of India located in Shastri Bhawan, New Delhi and the process starts for giving prior approval of the Central Government to the proposal. I will deal with the procedure in the following paragraphs.

In the Ministry of Mines there is a well laid down procedure in dealing with such cases and by and large it has been a very smooth process and I had never come across a single case in my fairly long tenure of eleven years as Director, Joint Secretary and Additional Secretary in the Ministry of Mines when the Office had ever indulged in any malpractices and generally visit by the applicant to the Ministry was unheard of. Under delegated power followed in the Ministry of Mines the power of granting prior approval for grant of Mining Lease in respect of scheduled minerals was being exercised by Joint Secretary rank officer in the Ministry till perhaps 1990-91 when I was Joint Secretary in the Ministry. In fact, prior to that there was a thinking in the Ministry that this power of the Central Government in granting prior approval could be delegated to some officer at Director level in certain categories of cases. The Ministry had never thought of delegating the power to any officer above the level of Joint Secretary as being unnecessary. Even the quasi-judicial revisional power of the Central Government under section 30 of the MMDR Act has been delegated to an officer of the rank of Joint Secretary and since it is a quasi-judicial power the cases are heard by a Bench consisting of a Joint

Secretary of the Ministry of Mines and a Joint Secretary from the Ministry of Law, popularly known as Tribunal. I understand presently no officer from the Ministry of Law is associated with the process. The entire procedure for grant of previous approval of the Central Government took a different course altogether sometime in the year 1991-92 giving rise to hitherto unheard of corrupt practices.

I would not mention the name of the Minister who initially did not know that the cases of grant of prior approval were being considered in the Ministry and such cases were being disposed of by the Joint Secretaries as per the allotment of states among the officers. I have known very closely most of the Secretaries of the Ministry of Mines during 1980 to 1996 and except for two Secretaries other Secretaries had been of impeccable integrity. Even the two Secretaries of doubtful inclination could not succeed directly as the other Senior Officers below them were men of integrity and they could not be influenced in the wrong way.

Somehow the Minister came to know that the cases of prior approval are being considered in the Ministry and in a most unusual manner a *suo motu* direction was issued by the Minister that all cases of prior approval should be put up before the Minister for his order followed by another order that copies of orders granting prior approval should be sent to the Office of the Minister. Another direction came from the Office of the Minister that a list of all Mining Lease holders in the country should be submitted to the Office of the Minister. Everybody was puzzled as the officers in the Ministry could not understand the rationale of all such *suo motu* directions/ orders emanating from the Office of the Minister. But it did not take time for all of us to know the real motive behind such orders/ directions and whenever there was any occasion to discuss the issue the silent smile on the faces of not only the officers but also the subordinate staff became more vocal than loud smile. Since, at that time word processing and computerization weren't in practice the sanction letters had to be manually typed and after the signature of the competent authority copies of such sanction letters were to be made for sending the same to all concerned including the State Government. Such letters were typed on stencil paper and the same were cyclostyled for providing copies of required number. If any local Delhi based representative of any applicant wanted to have a copy of the sanction letter in advance it was very easy for him as he could have got the same by paying a small amount of Rs. 5 or so to the typist. Why I am mentioning such apparently unimportant matter is that the father of one of the big players in non-ferrous metals production told me that the Private Secretary to the Minister told him on telephone that he could supply a copy of a certain recommendation of the Ministry on import duty to him on payment of Rs. 25,000. At that time his son was operating in a small way and the family was Mumbai based. The gentleman told me that the Private Secretary to the Minister was not perhaps in the know that procuring any government letter would not cost the interested party more than Rs. 10 as the typist or the office clerk never thought of making a fortune through such corrupt practices. I would not go into further details but in lighter vein I would comment that the amount to be paid by the applicant to the authority competent to grant prior approval at that time was a peanut compared to the alleged amount involved in 2G Spectrum cases, the word scam was not in circulation at that time. So what was a routine function of the Central Government in the grant of prior approval became a source of minting money and subsequently no Secretary had succeeded nor any Minister had voluntarily agreed to delegate the power of prior approval to the officers at appropriate level. Since individual Minister in charge of the Ministry has the power under the Rules of Transaction of Business to decide the administrative arrangement in dealing with any matter in the Ministry even the Prime Minister will be totally unaware of any such practice which was contrary to the sound and fundamental administrative principle of delegation and decentralization of power. I will cite three examples.

A very dubious practice was taken recourse to. It was like this. The common belief was that the Private Secretary to the Minister would get a letter signed by a Member of the Parliament (MP) addressed to the Minister alleging certain financial irregularities committed by some company. One such letter was received in the office and it related to alleged non-payment of custom duty on certain imported items. Since the matter related to the Department of Revenue, Ministry of Finance, the file was put up before the Minister with the suggestion that the letter could be forwarded to the Department of Revenue for appropriate action and accordingly a reply could be sent to the M.P. The Chairman of the company, a private company, was conveyed the message by the Private Secretary to the Minister that the matter would be referred to the CBI for investigation. The Chairman had no option but to satisfy the demand of the Minister and the matter ended there.

In my absence the Managing Director of a joint venture mining company in one of the north-eastern states left a message for me to my PA as I was out of station. The message was that he could manage prior approval of his case but not before handing over a little over Rs. 100, all that he had in his wallet, to the Private Secretary to the Minster.

Another case was a quite interesting one and at that time I was the Additional Secretary in the Ministry and the Ministry was renamed as Ministry of Steel and Mines with a common Minister (a different Minister). Since he was a new Minister without any previous background his demand was also unusually low. One of the senior officers of a Public Sector Undertaking had a complaint against him filed by somebody before the Minister. As the incident is more than fifteen years old I don't remember the name of the person but what he told me was quite revealing. He wanted to get the complaint dropped and met the Minister and succeeded in his effort. He told me that he thought that he would have to pay at least about Rs.1 million but after negotiations he could manage to get a favourable order at 25 per cent of the estimated cost.

In fact, from the early 1990's onwards things only deteriorated and it is beyond anybody's comprehension that a most routine procedure was converted into a procedure that begot such unhealthy practices. I had the opportunity to work in the Ministry of Steel and Mines and under such veteran Ministers like Mr. Pranab Mukherjee, the present President of India, Mr. Narayan Dutt Tiwari, Mr. M.L. Fotedar and Late Mr. Ashok Sen and nobody even could entertain any idea that any Minister could interfere in such small and routine decision-making process. In fact, I still remember that when Late Mr. Ashok Sen was Minister of Steel and Mines, I was then Joint Secretary in the Ministry, the question of allotment of work to the Minister of State (Mines) arose. Mr. Sen as the Cabinet Minister minuted in the file that as the Administrative Head, the Secretary, Department of Mines would decide the movement of file from the Department to the Minister. Having worked under such veterans I was almost shell-shocked to experience the state of corrupt practices being invented.

From whatever little I have stated above one can imagine the travails of a prospective miner in getting a Mining Lease.

I would not go into further details on the magnitude of bribe money and the harassment to the small miners after the level of the authority for grant of prior approval was upgraded. This will be discussed in the next section on governance as only good governance can ensure a corruption free process in the grant of prospecting licence or mining lease. I would now proceed to deal with the corrupt practices that have become an integral part of the process in the grant of prior environmental clearance by the MoEF.

Before I deal with the process involved in obtaining prior environmental clearance including the functioning of the EAC whose recommendations are essential for the Central Regulator, the Minister Incharge, MoEF to take a view I would very briefly mention the most common practices followed by the field functionaries who have the responsibility to protect the forest.

Pruning is a very common word with which even a non-forest officer like me is familiar and there is no dearth of humorous comments as to how in the name of pruning one can create havoc with the standing trees of good timber value. A farmer has to weed out unwanted grass and other plants in his paddy field to ensure good growth of paddy plant. Likewise, a forest officer has to undertake periodical pruning activity for healthy growth of the trees in a forest. Pruning means cutting dead or overgrown branches, etc. Earlier, I have explained the meaning of a tree which has a self-supporting main stem or trunk and usually the trunk does not have any branches upto certain distance above the ground. The tree for its growth gets nourishment from the soil. Most of the trees would have branches after a certain height above the ground and such branches would also have sub-branches and these branches also would draw their sustenance from the mother tree. Some of the branches specially those coming out of the main trunk at lower level would have also good timber value like the mother tree. In fact, the diameter of a branch up to certain length could be 20 centimetres or more. Therefore, for the main trunk of the tree to mature upto the desired level there is need to trim the branches in a way so that the branches do not overgrow the main tree. In the name of pruning a forest officer can very easily cut down the branches of higher diameter and with good timber value and one can leave it to the ingenuity of the officer to make money by selling such branches to some select traders. In other words, the forest officer would contrive a situation to make out a case that pruning of unwanted branches was essential for the growth of the mother tree. I can not help mentioning a story here narrated to me sometimes in 1972 by a District Collector who is also a very close friend of mine till date regarding use of the device of pruning by the local forest officer to supply a well developed branch of mahogany tree (a tropical tree of the genus Swietenia) to a very senior officer at the district headquarter. Mahogany is a very high quality tree whose number is limited and it is quite possible that it has become an extinct commodity in areas where it used to grow earlier. It was altogether a different matter that the officer could not succeed in his attempt to get the Mahogany branch. In the process the forest officer who was forced to cut down the branch could save his job.

Another opportunity the field functionaries of the forest department get to make money is provided by the process in granting permission of the MoEF to divert forest lands for non-forest purposes. The forest officer is supposed to count the number of trees to be felled. It is left to anybody's imagination about the capacity of the forest officer to manipulate the number and to make money from the prospective miners. This can be best appreciated if I could give a reference to similar activity performed by a Mining Inspector in calculating the amount of royalty to be paid by a brick-kiln owner under the State Minor Mineral Concession Rules. Usually a brick-kiln would contain bricks numbering between 300000 and 1000000 depending on the area where the brick-kiln is operated. One can imagine the ingenuity of the Mining Inspector in arriving at a particular figure of bricks in a kiln to manipulate the amount of royalty for the kiln to be paid.

I have cited two types of cases above only to prove that making money through bribery is almost in-built in the system where discretion plays a great role. I will now deal with the issue of corruption in obtaining prior environmental clearance for a mining project. As the recommendations of the EAC constitute the basis for the Ministry to take a decision on any proposal for grant of prior environmental clearance I would confine myself to the functioning of the EAC and the procedure followed in the ministry for grant of prior environmental clearance. And in doing so I would make an attempt to show how one can make money without doing any illegality in the grant of environmental clearance. I would also highlight the need for taking action against the field officers who have almost collectively decided to ensure that the well thought out conditions prescribed by the Ministry in the sanction letter are not complied with.

Having given some illustrations on the *modus-operandi* of the field functionaries in making money I would deal with the opportunities that are plenty for the Office in the MoEF including the Political Executive to make easy money without doing any irregular activities. In fact, if an official of the Ministry is clever enough to evolve a system under which the interested party, the "supplier's" side, gets the information promptly that his proposal is under process and the file movement has started there would be no delay in the disposal of the case and, therefore, the process leading to final decision would appear absolutely normal. In the absence of any interest shown by the party either directly or through his emissary in pursuing his case the movement of the file containing his application for prior environmental clearance is bound to be stymied. Of course, cell phones would be of use for conveying the message to the applicant to the effect that his visit to the Paryavaran Bhawan, where the Ministry Office is located, is urgently required in connection with his application for prior environmental clearance. A wise applicant would get the correct message and depending on his effective effort the file would start moving upward. I would now deal with the procedure followed in processing an application for prior environmental clearance for a mining project and the opportunities to make money in-built in the system.

The 14th September Notification prescribes detailed procedure to be followed in dealing with any proposal for prior environmental clearance for mining projects. The Notification ensures a transparent procedure and therefore the MoEF has nothing to hide. Recommendations of the EAC are essential for the Central Regulator, that is, the Minister in charge of MoEF to take a decision on any proposal. In fact, if the Minister does not agree with the recommendatio.ıs of the EAC he has the only option to refer back in the first place the proposal to the EAC for reconsideration on the grounds to be indicated by the Minister. On a reference of this type from the Minister, the Expert Appraisal Committee (EAC) would reconsider the matter and can take a view which could be a revised opinion with justification or EAC could stick to its original recommendations. Though it is not clearly mentioned in the Notification, it is most reasonable to presume that if the EAC does not change its original recommendations the Minster has the inherent power to take a different view though in actual practice such a contingency would not normally happen and during the three years of my tenure as Chairman of the EAC I had never come across a case where the Minister had not accepted the recommendations of the EAC. The EAC consists of members, numbering between 12 and 15, who are experts in different disciplines relevant for a mining project. It is to the credit of the Ministry that it selects the members who would be familiar with actual mining activities and the measures required for mitigating the adverse impacts due to mining activities. Some of the members are distinguished faculties from educational institutions some of whom are experts in suggesting appropriate CSR activities for the affected people. Usually the Chairman of the EAC is a person with adequate administrative experience who can secure a consensus among the members of the EAC so that EAC does not de-generate into a debating body without any concrete suggestions. That being so it is not for nothing that the recommendations of the EAC are the basic requirement for the Ministry to take a view and the recommendation of the EAC is given serious consideration.

As per the procedure followed in the Secretariat of the Ministry the recommendations of the EAC are to be put in the relevant file already opened in the Ministry with the original application filed by the applicant for prior environmental clearance. The Member Secretary of the Committee is usually a senior Director level Officer of the Ministry and normally he/

she is also in charge of the Section dealing with this subject. Since, the Member Secretary is a link between the Ministry and the EAC and usually he/she is free to give his/her candid opinion which is accepted as the views of the Ministry and the Member Secretary, whenever necessary, can discuss separately with the Chairman any particular issue. Therefore, when the Member Secretary records his/her opinion in the file he/she would give a gist of the recommendations of the EAC. The file moves upward. The files moves upwards through the concerned Advisor who is a technical person and the same is put up before the Minister either through the Additional Secretary or the Special Secretary in the Ministry. As far as I know such files are not routed through the Secretary but there is no such embargo on routing the file through the Secretary.

If the Ministry accepts the recommendations of the Committee nobody can fault the Ministry as it has accepted the recommendations of the Expert Committee it has constituted precisely for the purpose. As the minutes of the EAC are put on the website of the Ministry the same are in public domain and the sanction letter of the Ministry conveying the grant of prior environmental clearance is also in public domain, the system is completely transparent. The EAC, while making its recommendations, prescribes certain conditions which are partly of general nature and partly of specific nature relevant for the project. The Ministry has certain prescribed standard conditions and the sanction letter issued by the Ministry conveying grant of prior environmental clearance contains conditions prescribed by the Ministry and the conditions prescribed by the EAC.

Every miner is well conversant with the fact that unless money is paid nothing moves in the Ministry. For him time is money and, therefore, having crossed all the hurdles in obtaining a Mining Lease and in convincing the EAC for a positive recommendation it would be an absolute foolery not to spend some money in getting the final order granting prior environmental clearance for his project. It is widely believed that no file will be cleared by the final authority unless he is satisfied and quantum of money required to ensure his satisfaction would depend on the nature of his greed. It would be unfair to make a sweeping observation that every final authority in the Ministry is prone to the corrupt practices as there could be some honourable exceptions and the same is the case about the officers in the Ministry and it is not the case that every official is involved in the corrupt practices of making money. But this much is clear that usually no irregularity is committed by the Ministry in the grant of prior environmental clearance as the recommendations are that of an Expert Committee and the whole procedure is transparent. However, I would give few examples without my opinion and I would leave it to the readers to make their own conclusions.

This is a case relating to the proposal for grant of prior environmental clearance in a mining project submitted by a major aluminium producer operating in a major minerals bearing State. The EAC rejected the proposal more than once. There is a common belief that when the EAC rejects a particular proposal for prior environmental clearance in its first meeting, the aggrieved party need not give up hope as in the next meeting the EAC would definitely clear the case. This particular party proceeded with the same presumption and re-submitted its proposal for reconsideration by the EAC almost in a routine way without caring for the grounds on which the proposal was rejected. The EAC could not take a different view and again recommended rejection of the case. This particular company had another such proposal in the same state. The recommendations of the Committee were routed through a very senior Officer of the Ministry who submitted the same to the Minister for approval. The Officer agreed with the recommendations of the EAC in both the cases. In one case the EAC, no doubt, recommended rejection of the proposal but the Committee made certain observations giving an opportunity to the company to rectify the deficiencies and the implied recommendation was that the party is free to come back to the Ministry afresh. The senior Officer was prudent enough to conclude that the concerned party would submit its proposal for reconsideration in due course which, indeed, the party did and the Committee accepted the proposal in the revised form. In the other case the recommendations of the EAC were clear and there was no scope for any reconsideration as the life of the mine was only five years and if allowed it would mean avoidable miseries that would befall more than 200 tribal families living there for generations. The company gave a proposal that it would shift these families to a different location and when the mine is closed after five years such families would be brought back to their original places of residence. The EAC thought it was most inhuman to accept such a proposal and it was beyond the comprehension of the EAC that the company could come up with such inhuman proposal. Even after such clear cut rejection the party again submitted its proposal for reconsideration by the Ministry. The Ministry referred the matter to the EAC as required under the 14th September Notification. I was aghast by such a reference and I wanted to see the reasons for such reconsideration. I could see the related file and also the observations made by the senior officer who submitted the file to the Minister directly. While agreeing with the recommendations of the EAC for rejection the officer made an apparently innocuous observation that the party would have the right to file a representation against the rejection. Such an observation was totally irrelevant and uncalled for as in our system any person aggrieved by a decision of any authority is within his right to file a representation against such rejection and there is no limitation on the number of times such representation can be made. Even in the Higher Judiciary the system of review/revision is followed to ensure that nobody is denied justice. The tenure of the EAC of which I was the Chairman was to end shortly and since the party would have no chance, as per the assessment of the senior officer, of getting a positive recommendation the above innocuous observation would give the party a legitimate cause for submitting the proposal again as his right to make representation even after clear rejection has been confirmed by the Minister in the file as recommended by the officer and the party might have been informed in writing also as the decision of the Minister was to be conveyed faithfully. The newly constituted EAC had, I understand, in one of its early meetings cleared the case for prior environmental clearance.

It would be unfair on my part if I do not refer to the unsavoury behaviour of some of the expert Members of the EAC. The members who were already in active service in a government or government aided organization or in educational institution of repute were men of integrity and I had no occasion to doubt their sincerity and their honest observations during presentation made by a mining company on any proposal for prior environmental clearance. I can not make for certainty such statement about other members who were retired persons either from the government or from the private sector or who are working in some organizations in Advisory positions. As it was not possible for me to stop any undesirable activities taking place outside the meeting place and at times in an altogether different location the best I could do was to ensure that such members could not be effective in influencing the Committee's judgment in any particular case. As the members are selected by the Ministry I had no option but to suffer the presence of such members in the meeting. In one case I submitted a written report with a demi official letter to the Secretary of the Ministry against a particular member, who defrauded the government, with my recommendations to remove him from the Committee. The Ministry did not take any action on my recommendation and in fact the member concerned was rewarded by his inclusion in the newly constituted EAC after the tenure of the EAC ended in August 2009.

The scope for making money does not end with the issue of the sanction letter granting prior environmental clearance for any mining project. In fact, it is the beginning of a new and never ending opportunity to almost mint money by the field functionaries. Every sanction letter has large number of conditions prescribed and a miner is legally bound to comply with those conditions failing which the sanction letter can be cancelled with the result the mining activities would come to a halt. Some of the conditions are so critical that any failure on the part of the miner to comply with those conditions could result in serious environmental pollution. It is a common knowledge and the MoEF is fully aware that its field officers are not ensuring compliance with the prescribed conditions. This is a serious matter as the grant of prior environmental clearance is subject to the conditions prescribed in the sanction letter itself. That the Ministry has not evolved a system for assessing the compliance status is clear from the decision taken by the Secretary of the Ministry in a meeting with some Chairpersons of the EAC on 4th July, 2006 a reference to which has been made in Chapter-14. During my visit to a particular State as Chairman of a sub-group I casually enquired from a very senior field officer of MoEF about the system of inspection by the field functionaries of the various mining projects to see if the conditions prescribed by the MoEF while granting prior environmental clearance were being complied with. What I could gather from the comments of the Officer is quite revealing. I believe there is a procedure under which various field officers posted in the area are duty bound to inspect the area and submit the inspection report to the higher authority, but in actual practice they would fill in the prescribed form almost in a routine way without any application of mind and perhaps without actual site visit. This gives credence to the popular perception that field officers of the department in connivance with the supervisory senior officers make money and no action is taken against the erring miners. The massive construction activities done by M/s Vedanta Resources Plc in the forest lands in Orissa which created lot of hue and cry could not have taken place without the full knowledge of the field officers who are responsible for protecting the forest. Media reports suggest that the Ministry has withdrawn the grant of prior environmental clearance granted earlier. I have not come across any media report that indicates that the MoEF or the State Forest Department has taken any action against the Forest Officials responsible for allowing certain activities in violation of the prescribed conditions. I am not commenting on the role of Vedanta in the whole process as that is not the subject matter of this book. But the MoEF has come to the conclusion that the company had carried out the construction activities illegally. If that is so, it is more important to fix responsibilities on the Forest Officials who had allowed such alleged illegal activities as nobody could carry out such activities in forest lands without the knowledge of the Officers of the Department.

One can imagine the scope for making money by the Forest Officials throughout the country as the number of mining projects that have been granted prior environmental clearance would be in hundreds if not in thousands.

It is an empirically established fact that in any system where statutory permission is required for conducting any business activities the amount of bribe money to be paid to the government functionaries increases commensurate with the level of the authority and consequently the highest amount is to be paid to the final authority in every case and that amount is left to the discretion of the authority. If the top political executive of the Ministry is a man of integrity and he is transparent in his decision-making process the message goes down the line and chances are that the corrupt practices of bribing the officials could be greatly controlled though not likely to be stopped altogether. I will now go back to the observations of the Minister, MoEF published in the *Times of India* referred to earlier in the beginning of the Section on Corruption.

The Minister has admitted that forest officials posted in the field and perhaps the officials working in the Ministry itself are prone to corruption and therefore his statement that he can control the demand for corruption is relevant. One can control something existing. If something does not exist one can not control a non-existing thing. The appropriate expression should have been "*regulate*" instead of the expression "*control*" as, if it is not possible to eradicate the demand for corruption one can only regulate the demand for corruption perhaps fixing a ceiling for different levels of functionaries.

The Minister also observed that someone (read miner or his agent) has to control the supply side of corruption also as it is not within the competency of the Minister to stop that.

In essence the Minister is propounding a theory that if there is none to give (supply) bribe money to officers there would be no demand for such illegal money and he is absolutely right and cannot be faulted even by his strongest critic. It is not simple economic theory where market forces like demand for a commodity and its supply determine the price at which a consumer is ready to buy a particular commodity. In the past there was shortage of onion in Delhi market and the price of onion shot up from Rs. 10 per kilogram to Rs. 70 per kilogram within a span of two weeks' time. The customers who could pay extra for the onion as they could not curtail the consumption of the commodity continued to purchase onion at such an exorbitant rate. In normal circumstances the demand for a commodity and its supply would command a price at which the buyer and the seller reach a state of equilibrium. This market theory does not apply to the demand for bribe money and its supply. In the above example if the officer is used to have a lavish lifestyle which is possible only with extra income beyond his salary and other known income, if any, his demand for bribe money will go up to compensate the rise in the price of any particular commodity. Therefore, it would be erroneous to postulate that if supply of bribe money is stopped the demand for corruption would not be there. In fact, the converse is true. If the officials involved in the permit system do not raise any demand for bribe money there would be no supply of money for bribing the officials as no supply is required for a non-existing demand. The miner would be extremely happy and grateful to the Minister if he can completely stop the demand for bribe money as the money so saved can be put to better use in his project. In the above example of onion, or any other commodity, if there is no demand for the item there would be no supply thereof. In India there are some villages where people consume only vegetarian food. So there would be no demand for any non-vegetarian food items like mutton or chicken and the consequence will be that there would be no supply of these non-vegetarian items to such villages.

Earlier, in para three of this section, I promised to elaborate the use of simile. I must keep my promise. This I will do with some examples in the following paragraphs.

While using the simile I have only forest officials and the wildlife in mind. Let us deal with the behaviour of a hungry predator like lion and the behaviour of a greedy forest officer which I would narrate in the next paragraph.

Both the predator animals and their victims live in the same forest for their sustenance. The victims, say a deer, would never go out of the forest simply because a predator like lion or cheetah would pounce upon it and the victim would be killed in no time. When a predator like a lion is hungry and his hunger has reached a point beyond which he can not suffer that he (lion) will pounce upon his victim (deer). He would look for his victim, a deer, and is quite possible that a lion could run after the deer for few kilometres and once successful the lion would have a belly full of meals and would take long rest thereafter. Since usually other predators would not dare approach the lion he would not have to hide his victim from other hungry predators. The lion would not mind, however, if the left-over is eaten by other predators including vultures. The point that I am trying to make is that the lion would not kill another deer for consumption immediately and when he is hungry again he would repeat the same process. No wonder the lion sincerely believes and practises that fresh flesh of a deer is a healthy diet without any advice from a dietician but he also conserves the victims, co-residents in the same forest area, and does not indulge in wanton killing of his victims.

As compared to the behaviour of a hungry predator the behaviour of a greedy officer makes very interesting and contrasting reading. Before I proceed further I would highlight the value of money. I have never studied economics as a subject but during those days there was a subject called Civics which I studied as a student in what was then Intermediate Arts and the subject Civics included elementary knowledge about Political Science and Economics. So my knowledge is limited to that. In the context of demand and supply we were taught that since there is no limit to the number of commodities one can purchase with money there would be no end to the demand for money. Even if there is a temporary shortage of a particular commodity the purchaser would still have demand for more money to purchase such a commodity at a future time. Therefore, it is inconceivable that the demand for money by a greedy officer can be stopped. If the person is in the habit of taking bribe money his greed would only go on increasing. He would need money first for his immediate family members and he would have a problem for higher education for his children, possibly an impressive wedding ceremony for his daughter, having more than one residential houses in different urban areas and a commercial accommodation so that his sources of income do not get dried up. Otherwise, how could one think of a husband-wife couple (MP Cadre), both members of the Indian Administrative Service, the top most Civil Service in the country, as reported by the media, acquire properties worth Rs. 350 crores (Rs. 3.50 billions)?

One can see that the behaviour of a wild animal like a predator lion is more ethical as he knows that if he goes on killing his victims there would be a time when he may face starvation as there would be no deer or any other animal to satisfy his hunger. A greedy officer, in contrast, by his never ending demand for bribe money would create a situation that would force the miner to neglect his duty to control pollution and to take other mitigating measures and he would do only mining. Obviously, a greedy officer who is supposed to be the protector of the forest and the ecology would be its destroyer whereas the predator would be the real conservator of the wildlife.

While on the subject corruption and before I proceed to the next section on governance I cannot help referring to the ingenuity of a government functionary to make money and for that he must ensure that the bribe money is paid in advance as once the decision in favour of the miner is conveyed to him it might not be possible to get the promised money. No wonder that there is no transaction on credit in the business of corruption and everything is to be paid and in cash before the decision is taken. Here I would narrate one interesting story told to us by a senior officer posted in the Central Vigilance Commission (CVC) which is the watch dog to ensure that corrupt officers are punished. I was Chief Vigilance Officer (CVO) in the Ministry of Mines for a pretty long period and in that capacity I was required to attend the conferences organized by the CVC from time to time. In one such conference the senior officer from CVC narrated the story which I would briefly mention below.

He did not refer to any particular Minister by name. He only narrated the sequence of events of the case in which the prospective bribe giver failed to keep his promise to satisfy the Minister. Those who are familiar with the process in examining any application for a decision of the competent authority know that what is written in the file is commonly known as *note* or *noting*. That is to say, various officers and staff dealing with the subject would record their views by writing the note in a file. In one case the file was put up before the Minister for decision. The Minister wrote in his own handwriting '*Approved*'. The file was still in the office of the Minister. The Minister waited for considerable time but when the applicant did not turn up as promised earlier thinking that now that his work was done he could manage by not paying the promised money and perhaps thinking that he had proved to be smarter than the Minister without realizing that if somebody thought he could fool a politician he would be a greater fool himself. The Minister called back the file and wrote *'Not'* before the word *"Approved"* to make it read as *"Not Approved"*. The personal staff of the Minister could guess the reason for not approving the proposal by the Minister. In no time the applicant was informed and immediately the Minister was satisfied. Since, the file was still in the office of the Minister he called for the file again and added the alphabet *"e"* after the word *"not"* to appear as *"note"*. So finally the order of the Minister would read as *"Note Approved"*, i.e. from original order *approved* to the intermediate order *not approved* to the final order *note approved.*

We (CVOs) were told many such stories only to make us understand the novel ways of a corrupt government functionary to ensure that the bribe money is paid in advance, and in full, of course in cash.

Another story worth mentioning here relates to mid 1970's. A colleague of mine and I were posted in the same department under the State

Government with the same rank. That my colleague was corrupt was not in dispute. But his modus operandi in taking bribe money was undoubtedly a novel one. He introduced religious camouflaging in receiving bribe money. The story was like this.

He was staying in his own house in a posh locality and the house had a reasonably spacious compound and near the entry gate a small temple was constructed with the statue of the Presiding Deity installed. The temple was spacious enough to accommodate the offerings (at that time even 500 rupees currency notes were not in circulation) the officer had in mind. Gradually, people who would like to get decisions in their favour came to know that appropriate *Prasad* (offerings) was to be placed before the Deity. Since, it was a place of worship the devotees had the right to place their offerings before the Presiding Deity and that would satisfy the officer who would ensure orders in favour of the devotees. Nobody could question the integrity of the officer as the devotees were free to place appropriate offerings on their own just like so may devotees would be doing the same thing in any of the well known places of worship.

How the two ills, i.e., lack of clarity in the policy prescription and the menace of corruption can be tackled, would be the subject matter of the next Section on Governance.

GOVERNANCE

Undoubtedly lack of a clear cut policy prescription and corruption are the two ills that, if not taken care of, would frustrate all good intentions of the government to create a sense of confidence in the minds of the entrepreneurs who are willing to invest in any mining project, or for that matter, in any economic activity. This brings us to the need for good governance. There are certain fundamental principles of any sound administrative system which are briefly mentioned in the following paragraphs.

One such fundamental principle is to eliminate avoidable delay by streamlining the procedures and by decentralization of the decision-making power.

In certain business activity where the government has the legal power to issue permit and to regulate such business activity there is a distinct possibility that delays would take place in procuring statutory clearances. Mining is one such activity which requires that a miner must have a mining lease under Section 4 of the Mines and Minerals (Development and Regulation) Act, 1957 (MMDR Act). There is a procedure prescribed in the Mineral Concession Rule, 1960 (MCR) framed under Section 13 of the MMDR Act for obtaining a mining lease. I have narrated the procedure for filing an application for mining lease and its consideration at various levels of the government both at the State level and at the Central level in the Section on Corruption. The delay that takes place in the processing of an application for mining lease can be minimized considerably. For example, every District Mining Officer would have up to date data on mineral deposits within the geographical boundary of the district. He would also have the details of operating mining leases as also the details of mineral bearing areas over which no mining lease has so far been granted. He would also have the details of areas which have become available for fresh grant of mining lease on account of surrender of the mining lease of the previous lease holder or on account of termination of a mining lease and the areas are free and available for fresh grant of mining lease in accordance with the provisions of Rule 59 of the MCR. That being so the system of inspection and report by the Mining Inspector becomes redundant. If there is any need for inspection that should be confined to ascertaining the fact if there has been any encroachment involving human settlements in the area which might interfere with the proposed mining activities. If the need for inspection by the Mining Inspector could be dispensed with the major reason for delay at the initial stage gets automatically eliminated and consequently the scope for likely corrupt practices by the Mining Inspector is completely eliminated. It is possible for the District Mining Officer to complete the examination and obtain the approval of the District Collector and the proposal can be sent to the Director of Mines at the State headquarters within a week's time or so. If there is an intermediary officer like Deputy Director of mines between the Director of Mines and the District Mining Officer, a copy of the proposal submitted by the District Mining Officer to the Director of Mines can be sent to the Deputy Director of Mines for his record as this would help him to supervise the activities of the District Mining Officer in ensuring that the lease holder, after the lease is granted, operates the mines in accordance with the terms and conditions of the lease. Since, the Collector of the District has already approved the proposal submitted by the District Mining Officer there is no need for an intermediary officer to make any comments on the proposal.

At the State level, it is possible for the department to take a view with the approval of the Minister in charge within three weeks' time. However, if certain information and documents are to be obtained from the District Mining Officer there would be need for another fifteen days' time, or may be in some cases, thirty days' time. If the Directorate of Mines is an independent office and not amalgamated with the Secretariat Department, the proposal submitted by the District Mining Officer would take about two weeks' time for processing in the office of the Director of Mines. If the proposal is not complete and some information and documents are to be obtained from the District Mining Officer the Director of Mines would take between fifteen and thirty days' time for the purpose.

I understand in most of the States the proposal is to be approved by the State Cabinet as it involves leasing of lands. Normally, meeting of the State Cabinet takes place atleast once a week. Therefore, after the approval of the Minister of Mines, the Secretariat Department should be in a position to submit the Cabinet Note for consideration by the Cabinet within a week's time. The designated department of the State Government, in some states, the department is known as Cabinet Secretariat, would take about a week's time to place the proposal before the Cabinet in its next weekly meeting. As the proposal has already been concurred in by the related departments of the State Government such as Finance, Revenue, Legal, etc. as required under the Rules of Executive Business of the State Government and the Chief Minister has given his permission to place the matter before the Cabinet the proposal submitted by the Department of Mines would usually get the approval of the Cabinet. The whole process involved in obtaining the approval of the State Government could be completed within a period of three months from the date of filing the application for grant of a mining lease in the office of the District Mining Officer.

Once the State Cabinet has approved the proposal, the Department of Mines should be in a position to submit its proposal to the Ministry of Mines, Government of India within a week's time for obtaining previous approval of the Central Government under Section 5 (1) of the MMDR Act as the mineral, iron ore, for the purpose of this book iron ore has been taken as the mineral for all purposes, is included in the First Schedule to the Act.

On receipt of the proposal, a file is opened in the concerned Section of the Ministry of Mines located in Shastri Bhawan, New Delhi. Since, there is division of work among the Sections in the Ministry state-wise or mineral-wise, the proposal for grant of previous approval would be considered only in that particular Section to which the work is allotted. Normally, it should not take more than fifteen days in the Ministry to decide any such proposal received from the State Government. By and large the proposals submitted by the State Government are complete as the procedure has been in practice for long and, therefore, the State Governments are fully conversant with the requirements in obtaining previous approval of the Central Government. Even if there is a case for obtaining certain clarifications or documents from the State Government that would not take much time. Till early 1990s the power of the Central Government for grant of previous approval under the MMDR Act was being exercised by the concerned Joint Secretary and the movement of the file from the Section to the Joint Secretary would not take more than two working days. It is only when the concerned Deputy Secretary or Director through whom the file is to be put up before the Joint Secretary is out of station for a period of, say one or two days, there could be some delay. In the Ministry there is an established procedure that if the concerned officer is absent for a long period, the work is allotted temporarily to another officer and, therefore, file movement does not get affected. It was possible for the Joint Secretary to take a final decision on the proposal within two days. Once the proposal is approved by the Joint Secretary, the same is conveyed to the State Government in the next three to four days' time. The State Government, on receipt of the previous approval of the Central Government, would take a maximum of a week's time to convey its approval to the District Mining Officer. The District Mining Officer might take about two weeks' time to finalise and approve the lease deed. As there is a standard prescribed proforma in which the lease deed is to be executed it does not take much time to finalise and approve the lease deed which can be executed. The whole process should not take more than a month's time in the office of the District Mining Officer.

Therefore, the entire process, culminating in the execution of the lease deed, should not take more than six months from the date of receipt of the application for grant of mining lease in the office of the District Mining Officer. The miner would be fully satisfied as he would consider the period of six months necessary and reasonable as it involves independent processing and decision at the levels of two governments, one State and the other Central. This also eliminates the scope for bribe money being paid to a great extent though I would not say with certainty that scope for corruption could be totally eradicated.

I have earlier mentioned the circumstances under which sometime in the early 1990s the Minister Incharge took over the power of the Central Government to grant previous approval. As I had worked as Director in the Ministry of Mines and also exercised the power of granting previous approval as Joint Secretary in the same Ministry we all were greatly surprised with dismay to see how a single *suo motu* decision of the Minister Incharge to upgrade the level of the authority to grant previous approval could provide a fertile breeding ground to make money for a most routine activity. Delay is bound to happen if the level of the authority to grant approval is upgraded. Therefore, the only way to eliminate the avoidable delay is to delegate the power back to the Joint Secretary level officers that has stood the test of time.

The same principle applicable in respect of mining lease applies in respect of grant of prior environmental clearance by the MoEF. As is well known to the mining industry, the 14th September Notification prescribes a detailed and transparent procedure for grant of prior environmental clearance. The Notification also prescribes a time schedule for grant of prior environmental clearance. However, there is scope for reducing delay in obtaining the approval of the Central Regulatory Authority (CRA) and in the process a likely scope for corruption could be eliminated to a great extent.

The recommendations of the EAC are processed in the Ministry and the proposal is put up before the Minister, MoEF for his decision. I am not aware of the present status, but during the three years I was Chairman of the EAC I had never come across a case where the Ministry Officials and the Minister had disagreed with the recommendations of the EAC. I believe the situation continues to be the same. Since EAC is an expert Committee consisting of experts from various disciplines, in normal circumstances there would be no occasion for the Ministry to reject the recommendations of the EAC but in certain circumstances the Ministry could take a different view but only after reconsideration by the EAC. Even for the Minster to ask the EAC to reconsider a particular recommendation he has to give the grounds for reconsideration and this is very clear from sub-para (ii) of para 8 of the 14th September Notification which makes it binding on the Minister to state "the reasons for the disagreement". Under these circumstances, the Minister would be circumspect in a case of disagreement as the original recommendations of the EAC are already in the website of the Ministry and therefore in the public domain and hence subsequent decision of the Central Regulator to take a different view would also be in the public domain and the aggrieved party would be within his right to challenge the decision of the Minister in a court of law. This is perhaps the reason that cases of disagreement between the Minister and the EAC would not be a common phenomenon.

Therefore, there is a case for delegating the power for taking final decision on the recommendations of the EAC that would be in accordance with the sound and fundamental principle of delegation and decentralization of power in any administrative system. May be, the Minister can exercise such power in respect of such projects that might have adverse impact on certain critical and ecologically fragile areas and the like as specified by a notification.

Let me now refer to paragraph 2 of the 14th September Notification which is extracted below:

"**Requirements of prior Environmental Clearance (EC):** The following projects or activities shall require prior environmental clearance from the concerned regulatory authority, which shall hereinafter referred to be as the Central Government in the Ministry of Environment and Forests for matters falling under Category 'A' in the Schedule and at State level the State Environment Impact Assessment Authority (SEIAA) for matters falling under Category 'B' in the said Schedule, before any construction work, or preparation of land by the project management except for securing the land, is started on the project or activity:

(i) All new projects or activities listed in the Schedule to this notification;
(ii) Expansion and modernization of existing projects or activities listed in the Schedule to this notification with addition of capacity beyond the limits specified for the concerned sector, that is, projects or activities which cross the threshold limits given in the Schedule, after expansion or modernization; and
(iii) Any change in product – mix in an existing manufacturing unit included in Schedule beyond the specified range."

The above paragraph makes it very clear that for Category 'A' project the Regulatory Authority shall be the Central Government in the Ministry of Environment and Forests. The above paragraph does not say that the Central Government in the Ministry of Environment and Forests shall mean the Minister in charge of the Ministry. In fact, in no Act or Rule or Statutory Notification it is ever stipulated that Ministry means the Minister in charge of the Ministry. Under the Rules of Business the Minister in charge of the Ministry has the power to decide the level at which decision of certain category would be taken. This is done for smooth functioning of the Government. Thus in some cases the files would go up to the Minister and in many cases the final decision will be taken by the Officers of the Ministry and such officers could be the Secretary of the Ministry or Joint Secretary of the Ministry as per the delegation of power approved by the Minister in charge. For example, all policy matters, Statutory Notifications, Note for the Cabinet etc. are to be approved by the Minister in charge. It is within the competency of the Minister to take a view if cases of prior environmental clearance should be finally decided at the level of the Minister or at the level of officer of a particular rank.

There is a similarity between the requirement of grant of previous approval under Section 5(1) of the MMDR Act and the requirement of grant of prior environmental clearance under paragraph 2 of the 14th September Notification. Till early 1990s the power of grant of previous approval of the Central Government for mining lease in respect of certain minerals included in the First Schedule to the MMDR Act was being exercised by the officers at the level of Joint Secretary. However, for some unknown reasons the then Minister took over such power *suo motu* and that was the beginning of all malpractices. I do not see any reason as to why an officer of appropriate level can not be declared as the Central Regulator to take a final view on the recommendations of the EAC which is an independent expert body constituted by the Ministry under a Statutory Notification which also prescribes a detailed and transparent procedure to be followed by the EAC. If the power is delegated to an officer of appropriate level it would only expedite the cases of granting prior environmental clearance. An individual Minister might be honest and very quick in clearing any proposal brought before him but one should go by the past experience about the time taken to decide a case at the level of the Minister. I am talking of a system and not of a particular person.

As if the lengthy procedure and consequent delay experienced presently is not enough. The MoEF, without a critical application of mind, had issued guidelines regarding procedure for consideration of proposals for grant of environmental clearance under 14th September Notification vide the Ministry's Office Memorandum no. J-11015/200/2008-IA.II (M) dated 31st March, 2011, a copy of which is at Annexure-D. If implemented in letter and in spirit, the guidelines would not only cause long delay but also undue harassment to the project proponent for no fault of his own. The office memorandum itself is *ultra vires* of the Statutory Notification. The guidelines can not contain something that is not in accordance with the intent of the Statutory Notification. Therefore, *ab initio,* the office memorandum is not in accordance with the 14th September Notification and I would examine that in the subsequent paragraphs.

The office memorandum is, in the face of it, for clarifying the import of sub-paragraph (v) of paragraph 8 of the 14th September Notification which is extracted below:

> "Clearances from other regulatory bodies or authorities shall not be required prior to receipt of applications for prior environmental

> clearance of projects or activities, or screening, or scoping, or appraisal, or decision by the regulatory authority concerned, unless any of these is sequentially dependent on such clearance either due to a requirement of law, or for necessary technical reasons."

Even a cursory reading of para 8(v) would reveal that activities like screening, scoping, appraisal etc. leading to final decision involved in the procedure for grant of prior environmental clearance as prescribed under the 14th September Notification are independent and integral parts of the process unless there is express provisions in any law or any essential technical reasons that make it mandatory that all or any of such activities as are involved in the procedure (i.e. screening, scoping, appraisal, etc.) shall be done only after the requirement of any law or requirement of the technical reasons are complied with prior to the processing of the application for prior environmental clearance. I think there is a confusion here. It is the project activities, that is, the act of extracting the minerals in case of a mining project, which could be dependent on some other clearances like, say, forestry clearance under the Forest (Conservation) Act, 1980, if use of forest land for non-forest purposes is involved, and definitely not the prescribed procedure culminating in the issuing of the sanction letter granting prior environmental clearance. Nobody can miss the distinction between a decision-making process and the practical application of the decision in the form of actual physical activities (extracting of minerals, for example).

The reading of the office memorandum would also indicate that the MoEF has given preference to the last part of the paragraph, that is, *"unless any of these is sequentially dependent on such clearance either due to a requirement of law, or for necessary technical reasons"* over the substantive main thrust of sub-para (v). The sub-para is very clear as the Ministry was well aware that there would be requirement of certain other statutory clearances such as "consent to establish" under the Air Act and Water Act and may be other clearances from various Regulatory Authorities for starting a mining project and therefore grant of prior environmental clearance does not, *ipso facto*, confer any right on a project proponent to start his mining project unless he also secures clearances from other Regulatory Authorities like the State Pollution Control Board (SPCB) and many others. All these clearances are parallel and not sequential. Diversion of forest lands for non-forest purposes under Section 2 of the Forest (Conservation) Act, 1980 is a parallel activity for which the project proponent would have to apply to the Ministry of Environment and Forests. Therefore, clearance from the Ministry for diversion of forest lands for non-forest purposes, if so required, is a parallel activity and not sequential depending on the grant of environmental clearance even though there could be delay in securing the forestry clearance and in many cases forestry clearance might come much later than the prior environmental clearance. There could be laws or some technical reasons compliance wherewith becomes mandatory after the grant of environmental clearance for which the project proponent shall be required to take some action subsequent to the grant of prior environmental clearance and such clearances can be termed sequential. To me it looks preposterous that forestry clearance is not a parallel process but a sequential one as assumed in the office memorandum referred to above. The project proponent is well aware that he can not start mining activities in the forest land unless he has separately obtained the forestry clearance from the MoEF. And, therefore, asking the project proponent, as mandated in the office memorandum, to delete the forest land from the total lease hold area would be contrary to the intent of sub-para (v). The Ministry is within its rights to enforce the condition that any activity in forest lands would be allowed only after forestry clearance has been obtained and, for that, forcing the project proponent to delete the forest land would be contrary to the 14th September Notification. It would be perfectly in order to take an undertaking from the project proponent that he would not carry on any activity on forest land without clearance from the Central Government in the Ministry of Environment and Forests and the logical corollary would be that the MoEF would have to take many such undertakings relating to clearances from other Regulatory Authorities like SPCB etc.

Sub-para 'D' of para-I of the office memorandum is, more often than not, bound to delay the consideration of even a complete proposal that has been recommended by the EAC and approved by the Ministry. The paragraph is extracted below:

> "In accordance with the recommendations of EAC, such projects will be processed on file for obtaining approval of the MEF for grant of environment clearance. After MEF has approved, a communication will be sent to the project proponent informing that the Competent Authority has approved the project; however, the formal environmental clearance will be issued only after the stage-I forestry clearance for the forestland involved in the project has been obtained and submitted. For the purpose, a maximum

> time limit of one year will be provided to the proponent during which time the proposal will be kept in abeyance. In case, the formal forestry clearance is not submitted within this time frame, the proposal will stand rejected and the process for obtaining environmental clearance will have to be initiated, de-novo, as per the procedure prescribed under EIA Notification, 2006".

A perusal of the above paragraph and specially the last sentence would have definitely a frustrating impact on the project proponent as he is, like any other project proponent, too familiar with the delatory tactics very routinely adopted by the officials at various levels. In this particular context, let us find out who is competent to grant stage-I forestry clearance for the forest land involved in the project. For grant of forestry clearance the project proponent is required to file an application before the same Ministry that is empowered to grant prior environmental clearance. Whenever, forest lands form part of the lease hold area and if a certain part of the forest lands is to be used by the project proponent for non-forest purposes such as a passage for going over to the mine pit or for extracting the minerals that occur in that part of the forest lands or for any other purposes like setting up a small field office or small repair shop etc. the project proponent would never fail to file an application to the Forest Department of the concerned State Government for grant of permission to use forest lands for non-forest purposes. The experience that the EAC, of which I was the Chairman, had during the three year tenure is that in this type of cases the project proponent would always submit before the EAC the progress in his attempt to obtain forestry clearance. In many cases it was found that stage-I forestry clearance had been obtained and in some cases the subject was under process as there is a different procedure for grant of forestry clearance and like in other procedures in the government system many a time delays can not be avoided notwithstanding the sincere effort of the officials involved to expedite the process.

If the project proponent has not defaulted in filing an application for forestry clearance it would be most unfair to ask him to obtain the forestry clearance within a maximum period of one year failing which the project proponent would have to initiate the whole process *de-novo* in preparing the EIA Report and EMP including public consultation and come back to the EAC with the forestry clearance. For whose fault the application for forestry clearance could not be decided? There has to be some responsibility fixed on the concerned Division of the Ministry to decide the forestry clearance cases within a fixed time schedule so that the project proponent can work out when to submit the application for prior environmental clearance in the same way the 14th September Notification has a prescribed time frame to decide the cases of prior environmental clearance.

It is beyond my comprehension to think that while adding sub-para 'D' referred to above the Ministry Officials weren't aware of the implication of such a conditionality. Firstly, the project proponent has no control over the time to be taken by the concerned Division of the Ministry to take a final decision on his application for stage-I forestry clearance. Secondly, and most importantly, it is quite common that due to various reasons, not necessarily on account of any fault on the part of the officials involved in processing any application for forestry clearance, delays could take place and perhaps such delays would be unavoidable under certain circumstances. In such a contingency one can imagine the wasteful expenditure already incurred by the project proponent in preparing the EIA Report and the EMP as also in the travel costs of the consultant and the representative of the project proponent in presenting his case before the EAC. To add insult to injury, the project proponent whose case has already been recommended by the EAC but the sanction letter conveying grant of prior environmental clearance was declined because another Division of the same Ministry has failed to take a view on the application of the project proponent for forestry clearance. So my initial observation that the office memorandum does not indicate that it has been drafted after application of mind are not out of place. In fact, no guidelines should include any such conditionality which is not intended by the original Statutory Notification.

Sub-para 'D' of Para 1 of the above Office Memorandum extracted hereinbefore is, *ab initio*, void being inconsistent with and contrary to the statutory provision in Para 8 (iii) of the 14th September Notification that stipulates that if the decision of the Regulatory Authority is not communicated within the prescribed time the applicant may proceed as if the environment clearance sought for has been granted or denied by the Regulatory Authority in terms of the final recommendations of the Expert Appraisal Committee (EAC) already in the website of the MoEF. Since, the recommendations of the EAC are already in the public domain the stipulation that grant of environmental clearance will be kept in abeyance is expressly in violation of the statutory provision of Para 8(iii) of the 14th September Notification.

The office memorandum betrays some amount of ignorance about the procedure followed by the State Government in granting mining lease. I have touched upon this issue in another context in this book that some times the State Government would include certain areas in the mining lease that could be forest lands also which are not essential for operating the mining project. The reasons for such a decision of the State Government are that if the related areas are not included in the total lease hold area there could be encroachment over the area by unauthorized persons. If the area is shown as part of the lease hold area the miner becomes the lessee of the whole area and instantly responsibilities are cast on the lessee to protect the entire lease hold area from unauthorized encroachments. There is another reason for the State Government to include certain areas purely for recovering some money from the lease holder in the form of dead rent. Under the law if the lessee does not start mining operations he would have to pay dead rent for the entire lease hold area which is quite substantial and is a non-productive financial burden on the lessee. This would induce the lessee to take up mining operations at the earliest so that he pays only royalty to the State Government at the prescribed rate for the quantity of minerals extracted. He would always ensure that he does not have to pay any dead rent and his main activities would be only to extract minerals to get a fair return on his investment. The project proponent on his own can exercise the option to surrender the lands not essential for his mining activities and the office memorandum would be applicable in such a case. Surrender of the surplus lands is not that easy as would appear *prima facie*. Supposing on a direction by the Ministry the project proponent applies to the State Government for accepting the surrender of the forest lands but the State Government declines to accept the surrender for some reason or other or the State Government takes a very casual approach that may entail unusually long time to take a view the project proponent becomes helpless. To make the project proponent suffer for no fault of his would be an undue hardship as in such a case delays are inevitable.

Before I deal with the fact that any delay begets corruption, I would like to refer to the office memorandum issued by the MoEF on *Corporate Environmental Responsibility* which, according to my assessment, is bound to create certain amount of confusion on the professed role of the Board of Directors of a company *vis-à-vis* that of the MoEF. Accordingly, I have decided to deal with the implications of the above office memorandum in the four succeeding paragraphs.

Like the office memorandum no. J-11015/200/2008-IA-II (M) dated 31st March 2011, dealt with in the preceding paragraphs, another office memorandum no. J-11013/41/2006-IA.II (I) dated 26th April, 2011 on Corporate Environmental Responsibility issued by the MoEF would create some confusion in the minds of the miners. A copy of the above office memorandum is at Annexure-E.

It would not be a problem for any mining company to have a corporate environmental policy either independently or as a part of the company's CSR policy. The confusion on the scope of sub-para (iv) of para (B) would create some difficulty for the project proponent while dealing with the case of violation of environmental and forestry clearances conditions. While issuing the circular the MoEF has presumed that officers of the Ministry and other public authorities would, as their assigned duty, inspect the project site and report cases of violation of various terms and conditions to the company which would place the same before the Board of Directors of the company for deliberations and appropriate decisions. It is not clear to the miner if the Ministry would also initiate parallel proceedings against the project proponent for violation of the terms and conditions. If that is so the Board of Directors would not be sure if its decision to take corrective steps would be enough or the company would still be subject to parallel action by the Ministry. If, however, the purpose is to make the company conscious of its statutory responsibility to comply with the terms and conditions of various clearances, the circular would appear to be in order. A reading of sub-para (iv) give the impression that the role of taking corrective measures has been transferred to the company and if that is so the role of the Ministry is confined only to report the compliance status, both positive compliance and violations of certain terms and conditions, as prepared by the inspecting officers of the Government, to the company for placing the matter before its Board of Directors and obviously it will be reflected in the Annual Report of the company which is a public document and could be put on the website of the company.

The circular is in respect of major Public Sector Undertakings (PSUs) and companies as detailed in para (C). Major PSUs and companies have been defined as all Central PSUs and all major projects. In the absence of proper clarification all Central PSUs irrespective of the related environmental concerns would be covered by this circular. All Central PSUs are not treated as major PSUs as there is a classification of the PSUs as Navaratna, Miniratna, Schedule- A, Schedule-B, Schedule-C and Schedule-D companies. For example PSUs like Mines and Minerals Trading Corporation (MMTC), State Trading Corporation (STC), Food Corporation of India (FCI) and any other trading companies would not have much of the environmental concern. Therefore, it is advisable that the PSUs and companies should be appropriately classified having regards to their activities that create environmental concerns of such nature as to warrant the attention of the Board of Directors.

Any guidelines or circulars should be such that are easy to be understood by mining and other companies like thermal power plants, cement plants etc. which necessarily involve environmental concerns of serious nature.

As delay begets corruption the administrative system could be so designed as to curtail delays in taking decision thereby controlling the menace of corruption becomes easy. How delays can be an effective tool to make money even without doing any irregularity can best be understood if I can explain the *modus operandi* of a corrupt officer.

For a miner, or for that matter any entrepreneur, time is money. When an entrepreneur intends to apply for a mining lease he has a fairly clear idea about the future of his project. Usually he will make a study of the market trend of the minerals, say iron ore, its requirement for meeting the plan target of steel production of the country and also the export target fixed by the government to make an assessment of its likely foreign exchange earnings. He would then take a decision if taking up a mining project for iron ore is profitable or not. Mining of iron ore has a gestation period from two years to five years depending on the size of the project. He would try his best to curtail the gestation period by expediting the mine development activities before actually starting mining operations. Therefore, he would try to save on time as any delay would mean additional financial burden which no serious entrepreneur would like. Now supposing after filing his application for mining lease he realizes that even though his case is justified on merits and that he has the required priority compared to other applicants over the same area, if any, his effort would be to ensure that the officials involved in the processing of his application at various levels expedite his case. It is very easy for any office to delay the processing of a particular application on any number of pretext. For example, if the applicant meets a particular officer in the Ministry of Mines who deals with the question of granting previous approval of the Central Government as required under the MMDR Act at around 11 a.m. in the morning and the officer calls for his file from the Section in his presence and starts writing his views on the file in presence of the applicant the applicant will be impressed by the promptness of the officer who would also advise the applicant to leave his office with the assurance that the file would be sent to the next senior officer during the course of the day and the applicant would leave the officer fully satisfied that his case would get priority. The officer dealing with the file would not take any further interest and after few days the applicant or his agent would enquire from the office about the status of the case. The office will express its ignorance about the file and the applicant or his agent again would meet the same officer who had earlier given the assurance for expediting his case.

This time around the officer would tell a different story which could be real or imaginary. He might tell that all on a sudden certain very important jobs were to be done as per the wishes of the boss and probably of the office of the Minister and therefore he was very sorry that he could not keep his promise. If such scenes get repeated the applicant will be forced to satisfy the officer or otherwise his case will be further delayed. So the applicant gets the hint and satisfies the officer and his job done. The practice could be the same in the MoEF in dealing with the application of the same entrepreneur for grant of prior environmental clearance even after a clear recommendation by the EAC. At this point of time the entrepreneur would not mind spending more money as he has reached a point by crossing all hurdles and the only thing remains is to get a sanction letter for grant of prior environmental clearance and perhaps the forestry clearance in case forest lands are also involved. The expectation of the entrepreneur has climaxed and so is the maneuvering capacity of the officials and the final competent authority in extracting the maximum satisfaction. So the entrepreneur has no option but to fall in line. And remember, nobody in the government hierarchy has committed any irregularity and has not shown any undue favour to the entrepreneur. Therefore, even if an enquiry is ordered no irregularity would be found and in our system delay in taking a decision is not categorized as irregularity rather it (delay) is a normal feature in the bureaucratic system. On the contrary, if there is a time schedule prescribed in processing a proposal in the file after receipt of the recommendations of the EAC in the same way the 14th September Notification prescribes the time schedule for the EAC to finalise its recommendations and if every government functionary is required to give his opinion with reasons within the time schedule delays would not take place.

It is universally accepted, and I have not invented anything new, that deciding a case without delay is one of the signs of good governance and it is in sync with the widely publicised government policy for providing responsive administration.

I would now proceed to the most important element of good governance and that is transparency. Ironically, both the processing of application for a mining lease and application for grant of prior environmental clearance in terms of the 14th September Notification are transparent and still the omnipotent discretionary power has created an unmistakable belief in the minds of the entrepreneurs that the Government's professed belief in providing a transparent administrative system is only for public consumption while in actual practice things have become almost non-transparently transparent.

In any organization accountability and transparency always go together. If the final authority is accountable for any arbitrary decision which is not justified on merits or which is not permissible under the Rules and Regulations, transparency is automatically ensured. In our system of administration the accountability of the bureaucracy is there. And, therefore, no government official, whatever be his status in the organization, would, in the normal course of his duty, deliberately commit any irregularity or would not give any suggestion which is not in accordance with the Rules and Regulations and in conformity with the precedent on similar cases in the past. But there could be some officials having a purely career point of view who would not mind giving an opinion knowing that it is not correct but in their anxiety to satisfy the political executive they would not mind giving suggestion which is acceptable to the political boss. It is not uncommon when a verbal message is conveyed by the political executive that a case should be made out (clearly) to favour a particular person or company. It is only when there is no case that a case is to be made out and depending on the amenability of the Secretary of the Ministry the established procedure in which the officials at various level are required to give their independent opinion is given a good-bye. Without naming a particular Minister, once I was conveyed the comment of the Minister that if he was only to put his signature after the signature of the Secretary of the Ministry then what was the need for a Minister? In this context I would refer to an observation made by a Minister of a State Government in a file which was resubmitted to him by the officer who wanted the Minister to state the reasons for the decision which was not correct. In that particular case the Minister observed that he was not a Court of Law that he should give reasons for his decision. The Minister was perhaps right. But in such a case if a Minister does not agree with the official suggestion in the file and if the order of the Minister is blatantly wrong there should be proper justification as any decision of the final authority becomes a precedent for decision in similar cases in future and perhaps in many past cases also the government might have to revise accordingly its own decision if any aggrieved party prefers an application for that purpose citing the particular decision taken by the Government subsequently.

It is so easy to take action against any official for giving an opinion in which his intention could be questioned by the Government and also by a court of law. Even after retirement the officer is subject to action under the relevant laws. Media reports have highlighted the prosecution of the then Secretary, Department of Telecommunication who is presently in prison. The prosecution of the political executive takes place only when very grave charges are *prima facie* established. In some cases political executives are also prosecuted but it is not as common as in respect of a government servant.

Earlier I have narrated the procedure for giving previous approval of the Central Government under Section 5(1) of the MMDR Act and the procedure for grant of prior environmental clearance in terms of the 14th September Notification. I worked in the Ministry of Mines for quite some time after the Minster took over the power of the Central Government for grant of previous approval. I had not come across a single case of grant of previous approval in which the Minster took a view different from that of the official hierarchy. Since all such cases are screened at various levels and these cases are also cleared by the State Cabinet and therefore chances of refusal of prior approval by the Central Government are very rare. In fact, in one case (not a case of previous approval) the Minister passed an illegal order and justification thereof was that he (the Minister) was more interested in the development of minerals than in legal technicalities. The decision was so blatantly illegal that the suggestion of the Secretary that the opinion of the Law Ministry might be obtained was approved by the Minister. The matter went to the Law Ministry which upheld the official view. It was the courage of the Secretary of the Ministry that he could resubmit the case to the Minister for a reference to the Law Ministry.

I am not aware of the current status, but usually the recommendations of the EAC are accepted by the MoEF and, therefore, the question remains whether there is really a need for upgrading the status of the Central Regulatory Authority to the level of the Minister. Integrity or otherwise of the Political Executive is not the subject matter of this book and, therefore, an objective view needs to be taken whether all cases of approval should necessarily be put up before the Minister or there could be a well considered decision that only certain types of cases should be put up before the Minister for approval. It is not impossible to categorize cases both under the MMDR Act and under the 14th September Notification that should move upward for final approval as earlier suggested in one of the preceding paragraphs.

The discretionary power given to any authority has the potential to introduce arbitrariness and therefore transparency becomes the first casualty. The word "discretion" is more often than not subject to arbitrary exercise of the right of discretion. In a narrow sense one would tend to believe that if discretion is to be regulated then it is not discretion rather it is a power subject to so many conditions. If one looks at the meaning/ definition of discretion given in *Oxford English Dictionary* it would be very clear that discretion is the freedom of the person exercising such discretionary power to act and think as one wishes, usually within legal limits. Discretion is equivalent to being discreet, that is, the person exercising his discretion should be circumspect in his action. Unless the person exercising any discretionary power is also held accountable for wrong doing, existence of such power in terms of any provisions in any Act, Rules, Regulations, Guidelines, etc. is always influenced by the personal judgment of the person competent to exercise any discretionary power. Since, transparency is the most critical element of any responsive governance, existence of any discretionary power specially in cases where statutory permission is essential would appear to be anachronic, if not an anathema.

While on the discretionary power of the Government I would refer to two decisions of the MoEF as reported in the print media in the past. The *Times of India* and *The Statesman* in their Delhi edition dated 3 May, 2011 have reported that the Minister MoEF has cleared Posco project in Orissa. The South Korean steel giant POSCO proposes to set up an integrated steel plant with an investment of US$ 12 billion. It is undoubtedly one of the largest projects of this type. The project also involves diversion of forest land (1,253 hectares) for non-forest purposes. Reportedly, the clearance has been given on the basis of the state government's latest communication dated 29th April, 2011. Apparently, the state government has given the assurance that has prompted the Minister to clear the proposal. I am not going into the details of the terms and conditions as being not relevant for the purpose of dealing with the discretionary power. However, it is essential to refer to the condition that POSCO shall not export raw materials from the plant as this (condition) has serious implications.

The mining industry is undoubtedly confused about the implication of the condition that POSCO should not export raw materials (obviously iron ore) from the proposed plant. It is not clear as to how the MoEF could decide on the question of export of any raw materials as this falls within the administrative domain of the Ministry of Commerce that decides the question of export and import and every year the Ministry brings out what is commonly known as EXIM Policy that regulates the export and import of various commodities. Even if you set aside the administrative aspect, the two critical issues would continue to baffle the industry.

In a liberalized economy the project proponent is to decide the question of disposal of any surplus raw materials in accordance of the extant policy of the Government. I give an example to make the point clear. Suppose in a particular year POSCO has a plan to produce 1 million tonnes steel for which the company would need about, say, 1.6 million tonnes of iron ore. During the course of the year it is possible that the company would end up by extracting, say, an additional quantity of 0.10 million tonnes of iron ore. This excess production could not have been avoided as the mine benches in a particular pit were such that the extracting of this much extra quantity of iron ore became inescapable. If POSCO has complied with all the terms and conditions of the mining lease, the approved mining plan and the terms and conditions of the prior environmental clearance the company can not be faulted for excess production of iron ore. If as per the export policy, export of iron ore is allowed with whatever terms and conditions it is not for the MoEF to put a condition that export of raw material iron ore should not take place.

The Indian iron ore of hematite type is of high grade with Fe content of 60 per cent and above. It is not only in the process of converting iron ore into steel but also in the process of making other items, for example, cement with limestone as raw material, blending of a particular type of raw material (iron ore or limestone) as sweetener is a technological necessity. In this particular case if POSCO has to blend iron ore of a particular characteristic as a sweetener and if the company can import such iron ore at economic cost by exporting certain quantity of iron ore mined by the company it is not the concern of the MoEF or even of the Ministry of Commerce if the extant EXIM Policy does not expressly forbid such export and import. The MoEF will be perfectly within its rights to suggest use of state-of-the-art technology that is environment friendly. As regards the technology for making steel out of iron ore it is best left to the entrepreneur who has great stake in investing huge amount of money. It is understood that blending of ore of a different grade as a sweetener result in lesser consumption of energy and considering the fact that energy shortage is a global phenomenon if any plant saves, say, one unit of energy, it is virtually generating one extra unit of energy.

The *Times of India* in its Delhi edition dated 7 May, 2011 has quoted the Minister MoEF as saying that he has cleared certain projects under pressure from some politician named by him as also under pressure from the Prime Minister's Office (PMO). The Minister has also been quoted as saying that one has to be practical in deciding such cases and one of the reasons given is that large amount of money has already been spent and therefore grant of environmental clearance was justified. But at the same time the Minister has also stressed, as reported by the newspaper, that the project proponent is also to be warned that violation of environmental norms can not be accepted.

In the case of POSCO the MoEF has accepted the assurance of the State Government as the ground for giving clearance in favour of POSCO.

The 14th September Notification does not give any role to the State Government and to that extent this is a deviation from the procedure prescribed under the above Notification. This would mean that even in a case where the EAC recommends rejection of a particular proposal the Ministry can overrule the recommendations of the EAC if the concerned State Government gives an assurance to the satisfaction of the Minister, who is the final authority, that the State Government would ensure compliance with the provisions of green laws. Every State Government is keen to see that the state is industrially developed and the states like Orissa or Jharkhand or Chattisgarh which are very rich in mineral reserves would like to see that the natural wealth, that is, the minerals are fully exploited for the economic development of the state. Therefore, it is inconceivable to think that any state government would not give any assurance to comply with the provisions of the green laws which (compliance) even otherwise is legally binding on the state government. It is only on the recommendation of the State Government that the Central Government gives previous approval for grant of a mining lease for, say, iron ore, to the particular applicant and therefore on being approached by the applicant the State Government would always be ready to give the required assurances to comply with the provisions of green laws as it has already recommended the case for previous approval for grant of mining laws and hence it becomes almost its duty to ensure that the lessee also gets the necessary prior environmental clearance and forestry clearance, if any.

In the other instance cited above where grant of environment clearance has reportedly been granted on the ground that large amount of money has already been spent by the project proponent and also due to some pressure put on the Minister. If the spending of large amount of money and certain amount of pressure could influence the decision of the Ministry in favour of the project proponent it becomes that much easy for any project proponent to ensure grant of prior environmental clearance. In a democratic country like ours ensuring the required pressure from the right person is not a problem.

Legally a miner is under obligation to prepare the EIA report and the EMP and submit the same to the MoEF which would place it before the EAC for giving its recommendations as per the procedure prescribed under 14th September Notification. Suppose the miner also submits a copy of the letter of the State Government giving the required assurance and the miner also submits details of his expenditure on some of the project activities certified by a registered Chartered Accountant the predicament of the EAC becomes too obvious. The EAC is under obligation to consider the EIA report and the EMP and the clarification given by the project proponent during presentation of the proposal made to the EAC. The EAC is not under obligation to make any comment on the assurance of the State Government and the expenses already incurred by the project proponent as these are irrelevant for deciding whether it is a fit case for grant of prior environmental clearance. Suppose the EAC recommends rejection of the application for environmental clearance. The assurance letter of the State Government and the details of expenditure are already there before the Ministry. Can the Ministry ignore the plea of the project proponent that on the basis of the precedent of POSCO and other cases he is entitled to grant of prior environmental clearance for his project also? I leave to the Ministry to think about it.

The two cases of exercise of discretionary power by the Ministry as referred to in the preceding paragraphs would create an unhealthy practice as it would be impossible for the Government to take a different view in many such cases. This has already created confusion among the mining fraternity as the industry would have no idea about the nature of discretion that the Government would practise.

For the sake of argument let us conceive a situation in which the government has a clear cut policy prescription, a reasonably corruption free administrative machinery, decision is taken without much delay and that a transparent procedure is followed without any discretionary power at any level, still there could be perceptible deficiencies in the system when it comes to the implementation of a well conceived decision of the government.

Let us see the role of the official hierarchy involved in implementing the provisions of the MMDR Act and the Rules framed thereunder. Every State specially a major mineral bearing state has a well organized hierarchy in which the Director of Mines and the District Mining Officer play very crucial role. And to the best of my personal experience as Secretary, Mines and Geology of a major mineral bearing state I can with reasonable amount of certainty say that there is a system of regular inspection of mines and inspection reports being submitted to the Director of Mines who would in a routine way put up the matter before the Secretary. I would not say that the miner does not indulge in wrong doings. But if the inspection mechanism is properly activated the chances of illegal mining and violation of terms and conditions of a mining lease could largely be controlled if not completely eliminated. In the absence of an effective inspection mechanism and follow up action by the competent authority for any wrong doings all efforts of the government would be frustrated.

As regards the compliance with the terms and conditions of the sanction letter granting prior environmental clearance the existing system would appear to be inadequate. This has been admitted by the Ministry itself. I have in Chapter-14 of this book referred to a meeting taken by the Secretary of the Ministry on 4th July, 2006 with some of the Chairpersons of the EACs in which it was decided that the Ministry would evolve a system for random inspection of the projects which have been granted environmental clearance for assessing the compliance status. To my knowledge the above decision taken in a meeting Chaired by the Secretary of the Ministry is yet to be given a concrete shape. In fact, I had an occasion to informally discuss this matter with a very senior official of the Ministry who agreed that an inspection mechanism is essential. But in a lighter vein he also told me that in the past an attempt in that direction was indeed made but it proved to be disastrous as the so called inspection team was alleged to blackmail the project proponents with the result that the very purpose of the inspection got defeated.

As it is not always possible to select officers of absolute integrity in the present circumstances, the government has to make a beginning. It would not be difficult to select some officers who could be trusted with the task of doing random inspection in select cases to ensure that the terms and conditions of the sanction letter granting prior environmental clearance in such select cases are complied with. If such a mechanism is put in place government would not have to face an embarrassing situation when it is forced to withdraw prior environmental clearance granted in certain cases as reported in the print media quite recently.

So it is not always true that with a clear cut policy prescription, a reasonably corruption free administrative system and a transparent procedure without any discretionary power that ensures disposal of cases without delay, the action of the Government would automatically result in providing the required relief to the project proponent. In fact, the project proponent may not necessarily, in the absence of an effective inspection, mechanism, ensure compliance with the terms and conditions of a mining lease and the terms and conditions of the sanction letter granting prior environmental clearance. Even this (inspection mechanism) would not mean that the project proponent would be complying with all the terms and conditions. This brings us to the responsibility of the project proponent which I would be dealing with in the succeeding paragraphs.

While dealing with the role of various stakeholders in Chapter-14, I have also specially dealt with the role of the miner. The miner has a very critical and significant role in eradicating any scope for corruption. Imagine a situation when the miner refuses to oblige anybody in the government by paying bribe money for processing his case. If all the miners get united and take a collective decision which is binding on every miner that come what may a miner will never succumb to the pressure tactics taken recourse to by the greedy government servants involved in processing his application for a mining lease it is possible to check the never-ending demand for bribe money to a great extent. Let us imagine an ideal situation when the mining fraternity takes a vow and follows it up by ensuring that no miner would indulge in any corrupt or unethical practices. This is perhaps the intention of the Minister, MoEF when he was quoted as saying that somebody (read the bribe giver) has to control the supply (bribe money) side and the Minister could not be faulted for such an observation. It is easier said than done. But unless a beginning, may be in a limited way, is made the cancer of corruption would eat into the vital of the administrative system. Every miner can make his small contribution to the cause of a clean and corruption free administration, may be, to some extent.

The same logic would apply in respect of action taken by a miner to obtain prior environmental clearance in terms of 14th September Notification. In fact, it is not true that in every case bribe taking is necessarily involved. But the image of the government prevailing among the general public is that nothing moves unless money changes hands specially in cases where statutory permissions are essential before starting any economic activities and undoubtedly mining is treated by the corrupt system as a hassle free source for illegal gratification. Therefore, the mining fraternity can make effective contribution to the cause of a corruption free system in a limited way, still an achievement.

The ordeal of a miner does not end with the execution of a mining lease and with the issue of a sanction letter granting prior environmental clearance. Rather it (ordeal) starts with the execution of the mining lease and receipt of the sanction letter granting prior environmental clearance and this is the period when the role of a miner becomes important. I would try to highlight the matter with some examples in the sequel.

A lessee is aware of the terms and conditions of the mining lease and also the terms and conditions of the sanction letter granting prior environmental clearance. He is also aware that he is under legal obligation to comply with the terms and conditions specified in the lease deed and the sanction letter granting prior environmental clearance. The grant of mining lease and the grant of prior environmental clearance are subject to those conditions and, therefore, if a lessee fails to comply with those terms and conditions it amounts to an act of violation of legally enforceable conditionalties for which the mining lease granted earlier could be terminated and the environmental clearance already granted can be withdrawn. For example, as per the mining plan approved by the Indian Bureau of Mines (IBM), the miner is under obligation to do scientific mining which involves progressive mine closure and final mine closure. If the lessee fails to comply with this condition of mine closure the lease is liable to be terminated.

There are number of conditions prescribed in the lease deed and also in the prior environmental clearance letter. The miner is fully aware that these conditions have to be complied with for creating a pollution free atmosphere with development of green belt. If a miner, on his own or in collusion with the local field officers of both the Department of Mines and the Department of Forests and Environment, fails to comply with the terms and conditions, he would not only do a disservice to the cause of the environment but also would encourage corruption as the field officers would have to be satisfied with the bribe money and the miner would find it easy, and perhaps with a sense of impunity, to ignore the terms and conditions. On the other hand, if a miner sincerely complies with the terms and conditions, there would be no cause for him to pay bribe money to the field officers.

In this context, it would be perhaps useful, if I could refer to some of the unethical practices followed by some miners. If a project proponent has large financial resources, he would try to influence the political executive and perhaps the local influential politicians through unethical practices and also by hiring a retired bureaucrat with good clout on the Government both at the State level and the Central level and of course with hefty financial compensation so that he can carry on his mining activities without any regards for the terms and conditions. There could be another category of miners who would find it easy to engage a local muscleman to silence any voice of protest by the affected people against his mining activities being carried on in violation of the prescribed terms and conditions. These are dangerous practices fraught with grave consequences beyond the imagination of the miner himself. Such persons as have been patronized by the miner through the inducement of money would not remain satisfied unless their never ending greed for money is satisfied. The miner, to his dismay, would realize that in no time such persons have become a Frankenstein's monster that becomes terrifying to its maker, i.e., the miner himself.

This leads us to the conclusion that a clear cut policy prescription, a reasonably corruption free administration, decision without or with least delay, a transparent procedure followed by the government without any discretionary power, an effective inspection mechanism to ensure compliance with the terms and conditions of a mining lease and prior environment clearance and a truly professional miner who follows the terms and conditions of the lease deed and terms and conditions specified in the sanction letter granting prior environmental clearance, are *sine qua non,* i.e., an indispensable condition, of good governance. If a situation like this is achieved the miner will be pleasantly surprised that he might be degrading the lands as being inescapable while extracting the minerals but at the same time he would be leaving the mined out areas which would be not only environmental friendly but also a healthy place to live in. If the government fails to provide a good and responsive governance and the miner falls easy victim to greedy official machinery the alternative will be that the affected people would take law into their own hands and the aggrieved people know how to deal with unscrupulous miners and their patrons in the government.

Providing a good and responsive governance is easier said than done. There are two levels in every government which must perform in perfect harmony failing which the system can not provide a good governance. At the top level of the government in any Ministry is the political executive, that is, the Minister in charge of the Ministry. Below is the bureaucratic level headed by the Secretary of the Ministry who is assisted by officers and other staff. The Ministry has also field offices at convenient locations through out the country and each of such offices is headed by a senior officer. In the case of the MoEF, these field functionaries along with the field functionaries of the State Forest Department have the responsibilities to protect the forests and the wildlife. I have earlier narrated the administrative structure of the Department of Mines and Geology under the State Government with field functionaries headed by the Director of Mines, District Mining Officers etc. who were responsible for ensuring that the terms and conditions of a mining lease are complied with.

As far as the government servants are concerned they are subject to disciplinary action for any misconduct and dereliction of duty. If the charges are serious and are proved against the delinquent officer he can be dismissed from service and the Government is competent to withhold either full or part of the pension if the officer concerned is eligible for post-retirement pension. Therefore, it all depends on the Secretary of the Ministry to ensure that the officers and other employees discharge their duties with devotion and integrity. If there is any lapse on the part of the Secretary of the Ministry, the Minister can pull up of the Secretary and in justified cases action can be taken against the Secretary and other officers under the relevant Service Conduct Rules besides transfer of the officer to some other organization.

The real problem comes when the political executive takes some decision which is not correct and also not in accordance with the provisions of the Act, Rules, Regulations, Guidelines, etc. In such a case, Secretary of the Ministry becomes helpless except resubmitting the file with reasons for reconsideration of the Minister. If the Minister still sticks to his original decision which, according to the Secretary, is not correct, there is no option for the bureaucracy left except to carry out the order of the Minister. As per the Rules of Transaction of Business in the Central Government the Minister is the final authority except in cases where approval of the Council of Ministers, commonly known as the Cabinet, is required. Let us conceive a situation in which a particular decision of the Minister is blatantly irregular, what is the option available with the Secretary as the Administrative Head of the Ministry? Here comes the relevance of the Cabinet Secretary who is the head of the Civil Service and finally that of the Prime Minister. A solution in such a case is possible if there is a mechanism under which the Secretary of the Ministry can bring the matter to the notice of the Cabinet Secretary for direction and the Cabinet Secretary is empowered to give his opinion and put up the file before the Minister of a particular department and in exceptional cases the matter can be brought to the notice of the Prime Minister. Such a procedure is followed in accordance with the Rules of Executive Business of some of the State Governments. I will give two instances in the following paragraphs. In another context, in this chapter I have referred to a particular case that was referred to the Ministry of Law as it was proved that the decision of the Minister was clearly illegal.

The Rules of Executive Business that regulate the functioning of the Secretariat Department of the Government of Bihar have a clear cut procedure to deal with the cases of difference between the Secretary and the Minister of a Department. I was posted as Commissioner and Secretary, Department of Health and Medical Education, Government of Bihar for a short period during 1994-95. In one particular case I gave my recommendations with justification and the file was submitted before the Minister for his approval. The then Cabinet Minister in-charge of the Department who was a strict believer in the procedure laid down in the Rules of Executive Business did not agree with my recommendations and he minuted his own decision. The Minister could guess that I might submit the case to him for reconsideration as by that time he had already formed an opinion about my way of working and incidentally I had no difficulty in working with the Minister. The Minister minuted in the file that if I as the Secretary of the Department were not in agreement with the views of the Minister I would be free to submit the file to the Chief Minister through the Chief Secretary for decision as per the provisions of the Rules of Executive Business. But he added that before submitting the file to the Chief Secretary he might be shown the file for his information.

The other instance relates to a case when I was posted as Commissioner and Secretary of the Department of Mines and Geology under the State Government of Bihar during 1986-88. In one particular case the Cabinet Minister in charge of the Department, who was politically very close to the Chief Minister, recorded his views which were contrary to my views and he submitted the file directly to the Chief Minister for his approval. In this case the Minister called me to his office chamber and suggested that I should also read the notings of the Minister in the file which, indeed, I did as a disciplined bureaucrat. When I finished my reading the Minister looked at me and smiled with the observation that he knew that the Chief Minister would agree with my views and not with the views of the Minister. But in a lighter vein he told me that he had recorded these views under pressure from some legislators knowing very well that his views were not in accordance with the legal provisions. The Minister was so correct that after I was transferred to some other department as Secretary, the Chief Secretary called me to his chamber and discussed the matter with me as directed by the Chief Minister. I believe ultimately my views prevailed.

I have cited the two instances from my own experience only to justify that a procedure like the one followed in the State Government could be thought of also at the Central Government level which would work as an effective deterrent against the political executive of any Ministry as in that case the Minister in charge of the department would be circumspect in taking a decision as no Minister would like that any inappropriate decision could be brought to the knowledge of the Prime Minister which might be quite embarrassing for him. In fact such an institutional arrangement is more transparent than the present unofficial procedure of carrying out a verbal direction to take a particular decision in a case.

At the end I am wondering how and where to get an environment-friendly miner? We have seen in more than one place in this book how the forest dwelling people like the tribes and other traditional forest dwellers, a predator like a lion and its victim, say, a deer have been living in the same forest area for generations in complete harmony with one another and every section of these forest dwellers, that is, humans, wildlife and also the forests has allowed each section of the forest dwellers and the forests to survive and survive well. If a miner takes a lesson from these forest dwellers he should take no time, I am sure, to realize that mining can be equally environment-friendly and he can contribute a lot to ensure an environment which is liveable for not only humans but also for wildlife.

If a miner sincerely gives a chance to what have been suggested in this book based on my personal experience, and it is not a theoretical hyperbole, the existence of the environment-friendly miner is round the corner in no time.

Annexure-A

[Published in the Gazette of India, Extraordinary, Part-II, and Section 3, Sub-section (ii) Ministry of Environment and Forests]

New Delhi 14th September, 2006

NOTIFICATION

S.O. 1533 Whereas, a draft notification under sub-rule (3) of Rule 5 of the Environment (Protection) Rules, 1986 for imposing certain restrictions and prohibitions on new projects or activities, or on the expansion or modernization of existing projects or activities based on their potential environmental impacts as indicated in the Schedule to the notification, being undertaken in any part of India[1], unless prior environmental clearance has been accorded in accordance with the objectives of National Environment Policy as approved by the Union Cabinet on 18th May, 2006 and the procedure specified in the notification, by the Central Government or the State or Union territory Level Environment Impact Assessment Authority (SEIAA), to be constituted by the Central Government in consultation with the State Government or the Union territory Administration concerned under sub-section (3) of section 3 of the Environment (Protection) Act, 1986 for the purpose of this notification, was published in the Gazette of India, Extraordinary, Part II, section 3, sub-section (ii) vide number S.O. 1324 (E) dated the 15th September, 2005 inviting objections and suggestions from all persons likely to be affected thereby within a period of sixty days from the date on which copies of Gazette containing the said notification were made available to the public;

And whereas, copies of the said notification were made available to the public on 15th September, 2005;

And whereas, all objections and suggestions received in response to the above mentioned draft notification have been duly considered by the Central Government;

1. Includes the territorial waters.

Now, therefore, in exercise of the powers conferred by sub-section (1) and clause (v) of sub-section (2) of section 3 of the Environment (Protection) Act, 1986, read with clause (d) of sub-rule (3) of rule 5 of the Environment (Protection) Rules, 1986 and in supersession of the notification number S.O. 60 (E) dated the 27th January, 1994, except in respect of things done or omitted to be done before such supersession, the Central Government hereby directs that on and from the date of its publication the required construction of new projects or activities or the expansion or modernization of existing projects or activities listed in the Schedule to this notification entailing capacity addition with change in process and or technology shall be undertaken in any part of India only after the prior environmental clearance from the Central Government or as the case may be, by the State Level Environment Impact Assessment Authority, duly constituted by the Central Government under sub-section (3) of Section 3 of the said Act, in accordance with the procedure specified hereinafter in this notification.

2. Requirements of Prior Environmental Clearance (EC): The following projects or activities shall require prior environmental clearance from the concerned regulatory authority, which shall hereinafter referred to be as the Central Government in the Ministry of Environment and Forests (MoEF) for matters falling under Category 'A' in the Schedule and at State level the State Environment Impact Assessment Authority (SEIAA) for matters falling under Category 'B' in the said Schedule, before any construction work, or preparation of land by the project management except for securing the land, is started on the project or activity:

(i) All new projects or activities listed in the Schedule to this notification;

(ii) Expansion and modernization of existing projects or activities listed in the Schedule to this notification with addition of capacity beyond the limits specified for the concerned sector, that is, projects or activities which cross the threshold limits given in the Schedule, after expansion or modernization;

(iii) Any change in product - mix in an existing manufacturing unit included in Schedule beyond the specified range.

3. State Level Environment Impact Assessment Authority:

(1) A State Level Environment Impact Assessment Authority hereinafter referred to as the SEIAA shall be constituted by the Central Government under sub-section (3) of section 3 of the Environment (Protection) Act, 1986 comprising of three

Members including a Chairman and a Member-Secretary to be nominated by the State Government or the Union territory Administration concerned.

(2) The Member-Secretary shall be a serving officer of the concerned State Government or Union territory administration familiar with environmental laws.

(3) The Chairman shall be an expert in terms of the eligibility criteria given in APPENDIX-VI in one of the specified fields, with sufficient experience in environmental policy or management. *(Substituted by Notification dated 11th October, 2007)*

(4) The other Member shall be an expert fulfilling the eligibility criteria given in APPENDIX-VI in one of the specified fields. *(Substituted by Notification dated 11th October, 2007)*

(5) The State Government or Union territory Administration shall forward the names of the Members and the Chairman referred in sub-paragraph 3 to 4 above to the Central Government and the Central Government shall constitute the SEIAA as an authority for the purposes of this notification within thirty days of the date of receipt of the names.

(6) The non-official Member and the Chairman shall have a fixed term of three years (from the date of the publication of the notification by the Central Government constituting the authority).

(7) All decisions of the SEIAA shall be taken in a meeting and shall ordinarily be unanimous:

Provided that, in case a decision is taken by majority, the details of views, for and against it, shall be clearly recorded in the minutes and a copy thereof sent to MoEF. *(Substituted by Notification dated 1st December, 2009).*

4. Categorization of Projects and Activities: (i) All projects and activities are broadly categorized in to two categories—Category-A and Category-B, based on the spatial extent of potential impacts and potential impacts on human health and natural and manmade resources.

(ii) All projects or activities included as Category 'A' in the Schedule, including expansion and modernization of existing projects or activities and change in product mix, shall require prior environmental clearance from the Central Government in the Ministry of Environment and Forests (MoEF) on the recommendations of an Expert Appraisal Committee (EAC) to be constituted by the Central Government for the purposes of this notification;

(iii) All projects or activities included as Category 'B' in the Schedule, including expansion and modernization of existing projects or activities as specified in sub paragraph (ii) of paragraph 2, or change in product mix as specified in sub paragraph (iii) of paragraph 2, but excluding those which fulfil the General Conditions (GC) stipulated in the Schedule, *will* require prior environmental clearance from the State/Union territory Environment Impact Assessment Authority (SEIAA). The SEIAA shall base its decision on the recommendations of a State or Union territory level Expert Appraisal Committee (SEAC) as to be constituted for in this notification. In the absence of a duly constituted SEIAA or SEAC, a Category 'B' project shall be considered at Central Level as a Category 'B' project. *(Substituted by Notification dated 1st December, 2009).*

5. Screening, Scoping and Appraisal Committees: The same Expert Appraisal Committees (EACs) at the Central Government and SEACs (hereinafter referred to as the (EAC) and (SEAC) at the State or the Union territory level shall screen, scope and appraise projects or activities in Category 'A' and Category 'B' respectively. EAC and SEAC's shall meet at least once every month.

(a) The composition of the EAC shall be as given in Appendix-VI. The SEAC at the State or the Union territory level shall be constituted by the Central Government in consultation with the concerned State Government or the Union territory Administration with identical composition;

(b) The Central Government may, with the prior concurrence of the concerned State Governments or the Union territory Administrations, constitutes one SEAC for more than one State or Union territory for reasons of administrative convenience and cost;

(c) The EAC and SEAC shall be reconstituted after every three years;

(d) The authorised members of the EAC and SEAC, concerned, may inspect any site(s) connected with the project or activity in respect of which the prior environmental clearance is sought, for the purposes of screening or scoping or appraisal, with prior notice of at least seven days to the applicant, who shall provide necessary facilities for the inspection;

(e) The EAC and SEACs shall function on the principle of collective responsibility. The Chairperson shall endeavour to reach a consensus in each case, and if consensus cannot be reached, the view of the majority shall prevail.

6. Application for Prior Environmental Clearance (EC): *An application seeking prior environmental clearance in all cases shall be made by the project proponent*[2] in the prescribed Form-1 annexed herewith and Supplementary Form-1A, if applicable, as given in Appendix-II, after the identification of prospective site(s) for the project and/or activities to which the application relates, before commencing any construction activity, or preparation of land, at the site by the applicant. The applicant shall furnish, along with the application, a copy of the pre-feasibility project report except that, in case of construction projects or activities (item 8 of the Schedule) in addition to Form 1 and the Supplementary Form-1A, a copy of the conceptual plan shall be provided, instead of the pre-feasibility report.

7. Stages in the Prior Environmental Clearance (EC) Process for New Projects

7(i) The environmental clearance process for new projects will comprise of a maximum of four stages, all of which may not apply to particular cases as set forth below in this notification. These four stages in sequential order are:

- Stage (1) Screening (Only for Category 'B' projects and activities)
- Stage (2) Scoping
- Stage (3) Public Consultation
- Stage (4) Appraisal

I. Stage (1)—Screening:

In case of Category 'B' projects or activities, this stage will entail the scrutiny of an application seeking prior environmental clearance made in Form-1 by the concerned State Level Expert Appraisal Committee (SEAC) for determining whether or not the project or activity requires further environmental studies for preparation of an Environmental Impact Assessment (EIA) for its appraisal prior to the grant of

---

[2] Substituted by Notification dated 4th April, 2011.

environmental clearance depending up on the nature and location specificity of the project. The projects requiring an Environmental Impact Assessment report shall be termed Category 'B1' and remaining projects shall be termed Category 'B2' and will not require an Environment Impact Assessment report. For categorization of projects into B1 or B2 except item 8 (b), the Ministry of Environment and Forests shall issue appropriate guidelines from time to time.

II. Stage (2)—Scoping:

(i) "Scoping": refers to the process by which the Expert Appraisal Committee (EAC) in the case of Category 'A' projects or activities, and State level Expert Appraisal Committee in the case of Category 'B1' projects or activities, including applications for expansion and/or modernization and/or change in product mix of existing projects or activities, determine detailed and comprehensive Terms of Reference (TOR) addressing all relevant environmental concerns for the preparation of an Environment Impact Assessment (EIA) Report in respect of the project or activity for which prior environmental clearance is sought. The Expert Appraisal Committee or State level Expert Appraisal Committee concerned shall determine the Terms of Reference on the basis of the information furnished in the prescribed application Form1/Form 1A including Terms of Reference proposed by the applicant, a site visit by a sub-group of Expert Appraisal Committee or State level Expert Appraisal Committee concerned only if considered necessary by the Expert Appraisal Committee or State Level Expert Appraisal Committee concerned, Terms of Reference suggested by the applicant if furnished and other information that may be available with the Expert Appraisal Committee or State Level Expert Appraisal Committee concerned. All projects and activities listed as Category 'B' in item 8*(a)* of the schedule (building and construction projects) shall not require Scoping and will be appraised on the basis of Form-1/Form-1A and the conceptual plan. *(Substituted by Notification dated 4 April, 2011)*

(ii) The Terms of Reference (TOR) shall be conveyed to the applicant by the Expert Appraisal Committee or State Level Expert Appraisal Committee as concerned within sixty days of the receipt of Form-1. In the case of Category-A Hydroelectric projects Item 1(c) (i) of the Schedule the Terms of Reference shall be conveyed along with the clearance for pre-construction activities. If the Terms of Reference are not finalized and conveyed to the applicant within sixty days of the receipt of Form-1, the Terms of Reference suggested by the applicant shall be deemed as the final Terms of Reference approved for the EIA studies. The approved Terms of Reference shall be displayed on the website of the Ministry of Environment and Forests and the concerned State Level Environment Impact Assessment Authority.

(iii) Applications for prior environmental clearance may be rejected by the regulatory authority concerned on the recommendation of the EAC or SEAC concerned at this stage itself. In case of such rejection, the decision together with reasons for the same shall be communicated to the applicant in writing within sixty days of the receipt of the application.

III. Stage (3)—Public Consultation:

(i) "Public Consultation" refers to the process by which the concerns of local affected persons and others who have plausible stake in the environmental impacts of the project or activity are ascertained with a view to taking into account all the material concerns in the project or activity design as appropriate. All Category 'A' and Category B1 projects or activities shall undertake Public Consultation, except the following:

(a) modernization of irrigation projects (item 1(c) (ii) of the Schedule).

(b) all projects or activities located within industrial estates or parks (item 7(c) of the Schedule) approved by the concerned authorities, and which are not disallowed in such approvals.

(c) expansion of Roads and Highways (item 7 (f) of the Schedule) which do not involve any further acquisition of land.

(cc) Maintenance dredging provided the dredged material shall be disposed within port limits (Inserted by Notification dated 1st December, 2009)

(d) all Building or Construction projects or Area Development projects (which do not contain any category 'A' projects and activities) and Townships (item 8(a) and

8(b) in the Schedule to the notification). *(Substituted by Notification dated 1st December, 2009)*

(e) all Category 'B2' projects and activities.

(f) all projects or activities concerning national defence and security or involving other strategic considerations as determined by the Central Government.

(ii) The Public Consultation shall ordinarily have two components comprising of:

(a) a public hearing at the site or in its close proximity-districtwise, to be carried out in the manner prescribed in Appendix-IV, for ascertaining concerns of local affected persons;

(b) obtain responses in writing from other concerned persons having a plausible stake in the environmental aspects of the project or activity.

(iii) The public hearing at, or in close proximity to, the site(s) in all cases shall be conducted by the State Pollution Control Board (SPCB) or the Union Territory Pollution Control Committee (UTPCC) concerned in the specified manner and forward the proceedings to the regulatory authority concerned within 45 (forty-five) days of a request to the effect from the applicant.

(iv) In case the State Pollution Control Board or the Union Territory Pollution Control Committee concerned does not undertake and complete the public hearing within the specified period, and/or does not convey the proceedings of the public hearing within the prescribed period directly to the regulatory authority concerned as above, the regulatory authority shall engage another public agency or authority which is not subordinate to the regulatory authority, to complete the process within a further period of forty-five days,.

(v) If the public agency or authority nominated under the sub-paragraph (iii) above reports to the regulatory authority concerned that owing to the local situation, it is not possible to conduct the public hearing in a manner which will enable the views of the concerned local persons to be freely expressed, it shall report the facts in detail to the concerned regulatory authority, which may, after due consideration of the report and other reliable information that it may have, decide that the public consultation in the case need not include the public hearing.

(vi) For obtaining responses in writing from other concerned persons having a plausible stake in the environmental aspects of the project or activity, the concerned regulatory authority and the State Pollution Control Board (SPCB) or the Union Territory Pollution Control Committee (UTPCC) shall invite responses from such concerned persons by placing on their website the Summary EIA report prepared in the format given in Appendix-IIIA by the applicant along with a copy of the application in the prescribed form, within seven days of the receipt of a written request for arranging the public hearing. Confidential information including non-disclosable or legally privileged information involving Intellectual Property Right, source specified in the application shall not be placed on the web site. The regulatory authority concerned may also use other appropriate media for ensuring wide publicity about the project or activity. The regulatory authority shall, however, make available on a written request from any concerned person the Draft EIA report for inspection at a notified place during normal office hours till the date of the public hearing. All the responses received as part of this public consultation process shall be forwarded to the applicant through the quickest available means.

(vii) After completion of the public consultation, the applicant shall address all the material environmental concerns expressed during this process, and make appropriate changes in the draft EIA and EMP. The final EIA report, so prepared, shall be submitted by the applicant to the concerned regulatory authority for appraisal. The applicant may alternatively submit a supplementary report to draft EIA and EMP addressing all the concerns expressed during the public consultation.

IV. Stage (4)—Appraisal:

(i) Appraisal means the detailed scrutiny by the Expert Appraisal Committee or State Level Expert Appraisal Committee of the application and other documents like the Final EIA report, outcome of the public consultations including public hearing proceedings, submitted by the applicant to the regulatory authority concerned for grant of environmental clearance. This appraisal shall be made by Expert Appraisal Committee or State Level Expert Appraisal Committee concerned in a transparent manner in a proceeding to which the applicant shall be invited for furnishing necessary clarifications in person or through an authorized representative. On conclusion of this proceeding, the Expert Appraisal Committee or State Level Expert Appraisal Committee concerned shall make categorical recommendations to the regulatory authority concerned either for grant of prior environmental clearance on stipulated terms and conditions, or rejection of the application for prior environmental clearance, together with reasons for the same.

(ii) The appraisal of all projects or activities which are not required to undergo public consultation, or submit an Environment Impact Assessment report, shall be carried out on the basis of the prescribed application Form-1 and Form-1A as applicable, any other relevant validated information available and the site visit wherever the same is considered as necessary by the Expert Appraisal Committee or State Level Expert Appraisal Committee concerned.

(iii) The appraisal of an application shall be completed by the Expert Appraisal Committee or State Level Expert Appraisal Committee concerned within sixty days of the receipt of the final Environment Impact Assessment report and other documents or the receipt of Form-1 and Form-1A, where public consultation is not necessary and the recommendations of the Expert Appraisal Committee or State Level Expert Appraisal Committee shall be placed before the competent authority for a final decision within the next fifteen days. The prescribed procedure for appraisal is given in Appendix-V;

7 (ii). Prior Environmental Clearance (EC) process for Expansion or Modernization or Change of product mix in existing projects:

All applications seeking prior environmental clearance for expansion with increase in the production capacity beyond the capacity for which prior environmental clearance has been granted under this notification or with increase in either lease area or production capacity in the case of mining projects or for the modernization of an existing unit with increase in the total production capacity beyond the threshold limit prescribed in the Schedule to this notification through change in process and or technology or involving a change in the product–mix shall be made in Form-I and they shall be considered by the concerned Expert Appraisal Committee or State Level Expert Appraisal Committee within sixty days, who will decide on the due diligence necessary including preparation of EIA and public consultations and the application shall be appraised accordingly for grant of environmental clearance.

8. Grant or Rejection of Prior Environmental Clearance (EC)

(i) The regulatory authority shall consider the recommendations of the EAC or SEAC concerned and convey its decision to the applicant within forty five days of the receipt of the recommendations of the Expert Appraisal Committee or State Level Expert Appraisal Committee concerned or in other words within one hundred and five days of the receipt of the final Environment Impact Assessment Report, and where Environment Impact Assessment is not required, within one hundred and five days of the receipt of the complete application with requisite documents, except as provided below.

(ii) The regulatory authority shall normally accept the recommendations of the Expert Appraisal Committee or State Level Expert Appraisal Committee concerned. In cases where it disagrees with the recommendations of the Expert Appraisal Committee or State Level Expert Appraisal Committee concerned, the regulatory authority shall request reconsideration by the Expert Appraisal Committee or State Level Expert Appraisal Committee concerned within forty five days of the receipt of the recommendations of the Expert Appraisal Committee or State Level Expert Appraisal Committee concerned while stating the reasons for the disagreement. An intimation of this decision shall be simultaneously conveyed to the applicant. The Expert Appraisal Committee or State Level Expert Appraisal Committee concerned, in turn, shall consider the observations of the regulatory authority and furnish its views on the same within a further period of sixty days. The decision of the regulatory authority after considering the views of the Expert Appraisal Committee or State Level Expert Appraisal Committee concerned shall be final and conveyed to the applicant by the regulatory authority concerned within the next thirty days.

(iii) In the event that the decision of the regulatory authority is not communicated to the applicant within the period specified in sub-paragraphs (i) or (ii) above, as applicable, the applicant may proceed as if the environment clearance sought for has been granted or denied by the regulatory authority in terms of the final recommendations of the Expert Appraisal Committee or State Level Expert Appraisal Committee concerned.

(iv) On expiry of the period specified for decision by the regulatory authority under paragraph (i) and (ii) above, as applicable, the decision of the regulatory authority, and the final recommendations of the Expert Appraisal Committee or State Level Expert Appraisal Committee concerned shall be public documents.

(v) Clearances from other regulatory bodies or authorities shall not be required prior to receipt of applications for prior environmental clearance of projects or activities, or screening, or scoping, or appraisal, or decision by the regulatory authority concerned, unless any of these is sequentially dependent on such clearance either due to a requirement of law, or for necessary technical reasons.

(vi) Deliberate concealment and/or submission of false or misleading information or data which is material to screening or scoping or appraisal or decision on the application shall make the application liable for rejection, and cancellation of prior environmental clearance granted on that basis. Rejection of an application or cancellation of a prior environmental clearance already granted, on such ground, shall be decided by the regulatory authority, after giving a personal hearing to the applicant, and following the principles of natural justice.

9. Validity of Environmental Clearance (EC): The "Validity of Environmental Clearance" is meant the period from which a prior environmental clearance is granted by the regulatory authority, or may be presumed by the applicant to have been granted under sub-paragraph (iv) of paragraph 7 above, to the start of production operations by the project or activity, or completion of all construction operations in case of construction projects (item 8 of the Schedule), to which the application for prior environmental clearance refers. The prior environmental clearance granted for a project or activity shall be valid for a period of ten years in the case of River Valley projects (item 1(c) of the Schedule), project life as estimated by Expert Appraisal Committee or State Level Expert Appraisal Committee subject to a maximum of thirty years for mining projects and five years in the case of all other projects and activities. However, in the case of Area Development projects and Townships [item 8(b)], the validity period shall be limited only to such activities as may be the responsibility of the applicant as a developer. This period of validity may be extended by the regulatory authority concerned by a maximum period of five years provided an application is made to the regulatory authority by the applicant within the validity period, together with an updated Form-1, and Supplementary Form-1A, for Construction projects or activities (item 8 of the Schedule). In this regard the regulatory authority may also consult the Expert Appraisal Committee or State Level Expert Appraisal Committee as the case may be.

10. Post Environmental Clearance Monitoring:

(i) (a) In respect of Category 'A' projects, it shall be mandatory for the project proponent to make public the environmental clearance granted for their project along with the environmental conditions and safeguards at their cost by prominently advertising it at least in two local newspapers of the district or State where the project is located and in addition, this shall also be displayed in the project proponent's website permanently. *(Inserted by Notification dated 1st December, 2009)*

(b) In respect of Category 'B' projects, irrespective of its clearance by MoEF/SEIAA, the project proponent shall prominently advertise in the newspapers indicating that the project has been accorded environment clearance and the details of MOEF website where it is displayed. *(Inserted by Notification dated 1st December, 2009)*

(c) The Ministry of Environment and Forests and the State/Union Territory Level Environmental Impact Assessment Authorities (SEIAAs), as the case may be, shall also place the environmental clearance in the public domain on Government portal. *(Inserted by Notification dated 1st December, 2009)*

(d) The copies of the environmental clearance shall be submitted by the project proponents to the Heads of local bodies, Panchayats and Municipal Bodies in addition to the relevant offices of the Government who in turn has to display the same for 30 days from the date of receipt." *(Inserted by Notification dated 1st December, 2009)*

(ii) It shall be mandatory for the project management to submit half-yearly compliance reports in respect of the stipulated prior environmental clearance terms and conditions in hard and soft copies to the regulatory authority concerned, on 1st June and 1st December of each calendar year. *(Para re-numbered by Notification dated 1st December, 2009)*

(iii) All such compliance reports submitted by the project management shall be public documents. Copies of the same shall be given to any person on application to the concerned regulatory authority. The latest such compliance report shall also be displayed on the web site of the concerned regulatory authority. *(Para re-numbered by Notification dated 1st December, 2009)*

11. Transferability of Environmental Clearance (EC): A prior environmental clearance granted for a specific project or activity to an applicant may be transferred during its validity to another legal person entitled to undertake the project or activity on application by the transferor, or by the transferee with a written "no objection" by the transferor, to, and by the regulatory authority concerned, on the same terms and conditions under which the prior environmental clearance was initially granted, and for the same validity period. No reference to the Expert Appraisal Committee or State Level Expert Appraisal Committee concerned is necessary in such cases.

12. Operation of EIA Notification, 1994, till Disposal of Pending Cases: From the date of final publication of this notification the Environment Impact Assessment (EIA) notification number S.O.60 (E) dated 27th January, 1994 is hereby superseded, except in supersession of the things done or omitted to be done before such supersession to the extent that in case of all or some types of applications made for prior environmental clearance and pending on the date of final publication of this notification, the Central Government may relax any one or all provisions of this notification except the list of the projects or activities requiring prior environmental clearance in Schedule I, or continue operation of some or all provisions of the said notification, for a period not exceeding *twenty-four months* from the date of issue of this notification.

(Substituted by Notification dated 11th October, 2007)

[No. J-11013/56/2004-IA-II (I)]

(R. Chandramohan)
Joint Secretary to the Government of India

SCHEDULE
(See Paragraph 2 and 7)

LIST OF PROJECTS OR ACTIVITIES REQUIRING PRIOR ENVIRONMENTAL CLEARANCE

Project or Activity		*Category with threshold limit*		*Conditions if any*
		A	B	
(1)	(2)	(3)	(4)	(5)
1.	**Mining, extraction of natural resources and power generation (for a specified production capacity)**			
1(a)	(i) Mining of minerals. (Substituted by Notification dated 1st December, 2009) (ii) Slurry pipelines (coal, lignite and other ores) passing through national parks/sanctuaries, coral reefs, ecologically sensitive areas. (Substituted by Notification dated 1st December, 2009)	$\geq$ 50 ha. of mining lease area in respect of non-coal mine lease. (Substituted by Notification dated 1st December, 2009) $\geq$ 150 ha of mining lease area in respect of coal mine lease. (Substituted by Notification dated 1st December,	<50 ha $\geq$5 of mining lease area in respect of non-coal mine lease. (Substituted by Notification dated 1st December, 2009) $\geq$150 ha $\geq$5 ha of mining lease area in respect of coal mine lease. (Substituted by Notification dated 1st December, 2009)	General Condition shall apply. *Note*: Mineral prospecting is exempted. is (Substituted by Notification dated 1st December, 2009) (i) Prior environmental clearance is as well required at the stage of renewal of mine lease for which application should be made up to one year prior to date of renewal. (ii) Mineral prospecting is exempted. (Substituted by Notification dated

(1)	(2)	(3)	(4)	(5)
		2009) Asbestos mining irrespective of mining area. All projects. (Substituted by Notification dated 1st December, 2009)		4 April, 2011)
1(b)	Offshore and onshore oil and gas exploration, development and production	All projects		*Note*: Seismic surveys which are part of— Exploration Surveys (Substituted by Notification dated 11th October, 2007) are exempted provided the concession areas have got previous clearance for physical survey
1(c)	River Valley projects	(i) $\geq$ 50 MW hydroelectric power generation; (ii) $\geq$ 10,000 ha. of culturable	(i) < 50 MW $\geq$ 25 MW hydroelectric power generation; (ii) < 10,000 ha. of culturable command area	General Condition shall apply. *Note*: Irrigation projects not involving submergence or inter-state domain shall be appraised by the SEIAA as Category 'B' Projects." (Substituted by Notification dated 1st December,

(1)	(2)	(3)	(4)	(5)
		command area		2009)
1(d)	Thermal Power Plants	< 500 MW (coal/lignite/naptha and gas based); ≥ 50 MW (Pet coke, diesel and all other fuels including refinery residual oil waste except biomass); (Substituted by Notification dated 1st December, 2009) ≥ 20 MW (based on biomass or non-hazardous municipal solid waste as fuel). (Substituted by Notification dated 1st December, 2009)	> 500 MW (coal/lignite/naptha and gas based); <50 MW ≥ 5MW (Pet coke, diesel and all other fuels including refinery residual oil waste except biomass); < 20 MW > 15 MW (based on biomass or non-hazardous municipal solid waste as fuel). (Substituted by Notification dated 1st December, 2009)	General Condition shall apply. *Note*: (i) Power plants up to 15 MW, based on biomass and using auxiliary fuel such as coal/lignite/petroleum products up to 15 per cent are exempt. (ii) Power plants up to 15 MW, based on non-hazardous municipal waste and using auxiliary fuel such as coal/lignite/petroleum products up to 15 per cent are exempt. (iii) Power plants using waste heat boiler without any auxiliary fuel are exempt." (Substituted by Notification dated 1st December, 2009)

(1)	(2)	(3)	(4)	(5)
1(e)	Nuclear power projects and processing of nuclear fuel	All projects	–	
2.	**Primary Processing**			
2(a)	Coal washeries	≥ 1 million tonne/ annum throughput of coal	< 1 million tonne/annum throughput of coal	General Condition shall apply (If located within mining area the proposal shall be appraised together with the mining proposal)
2 (b)	Mineral beneficiation	≥ 0.1million tonne/ annum mineral throughput	< 0.1 million tonne/annum mineral throughput	General Condition shall apply (Mining proposal with Mineral beneficiation shall be appraised together for grant of clearance)
3	**Materials Production**			
3(a)	Metallurgical industries (ferrous and non-ferrous)	(a) Primary metallurgical industry All projects (b) Sponge iron manufacturing ≥ 200TPD	Sponge iron manufacturing < 200TPD Secondary metallurgical processing industry (i) All toxic and heavy metal pro-ducing units	General Condition shall apply. *Note*: (i) The recycling industrial units registered under the HSM Rules, are exempted. (ii) In case of secondary metallurgical processing industrial units, those

(1)	(2)	(3)	(4)	(5)
		(c) Secondary metallurgical processing industry All toxic and heavy metal producing units ≥ 20,000 tonnes/annum	< 20,000 tonnes/annum (ii) All other non – toxic secondary metallurgical processing industries > 5000 tonnes/annum	projects involving operation of furnaces only such as induction and electric are furnace, submerged arc furnace, and cupola with capacity more than 30,000 tonnes per annum (TPA) would require environmental clearance. (iii) Plant/units other than power plants (given against entry no. 1(d) of the schedule), based on municipal solid waste (non-hazardous) are exempted." (Substituted by Notification dated 1st December, 2009)
3(b)	Cement plants	≥ 1.0 million tonnes/annum production capacity	< 1.0 million tonnes/annum production capacity. All Stand alone grinding units	General Condition shall apply
4	**Materials Processing**			
4(a)	Petroleum refining industry	All projects	—	—
4(b)	Coke oven plants	≥ 2,50,000	< 2,50,000 and ≥ 25,000	"General conditions shall apply".

(1)	(2)	(3)	(4)	(5)
		tonnes/annum -	tonnes/annum	(Substituted by Notification dated 1st December, 2009)
4(c)	Asbestos milling and asbestos based products	All projects	–	–
4(d)	Chlor-alkali industry	≥ 300 TPD production capacity or a unit located outside the notified industrial area/estate	(i) All projects irrespective of the size, if it is located in a Notified Industrial Area/Estate. (ii) < 300 tonnes per day (TPD) and located outside a Notified Industrial Area/Estate. (Substituted by Notification dated 1st December, 2009)	General as well as specific condition shall apply. No new Mercury Cell based plants will be permitted and existing units converting to membrane cell technology are exempt from the notification." (Substituted by Notification dated 1st December, 2009)
4(e)	Soda ash Industry	All projects	–	–
4(f)	Leather/skin/hide processing industry	New projects outside the industrial area or expansion of existing units	All new or expansion of projects located within a notified industrial area/estate	General as well as specific conditions shall apply. (Substituted by Notification dated 1st December, 2009)

(1)	(2)	(3)	(4)	(5)
		outside the industrial area		
5	**Manufacturing/Fabrication**			
5(a)	Chemical fertilizers	All projects except Single Super Phosphate (Substituted by Notification dated 1st December, 2009)	Single Super Phosphate	—
5(b)	Pesticides industry and pesticide specific intermediates (excluding formulations)	All units producing technical grade pesticides	—	—
5(c)	Petro-chemical complexes (industries based on processing of petroleum fractions and natural gas and/or reforming to aromatics)	All projects	—	—
5(d)	Manmade fibres manufacturing	Rayon	Others	General Condition shall apply

(1)	(2)	(3)	(4)	(5)
5(e)	Petrochemical based processing (processes other than cracking and reformation and not covered under the complexes)	Located outside the notified industrial area/estate —	Located in a notified industrial area/estate	General as well as specific conditions shall apply. (Substituted by Notification dated 1st December, 2009)
5(f)	Synthetic organic chemicals industry (dyes and dye intermediates; bulk drugs and intermediates excluding drug formulations; synthetic rubbers; basic organic chemicals, other synthetic organic chemicals and chemical intermediates)	Located outside the notified industrial area/estate	Located in a notified industrial area/estate	General and specific conditions shall apply. (Substituted by Notification dated 1st December, 2009)
5(g)	Distilleries	(i) All Molasses based distilleries (ii) All Cane juice/ non-molasses based distilleries ≥30 KLD	All Cane juice/non-molasses based distilleries – <30 KLD	General Condition shall apply

(1)	(2)	(3)	(4)	(5)
5(h)	Integrated paint industry	—	All projects	General Condition shall apply
5(i)	Pulp and paper industry excluding manufacturing of paper from waste paper and manufacture of paper from ready pulp without bleaching	Pulp manufacturing and Pulp and Paper manufacturing industry —	Paper manufacturing industry without pulp manufacturing	General Condition shall apply
5(j)	Sugar Industry	—	≥ 5000 tcd cane crushing capacity	General Condition shall apply
5(k)	**(Omitted by Notification dated 1st December, 2009)**			
6	**Service Sectors**			
6(a)	Oil and gas transportation pipe line (crude and refinery/ petrochemical products), passing through national parks/sanctuaries/coral reefs/ecologically sensitive areas including LNG Terminal	All projects —	—	—

(1)	(2)	(3)	(4)	(5)
6(b)	Isolated storage and handling of hazardous chemicals (As per threshold planning quantity indicated in column 3 of schedule 2 and 3 of MSIHC Rules 1989 amended 2000)	—	All projects	General Condition shall apply
7	**Physical Infrastructure including Environmental Services**			
7(a)	Airports	All projects including airstrips, which are for commercial use. (Substituted by Notification dated 1st December, 2009)	—	*Note*: Air strips, which do not involve bunkering/refueling facility and or Air Traffic Control, are exempted. (Substituted by Notification dated 1st December, 2009)
7(b)	All ship breaking yards including ship breaking units	All projects	—	—

(1)	(2)	(3)	(4)	(5)
7(c)	Industrial estates/parks/ complexes/areas, export processing Zones (EPZs), Special Economic Zones (SEZs), Biotech Parks, Leather Complexes.	If at least one industry in the proposed industrial estate falls under the Category A, entire industrial area shall be treated as Category A, irrespective of the area. Industrial estates with area greater than 500 ha. and housing at least one Category B industry.	-Industrial estates housing at least one Category B industry and area <500 ha. Industrial estates of area> 500 ha. and not housing any industry belonging to Category A or B.	General as well as specific conditions shall apply. *Note*: 1. Industrial Estate of area below 500 ha. and not housing any industry of Category 'A' or 'B' does not require clearance. 2. If the area is less than 500 ha. but contains building and construction projects > 20,000 sq. mtr. and or development area more than 50 ha it will be treated as activity listed at serial no. 8(a) or 8(b) in the Schedule, as the case may be." (Submitted by Notification dated 1st December, 2009)
7(d)	Common hazardous waste treatment, storage and disposal facilities (TSDFs)	All integrated facilities having incineration and landfill or incineration alone	All facilities having land fill only	General Condition shall apply

(1)	(2)	(3)	(4)	(5)
7(e)	Ports, harbours, break waters, dredging. (Submitted by Notification dated 1st December, 2009)	≥ 5 million TPA of cargo handling capacity (excluding fishing harbours)	< 5 million TPA of cargo handling capacity and/or ports/harbours ≥10,000 TPA of fish handling capacity	General Condition shall apply. *Note*: 1. Capital dredging inside and outside the ports or harbours and channels are included; 2. Maintenance dredging is exempt provided it formed part of the original proposal for which Environment Management Plan (EMP) was prepared and environmental clearance obtained. (Submitted by Notification dated 1st December, 2009)
7(f)	Highways	(i) New National Highways; and (ii) Expansion of National Highways greater than 30 km, involving additional right of way greater	(i) All New State Highway Projects (Substituted by Notification dated 4 April, 2011) (ii) State Highways expansion projects in hilly terrain (above 1,000 m AMSL) and or ecologically sensitive areas. (Substituted by	General Condition shall apply. *Note*: Highways include expressways. (Submitted by Notification dated 1st December, 2009)

(1)	(2)	(3)	(4)	(5)
		than 20m involving land acquisition. (Substituted by Notification dated 11th October, 2007)	Notification dated 1st December, 2009)	
7(g)	Aerial ropeways	(1) All Projects located at altitude of 1,000 mtr and above (2) All Projects located in notified ecologically sensitive areas (Substituted by Notification dated 1st December, 2009)	All projects except those covered in column (3). (Substituted by Notification dated 1st December, 2009)	General Condition shall apply

(1)	(2)	(3)	(4)	(5)
7(h)	Common Effluent Treatment Plants (CETPs)		All projects	General Condition shall apply
7(i)	Common Municipal Solid Waste Management Facility (CMSWMF)		All projects	General Condition shall apply
8	**Building/Construction projects/Area Development projects and Townships**			
8(a)	Building and Construction projects		≥20000 sq.mtrs and <1,50,000 sq.mtrs. of built-up area#	#(The built up area for the purpose of this Notification is defined as "the built up or covered area on all floors put together including basement(s) and other service areas, which are proposed in the building/construction projects". (Substituted by Notification dated 4 April, 2011)
8(b)	Townships and Area Development projects.		Covering an area ≥ 50 ha and or built up area ≥ 1,50,000 sq. mtrs ++	++All projects under Item 8(b) shall be appraised as Category B1

Note:

General Condition (GC)

Any project or activity specified in Category 'B' will be treated as Category 'A', if located in whole or in part within 10 km from the boundary of:

(i) Protected areas notified under the Wildlife (Protection) Act, 1972;
(ii) Critically polluted areas as identified by the Central Pollution Control Board from time to time;
(iii) Eco-sensitive areas as notified under Section 3 of the Environment (Protection) Act, 1986, such as Mahabaleshwar Panchgani, Matheran, Pachmarhi, Dahanu, Doon Valley, and
(iv) Inter-State boundaries and international boundaries:

Provided that the requirement regarding distance of 10 km of the Inter-State boundaries can be reduced or completely done away with by an agreement between the respective States or UTs sharing the common boundary in case the activity does not fall within 10 kilometres of the areas mentioned at item (i), (ii) and (iii) above." (Substituted by Notification dated 1st December, 2009).

Specific Condition (SC)

If any Industrial Estate/Complex/Export processing Zones/Special Economic Zones/Biotech Parks/Leather Complex with homogeneous type of industries such as Items 4(d), 4(f), 5(e), 5(f), or those Industrial estates with pre-defined set of activities (not necessarily homogeneous, obtains prior environmental clearance, individual industries including proposed industrial housing within such estates/complexes will not be required to take prior environmental clearance, so long as the Terms and Conditions for the industrial estate/complex are complied with (Such estates/complexes must have a clearly identified management with the legal responsibility of ensuring adherence to the Terms and Conditions of prior environmental clearance, who may be held responsible for violation of the same throughout the life of the complex/estate).

APPENDIX-I
(See Paragraph – 6)

FORM -1
(SUBSTITUTED BY NOTIFICATION DATED 1ST DECEMBER, 2009)

(I) BASIC INFORMATION

Serial Number	*Item*	*Details*
1.	Name of the project/s	
2.	S. No. in the schedule	
3.	Proposed capacity/area/length/tonnage to be handled/command area/lease area/number of wells to be drilled	
4.	New/Expansion/Modernization	
5.	Existing Capacity/Area etc.	
6.	Category of Project i.e. 'A' or 'B'	
7.	Does it attract the general condition? If yes, please specify.	
8.	Does it attract the specific condition? If yes, please specify.	
9.	Location Plot/Survey/Khasra No. Village Tehsil District State	
10.	Nearest railway station/airport along with distance in kms.	
11.	Nearest Town, City, District Headquarters along with distance in kms.	
12.	Village Panchayats, Zilla Parishad, Muncipal Corporation, Local body (complete postal addresses with telephone nos. to be given)	

Serial Number	*Item*	*Details*
13.	Name of the applicant	
14.	Registered Address	
15.	Address for correspondence: Name Designation (Owner/Partner/CEO) Address Pin Code E-mail Telephone No. Fax No.	
16.	Details of Alternative Sites examined, if any. Location of three sites should be shown on a topo sheet.	Village-District-State 1. 2. 3.
17.	Interlinked Projects	
18	Whether separate application of interlinked project has been submitted?	
19.	If yes, date of submission	
20.	If no, reason	
21.	Whether the proposal involves approval/clearance under: if yes, details of the same and their status to be given. (a) The Forest (Conservation) Act, 1980? (b) The Wildlife (Protection) Act, 1972? (c) The C.R.Z. Notification, 1991?	
22.	Whether there is any Government Order/Policy relevant/relating to the site?	
23.	Forest land involved (hectares)	
24.	Whether there is any litigation pending against the project and/or land in which the project is proposed to be set up? (a) Name of the Court (b) Case No.	

Serial Number	*Item*	*Details*
	(c) Order/directions of the Court, if any and its relevance with the proposed project.	

"I hereby an undertaking that the data and information given in the application and enclosures are true to the best of my knowledge and belief and I am aware that if any part of the data and information submitted is found to be false or misleading at any stage, the project will be rejected and clearance given, if any, to the project will be revoked at our risk and cost.

Date: ....

Place: ....

Signature of the applicant
With Name and Full Address
(Project Proponent/Authorised Signatory)

Note:

1. The projects involving clearance under Coastal Regulation Zone Notification, 1991 shall submit with the application a CRZ map duly demarcated by one of the authorized agencies, showing the project activities, w.r.t. CRZ (at the stage of TOR) and the recommendations of the State Coastal Zone Management Authority (at the stage of EC). Simultaneous action shall also be taken to obtain the requisite clearance under the provisions of the CRZ Notification, 1991 for the activities to be located in the CRZ.
2. The projects to be located within 10 km of the National Parks, Sanctuaries, Biosphere Reserves, Migratory Corridors of Wild Animals, the project proponent shall submit the map duly authenticated by Chief Wildlife Warden showing these features *vis-à-vis* the project location and the recommendations or comments of the Chief Wildlife Warden thereon (at the stage of EC).
3. All correspondence with the Ministry of Environment and Forests including submission of application for TOR/Environmental Clearance, subsequent clarifications, as may be required from time to time, participation in the EAC Meeting on behalf of the project proponent shall be made by the

authorized signatory only. The authorized signatory should also submit a document in support of his claim of being an authorized signatory for the specific project.

(II) ACTIVITY

1. Construction, operation or decommissioning of the Project involving actions, which will cause physical changes in the locality (topography, land use, changes in water bodies, etc.)

S. No.	*Information/Checklist confirmation*	*Yes/No*	*Details thereof (with approximate quantities/rates, wherever possible) with source of information data*
(1)	(2)	(3)	(4)
1.1	Permanent or temporary change in land use, land cover or topography including increase in intensity of land use (with respect to local land use plan)		
1.2	Clearance of existing land, vegetation and buildings?		
1.3	Creation of new land uses?		
1.4	Pre-construction investigations e.g. bore houses, soil testing?		
1.5	Construction works?		
1.6	Demolition works?		
1.7	Temporary sites used for construction works or housing of construction workers?		
1.8	Above ground buildings, structures or earthworks including linear structures, cut and fill or excavations		
1.9	Underground works including mining or tunnelling?		
1.10	Reclamation works		

(1)	(2)	(3)	(4)
1.11	Dredging?		
1.12	Offshore structures?		
1.13	Production and manufacturing processes?		
1.14	Facilities for storage of goods or materials?		
1.15	Facilities for treatment or disposal of solid waste or liquid effluents?		
1.16	Facilities for long-term housing of operational workers?		
1.17	New road, rail or sea traffic during construction or operation?		
1.18	New road, rail, air waterborne or other transport infrastructure including new or altered routes and stations, ports, airports, etc.?		
1.19	Closure or diversion of existing transport routes or infrastructure leading to changes in traffic movements?		
1.20	New or diverted transmission lines or pipelines?		
1.21	Impoundment, damming, culverting, realignment or other changes to the hydrology of watercourses or aquifers?		
1.22	Stream crossings?		
1.23	Abstraction or transfers of water form ground or surface waters?		
1.24	Changes in water bodies or the land surface affecting drainage or run-off?		
1.25	Transport of personnel or materials for construction, operation or decommissioning?		

(1)	(2)	(3)	(4)
1.26	Long-term dismantling or decommissioning or restoration works?		
1.27	Ongoing activity during decommissioning which could have an impact on the environment?		
1.28	Influx of people to an area in either temporarily or permanently?		
1.29	Introduction of alien species?		
1.30	Loss of native species or genetic diversity?		
1.31	Any other actions?		

2. Use of Natural resources for construction or operation of the Project (such as land, water, materials or energy, especially any resources which are non-renewable or in short supply):

S. No.	*Information/checklist confirmation*	*Yes/No*	*Details thereof (with approximate quantities/ rates, wherever possible) with source of information data*
2.1	Land especially undeveloped or agricultural land (ha)		
2.2	Water (expected source and competing users) unit: KLD		
2.3	Minerals (MT)		
2.4	Construction material – stone, aggregates, sand/soil (expected *source* – MT)		
2.5	Forests and timber (*source* – MT)		
2.6	Energy including electricity and fuels (*source*, competing users) Unit: fuel (MT), energy (MW)		
2.7	Any other natural resources (use appropriate standard units)		

3. Use, storage, transport, handling or production of substances or materials, which could be harmful to human health or the environment or raise concerns about actual or perceived risks to human health.

S. No.	*Information/Checklist confirmation*	*Yes/No*	*Details thereof (with approximate quantities/rates, wherever possible) with source of information data*
3.1	Use of substances or materials, which are hazardous (as per MSIHC rules) to human health or the environment (flora, fauna, and water supplies)		
3.2	Changes in occurrence of disease or affect disease vectors (e.g. insect or water borne diseases)		
3.3	Affect the welfare of people e.g. by changing living conditions?		
3.4	Vulnerable groups of people who could be affected by the project e.g. hospital patients, children, the elderly etc.		
3.5	Any other causes		

4. Production of solid wastes during construction or operation or decommissioning (MT/month)

S. No.	*Information/Checklist confirmation*	*Yes/No*	*Details thereof (with approximate quantities/rates, wherever possible) with source of information data*
(1)	(2)	(3)	(4)
4.1	Spoil, overburden or mine wastes		
4.2	Municipal waste (domestic and or commercial wastes)		

(1)	(2)	(3)	(4)
4.3	Hazardous wastes (as per Hazardous Waste Management Rules)		
4.4	Other industrial process wastes		
4.5	Surplus product		
4.6	Sewage sludge or other sludge from effluent treatment		
4.7	Construction or demolition wastes		
4.8	Redundant machinery or equipment		
4.9	Contaminated soils or other materials		
4.10	Agricultural wastes		
4.11	Other solid wastes		

5. Release of pollutants or any hazardous, toxic or noxious substances to air (kg/hr)

S.No.	*Information/Checklist confirmation*	*Yes/No*	*Details thereof (with approximate quantities/rates, wherever possible) with source of information data*
(1)	(2)	(3)	(4)
5.1	Emissions from combustion of fossil fuels from stationary or mobile sources		
5.2	Emissions from production processes		
5.3	Emissions from materials handling including storage or transport		

(1)	(2)	(3)	(4)
5.4	Emissions from construction activities including plant and equipment		
5.5	Dust or odours from handling of materials including construction materials, sewage and waste		
5.6	Emissions from incineration of waste		
5.7	Emissions from burning of waste in open air (e.g. slash materials, construction debris)		
5.8	Emissions from any other sources		

6. Generation of Noise and Vibration, and Emissions of Light and Heat:

S. No.	*Information/Checklist confirmation*	*Yes/No*	*Details thereof (with approximate quantities/rates, wherever possible) with source of information data with source of information data*
6.1	From operation of equipment e.g. engines, ventilation plant, crushers		
6.2	From industrial or similar processes		
6.3	From construction or demolition		
6.4	From blasting or piling		
6.5	From construction or operational traffic		
6.6	From lighting or cooling systems		
6.7	From any other sources		

7. Risks of contamination of land or water from releases of pollutants into the ground or into sewers, surface waters, groundwater, coastal waters or the sea:

S. No.	*Information/Checklist confirmation*	*Yes/No*	*Details thereof (with approximate quantities/rates, wherever possible) with source of information data*
7.1	From handling, storage, use or spillage of hazardous materials		
7.2	From discharge of sewage or other effluents to water or the land (expected mode and place of discharge)		
7.3	By deposition of pollutants emitted to air into the land or into water		
7.4	From any other sources		
7.5	Is there a risk of long-term build up of pollutants in the environment from these sources?		

8. Risk of accidents during construction or operation of the Project, which could affect human health or the environment

S. No.	*Information/Checklist confirmation*	*Yes/No*	*Details thereof (with approximate quantities/rates, wherever possible) with source of information data*
(1)	(2)	(3)	(4)
8.1	From explosions, spillages, fires etc. from storage, handling, use or production of hazardous substances		

(1)	(2)	(3)	(4)
8.2	From any other causes		
8.3	Could the project be affected by natural disasters causing environmental damage (e.g. floods, earthquakes, landslides, cloudburst etc)?		

9. Factors which should be considered (such as consequential development) which could lead to environmental effects or the potential for cumulative impacts with other existing or planned activities in the locality

S. No.	*Information/Checklist confirmation*	*Yes/No*	*Details thereof (with approximate quantities/rates, wherever possible) with source of information data*
9.1	Lead to development of supporting, lities, ancillary development or development stimulated by the project which could have impact on the environment e.g.: • Supporting infrastructure (roads, power supply, waste or waste water treatment, etc.) • housing development • extractive industries • supply industries • other		
9.2	Lead to after-use of the site, which could have an impact on the environment		
9.3	Set a precedent for later developments		
9.4	Have cumulative effects due to proximity to other existing or planned projects with similar effects		

(III) ENVIRONMENTAL SENSITIVITY

S. No.	*Areas*	*Name/Identity*	*Aerial distance (within 15 km.)Proposed project location boundary*
(1)	(2)	(3)	(4)
1.	Areas protected under international conventions, national or local legislation for their ecological, landscape, cultural or other related value		
2.	Areas which are important or sensitive for ecological reasons — Wetlands, watercourses or other water bodies, coastal zone, biospheres, mountains, forests		
3.	Areas used by protected, important or sensitive species of flora or fauna for breeding, nesting, foraging, resting, over wintering, migration		
4.	Inland, coastal, marine or underground waters		
5.	State, National boundaries		
6.	Routes or facilities used by the public for access to recreation or other tourist, pilgrim areas		
7.	Defence installations		
8.	Densely populated or built-up area		
9.	Areas occupied by sensitive man-made land uses (hospitals, schools, places of worship, community facilities)		
10.	Areas containing important, high quality or scarce resources (groundwater resources, surface		

(1)	(2)	(3)	(4)
	resources, forestry, agriculture, fisheries, tourism, minerals)		
11	Areas already subjected to pollution or environmental damage. (those where existing legal environmental standards are exceeded)		
12	Areas susceptible to natural hazard which could cause the project to present environmental problems (earthquakes, sub-sidence, landslides, erosion, flooding or extreme or adverse climatic conditions)		

(IV) PROPOSED TERMS OF REFERENCE FOR EIA STUDIES

APPENDIX–II
(See Paragraph-6)

FORM–1 A
(Only for Construction Projects Listed under Item 8 of the Schedule)

CHECK LIST OF ENVIRONMENTAL IMPACTS

(Project proponents are required to provide full information and wherever necessary attach explanatory notes with the Form and submit along with proposed environmental management plan and monitoring programme)

1. Land Environment (Attach Panoramic View of the Project Site and the Vicinity)

1.1. Will the existing landuse get significantly altered from the project that is not consistent with the surroundings? (Proposed landuse must conform to the approved Master Plan/ Development Plan of the area. Change of landuse if any and the statutory approval from the competent authority be submitted). Attach Maps of (i) site location, (ii) surrounding features of the proposed site (within 500 meters) and (iii) the site (indicating levels and contours) to appropriate scales. If not available attach only conceptual plans.

1.2. List out all the major project requirements in terms of the land area, built up area, water consumption, power requirement, connectivity, community facilities, parking needs etc.

1.3. What are the likely impacts of the proposed activity on the existing facilities adjacent to the proposed site? (Such as open spaces, community facilities, details of the existing landuse, disturbance to the local ecology).

1.4. Will there be any significant land disturbance resulting in erosion, subsidence and instability? (Details of soil type, slope analysis, vulnerability to subsidence, seismicity etc may be given).

1.5. Will the proposal involve alteration of natural drainage systems? (Give details on a contour map showing the natural drainage near the proposed project site)

1.6. What are the quantities of earthwork involved in the construction activity-cutting, filling, reclamation, etc. (Give details of the quantities of earthwork involved, transport of fill materials from outside the site, etc.)

1.7. Give details regarding water supply, waste handling, etc. during the construction period.

1.8. Will the low lying areas and wetlands get altered? (Provide details of how low lying and wetlands are getting modified from the proposed activity)

1.9. Whether construction debris and waste during construction cause health hazard? (Give quantities of various types of wastes generated during construction including the construction labour and the means of disposal)

2. Water Environment

2.1. Give the total quantity of water requirement for the proposed project with the breakup of requirements for various uses. How will the water requirement met? State the sources and quantities and furnish a water balance statement.

2.2. What is the capacity (dependable flow or yield) of the proposed source of water?

2.3. What is the quality of water required, in case, the supply is not from a municipal source? (Provide physical, chemical, biological characteristics with class of water quality)

2.4. How much of the water requirement can be met from the recycling of treated wastewater? (Give the details of quantities, sources and usage)

2.5. Will there be diversion of water from other users? (Please assess the impacts of the project on other existing uses and quantities of consumption)

2.6. What is the incremental pollution load from wastewater generated from the proposed activity? (Give details of the quantities and composition of wastewater generated from the proposed activity)

2.7. Give details of the water requirements met from water harvesting? Furnish details of the facilities created.

2.8. What would be the impact of the landuse changes occurring due to the proposed project on the runoff characteristics (quantitative as well as qualitative) of the area in the post construction phase on a long-term basis? Would it aggravate the problems of flooding or water logging in any way?

2.9. What are the impacts of the proposal on the groundwater? (Will there be tapping of groundwater; give the details of groundwater table, recharging capacity, and approvals obtained from competent authority, if any)

2.10. What precautions/measures are taken to prevent the run-off from construction activities polluting land and aquifers? (Give details of quantities and the measures taken to avoid the adverse impacts)

2.11. How is the storm water from within the site managed? (State the provisions made to avoid flooding of the area, details of the drainage facilities provided along with a site layout indication contour levels)

2.12. Will the deployment of construction labourers particularly in the peak period lead to unsanitary conditions around the project site (Justify with proper explanation)

2.13. What on-site facilities are provided for the collection, treatment and safe disposal of sewage? (Give details of the quantities of wastewater generation, treatment capacities with technology and facilities for recycling and disposal)

2.14. Give details of dual plumbing system if treated waste used is used for flushing of toilets or any other use.

3. Vegetation

3.1. Is there any threat of the project to the biodiversity? (Give a description of the local ecosystem with it's unique features, if any)

3.2. Will the construction involve extensive clearing or modification of vegetation? (Provide a detailed account of the trees and vegetation affected by the project)

3.3. What are the measures proposed to be taken to minimize the likely impacts on important site features (Give details of proposal for tree plantation, landscaping, creation of water bodies etc. along with a layout plan to an appropriate scale)

4. Fauna

4.1. Is there likely to be any displacement of fauna—both terrestrial and aquatic or creation of barriers for their movement? Provide the details.

4.2. Any direct or indirect impacts on the avifauna of the area? Provide details.

4.3. Prescribe measures such as corridors, fish ladders etc to mitigate adverse impacts on fauna

5. Air Environment

5.1. Will the project increase atmospheric concentration of gases and result in heat islands? (Give details of background air quality levels with predicted values based on dispersion models taking into account the increased traffic generation as a result of the proposed constructions)

5.2. What are the impacts on generation of dust, smoke, odorous fumes or other hazardous gases? Give details in relation to all the meteorological parameters.

5.3. Will the proposal create shortage of parking space for vehicles? Furnish details of the present level of transport infrastructure and measures proposed for improvement including the traffic management at the entry and exit to the project site.

5.4. Provide details of the movement patterns with internal roads, bicycle tracks, pedestrian pathways, footpaths etc., with areas under each category.

5.5. Will there be significant increase in traffic noise and vibrations? Give details of the sources and the measures proposed for mitigation of the above.

5.6. What will be the impact of DG sets and other equipment on noise levels and vibration in and ambient air quality around the project site? Provide details.

6. Aesthetics

6.1. Will the proposed constructions in any way result in the obstruction of a view, scenic amenity or landscapes? Are these considerations taken into account by the proponents?

6.2. Will there be any adverse impacts from new constructions on the existing structures? What are the considerations taken into account?

6.3. Whether there are any local considerations of urban form and urban design influencing the design criteria? They may be explicitly spelt out.

6.4. Are there any anthropological or archaeological sites or artefacts nearby? State if any other significant features in the vicinity of the proposed site have been considered.

7. Socio-Economic Aspects

7.1. Will the proposal result in any changes to the demographic structure of local population? Provide the details.

7.2. Give details of the existing social infrastructure around the proposed project.

7.3. Will the project cause adverse effects on local communities, disturbance to sacred sites or other cultural values? What are the safeguards proposed?

8. Building Materials

8.1. May involve the use of building materials with high-embodied energy. Are the construction materials produced with energy efficient processes? (Give details of energy conservation measures in the selection of building materials and their energy efficiency)

8.2. Transport and handling of materials during construction may result in pollution, noise and public nuisance. What measures are taken to minimize the impacts?

8.3. Are recycled materials used in roads and structures? State the extent of savings achieved?

8.4. Give details of the methods of collection, segregation and disposal of the garbage generated during the operation phases of the project.

9. Energy Conservation

9.1. Give details of the power requirements, source of supply, backup source etc. What is the energy consumption assumed per square foot of built-up area? How have you tried to minimize energy consumption?

9.2. What type of, and capacity of, power back-up to you plan to provide?

9.3. What are the characteristics of the glass you plan to use? Provide specifications of its characteristics related to both short wave and long wave radiation?

9.4. What passive solar architectural features are being used in the building? Illustrate the applications made in the proposed project.

9.5. Does the layout of streets and buildings maximise the potential for solar energy devices? Have you considered the use of street lighting, emergency lighting and solar hot water systems for use in the building complex? Substantiate with details.

9.6. Is shading effectively used to reduce cooling/heating loads? What principles have been used to maximize the shading of Walls on the East and the West and the Roof? How much energy saving has been effected?

9.7. Do the structures use energy-efficient space conditioning, lighting and mechanical systems? Provide technical details. Provide details of the transformers and motor efficiencies, lighting intensity and air-conditioning load assumptions? Are you using CFC and HCFC free chillers? Provide specifications.

9.8. What are the likely effects of the building activity in altering the micro-climates? Provide a self assessment on the likely impacts of the proposed construction on creation of heat island and inversion effects?

9.9. What are the thermal characteristics of the building envelope? (a) roof; (b) external walls; and (c) fenestration? Give details of the material used and the U-values or the R values of the individual components.

9.10. What precautions and safety measures are proposed against fire hazards? Furnish details of emergency plans.

9.11. If you are using glass as wall material provides details and specifications including emissivity and thermal characteristics.

9.12. What is the rate of air infiltration into the building? Provide details of how you are mitigating the effects of infiltration.

9.13. To what extent the non-conventional energy technologies are utilised in the overall energy consumption? Provide details of the renewable energy technologies used.

10. Environment Management Plan

The Environment Management Plan would consist of all mitigation measures for each item wise activity to be undertaken during the construction, operation and the entire life cycle to minimize adverse environmental impacts as a result of the activities of the project. It would also delineate the environmental monitoring plan for compliance of various environmental regulations. It will state the steps to be taken in case of emergency such as accidents at the site including fire.

APPENDIX-III
(See Paragraph-7)

GENERIC STRUCTURE OF ENVIRONMENTAL IMPACT ASSESSMENT DOCUMENT

S. No.	*EIA Structure*	*Contents*
1.	Introduction	• Purpose of the report • Identification of project and project proponent • Brief description of nature, size, location of the project and its importance to the country, region • Scope of the study – details of regulatory scoping carried out (As per Terms of Reference)
2.	Project Description	• Condensed description of those aspects of the project (based on project feasibility study), likely to cause environmental effects. Details should be provided to give clear picture of the following:

S. No.	*EIA Structure*	*Contents*
		• Type of project • Need for the project • Location (maps showing general location, specific location, project boundary and project site layout) • Size or magnitude of operation (incl. Associated activities required by or for the project • Proposed schedule for approval and implementation • Technology and process description • Project description. Including drawings showing project layout, components of project etc. Schematic representations of the feasibility drawings which give information important for EIA purpose • Description of mitigation measures incorporated into the project to meet environmental standards, environmental operating conditions, or other EIA requirements (as required by the scope) • Assessment of New and untested technology for the risk of technological failure
3.	Description of the Environment	• Study area, period, components and methodology • Establishment of baseline for valued environmental components, as identified in the scope • Base maps of all environmental components
4.	Anticipated Environmental Impacts and Mitigation Measures	• Details of Investigated Environmental impacts due to project location, possible accidents, project design, project construction, regular operations, final decommissioning or rehabilitation of a completed project • Measures for minimizing and/or offsetting adverse impacts identified • Irreversible and Irretrievable commitments of environmental components

S. No.	*EIA Structure*	*Contents*
		• Assessment of significance of impacts (Criteria for determining significance, Assigning significance) • Mitigation measures
5.	Analysis of Alternatives (Technology and Site)	• In case, the scoping exercise results in need for alternatives: • Description of each alternative • Summary of adverse impacts of each alternative • Mitigation measures proposed for each alternative, and • Selection of alternative
6.	Environmental Monitoring Programme	• Technical aspects of monitoring the effectiveness of mitigation measures (incl. measurement methodologies, frequency, location, data analysis, reporting schedules, emergency procedures, detailed budget and procurement schedules)
7.	Additional Studies	• Public Consultation • Risk assessment • Social Impact Assessment. R&R Action Plans
8.	Project Benefits	• Improvements in the physical infrastructure • Improvements in the social infrastructure • Employment potential –skilled; semi-skilled and unskilled • Other tangible benefits
9.	Environmental Cost Benefit Analysis	If recommended at the Scoping stage
10.	EMP	• Description of the administrative aspects of ensuring that mitigative measures are implemented and their effectiveness monitored, after approval of the EIA

S. No.	*EIA Structure*	*Contents*
11	Summary and Conclusion (This will constitute the summary of the EIA Report)	• Overall justification for implementation of the project • Explanation of how, adverse effects have been mitigated
12.	Disclosure of Consultants engaged	• The names of the Consultants engaged with their brief resume and nature of Consultancy rendered

APPENDIX-III (A)
(See Paragraph-7)

CONTENTS OF SUMMARY ENVIRONMENTAL IMPACT ASSESSMENT

The Summary EIA shall be a summary of the full EIA Report condensed to ten A-4 size pages at the maximum. It should necessarily cover in brief the following Chapters of the full EIA Report:

1. Project Description
2. Description of the Environment
3. Anticipated Environmental impacts and mitigation measures
4. Environmental Monitoring Programme
5. Additional Studies
6. Project Benefits
7. Environment Management Plan

APPENDIX-IV
(See Paragraph-7)
(Substituted by Notification Dated 1st December, 2009)

PROCEDURE FOR CONDUCT OF PUBLIC HEARING

1.0 The Public Hearing shall be arranged in a systematic, time bound and transparent manner ensuring widest possible public participation at the project site(s) or in its close proximity District-wise, by the concerned State Pollution Control Board (SPCB) or the Union Territory Pollution Control Committee (UTPCC).

2. 0 The Process

2.1 The Applicant shall make a request through a simple letter to the Member Secretary of the SPCB or Union Territory Pollution Control Committee, in whose jurisdiction the project is located, to arrange the public hearing within the prescribed statutory period. In case the project site is *covering more than one District or* State or Union Territory, the public hearing is mandated in each *District*, State or Union Territory in which the project is *located* and the applicant shall make separate requests to each concerned SPCB or UTPCC for holding the public hearing as per this procedure.

2.2 The Applicant shall enclose with the letter of request, at least 10 hard copies and an equivalent number of soft (electronic) copies of the draft EIA Report with the generic structure given in Appendix-III including the Summary Environment Impact Assessment report in English and in the *official* language *of the state/local language*, prepared strictly in accordance with the Terms of Reference communicated after Scoping (Stage-2). Simultaneously the applicant shall arrange to forward copies, one hard and one soft, of the above draft EIA Report along with the Summary EIA report to the *following authorities or offices*, within whose jurisdiction the project will be located:

(a) District Magistrate/District collector/Deputy Commissioner/s

(b) Zila Parishad or Municipal Corporation or Panchayats Union

(c) District Industries Office

(d) Urban Local Bodies (ULBs)/PRIs Concerned/ Development authorities

(e) Concerned Regional Office of the Ministry of Environment and Forests.

2.3 On receiving the draft Environmental Impact Assessment report, the above-mentioned authorities except the *Regional Office of* MoEF, shall arrange to widely publicize it within their respective jurisdictions requesting the interested persons to send their comments to the concerned regulatory authorities. They shall also make available the draft EIA Report for inspection electronically or otherwise to the public during normal office hours till the Public Hearing is over.

2.4 The SPCB or UTPCC concerned shall also make similar arrangements for giving publicity about the project within the

State/Union Territory and make available the Summary of the draft Environmental Impact Assessment report (Appendix-IIIA) for inspection in select offices or public libraries or *any other suitable location* etc. They shall also additionally make available a copy of the draft Environmental Impact Assessment report to the above five authorities/offices.

3.0 Notice of Public Hearing

3.1 The Member-Secretary of the concerned SPCB or UTPCC shall finalize the date, time and exact venue for the conduct of public hearing within 7 (seven) days of the date of receipt of the draft Environmental Impact Assessment report from the project proponent, and advertise the same in one major National Daily and one Regional vernacular Daily/*Official State Language*. A minimum notice period of 30 (thirty) days shall be provided to the public for furnishing their responses;

3.2 The advertisement shall also inform the public about the places or offices where the public could access the draft Environmental Impact Assessment report and the Summary Environmental Impact Assessment report before the public hearing. *In places where the newspapers do not reach, the Competent Authority should arrange to inform the local public about the public hearing by other means such as by way of beating of drums as well as advertisement/announcement on radio/television*;

3.3 No postponement of the date, time, venue of the public hearing shall be undertaken, unless some untoward emergency situation occurs and only on the recommendation of the concerned *District Magistrate/District Collector/Deputy Commissioner*, the postponement shall be notified to the public through the same National and Regional vernacular dailies and also prominently displayed at all the identified offices by the concerned SPCB or Union Territory Pollution Control Committee;

3.4 In the above exceptional circumstances, fresh date, time and venue for the public consultation shall be decided by the Member-Secretary of the concerned SPCB or UTPCC only in consultation with the District Magistrate/*District Collector/ Deputy Commissioner* and notified afresh as per procedure under 3.1 above.

4.0 Supervision and Presiding Over the Hearing

4.1 The *District Magistrate/District Collector/Deputy Commissioner* or his or her representative not below the rank of an Additional District Magistrate assisted by a representative of SPCB or UTPCC, shall supervise and preside over the entire public hearing process.

5.0 Videography

5.1 The SPCB or UTPCC shall arrange to video film the entire proceedings. A copy of the videotape or a CD shall be enclosed with the public hearing proceedings while forwarding it to the Regulatory Authority concerned.

6.0 Proceedings

6.1 The attendance of all those who are present at the venue shall be noted and annexed with the final proceedings.

6.2 There shall be no quorum required for attendance for starting the proceedings.

6.3 A representative of the applicant shall initiate the proceedings with a presentation on the project and the Summary EIA report.

6.4 Person present at the venue shall be granted the opportunity to seek information or clarifications on the project from the applicant. The summary of the public hearing proceedings accurately reflecting all the views and concerns expressed shall be recorded by the representative of the SPCB or UTPCC and read over to the audience at the end of the proceedings explaining the contents in the *local*/vernacular language and the agreed minutes shall be signed by the *District Magistrate/District Collector/Deputy Commissioner* or his or her representative on the same day and forwarded to the SPCB/UTPCC concerned.

6.5 A Statement of the issues raised by the public and the comments of the applicant shall also be prepared in the local language *or the Official State language, as the case may be, and in English* and annexed to the proceedings.

6.6 The proceedings of the public hearing shall be conspicuously displayed at the office of the Panchayats within whose jurisdiction the project is located, office of the concerned Zila Parishad, *District Magistrate/District Collector/Deputy*

Commissioner and the SPCB or UTPCC. The SPCB or UTPCC shall also display the proceedings on its website for general information. Comments, if any, on the proceedings may be sent directly to the concerned regulatory authorities and the applicant concerned.

7.0 Time Period for Completion of Public Hearing

7.1 The public hearing shall be completed within a period of forty five days from date of receipt of the request letter from the Applicant. Thereafter the SPCB or UTPCC concerned shall send the public hearing proceedings to the concerned regulatory authority within eight days of the completion of the public hearing. *Simultaneously, a copy will also be provided to the project proponent*. The applicant may also directly forward a copy of the approved public hearing proceedings to the regulatory authority concerned along with the final Environmental Impact Assessment report or supplementary report to the draft EIA report prepared after the public hearing and public consultations *incorporating the concerns expressed in the public hearing along with action plan and financial allocation, item-wise, to address those concerns*.

7.2 If the SPCB or UTPCC fails to hold the public hearing within the stipulated 45(forty-five) days, the Central Government in Ministry of Environment and Forests for Category 'A' project or activity and the State Government or Union Territory Administration for Category 'B' project or activity at the request of the SEIAA, shall engage any other agency or authority to complete the process, as per procedure laid down in this Notification.

APPENDIX–V
(See Paragraph-7)
(Substituted by Notification Dated 1st December, 2009)

PROCEDURE PRESCRIBED FOR APPRAISAL

1. The applicant shall apply to the concerned regulatory authority through a simple communication enclosing the following documents where public consultations are mandatory:
   - Final Environment Impact Assessment Report [20 (twenty) hard copies and 1 (one) soft copy)]

- A copy of the video tape or CD of the public hearing proceedings
- A copy of final layout plan (20 copies)
- A copy of the project feasibility report (1 copy)

2. The Final EIA Report and the other relevant documents submitted by the applicant shall be scrutinized in office within 30 days from the date of its receipt by the concerned Regulatory Authority strictly with reference to the TOR and the inadequacies noted shall be communicated electronically or otherwise in a single set to the Members of the EAC/SEAC enclosing a copy each of the Final EIA Report including the public hearing proceedings and other public responses received along with a copy of Form-1 or Form-1A and scheduled date of the EAC/SEAC meeting for considering the proposal.
3. Where a public consultation is not mandatory, the appraisal shall be made on the basis of prescribed application Form-1 and EIA report, in the case of all projects and activities other than Item 8 of the Schedule. In the case of Item 8 of the Schedule, considering its unique project cycle, the EAC or SEAC concerned shall appraise projects or activities on the basis of Form-1, Form-1A, conceptual plan and the EIA report [required only for projects listed under 8(b)] and make recommendations on the project regarding grant of environmental clearance or otherwise and also stipulate the conditions for environmental clearance. *(Substituted by Notification dated 25th January, 2012)*
4. Every application shall be placed before the EAC/SEAC and its appraisal completed within 60 days of its receipt with requisite documents/details in the prescribed manner.
5. The applicant shall be informed at least 15 (fifteen) days prior to the scheduled date of the EAC/SEAC meeting for considering the project proposal.
6. The minutes of the EAC/SEAC meeting shall be finalised within 5 working days of the meeting and displayed on the website of the concerned regulatory authority. In case the project or activity is recommended for grant of EC, then the minutes shall clearly list out the specific environmental safeguards and conditions. In case the recommendations are for rejection, the reasons for the same shall also be explicitly stated.

APPENDIX-VI
(See Paragraph-5)

COMPOSITION OF THE SECTOR/PROJECT SPECIFIC EXPERT APPRAISAL COMMITTEE (EAC) FOR CATEGORY-A PROJECTS AND THE STATE/UT LEVEL EXPERT APPRAISAL COMMITTEES (SEACS) FOR CATEGORY-B PROJECTS TO BE CONSTITUTED BY THE CENTRAL GOVERNMENT

1. The Expert Appraisal Committees [EAC(s)] and the State/UT Level Expert Appraisal Committees (SEACs) shall consist of only professionals and experts fulfilling the following eligibility criteria:

   Professional: The person should have at least (i) 5 years of formal University training in the concerned discipline leading to a MA/MSc. Degree, or (ii) in case of Engineering/ Technology/Architecture disciplines, 4 years formal training in a professional training course together with prescribed practical training in the field leading to a B.Tech/B.E./B.Arch. Degree, or (iii) Other professional degree (e.g. Law) involving a total of 5 years of formal University training and prescribed practical training, or (iv) Prescribed apprenticeship/article ship and pass examinations conducted by the concerned professional association (e.g. Chartered Accountancy), or (v) a University degree, followed by 2 years of formal training in a University or Service Academy (e.g. MBA/IAS/IFS). In selecting the individual professionals, experience gained by them in their respective fields will be taken note of.

   Expert: A professional fulfilling the above eligibility criteria with at least 15 years of relevant experience in the field, or with an advanced degree (e.g. Ph.D.) in a concerned field and at least 10 years of relevant experience.

   Age: Below 70 years. However, in the event of the non-availability of/paucity of experts in a given field, the maximum age of a member of the Expert Appraisal Committee may be allowed up to 75 years

2. The Members of the EAC shall be Experts with the requisite expertise and experience in the following fields *or* disciplines. In the event that persons fulfilling the criteria of "Experts" are

not available, Professionals in the same field with sufficient experience may be considered:

- *Environment Quality Experts*: Experts in measurement, monitoring, analysis and interpretation of data in relation to environmental quality.
- *Sectoral Project Management*: Experts in Project Management or Management of Process *or* Operations *or* Facilities in the relevant sectors.
- *Environmental Impact Assessment Process*: Experts in conducting and carrying out Environmental Impact Assessments (EIAs) and preparation of Environmental Management Plans (EMPs) and other Management plans and who have wide expertise and knowledge of predictive techniques and tools used in the EIA process.
- *Risk Assessment*
- *Life Science* (Floral and Faunal Management)
- *Forestry and Wildlife*
- *Environmental Economics with experience in project appraisal*
- *Public Administration or Management.*

(*Substituted by Notification dated 11th October, 2007*)

3. The Membership of the EAC shall not exceed 15 (fifteen) regular Members. However, the Chairperson may co-opt an expert as a Member in a relevant field for a particular meeting of the Committee.
4. (Omitted by Notification dated 11th October, 2007)
5. The Chairperson shall nominate one of the Members as the Vice Chairperson who shall preside over the EAC in the absence of the Chairman/Chairperson.
6. A representative of the Ministry of Environment and Forests shall assist the Committee as its Secretary.
7. The maximum tenure of a Member, including Chairperson, shall be for 2 (two) terms of 3 (three) years each.
8. The Chairman/Members may not be removed prior to expiry of the tenure without cause and proper enquiry.

Annexure-B

Revised (April, 2008) Model Terms of Reference for the Preparation of Environmental Impact Assessment (EIA) Report and Environment Management Plan (EMP) on Mining Projects for Consideration by Expert Appraisal Committee

IMPORTANT

1. The revised TOR has been devised to facilitate the project proponents and their consultants to prepare the EIA Report and the EMP which are informative, compact and easy to comprehend. In short, the revised TOR is expected to be user friendly for all concerned. Its salient features are as under:
   - EIA Report and the EMP shall contain in the beginning an Executive Summary which shall be a miniature EIA Report and EMP.
   - It has five chapters as against six in the earlier TOR.
   - One chapter (chapter-3) has been exclusively allotted to environmental issues with a separate section for each component of the environmental issues.
   - Each component of environmental issues has been dealt with in all its ramifications such as baseline status, anticipated impacts due to mining activities and proposed mitigating measures to contain the adverse impact, in that sequence, in one section assigning sub-section 1 to baseline status, sub-section 2 to anticipated impacts and sub-section 3 to proposed mitigating measures.
2. Even if different chapters/sections are prepared by separate experts with separate page numbers for individual chapter/ section, the consolidated and composite EIA Report and the EMP shall have consecutive page numbers beginning with Executive Summary using automatic numerator (English Numbering Machine), if necessary.
3. In the beginning of the EIA Report and the EMP, proper and correct reference to the page numbers of various chapters, sections and sub-section with the appropriate title/sub-title of

the subject shall be clearly indicated under the heading CONTENTS. The pages of the CONTENTS shall be numbered in Numerical Numerals like I, II etc.

4. The project proponents and their consultants must adhere to the framework of the revised TOR in the preparation of the EIA Report and the EMP as also in the presentation to be made to the Expert Appraisal Committee in its meetings failing which the proposal shall be treated as incomplete and hence liable to be rejected outright.

REVISED (APRIL, 2008) Model Terms of Reference for the Preparation of Environmental Impact Assessment (EIA) Report and Environment Management Plan (EMP) on Mining Projects for Consideration by Expert Appraisal Committee

The Environmental Impact Assessment (EIA) Report and Environment Management Plan (EMP) shall, *inter alia*, cover following major aspects:

Executive Summary: The executive summary shall consist of gist of all relevant details chapter-wise and section-wise of the EIA Report and the EMP. For example, If mining is intersecting groundwater or not and if yes, a brief mention of the studies carried out and environment management plan, i.e., mitigating measures to be mentioned. Further, the nature of possible impact on the socio-economic aspects of the people in the buffer zone with special emphasis on the people in the core zone shall be briefly mentioned along with proposed mitigating measures as a component of the Corporate Social Responsibility (CSR). Likewise, if the area is ecologically fragile with flora and fauna, a brief mention about the impact on flora and fauna and mitigating measures like conservation plan for wildlife to be mentioned. The executive summary shall give a prima facie idea about the objectives of the proposai, use of the minerals to be mined, justification, etc. and should be co-related to the details given in the EIA Report and the EMP. Post project plan in brief should also be included. **In a nutshell, the executive summary shall be a miniature EIA Report and EMP.**

CHAPTER 1—INTRODUCTION

- Profile of project proponent and background to establish the financial and entrepreneurial competency to undertake the project.
- Genesis and objectives of the project to clearly state use of the minerals through sale or use as intermediate or final raw materials for end-use product.
- Brief description of nature, size and location of the project and its importance to the region and the country giving the nature and details of the lease-hold area indicating total mineable reserves, rated capacity and the life of the mine highlighting how the project would benefit the surrounding areas and the country's economic development.
- If the lease area/buffer zone is ecologically fragile justification for the project clearly stating as to why some other deposits cannot be exploited so as to save the fragile ecology of the area.
- Status and stage of regulatory clearances like approval of the mining plan, forestry clearance and other statutory clearances essential before starting mine development activities leading to mining.

CHAPTER 2—PROJECT DESCRIPTION

- A site map to 1:50,000 scale, presenting recent features of the area with the help of satellite imagery (NRSA), of a larger area, showing all relevant details like habitation (both rural and urban areas), cropping pattern, water bodies, drainage systems, nallahs, river, water reservoir, forests, on a scale of 1:50,000 and contour at not more than 15 metres, world heritage site, historical places and other sensitive objects distinctly indicating the core zone and the buffer zone, on key plan and their current management status (whether Reserve Forest, Protected Forest, National Park, Sanctuary, Biosphere Reserve, Elephant Reserve, Tiger Reserve, etc.)
- General description of Project:
    - ❑ Project profile, need for the project, location: latitude, longitude and elevation of the site (maps to the scale showing general location, specific location, project boundary and project site layout), topographic (map showing topography of cadastral area), topo sheet no.,

geology of mining lease area (local and regional) with remote sensing satellite map (if available) geological plan showing all lithological units/structural details viz. strike/dip, fold/fault/plunge of the deposit, mining area dimensions, year wise mining plan and production of Overburden (OB) and O.B. dump sites, conceptual mine plan for every five year period for the life of the mine, mining closure plan, production capacity both present and planned

- Project details:
  - ❑ Drawings showing project layout, components of project, schematic representations of feasibility drawings, lease hold area, nature of mineralisation, associated minerals, mineralogical analysis of ore, elemental composition of ore, nature and behaviour of ore body, reserves and quality, use of minerals, surface subsidence, protective measures for subsidence during extraction, rock mechanics, physico-mechanical properties of rocks (compressive/shear/strength),
- Additional details:
  - ❑ Surface plan with every prominent surface features, transverse sections of mineral deposits through drilled bore holes, contour maps at intervals of not more than 15 meters, physiography and drainage pattern
- Details of Mining:
  - ❑ Exploration and reserves, characteristics of ore and waste rocks, estimation of mineral reserves, estimation of proven and mineable reserves, proposed method of working, stripping ratio, method of mining, proposed working depths, in bgl and msl, proposed mechanization, proposed manpower, drilling method—its pattern, blasting, blast hole design, types of explosives, its optimum utilization, frequency of blasting, powder factor, intensity of ground vibration in ppv/distance of Max ppv with proposed charge of explosives, level of sound over pressure during blasting in dB, maximum size of fragments generated and distance of flying in meters, control measures, storage of overburden/solid waste to be marked on map with their quantity, angle of repose for development of waste dumps, particle size distribution of surface soil/overburden, number of benches in ore and

OB with physical dimensions based on conceptual mine plan, mining equipment, their deployment and frequency of possible break down, preventive maintenance, techno-economic basis for selection of the mining technology with environmental compatibility *vis-à-vis* available other alternative mining geometry, groundwater contour plan (both pre and post monsoon), impact of mining on hydrology of core zone and buffer zone indicating if mining is intersecting groundwater and hydrological monitoring for life of the mine.

- Steps to ensure "**zero-waste**" mining, i.e., extracting all the minerals as are geologically extractable and utilizing the same through beneficiation process so as to ensure that all the ore, whether low grade or high grade, is optimally utilized. For example, if iron ore is extracted the beneficiation process would involve sintering/pelletisation including direct supply of low grade ore to units that can consume such ore.
- Steps to fully utilize the associated minerals, if any, either as directly mined or as by-products, for productive purposes.
- **Zero-waste** mining and recovery of **associated minerals** shall be treated as effective tools to increase the resource base of the minerals – steps like beneficiation, utilization of low grade ore and rejects shall be elaborated in the EMP.

CHAPTER 3—BASELINE DATA: DESCRIPTION OF BASELINE STATUS OF ENVIRONMENT, ANTICIPATED ENVIRONMENTAL IMPACTS AND PROPOSED MITIGATING MEASURES:

The details of baseline data to be collected from core zone and buffer zone with respect to different components of environment viz. air, noise, water, land, biology and socio-economic shall be given in **Table 1**. The air quality and noise are to be monitored at all environmental/ecological sensitive areas. The details (component-wise) are given below:

3.1 Air Environment

3.1.1 Baseline Status

- Climate and Meteorology (Source: nearest IMD Station)
    - ❑ Distance as the crow flies from the nearest IMD station.
    - ❑ Climatological data in respect of temperature, humidity, wind speed and direction, wind rose and rainfall.

- On site hourly meteorological data in respect of wind speed and direction, temperature, relative humidity, cloud amount and height (type) and average daily rainfall.
- Hourly mixing heights extracted from CPCB publications and interpolated for the site.
- Wind rose at site.

- Location (distance and direction) of monitoring stations (i) chosen/to be selected conforming to wind rose; (ii) selection of the dominant wind direction with higher frequency; (iii) computation of coverage factor using formula (Ajk = frequency(k)[1/1+Dj] where D is distance of the proposed site; and (iv) sites having high coverage factor should be selected as potential monitoring stations.
- Terrain features around air quality monitoring stations to assess likely impact of the terrain characteristics on air quality.
- Air pollutants: SPM, RSPM, SO_2, NOx, CO, trace or heavy metals (Fe, Mn, Pb etc) in SPM in core zone and buffer zone (24 hourly monitoring indicating the season/months and the year) and any other project specific pollutants like radiological parameters e.g. radon in mine exhaust air, radium and uranium in mine water and radionuclides etc. from atomic minerals for one season other than monsoon are to be monitored as per CPCB norms.
- Maximum, minimum and 98 percentile of air quality data and applicable air quality standards.
- Fugitive emissions in and around the area of mining operations, crushing operations, ore processing operations and ore beneficiation plant as also along the transportation routes.

3.1.2 Anticipated Impacts

- Emission inventory of SPM (including RPM), SO_2, NOx.
- Prediction for fugitive dust emissions due to mining activities, crushing plant and transportation activity by road, rail or conveyor (covered or open to be specified).
- Impact of fugitive emissions on flora and fauna.
- Prediction of impacts on ambient air quality using appropriate mathematical models, ISCST or FDM Model be used for Air Quality Impact Prediction (AQIP).
- Brief description of models, input requirement and how they are derived with references, if any.

- Output of models, 24 hourly concentrations at all monitoring stations (indicating the month(s) and the year), isopleth distribution of major pollutants of concern over 10 km radius of the study area.
- Representation of SPM, RSPM, SO_2 and NOx to be indicated in a tabular form given below:

S. No.	Location of Monitoring Station (name, distance and direction)	Background Level	Predicted Concentration	Resultant concentration	Air Quality Standard

3.1.3 Proposed Mitigating Measures

- Mitigating measures to lower the emission of pollutants and to maintain the air quality.
- Mitigating measures to contain impact of fugitive emissions on flora and fauna.
- Scientific mining methods to reduce the dust emission from point and line sources.
- Alternate solutions such as conveyor belt (covered or open to be specified).

3.2 Noise Environment

3.2.1 Baseline Status

- Locations of monitoring stations in accordance with direction and distance from the sources preferably at the same air quality monitoring sites.
- Day Time and Night Time noise levels are to be monitored.
- Noise levels monitoring should be done considering all the cardinal directions with average of at least 15 minutes and time and date of measurements to be specified.
- Terrain feature to be provided along with noise quality monitoring stations to assess the likely impact of the terrain characteristics on noise quality.
- Noise levels i.e. Leq (day) and Leq (night) for each station in core zone and buffer zone along with applicable standards.
- Noise levels due to mining activity, ore processing units, beneficiation plant and transportation routes separately for

surface transportation (vehicular or rail) and conveyor belt (covered or open to be specified).

- Vibrations caused due to blasting operations.

3.2.2 Anticipated Impacts

- Impact of vibrations on the surrounding environment including damage to materials/structures.
- Prediction of noise levels through modelling at different and representative monitoring stations.
- Impact due to noise levels generated by existing and proposed activities in relation to human environment and wild life including avi-fauna.
- Impact due to present and future surface transportation activities by road/rail as also by conveyor belt (covered or open), if any.
- Impact of noise levels on auditory function, i.e. hearing activity.

3.2.3 Proposed Mitigating Measures

- Identification and adoption of mitigating measures for noise abatement including noise barriers for point sources and line sources as also measures to minimize effect of vibrations due to blasting.
- Evaluation of adequacy of the proposed pollution control devices periodically to minimize occupational exposure and to suggest modifications, if required, as a continuous process.

3.3 Water Environment

3.3.1 Baseline Status

- Locations of representative monitoring stations with direction and distance from the core zone.
- Rainfall data, run off and sediment data from nearby reputed institution including IMD station should be used.
- Details of springs, lakes, reservoirs, rivers etc. within core zone and buffer zone.
- Physico-chemicals including toxic/trace/heavy metals/elements, biological and bacteriological and radiological characterization of surface and groundwater resources for assessment of water quality, upstream and downstream surface water quality with reference to mining lease area.

- Biological characteristics should include the algae population and species available in the surface water and groundwater.
- Iron/manganese level in the water and fish fleshes should be analysed.
- Delineation of water sheds and water drainage pattern in study area using cadastral/aerial/remote sensing satellite imageries as are available.
- If mining results in shifting of water courses (rivers, nallahs etc.), the meandering effect should be indicated.
- Surface water balance of river/stream in study area and withdrawal of surface water for project activity.
- Hydrogeology and Aquifer Characteristics of the area indicating the water absorbing and water transmitting capacity of Aquifer.
- If mining will be intersecting ground water, indicate radius of influence from the mine pit.
- Groundwater potential including water harvesting, recharge and water balance of the area: Groundwater recharge and balance available for present and future use.
- Water requirement and wastewater production from mine lease area, mining townships, ore processing and beneficiation plant and other facilities.
- Wastewater treatment, recycling and reuse of effluent.
- Possibility of rainwater harvesting to replenish groundwater.
- Details of sea water intrusion, wherever applicable.
- Details of existing water bodies and water bodies likely to be created as a result of mining activities both in the core zone and buffer zone.

3.3.2 Anticipated Impacts

- Impact on water sources due to shifting of water courses, if any.
- Impact of water withdrawal on surface water/groundwater resources.
- Impact on exploitation of surface/ground water.
- Impact of mining on hydrogeology with special reference to a situation when mining will intersect groundwater.
- Impact on proper planning for withdrawal of surface/groundwater below the threshold level of replenishment.

- Impact of mining activity including tailings pond on surface and groundwater quality.

3.3.3 Proposed Mitigating Measures

- Model study for prediction of groundwater contamination and suggested mitigating measures to minimize the pollution level.
- Construction of gully checks, check dams, sedimentation ponds, settling tanks, water weirs and retaining walls etc with design and sitting aspects.
- Creation or conservation of water holes in forest for wildlife.
- Scientific mining methods for management of waste water from mining area and OB dumps with design and schematic flow diagrams including those for treatment of water/waste water.
- Slope stabilisation through retaining walls, vegetation etc.
- Management of waste water sources viz. industries, workshop, townships etc. to contain the adverse impact on water resources in core zone and buffer zone.
- Details of mitigating steps to contain adverse impact on water table in case of mining intersecting ground water.
- Details of mitigating measures where there is sea water intrusion in the core zone.
- Mangrove plantation if the mining lease area is near the estuary/sea.
- Suggested exploitation of surface/groundwater to protect aquatic biodiversity and groundwater development.
- Steps to neutralize the solid and liquid elements of the tailing pond.
- Rainwater harvesting to maintain the water level.
- Construction of water harvesting structures.
- Steps to preserve the existing water bodies and water bodies likely to be created as a result of mining activities both in the core zone and buffer zone by developing such water bodies as fisheries, irrigation sources and recreational facilities.

3.4 Land Environment

3.4.1 Baseline Status

- Representative locations of monitoring stations with direction and distance from the core zone considering land use pattern.
- Collection of soil samples from monitoring stations and their texture representing core zone and buffer zone, physico-

chemical and microbiological characterization, water holding capacity, porosity, wilting co-efficient, toxic contaminants, sodium absorption ratio (SAR) and cation exchange capacity.

- Fertility status of soil samples at different and representative sampling stations.
- Study of pre-mining land use pattern, cropping pattern, vegetation cover etc. employing remote sensing techniques (if available) and ground truthing and also through secondary data sources.
- Study on the run off and siltation of the water shed area through run off and sediment monitoring station at the tail end of selected water shed.
- Study about the trend of change in land use pattern, if any, with reasons thereof for the last 10 years based on remote sensing data and its extrapolation to future 10 to 20 years with and without EMP for mining activity.
- Determination of leaching properties of overburden samples to define the load of heavy metal pollutants in run-off water.

3.4.2 Anticipated Impacts

- Estimation of anticipated impacts of proposed mining activity on topography, water drainage pattern, land use pattern with respect to agriculture, forestry and fisheries.
- Impact of leachate water from overburden on surface and groundwater quality.
- Study of the problem of landslides and assessment of soil erosion potential and their impact.
- Impact of mining activity on the fertility status of soil in the study area.
- Prediction of groundwater pollution due to seepage of pollutants through soil column.
- Impact of mining on the top fertile soil cover in mining area.
- Impact of mining on local biodiversity and forest cover.

3.4.3 Proposed Mitigating Measures

- Scientific mining methods to mitigate the impacts of mining activity on land resource.
- Delineation of Mining Closure Plan/exit protocol to rehabilitate the mined out land to match its surrounding land use including removal, storage and reuse of top soil from mining area to cover reclaimed area.

- Plan for restoration/rehabilitation of mined out area to forestry productive land.
- Model study for potential soil erosion from core zone and buffer zone with a view to planning preventive measures.
- Management plan including technological package of practices for checking soil erosion and soil loss in core zone and buffer zone.
- Methods for treatment and disposal of domestic solid waste.
- Selection of suitable local plant species for greenbelt development in and around mine sites, ore processing plant and beneficiation plant and also on overburden dump sites and mined out areas and for avenue plantation in workers colony.
- Top soil conservation plan and its reutilization depending on its quality.

3.5 Biological Environment

3.5.1 Baseline Status

- Locations of monitoring stations (representative) with direction and distance from the core zone.
- Biodiversity, terrestrial and aquatic.
- Assessment of plant species with respect to dominance, density, frequency, abundance, diversity index, similarity index, Importance Value Index etc. within the study area in different ecosystems, mangroves in wet land area, wherever applicable.
- Collection of primary data through field survey and authenticated secondary data on forest and non-forest flora in impact zone with respect to parameters in the preceding paras and forest area and floristic structure, rare and endangered species, endemic species, ethnobotanical aspects, medicinal plants, major and minor forest produce, afforestation/social forestry.
- Characterization of forest litter fauna.
- Collection of primary data through field survey and authenticated secondary data on fauna including avi-fauna indicating endangered and endemic species, if any, with scientific name as well as common (including) local name in English clearly indicating the Schedule of the Wild Life (Protection) Act under which the species fall.
- Information on the dependence of the local people on minor forest produce and their cattle grazing rights in the forest land.

- Collection of secondary data on fishery resource in study area.
- Collection of secondary data on agricultural activity, crops and their productivity, and irrigation facilities.
- Existence of National Park, Sanctuary, Biosphere Reserve, Tiger Reserve, Elephant Reserve, Conservation Reserve, Community Reserve, etc. in the study area and in case such an area (National Park, Sanctuary, etc.) exists within ten km radial distance from the boundary of mining lease area, its location (s) along with name(s) shall be clearly shown on a 1:50,000 scale map.
- Estimation of number and types of trees and shrubs which would be cut during deforestation for mining activity and other facilities.
- Some photographs showing the vegetation cover before and after mining in case of on going mining activities and the existing vegetation in case of a new mine.

3.5.2 Anticipated Impacts

- Loss of forest resource, economically important plants, medicinal plants, and threat to rare, endemic and endangered species due to deforestation.
- Impact of mining activity on terrestrial and aquatic biodiversity.
- Impact of mining activity on wildlife including avifauna.
- Impacts of mining activity on biodiversity, wildlife habitats, migratory corridors, migratory avifauna, rare, endemic and endangered species and medicinal plants.
- Assessment of likely damage to flora and fauna due to air emissions, noise and vibrations, illumination, vehicular movement, waste water discharges, change in land use pattern and anthropogenic impact.
- Impact of mining activity on fishery resource and agricultural production.
- Habitat fragmentation and blocking of migratory corridors due to project activities.

3.5.3 Proposed Mitigating Measures

- Mitigating measures to compensate the loss of forest cover in addition to the obligatory compensatory afforestation under various laws.

- Regeneration/Restoration of rare plants of economic importance including medicinal plants and wildlife species which require protection and conservation.
- Scientific mining and other management methods resulting in improvement of biodiversity, wildlife and forest cover.
- Stabilization of mining benches and overburdens by development of vegetation cover over them.
- Afforestation of reclaimed mined out areas, composite of grass, shrubs and trees, priority for native hardwood varieties.
- Delineation and implementation of pollution control measures to minimize the pollutants due to air emissions, noise and vibrations, illumination, vehicular movement, waste water discharge, change in land use pattern and anthropogenic factor that have impact on biotic environment.
- Identification of measures through scientific conservation plan for protection and conservation of flora, fauna including wildlife, migratory avifauna, rare, endemic and endangered species and medicinal plants etc.
- Compensatory afforestation to compensate the deforested forest area and loss of biodiversity, identification of suitable native tree species for compensatory afforestation, polyculture (fast growing species), plantation of economically beneficial shrubs/trees, floriculture, green belt in and around mine lease areas, mining benches, crushing plant, ore beneficiation plan, sewerage treatment plant, tailing pond and for avenue plantation along haul roads.
- Development of at least 50 meter wide thick green belt between the nearby natural water course and the lease boundary to preserve the natural flow of the water course and prevent it from getting polluted.
- Development of forest floor by litter fauna in the reclaimed area
- **Institutional mechanism (like separate cell) to supervise and monitor various mitigating measures.**

3.6 Socio-Economic Environment

3.6.1 Baseline Status

- Collection of baseline data on human settlements, health status of the community and existing infrastructure facilities for social welfare including sources of livelihood, job opportunities and safety and security of workers and surrounding population.

- Collection of information with respect to social awareness about the developmental activity in the area and existing social welfare measures and those proposed by project proponent.
- Collection of information on sensitive habitats of historical, cultural, and ecological importance.
- Details of the private lands with ownership in the core zone indicating loss of annual income of the lands on account of crop loss and or loss of surface rights to the owners and if such private land owners will be ousted from their lands a detailed socio-economic profile of such land owners based on field survey.
- Details of the public lands including common property resources in the core zone and nature of loss of right of easement in terms of cattle grazing land, convenient access route to the usual places/roads frequented by the locals including their domestic animals, if any.
- Primary data through household-wise field survey about the employable young boys and girls, sources of livelihood of the household, traditional skills like poultry farming, piggery, goat/sheep rearing, basket making, floriculture, pisciculture, collection of minor forest produce, etc. besides various community facilities, of the people living within 3 kms. (as the crow flies) from the core zone and available natural resources for productive purposes.
- Socio-economic profile of the people within 2, 5 and 10 kms. of buffer zone.
- Certain relevant data should be in the format provided in the **Annexures.**

3.6.2 Anticipated Impacts

- Projection of anticipated changes both positive and negative with respect to the details in 3.6.1 above.
- Impact on the cropping pattern and crop productivity within 2 kms. of the core zone.
- Impact on the sources of livelihood of the people with special emphasis on the most vulnerable section as may be affected by mining activities.

- Nature of Impacts on land holdings specially of persons with small land holdings indicating if such people are land owners or share croppers.
- Impact on the grazing lands and on the right of easement of the people such as access to usual places/roads frequented by them.
- If mining activity would displace human settlements any time during the life of the mine.

3.6.3 Proposed Mitigating Measures

Note: The Corporate Social Responsibility (CSR) should not be treated only as philanthropy, rather it should be the Corporate Mission of the project proponent—

- While formulating schemes for socio-economic welfare activities distinction shall be made between community oriented development activities and household-wise oriented economic activities and the latter being divided into individual oriented (like vocational training) and family oriented (like providing gainful economic activities on sustained basis).
- Mitigating measures should take into account the needs of the people based on primary data as obtained through Need Assessment Survey/Study (NAS).
- Certain schemes can be dovetailed with identical/related similar schemes being executed by various Govt. depts./agencies.
- While preparing the rehabilitation action plan for land oustees special emphasis should be given on the interest of the economically weaker section of the population who will be more affected due to the proximity of their habitation to the mine site and should be based on the needs of such people as found through need based field survey (any rehabilitation action plan shall be in position during the mine development activities and before mining starts).
- Criteria and method of calculating compensation for loss of land and or loss of crop.
- Criteria and method of calculating compensation for loss of surface rights, if such lands do not have any income for the land owners the compensation amount should be assessed with reference to the advantage the lessee would gain for the surface rights with periodicity of payment (one time or annual)

till the land with proper development is restored by the lessee to the owners.

- In case of loss of cattle grazing rights or other rights of easement on public/private lands for access to roads etc. alternative arrangements to be specified.
- Arrangement for vocational training for eligible boys and girls of the locality with tie-up for employment and or financial assistance and training for self employment.
- Economic package with initial financial assistance for providing gainful economic activities on sustained basis for the households consistent with their skills such as poultry farming/piggery/goat (sheep) rearing in the backyard (of the houses), coir making, mushroom cultivation and other potential activities as identified during the field survey and proper marketing tie-up for their products including convenient collection centers for minor forest produce.
- Activities like fishery development in the existing water bodies as also in the water bodies likely to be created due to mining activities, floriculture, coir making and basket making can best be organized through Cooperative Society with economically weaker section of the people as members by providing initial financial support in the form of membership fee and minimum share money with tie up with nearest market and managerial assistance by the project proponent for proper maintenance of records and to train such members for shouldering responsibility on their own in due course.
- In plantation work, local species especially fruit bearing trees/orchards based on primary survey should be planted by involving local people especially women self help group and if practicable in private homestead land of poor people to provide a regular source of income in the long run.
- Local people especially the women and women self help group should be involved in selecting alternative vocation to be made available to the affected people.
- If displacement of human settlements is involved, the project authority shall indicate the proposed Rehabilitation Action Plan (RAP) in the EIA Report and EMP which shall include the plan to construct alternative dwelling units for the displaced families and they shall be shifted to the new sites during mine development activities and before actual mining starts.

- Scholarship in the form of books and stationary, school uniform and tuition fee for the needy may be provided with special monitory scholarship to few select meritorious students.

3.7 Occupational Health Environment

3.7.1 Baseline Status

- Primary data through field survey of the existing prevalent diseases in the locality and facilities for treatment.
- Number of workers to be employed and category of hazardous jobs assigned and the duration.
- List of likely hazardous operations/activities.
- The existing practices adopted for assessment of occupational health including the details of medical examination and the facilities.
- Principal environmental and occupational risks likely to be created.
- Ranking the risks to public health in order of severity.
- Methodology of risk assessment.
- Methodology of the health impact assessment to be undertaken, if needed, the plan, the project authority to provide for hiring a person with established credentials to be able to undertake such activities.
- Name(s) of specialized agency to undertake an environmental health study, if needed.
- Methodology of assessment of workplace exposures and mode of communicating and explaining the same (exposures) to the workers.
- Authority to conduct training and education in occupational health and safety.
- Place(s) where health surveillance will be undertaken including tests, e.g., x-rays, pulmonary function tests, and tests for hearing, and identifying tuberculosis.

3.7.2 Anticipated Impacts

- Anticipated occupational illness in view of the hazardous exposures – exhaustive list of such diseases to be given. An illustrative list of possible diseases as a sequel to mining activities will be as under:
  (i) Silicosis
    – Acute

– accelerated
– chronic

(ii) Silicotuberculosis
(iii) Progressive pulmonary fibrosis
(iv) Chronic obstructive pulmonary disease (chronic bronchitis, emphysema)
(v) Lung cancer
(vi) Higher risk for tuberculosis
(vii) Rheumatoid arthritis
(viii) Scleroderma
(ix) Systemic lupus erythematosus
(x) Small vessel vasculitides
(xi) Manganism
(xii) Dust related Pneumonias
(xiii) Siderosis
(xiv) Whole Body Vibration
(xv) Segmental Vibration
(xvi) Joint, Tendon and Muscle inflammation
(xvii) Miners's Nystagmus

3.7.3 Proposed Mitigating Measures

- Measures to communicate the risks before starting mining to people and steps for prevention and control.
- Arrangement for induction training for workers on health and safety and first aid facility.
- Education and training to the workers about their safety and the risk in contaminating various occupational health risks unless personal protective equipments are used and if necessary denial of work and wages for the recalcitrant to ensure use of the personal protective equipments be resorted to.
- Adequate budget for environmental and occupational health activities.
- Break up of the budgetary provision for every activity proposed to be undertaken.
- Constitution of a safety committee and its members including the head of the committee.
- Proper delineation of the function of the safety committee.
- Agency to pay for the tests and the treatment of non-occupational illness.

- Responsibility to compensate the workers for health impairment due to injury or illness and feasibility of health insurance for the mine workers (can be combined with such scheme of the government, if any).
- The amount of compensation; list the minimum and maximum amount stipulated.
- Duration for which the records of health check up be kept and maintaining the records when the project ends for future reference, if any.
- Nomination of a person to identify occupational disease early to prevent serious damage.
- Measures to be undertaken for following:
  (i) Preventing heat stress
  (ii) Preventing noise exposure; and
  (iii) Preventing injuries
- Providing ergonomic support.
- Designating a person to undertake administration of personal protective equipments.
- Employment of trained doctor in occupational health risk and arrangement for referral facilities to be identified.
- Periodical survey (every 3 to 5 years) should be conducted to see the impact on the health status of the local people and the workers as a result of various mitigating measures adopted by the project authorities and to take remedial measures, wherever required.
- Action proposed when the project ends and the workers become exposed to latent disease which may appear in future.

CHAPTER 4—ADDITIONAL STUDIES

- Public consultation (during EIA study as well as public hearing) with the issues raised by the public and response of the project proponent in tabular form.
- *Risk Assessment and Disaster Management Plan*: Risk assessment should be done covering, *inter alia*, following aspects.
- Roof-fall inside the mine, surface subsidence, inundation, surface fire (electrical and oil, as also forest fire during summer season common in certain areas, if any), possible danger due to storage of explosive and sabotage, radioactive hazard, failure of mine benches, accident due to explosive,

accident due to heavy earth moving machinery, accident due to blasting etc.

CHAPTER 5 —ENVIRONMENT MANAGEMENT PLAN AND POST-PROJECT MONITORING PROGRAMME

- Description of the administrative and technical set-up i.e. EMP implementation organizational structure for ensuring that mitigative measures are implemented and their effectiveness monitored after environmental approval from the Impact Assessment Agency.
- Environment plan of the mining lease area on 1:50,000 scale within 500 metres of the boundary and contour lines at 10 meters intervals, indicating all surface features, area occupied by mine workings, area deforested, area covered by dumps (with height), processing plant, surface buildings, mining workshop, area reclaimed and afforested and course of discharge of mine water.
- Monitoring the effectiveness of adopted EMP and scientific mining measures to enable the project authority to take corrective actions, *inter alia,* validation of predictions made in the EIA Report, mid-course corrections to make effective environment management plan if the mitigating measures being implemented not yielding expected results.
- Delineation of technical aspects of environmental monitoring to examine the effectiveness of the adopted EMP and scientific mining measures (including measurement methodologies, frequency, location, data analysis, reporting schedules, emergency procedures, detailed budget and procurement schedules) and to take corrective steps, if necessary.
- Post project hydrogeological monitoring for the entire mine life, restrictive monitoring thereafter during reclamation for collection of hydrogeological and hydrological data.
- Plantation monitoring programme during post project period for ensuring survival and growth rate of plantations in reclaimed area.

Table 1: Details of Parameters, Procedures, and Methods for Description of Environment for Mining Projects

Parameters	*Sampling*		*Measurement Method and Standards*	*Remarks*
	Network	*Frequency*		
A. Air Environment				
Meteorological i.e. wind speed, wind direction, temperature, cloud cover (amount and height), humidity and rainfall	One site in the project impact area	1 hourly, continuous one season simultaneously with air quality monitoring	automatic weather station, or Secondary data from IMD, New Delhi, If data is not available from IMD site specific primary data will be collected	
Wind rose	Project site	Seasonal	To be plotted for one season	
Air Pollutants				
• SPM	Locations to be selected on the basis of coverage factor as described under 3.1 of the document	24 hourly twice a week — one season other than monsoon	Gravimetric (High-Volume sampler)	Fugitive Dust Model or Industrial Source Complex—Short Term version 3 (ISCST-3) be used for prediction of impacts
• RPM	-- do --,	-- do --	Gravimetric (High-Volume with Cyclone)	

Parameters	*Sampling*		*Measurement Method and Standards*	*Remarks*
	Network	*Frequency*		
• SO_2	-- do --,	-- do --	EPA modified West and Gaeke method	
• NOx	-- do --,	-- do --	Arsenite modified Jacob and Hochheiser	
B. Noise				
Hourly equivalent noise levels	Study area Core and buffer zone	Once in each season	Instrument: Noise level meter IS: 4954-1968 as adopted by CPCB	
Hourly equivalent noise levels, Leq day and night separately		Once in each season	Instrument: Noise level meter CPCB/OSHA	Wave propagation or attenuation model for modelling
C. Water				
Water Quality (Surface and Groundwater)				
pH, temp, turbidity, total dissolved solids, total suspended solids, toxic algae	Set of grab samples of surface	Once in each season	• IS: 2488 (Part 1-5) Methods for Sampling and	Surface water to perform 35 or more

Parameters	*Sampling*		*Measurement Method and Standards*	*Remarks*
	Network	*Frequency*		
in surface as well as bore water, to submit raw data instead of BDL, to check waterborne parasites in drinking water, conductivity, total hardness, calcium hardness, total alkalinity, chloride, fluoride, sulphate, sodium, potassium, nitrate, total phosphates, dissolved oxygen, pesticides, heavy metals Bacteriological (total coliforms, E.coli, Indicators of water quality (Benthos, Phytoplankton, Zooplankton, Fishery production, Macrophytes, Productivity)	(flowing and stagnant water) and groundwater for study area. Sediment samples in surface water to be collected for estimation of heavy metals		Testing of Industrial Effluents • Standard Methods for Examination of Water and Wastewater Analysis published by American Public Health Association (APHA)	parameters and to follow IS 2296 standard Groundwater/ drinking water to perform 37 parameters and follow IS 10500 standard
Wastewater Characterization				
Temp, colour, odour, turbidity, TSS, TDS pH, alkalinity as $CaCO_3$, chloride as Cl, total hardness as $CaCO_3$, sulphate as SO_4, Nitrate as NO_3, Fluoride as F, Phosphate as PO_4, Chromium as Cr (Hexavalent, total), Ammonical as N, TKN, % sodium,	Core zone composite sampling	Once in each season	IS: 2488 (Part 1-5) Methods for Sampling and Testing of Industrial Effluents Standard Methods for Examination of Water and Wastewater	Beneficiation mine wastewater

Parameters	Sampling		Measurement Method and Standards	Remarks
	Network	Frequency		
C.O.D., DO, oil and grease, sulphide			Analysis published by APHA	
Heavy metals in leachate water from overburdens		Once in study period		
D. Land Environment				
Soil				
Particle size distribution, texture, pH, electrical conductivity, cation exchange capacity, alkali metals, sodium absorption ratio (SAR), soil fertility, permeability, water holding capacity, porosity	Sample stations shall be of representative character for the coverage area	One surface sample from each selected station (soil samples are collected as per BIS specifications)	Collected and analysed as per soil analysis reference book, M.I. Jackson and soil analysis reference book by C.A. Black	
Overburden: pH, heavy metal content	Representative sample(s)	Once in study period	pH meter,	
Land use/Landscape Location code, total project area, topography, cultivated area, forest, plantations, barren land, water bodies, and settlements	Study area	Before and after Project Activity	Global positioning system, topo sheets, satellite imageries. (1:50,000)	

Parameters	*Sampling*		*Measurement Method and Standards*	*Remarks*
	Network	*Frequency*		
Trend analysis for the last 10 years and future predictions if possible	Buffer zone	—	Remote sensing data before 5 and 10 years	
Impact of mining operations on topography of land	Core zone			
Solid Waste: overburden dumps and domestic waste				
Scientific mining methods for all operations				
E. Biological Environment				
Aquatic Aquatic weeds, Phytoplankton, zooplankton, fisheries, diversity indices, trophic levels, rare, endemic and endangered species, marine parks/sanctuaries/closed areas/coastal regulation zone (CRZ)	• Sampling points are selected considering impact area • Water samples from upstream and downstream of discharge	Once in each season	Standard Methods (APHA 1995), Rau and Wooten (1980) for sampling and measurements	• Seasonal sampling for aquatic biota • Macrophytes, Microscopic analysis of plankton and application of indices viz. Shannon,

Parameters	Sampling		Measurement Method and Standards	Remarks
	Network	Frequency		
	points, and dug wells close to activity site			Palmer etc. • Plankton net, microscope • Secondary data from government offices, NGO's
Terrestrial • Vegetation – species list, economic importance, forest produce, medicinal value • Fauna, avifauna, migratory birds • Habitat, migratory paths • Rare, endemic and endangered species • Sanctuaries/national parks/biosphere reserve/tiger reserve/elephant reserve/conservation reserve/ community reserve	• Sampling points are selected considering impact area	Once before project activity in Winter Season/Post Monsoon	Standard Methods (APHA 1995), Rau and Wooten (1980) for sampling and measurements	1. Quadrate method or point quarter plot less method for terrestrial vegetation survey 2. Secondary data from government offices, NGO's
F. Socio-economic and Health Component				
Infrastructure resource base, economic resource base, health status (morbidity			Primary data collection through questionnaire	Secondary data from census records,

Parameters	*Sampling*		*Measurement Method and Standards*	*Remarks*
	Network	*Frequency*		
pattern), Cultural and aesthetic attributes, education, awareness about bio-energy and green energy			based on NAS which should relate to the periods before, during and post project activities. Such socio-economic survey may be based on random sampling method	statistical hand books, toposheets, health records and relevant official records available with Govt. agencies

Annexure-C

Table 1: Demographic Profiles of the Villages in the Core Zone and Buffer Zone

Sr. No.	*Name of the village*	*Distance from the core*	*Name of the GP*	*Name of the Tehsil*	*No. of Households*				*Number of population*				*Literacy rate*	
					SC	*ST*	*Others*	*Total*	*SC*	*ST*	*Others*	*Total*	*Male*	*Female*

Table 2: Occupation of Population and Work Forces of the Buffer Zone

Sr. No.	*Name of the village*	*Main activity/occupation of households of the village*						*Worker's classification*					
		Agriculture/farming	*Business*	*Service*	*Agr. Labour*	*Allied to Agri. Activity*	*Non-agri. Labour*	*Workers (Male)*	*Workers (Female)*	*Marginal workers (Male)*	*Marginal Workers (Female)*	*Non-workers (Male)*	*Non-Workers (Female)*

Table 3: Land use and Cropping Patterns of the Core zone and Buffer Zone (Pie chart to be provided along with the report if possible)

Sr. No.	*Name of the village*	*Land use patterns (in acres)*								*Land used for public utilities*
		Total area	*Forests*	*Homestead area*	*Agriculture land*		*Grazing land*	*Waste land*		*Give schools, temple, roads, ponds, monuments etc.*
					Irrigated	*Non-irrigated*		*Fallow*	*Current fallow*	

Table 4: Educational Facilities and CBOs within the Study Area

Sr. No.	*Name of the Village*	*Primary School*	*Middle School*	*Sr. Secondary School*	*College*	*Training School*	*Adult Literacy Centre*	*CBOs*	
								SHGs	*Other comm. Org.*
1.									
2.									
3.									
4.									

CBOs: Community Based Organizations

Table 5: Medical Facilities within the Study Area

Sr. No.	*Name of the Village*	*MEDI FAC*	*MCW CNTR*	*M HOME*	*CWC*	*H CNTR*	*PH CNTR*	*PHS CNTR*	*FWC CNTR*	*TB CLN*	*N HOME*	*RMP*	*SMP*	*CHC*	*OTH CNTR*
1.															
2.															
3.															

Note: *MEDI FAC*: Medical Facilities; *FWC CNTR*: Family Welfare Centre; *MCW CNTR*: Maternity and Child Care Centre; *TB CLN*: TB Clinic; *M HOME*: Maternity Home; *N HOME*: Nursing Home; *CWC*: Child Welfare Centre; *RMP*: Registered Medical Practitioners; *H CNTR*: Health Centre; *SMP*: Subsidized Medical Practitioners; *PH CNTR*: Primary Health Centre; *CHC*: Community Hall Centre; *PHS CNTR*: Primary Health Sub-Centre; *OTH CNTR*: Other Centre

Table 6: Other Infrastructural Facilities Available in the Study Area

Sr. No.	*Name of the Village*	*DWF*	*Tp*	*W*	*T*	*TW*	*HP*	*R*	*C*	*L*	*S*	*O*	*PO*	*TO*	*PT*	*P*	*B*	*RS*	*NW*	*CB*	*CoB*

Note: *DWF*: Drinking Water Facility; *C*: Canal *P*: Phone; *Tp*: Tap; *L*: Lake; *B*: Bus; *W*: Well; *S*: Spring; *RS*: Railway Service; *T*: Tank; *O*: Others; *NW*: Navigable Waterways; *TW*: Tube-Well; *PO*: Post Office; *CB*: Commercial Bank; *HP*: Hand Pump; *TO*: Telegraph Office; *CoB*: Co-operative Bank; *R*: River; *PT*: Post & Telegraph Offices

Annexure-D

F. NO. J-11013/77/2004- IA II (I)

GOVERNMENT OF INDIA
MINISTRY OF ENVIRONMENT AND FORESTS
(I. A. DIVISION)

Paryavaran Bhawan
CGO Complex, Lodhi Road
New Delhi – 110 003

Dated 2nd December, 2009

OFFICE MEMORANDUM

***Subject*:** Accreditation of the EIA Consultants with Quality Council of India (QCI)/National Accreditation Board of Education and Training (NABET)

1. The Environmental Appraisal of Development Projects is undertaken as per the provisions of the Environmental Impact Assessment (EIA) Notification, 2006 based on the EIA and EMP Reports prepared by the project proponents in assistance with their Consultants. It has been felt in the Ministry that there is a need to enhance the quality of EIA Reports as the Consultants generally, undertake preparation of EIA/EMP Reports in many sectors and in some instances without requisite expertise and supporting facilities like laboratories for testing of samples, qualified staff etc. The good quality EIA Reports are pre-requisite for improved decision-making.

2. In view of the above, a series of discussions were held with the National Accreditation Board of Education and Training (NABET) and the Quality Council of India (QCI) to evolve a framework for registration of the Consultants including those working in Public Sector Undertakings/Laboratories.

3. After detailed consideration of the issues relating to accreditation of the Consultants, following decisions have been taken:

   - All the Consultants/Public Sector Undertakings (PSUs) working in the area of Environmental Impact Assessment would be required to get themselves registered under the scheme of Accreditation and Registration of the NABET/QCI.
   - Consultant would be confined in the consultancy only to the accredited sectors and parameters for bringing in more specificity in the EIA document.
   - The QCI would put in place detailed procedure for registration of Consultants for taking up the assignments in category 'A' and 'B' projects as detailed in EIA Notification, 2006. The QCI would maintain full transparency on accredited Consultants, procedure followed for accreditation, feedback and evaluation mechanism for Consultants for quality of EIA/EMP Reports.
   - After accreditation, the Consultants would need to include a Certificate in this regard in the EIA/EMP Reports prepared by them and data provided by other Organizations/Laboratories including their status of approvals, etc.
   - The EIA Consultants may like to see further clarification on the subject through the website of NABET/QCI (www.qcin.org).
   - All the Member Secretaries of various Expert Appraisal Committee (EACs) would inform the Consultants in their respective meetings, the need to get accredited with NABET/QCI.

4. It is decided, in the above factual matrix that no EIA/EMP Reports prepared by such Consultants who are not registered with NABET/QCI shall be considered by the Ministry after 30th June, 2010.

This issues with the approval of the Competent Authority.

(Dr. P.B. Rastogi)
Director

Annexure-E

NO. J-11015/200/2008-IA.II(M)

GOVERNMENT OF INDIA
MINISTRY OF ENVIRONMENT AND FORESTS

Paryavaran Bhawan
CGO Complex, Lodhi Road
New Delhi – 110 003
Telefax: 24362434

Dated the 31st March, 2011

OFFICE MEMORANDUM

Sub: Consideration of projects for grant of environmental clearance under EIA Notification, 2006 which involve forestland — Procedure to be followed — Regarding

Ref: Office Memorandum No.-11013/41/2006-IA.II(I) dated 2nd December, 2009 regarding procedure for consideration of proposals for grant of environmental clearance under EIA Notification, 2006, which involve forestland and or wildlife habitat

The issue regarding consideration of proposals especially mining projects for grant of environmental clearance under EIA Notification, 2006, which also involve diversion of forestland has been under consideration for quite some time and circulars/guidelines have been issued in the past in this regard from time to time. In this regard, reference is also invited to para 8(v) of the EIA Notification, 2006 reads as follows:

> "Clearances from other regulatory bodies or authorities shall not be required prior to receipt of applications for prior environmental clearance of projects or activities, or screening, or scoping, or appraisal, or decision by the regulatory authority concerned, unless any of these is sequentially dependent on such clearance either due to a requirement of law, or for necessary technical reasons."

According to the above provision, the environmental clearance under EIA Notification, 2006 is independent of other clearances and submission of clearances under other relevant Acts and Rules as may by applicable to a project is not a perquisite for obtaining environmental clearance except in specific cases where it is sequentially dependent on such clearance either due to requirement of law or for necessary technical reason. This aspect was earlier discussed and deliberated and deliberated and the office memorandum dated 2nd December, 2009 referred to above was an outcome of the same.

However, in view of the complexity of the issues involved, the matter has been considered further in the Ministry and in supersession of the earlier instructions, it has now been decided to adopt the following procedure for consideration of such projects.

I. PROJECTS IN PIPELINE:

(A) **Projects received for TORs and yet to be considered by EAC:** In case of the proposals which have been received for prescribing TORs and involve forestland, in part or in full, and are yet to be considered by the EAC, during consideration of such proposals, clarifications will be obtained from the project proponent regarding feasibility of undertaking the project only in non-forestland. In case, the project proponent confirms to undertake the project in non-forest areas only, the proponent may be advised to submit the revised proposal by deleting the forestland involved in the project. In case, it is not possible to undertake the project without involving diversion of forestland, the project proponent will be asked to first apply for stage-I forestry clearance for the forestland involved in the project and thereafter submit the proposal for obtaining terms of reference as per the procedure prescribed under EIA Notification, 2006.

(B) **Projects for which TORs have already been prescribed but the proposal for environmental clearance is yet to be submitted:** In case of the proposals, which involve forestland, in part or in full, and for which TORs have already been prescribed, the project proponents are advised to ensure that the requisite stage-I forestry clearance has been granted and its copy is submitted along with their application/proposal for environment clearance. Alternatively, the proponent should delete from their land requirement, the forestland involved in the project and the proposal so amended without any forestland may be submitted for appraisal by the EAC.

In case of projects where forest diversion (Stage I Clearance) has been approved for past of the total forestland involved in the project, the proposal will be considered only for the land for which forest diversion has been approved and the non-forestland, if any. For the purpose, the onus of demonstrating that the project activities will be limited to that much area only would like with the project proponent and necessary supporting documents will be submitted in this regard.

(C) **Projects submitted for environmental clearance based on the TORs prescribed by EAC:** The proposals already submitted for environmental clearance will be appraised by the EAC on their merit and in case of involvement of forestland, the proponent will be asked to delete the forestland and submit the revised or approach the EAC after the stage-I forestry clearance for the forestland involved in the project has been granted, till which time the proposal will stand delisted.

In case of projects for which diversion of forestland has been granted for part of the forestland, the proposal will be appraised taking into account that much of land only (land for which FC granted+Non-forestland) for the project activities and the proponent should demonstrate the viability of the project with requisite supporting documents.

(D) **Projects already considered by EAC and recommended for grant of environmental clearance:** In accordance with the recommendations of EAC, such projects will be processed on file for obtaining approval of the MEF for grant of environment clearance. After MEF has approved, a communication will be sent to the project proponent informing that the Competent Authority has approved the project; however, the formal environmental clearance will be issued only after the stage-I forestry clearance for the forestland involved in the project has been obtained and submitted. For the purpose, a maximum time limit of one year will be provided to the proponent during which time the proposal will be kept in abeyance. In case, the formal forestry clearance is not submitted within this time frame, the proposal will stand rejected and the process for obtaining environmental clearance will have to initiated, de-novo, as per the procedure prescribed under EIA Notification, 2006.

II. EXPANSION PROJECTS:

(i) Mining projects involving enhancement of production by increasing the depth and or number of shifts, without any increase in lease area and having already obtained the forestry clearance for the forestland involved in the mine lease, shall be considered on merit and decision taken.

(ii) The Expansion projects involving horizontal spread with additional land requirement will be dealt with as green field projects, if additional forestland is to be diverted.

III. GREENFIELD PROJECTS:

(i) If any Greenfield project does not envisage any diversion of forestland, it would be considered as per the provisions of EIA Notification, 2006.

(ii) In case of any Greenfield project, which involves diversion of forestland, the project proponents are advised to re-examine the requirement of forestland and submit the proposal without forestland for consideration of the EAC. Otherwise, the proponent should submit the proposal for TORs under the EIA Notification, 2006 only after applying the stage-I forestry clearance for the forestland involved in the project.

(iii) All cases of grant/renewal of EC for any abandoned mine or sick project under revival etc. would be considered as a green field project for appraisal under EIA Notification, 2006 and the procedure mentioned above will be followed.

This issues with the approval of the Competent Authority.

(Dr. S K Aggarwal)
Director

To

1. All the Officers of IA Division.
2. Chairpersons/Member Secretaries of all the SEIAAs/ SEACs

Copy to:-

1. PS to MEF
2. PPS to Secretary (E&F)
3. PPS to SS (JMM)
4. Advisor (NB)
5. Website, MoEF
6. Guard File

Annexure-F

NO. J-11013/41/2006-IA.II(I)

GOVERNMENT OF INDIA
MINISTRY OF ENVIRONMENT AND FORESTS

Paryavaran Bhawan
CGO Complex, Lodi Road
New Delhi – 110 003

Dated 26th April, 2011

OFFICE MEMORANDUM

Sub: Corporate Environmental Responsibility

(A) BACKGROUND

1. The Ministry of Environment and Forests has notified various Acts and Rules for environmental governance. The EIA Notification, 2006 elaborates the procedure for seeking environmental clearance and preparation of EIA Reports and Environmental Management Rules. However, there is a need to integrate the environmental concerns including those related to forestry, wildlife and bio-diversity, wherever applicable, into the main stream of the Corporate Policies. It would, therefore, be appropriate that the Corporate Houses, major Public Sector Undertakings (PSUs) and Companies in place Corporate Environmental policies for protection of environment.
2. In light of the recommendations made by the Committee on Monitoring of projects, a separate OM was issued on 6th April, 2011 to stipulate additional conditions in respect of major projects which have already been accorded environmental clearance.

3. Now the matter has been further reviewed and deliberated to bring into focus environmental commitment in the Corporate Sector, so that all the project proponents integrate environmental concerns into their day-today-functioning especially the compliance with the conditions of the clearances.

(B) CORPORATE ENVIRONMENT POLICY

In view of the above, it is felt appropriate that all the major PSUs and Companies, as detailed in Section 'C' below, need to:

(i) Adopt well laid down Corporate Environment Policy;
(ii) Ensure, as a part of this Policy, adherence with the environmental clearances and forestry clearances wherever applicable, granted to the Company;
(iii) Ensure that *inter-alia* the Company functions in conformity with the Policy;
(iv) Ensure that deviations, if any, from this Policy and cases of violations of environmental and forestry clearances conditions that have been found by this Ministry or other public authorities should be duly reported to its Board of Directors and desirably reflected thereafter on its website and its Annual Report;
(v) Identify and designate responsible persons(s) at all levels of their hierarchy for ensuring adherence to this Policy and compliance with the Environmental Laws and Regulations.

These measures to promote environmental consciousness and secure compliance will surely protect the project's stakeholders just like financial systems and audit mechanisms protect the shareholders of a company.

(C) MAJOR PSUs AND COMPANIES

The above measures may be adopted by major PSUs and Companies namely:

(i) All Central PSUs
(ii) All Major Projects
  - Coal based thermal power plants with capacity of 500 MW and above
  - Integrated steel plants with capacity of 1 MTPA and above and

- Cement plant with capacity of 3 MTPA and above
- Petroleum refining industries

The respective EACs would henceforth suitably incorporate appropriate Terms of Reference (TOR) in respect of the status of Corporate Environment Policy and its implementation, as at B above, which would need to be addressed in the EIA/EMP Reports. For all projects proposals in future at the at the appraisal state the EACs and FACs where appropriate, would deliberate on the aspects related to the Corporate Environment Policy, especially with regard to adequacy and comprehensiveness.

(D) OTHER PROJECTS NOT COVERED IN (C) ABOVE

In respect of projects proponents other than those specified in Section C above, the respective EACs and the FACs, where applicable, on a case to case basis, based on sectoral imperatives, locational aspects, size of the company, past track record etc, may stipulate, through a speaking recommendation the course of action as in Section B at TOR or appraisal stage, as the case may be.

This issues with the approval of the Competent Authority.

(Dr. S K Aggarwal)
Director

To

1. All the Officers of IA Division.
2. Chairpersons/Member Secretaries of all the EACs/SEIAAs/ SEACs

Copy to:-

1. PS to MEF
2. PPS to Secretary (E&F)
3. PPS to SS (JMM)
4. Advisor (NB)
5. Website, MoEF
6. Guard File

Index